Strategy and Choice

Strategy and Choice

edited by
Richard J. Zeckhauser

The MIT Press
Cambridge, Massachusetts
London, England

This book was set in Palatino by Asco Trade Typesetting Ltd., Hong Kong and printed and bound in the United States of America.

Library of Congress Cataloging-in-Publication Data

Strategy and choice / edited by Richard J. Zeckhauser.
    p.   cm.
  Includes bibliographical references and index.
  ISBN 0-262-24033-5
  1. Decision-making. 2. Choice (Psychology). I. Zeckhauser,
Richard.
HD30.23.S77   1991
658.4'03—dc20   91-15837
                                                              CIP

To Thomas Schelling,
our teacher

Contents

Acknowledgments

This volume, a tribute to Thomas Schelling, reflects his influence in many ways. By teaching and by example, he has encouraged us to think and write clearly, and to probe to the heart of matters. The book benefited as well from the comments of a working seminar at Harvard's Kennedy School of Government that met regularly in the early months of 1990 to critique individual chapters. Participants in that seminar were Arthur Applbaum, Glenn Blackmon, Darryll Hendricks, Avon Leong, Ted Parson, Jay Patel, Harold Pollack, John Pratt, Han Shi, Alan Wertheimer, and Richard Zeckhauser. In May 1990, the chapters were presented formally at a conference in Cambridge, Massachusetts, which was attended by a large number of Schelling's former students and current admirers. Finally, Nancy Jackson and Wendy Wyatt expertly edited and oversaw production of the book.

1   The Strategy of Choice

Richard J. Zeckhauser

From the refusal of key Soviet military officers to support the August coup to the dieter's duel with himself in the midnight kitchen, strategic choices determine destinies. In activities from gift giving to political wheeling and dealing, men and women strive ingeniously, though sometimes counterproductively, to secure desired outcomes. Whatever the arena, students of strategic behavior come back to the same fundamental questions: What factors motivate individuals' values and actions? What are the principles for effective bargaining? How can incentives and decision processes be structured to yield desirable collective outcomes? How is the flow of useful information impeded or stimulated?

Individuals and larger social units must make strategic choices in many phases of everyday life. To be strategic usually requires that we anticipate the responses of other parties, possibly ourselves at a later moment. The problems of strategic choice go beyond tactics, however. We also need to find ways to cope with the unpredictability of outcomes and to expand our concept of preferences. For example, fairness or relative standing may be as significant a concern as the absolute payoffs to the players.

Insights into strategic choice will find application in economics and political science as well as international affairs and personal behavior. The issues on which we focus in this book—such as trust, envy, bribes, contrast effects in judgments of well-being, free riding, and systems effects—are likely to be relevant to all actors, from industrial firms seeking a reputation for quality in new markets to the people of Eastern Europe demanding democracy.

The One-Minute Strategist

The first step in strategic choice is to identify the players, their possible actions, and the outcomes and payoffs that will result from each

Figure 1.1

possible set of actions. To choose effectively, one must know oneself and predict the likely choices of others. The key concepts in fulfilling these tasks can be organized around the three ideas of incentives, information, and valuation, which might be thought of as the "golden triangle" of strategic choice (figure 1.1).

These three ideas are central to virtually any strategic situation, as readers of this volume will discover. Usually they must work in concert. Let me illustrate with the principal-agent model, a paradigm that comes into play whenever one person (the agent) acts on behalf of another (the principal). Principal and agent could be client and lawyer, company owner and manager, or citizen and elected representative. In each case the pair are in a joint dilemma. The challenge is that preferences diverge and not all information is costlessly monitored. The owner would like the manager to work hard on her behalf at all times. The manager would like to be a little more relaxed in his approach to the job, increase his perks and compensation, and perhaps pursue some projects of greater benefit to himself than to the owner. If the manager cannot find a believable way to commit to working diligently and frugally, he will suffer, for the owner will not be willing to pay him as much. One possible way to improve matters would be for the owner to hire someone whose payoffs correspond with hers (e.g., a relative). Alternatively, she could provide strong incentives to the manager, say a substantial bonus depending on performance. Finally, she could attempt to monitor the manager's actions, perhaps by requiring frequent reports. Any effective real-world solution, we suspect, will attend to all three elements of the golden triangle: sturdy incentives, reasonable oversight, and some alignment of values.

Before proceeding further, the reader might ponder the principal-agent paradigm, which undoubtedly applies in many situations in

Table 1.1
Setter-decider example—sale of an object

		BUYER Object worth 4	
		Accept	Reject
SELLER Object worth 1	Offer at 3	1 / 2	0 / 0
	Offer at 2	2 / 1	0 / 0

your own experience. A fundamental principle of this book is that the same strategic structures reappear in different guises across a wide range of applications. The best practice for thinking about strategic choices is to proceed both from abstract model to application and vice versa, always seeking to generalize insights and identify the critical elements in specific situations.

Models and Metaphors

Abstraction is at the core of effective strategic thinking. I shall illustrate by discussing two models that have wide application, one involving two players, the other many.

1. Setter-Decider Model. The actors, actions, and outcomes of a strategic situation can be structured as a payoff matrix, as the following bargaining example illustrates. Suppose a seller has an object that is worth 1 to him. To the potential buyer it is worth 4. The matrix diagram in table 1.1 shows the value of the outcomes to seller and buyer (in the lower left and upper right corners of each cell, respectively) if the seller offers the object for a price of 3 or 2, and in each case the buyer decides to accept or reject the offer.

It appears that the seller should offer at 3, a price that the buyer will accept and that will yield a payoff of 2 (i.e., a net gain of $3 - 1$) to the seller. Note two points. First, although we are discussing a seller and a buyer, the matrix could equally well represent any number of other situations—for example, the Congress sending a bill to the president, who may veto the measure if it is too different from his expressed wishes.

Second, even the simplest context is extremely rich. What happens, for example, if the buyer states in advance that he will not accept a price of 3, or if the president threatens to veto a bill that doesn't honor his preferences? The nature of the game has changed; we have a new first mover. Would such commitments be credible? Almost assuredly yes, if an equivalent game were to be played many times, or even once again if the buyer rejected the initial offer.

The preceding paradigm assumes that one player sets the terms of a deal and the other decides whether or not to accept the offer. This so-called setter-decider framework obviates many of the difficulties that small groups encounter in real-world attempts to reach agreement. In particular, the buyer's share of the gains from trade (often a sticking point in practice) is not an issue.[1] Effective strategic choice recognizes that the first choice made is usually what game to play.

Stores post prices; they are the setters, it seems. But smart buyers occasionally risk potential embarrassment and say, "If you'd be willing to sell that object [marked at $250] for $200, I would be happy to take it," or let the store owner save face (and price), by asking instead whether he'd "throw in the firescreen with the andirons."

2. Multi-Player Externalities. When we move from the context of bargaining between individuals to establishing prices in large groups, the market comes into play. The most widely praised virtue of competition is that it secures whatever is produced at lowest cost. But there is an additional area of gain. No one has the ability to seek an extra share of the pie; bargaining losses are eliminated. Feasible agreements will quickly be reached.

From these considerations we might conclude that operating in large groups is an advantage. And so it will be in cases that meet the conditions for a relatively competitive market. But such conditions are stringent. The section of this volume titled "Micromotives and Macrobehavior" discusses many-player situations in which we can not expect market-like competitive processes to arise. Two major classes of problems are encountered: inappropriate incentives and impeded information flow.

Incentives

Inappropriate incentives arise because the actions of one actor may affect the welfare of others; that is, there are externalities. Figure 1.2

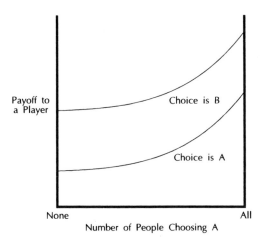

Figure 1.2

illustrates the role of externalities in a binary choice situation. The number of people choosing option A is indicated along the horizontal axis. The payoff to an individual choosing A or B is indicated along the vertical axis, with a different curve for each action. The curves slope upward, indicating that whether one chooses A or B, one prefers that other people choose A. A might represent a decision to pick up litter as one walks along public paths. Or for the partners in a law firm, A might mean investing effort to nurture new employees. Given the curves of figure 1.2, no one would engage in the socially desirable behavior, because each individual's payoff to choosing B is always greater, no matter how many others select A. Good deeds benefit many, but return only a small reward to their author. Note once again the span of application of this strategic model.[2]

To cope with such situations, all manner of social institutions arise. Apprentices learn to return the loyalty of their mentors, so there is at least some reciprocal benefit. The society as a whole inculcates values, hoping to make litterers uncomfortable. And when neither indoctrination nor personal benefits can be sufficient, often society imposes extreme penalties for nonsocial behavior. During war, for example, the army may not be confident that young men will risk their lives for honor and duty. The penalties for desertion, as a consequence, are draconian.

Information

Information is often described as the quintessential public good, for its use by one individual does not reduce the amount available to another. Of course, the value of information may depend on its not being generally available. If Lucy discovers that IBM is undervalued, she will hardly wish to tell the world until she has made her own purchases at the prevailing bargain price. And if IBM itself determines that parallel processing is the key to economical data compression and ultimately high-definition TV, and if such information is not patentable, it will hardly rush to announce its findings to its rivals. At the more mundane level, all of us recognize the tension when we decide whether to share the name of our wonderful little-known restaurant, or for that matter a recipe.

In many situations, however, the value of information is unaffected, or even increased, by wide distribution. If I know the best way to balance my investment portfolio between bonds and stocks, I am no worse off if you copy my methods. And if we find a ski resort more fun when our friends are on the same slopes, then we have a positive incentive to share information. So too, manufacturers have learned that it is frequently desirable to have others adopt their technology, even if they will lose some of the benefits from any particular use of the technology. Most computer companies now freely provide information on their operating systems, so that other companies will develop compatible software, which in turn will make their system more desirable. Sony's Betamax experience showed that a superior technology can be defeated if it does not achieve wide use. The company's later purchase of Columbia Pictures was designed to ensure that enough software would be available for its new products. The Japanese, more generally, have learned the advantages of coordinating on industry standards.

As interconnectability and networks become more and more the norm, compatibility concerns will become ever more important. The danger, of course, is that we may QWERTY ourselves by choosing the wrong technology (as with the infamous typewriter keyboard that met the needs of the nineteenth century and could not be dislodged in the twentieth). We may lock ourselves in the wrong equilibrium. Where compatibility is critical, it is exceedingly costly to be out of the mainstream. Inappropriately chosen technologies may take decades to reverse.

The United States, for example, has effectively dropped out of the business of developing new nuclear power plants, even though this technology is less harmful environmentally than either coal or oil. Given the antinuclear regulatory climate, a company that had developed a substantially cheaper and safer nuclear technology might not have been able to make much headway in the United States in the last decade. And should we decide to begin building nuclear power plants again, we will have to catch up on many years of missed opportunities for learning to work with the latest technical advances. What was the problem? Why did our competitive system break down? The answer lies in externalities, the lack of an ability to commit to safe practices, and a highly imperfect regulatory process. Given the magnitude of the potential liabilities that would result from a Chernobyl-style accident, no company can guarantee to pay for all damages. Indeed, by law the U.S. government is the residual claims payer (over $600 million) should a nuclear accident occur. Normally companies investing in new products merely commit their own money. When they put the health or dollars of others on the line, those others claim the right to be consulted. That is why we have risk-control regulation for technologies such as power generation. Given the way the process operates, unfortunately, decisions are shaped as much by battling advocates as by deliberating regulators.

In principle, the advocacy system generates information and the truth is revealed. In practice, it appears, few minds are swayed, with ample reason. First, there is no expectation that one will reveal all relevant information or present information in a nondistorting fashion. Second, there is no requirement that critics or advocates must put their money where their mouths are; there is little penalty for being proved wrong. Third, enormous rents shuttle back and forth depending on the outcome of the process: Is the power plant approved, is the corporate takeover permitted, is the new drug placed on the market? The incentive to distort is tremendous.

Parimutuel gambling and investing in the stock market represent a very different approach to aggregating information. Each participant has a strong incentive to question his own information, and pay heed to the data provided directly or indirectly by others. If I have information suggesting a company is underpriced, I must be concerned about why its stock is not higher (that is, why other investors are betting against me). And if I bet and am wrong, I pay the consequences.

Where information affects the welfare of many, we can think of a continuum. At one end we have betting situations, in which information is not freely shared but will emerge through prices in the market or odds at the track. At the other end we have advocacy processes, in which the payoff depends less on the correctness of one's view than on whether one is able to convince others; information unfavorable to either side's point of view gets suppressed.

Finally, consider information acquisition and sharing when there is herd behavior. Like lemmings or migrating butterflies, human beings like to travel in herds, particularly if quality or appropriate behavior is difficult to judge, so that comparative standards are employed. Both individuals and institutions hesitate to get too far out of line with their peers. (Company A knows that observers will be comparing its balance sheet with B's. Bank C's lending to Third World borrowers will be weighed against the practices of other institutions.) The sticky question is who decides what the balance sheet should look like, or what level of Third World debt is appropriate. This consensus activity poses at least two problems. First, no one has a sufficient incentive to gather information that will be of benefit to the group, and as each participant seeks to be in the center of the herd, no one is really responsible for its location or direction. Second, payment asymmetries may complicate the situation. If each bank wishes to earn just a little more than the norm, each will pay just a smidgen to move toward the head of the herd. What we thought of as a migration may turn into a stampede, a bubble, or merely a fad.

We have organized the essays of this volume into three sections, defined by the number of players in a strategic situation. The reader will find that situations involving many players possess important common elements, as do those with few players and just one. We have titled our three sections "Micromotives and Macrobehavior," "Commitment and the Strategy of Conflict," and "Choice and Consequence." Devotees of the field will recognize allusions to works by Thomas Schelling, to whom we dedicate this book.

Part I. Micromotives and Macrobehavior: Many Players

Riots and revolutions have many players. So too do fashion crazes. There is a risk, with no one in charge, that the outcome will be undesirable for everyone. The anonymous city becomes litter-strewn. In the rush to the theater exit, many get trampled. Many-player situations are explored in the first five chapters of this volume, which highlight a few central questions. What is the legitimacy and nature of outcomes when an individual's welfare depends on comparisons with the welfare of another? Under what circumstances can we assure that collective outcomes will resemble what the participants desire? And more generally, how can we organize society to promote desirable outcomes?

Externalities of Valuation

Economists usually assume that individuals evaluate their welfare on some absolute basis: what utility do I reap from the goods and services available to me? Often, however, one is judged in relation to others. Teachers grade on a curve; girls try to attract the cutest boys in their school; promotions are given to employees who perform better than their peers. When judgments and big prizes, such as promotions, are awarded on the basis of relative standing, rat races may result.[3] To inhibit such destructive competitions, society frequently develops norms against excessive efforts. Among undergraduates on many campuses, there is an ethic against studying too hard. One student of my acquaintance gamed against this norm. He holed up in a room in Boston to study for exams, but purchased a sunlamp. When he reemerged, he told all his friends he'd had a lovely time in Jamaica.

Robert Frank's chapter 2, "Positional Externalities," evaluates situations in which an individual's welfare depends on comparisons with others. The comparison may be made by a player on the other side of the market, such as a boss considering whom to promote or a customer seeking a motel along a strip in a small town, or by the individual himself. In many workplaces, including most universities, salaries are not publicized. Many of us would find our welfare substantially diminished, even though our income remained the same, if we discovered that our colleagues were earning more than we were. In part that is because the discovery would reveal the boss's view of us. In part our reaction would be merely envy.

Envy is a subtle and powerful feeling, motivating everything from political movements to murders. Jon Elster's chapter 3, "Envy in Social Life," starts with the simple observation that envy diminishes the welfare of the envious. Operationally, an envious person—whatever his own holdings—would prefer that others have less, and he might even sacrifice a little of his own wealth to achieve that end. From these simple observations, all manner of strategic predictions and prescriptions follow. Whereas society is supposedly organized to help create value, envy may help to destroy it. Individuals may choose their associations to control or avoid envy.

If envy may be a powerful force from the dark side, understanding may be a weapon to control it. I like to ask my American students whether, when they come back for their tenth reunion, they would prefer to find that per capita income is $25,000 in Japan and $24,000 in the United States, or that Japan is at $22,000 with the United States at $23,000. Many choose the latter. But as powerful as envy may be, it is vulnerable to intellectual and moral scrutiny. Even a brief reminder that envy may be a base emotion, and that a generous-spirited individual would wish the Japanese well, seems to be sufficient to sway many votes.[4]

Complex Systems

In simple systems, patterns of causality and payoffs are known. Strategic choices are relatively easy. But when there are many players, as our early chapters reveal, the uncoordinated social result can be far inferior to what might be achieved through incentives and cooperative action. The challenge to the analyst is to design (or at least describe) mechanisms that induce choices by individual actors that redound to the welfare of all. Chapter 4, "Free Riding versus Cooperation," by Howard Margolis, takes us through the array of possible strategies for securing cooperation in interactive situations of this sort, but soberly describes as well the need to allow for potential free riding. Once we take even a small move away from simple binary choices, such as the decision whether to free ride or cooperate, the analytic challenge multiplies. We cannot prescribe what we want people to do before we predict what consequences will result from various patterns of action.

Competitive markets can coordinate the actions of millions of individuals and produce an efficient allocation of resources. Forces of natural selection create evolutionary patterns that we believe more or less optimize the survival fitness of species over millions of generations. And most ecosystems, if left undisturbed by human beings, achieve elegant balances. The danger is that these examples will lead us to underestimate the difficulty of both prediction and coordination. In fact, no individual or group could possibly plan an outcome as effective as the uncoordinated market achieves. As science advances, we have become more humble in many areas. In comparison with a few decades ago, economists are more suspicious of market interventions, and ecologists less likely to think we can beneficially intervene in the natural environment. Moreover, unplanned systems for resource allocation (e.g., pluralistic politics) often achieve not only acceptable results but far greater legitimacy than would be accorded any centrally controlled system.

Benign neglect is not the answer to every problem, however. In many situations, the question is not whether to intervene at all in a complex system, but how to act in a manner that has a reasonable chance of leading to a desirable outcome. The strategic analyst must frequently be concerned with prediction tasks in unexplored domains. Will the collapse of the Soviet Union and Eastern Bloc hamper efforts to control nuclear proliferation? Will the economic conditions of these nations deteriorate over many years, or will downward spirals engender corrective forces? How can a federal system operate when units at all levels are running substantial deficits? In chapter 5, "Systems Effects," Robert Jervis explores situations in which the choice of all is the choice of none—that is, the effects of many individual actions cumulate in nonlinear fashion, and straightforward policy interventions are often counterproductive. This discussion reveals the difficulties of trying to act effectively within systems that are not subject to a powerful coordinating force such as the market or natural selection.

The grandest system question of all is how to organize our governments and our economies. The two questions are inextricably linked. Most socialist countries, it appears, sacrificed economic well-being along with democracy. European countries are now pondering political unification, giving up centuries of individual national political tradition, to bolster economic competitiveness. Japan and some of its smaller neighbors, roaring successes in the economic realm, have their own, distinctively soft-pedaled, approaches to democracy. Mancur Olson's chapter 6, "Autocracy, Democracy, and Prosperity," engages the government-prosperity relationship at its roots. It examines the expected performance of these polar forms of government in promoting the well-being of the citizenry, and concludes for democracy.

Part II. Commitment and the Strategy of Conflict: A Few Players

When players are few, outcomes are difficult to predict, because each player's action substantially influences the welfare of others. How can we assure people that we will do what we say we will do? From whence comes trust? And thinking in terms of trust and relationships, how can we draw the not-so-obvious distinction between gifts and bribes? How can we employ third parties to tie our hands and thereby improve outcomes? These questions are discussed in the chapters that follow, with a concluding overview chapter that places them in context.

A few-player situation—be it a squabbling married couple, two competing stores, or a boss and her subordinates—has strong elements of both cooperation and conflict. Because individual participants can affect outcomes more significantly than in many-player contexts, this is a tempting arena for strategic ploys, such as issuing threats or misrepresenting preferences.

Trust and Credibility

The problems of trust and credibility are central to the function of governments, friendships, and business relationships. Even supposed enemies are likely to have sufficient overlap of interests that the ability to make a commitment is critical. Would it not be in the interest of the Palestinians to make a binding commitment to Israel to facilitate a trade of land for peace? With friends, credibility is stronger, but how strong can it be? Business and marriage partnerships can deteriorate swiftly, turning allies into enemies.

To the cynical analyst, trust is a matter of a common interest or an established relationship. Parents and children or members of an ethnic group may benefit from a natural element of common interest, which helps to explain ethnic voting patterns and the inheritance process. Most dealings have no such benefits. Credibility may be built slowly through reputation and mutually beneficial transactions, or more quickly by establishing appropriate patterns of payoffs. In chapter 7, "Making Strategies Credible," Avinash Dixit and Barry Nalebuff provide an insightful guide to that subject. They focus on informational approaches (e.g., cutting off communication), the alteration of payoffs to make threats and promises credible, and the use of outside players (e.g., to carry out your promises or act on your behalf).

Trust might be thought of as a game. Each successful play provides reinforcement. We start with small investments and small risks. We may lose, but should we gain we are led to a land of greater payoffs. In this formulation, as Russell Hardin phrases it in chapter 8, "Trusting Persons, Trusting Institutions," the public good of trust may be primarily a manifestation of encapsulated interest. That is, a trusting environment can be a strategic outcome, not a norm built on moral reasoning. It is a great advantage to a society to have established a norm of trust rather than distrust. Contracts, relationships, and business and political dealings are all facilitated. Replaying a theme from part I, there are likely to be significant externalities from one relationship to another. If A proves trustworthy with B, then B may believe the odds favor his trusting C. Given the same set of members, a society may have sustainable high- and low-trust equilibria. I am willing to behave in a more trustworthy manner if everyone else does too. Then I will not only have greater confidence in my peers, but I will worry that any cheating on my part might catalyze an unraveling to the low-trust equilibrium. Presumably when trust is high, untrustworthy behavior will be more severely censured.

Our chapter on trust opens with the story of a lieutenant colonel who parks army funds with a merchant, who rewards him under the table. When the officer is abruptly relieved of his command, the merchant denies ever having received such funds. The general lesson is that expectations of mutually acceptable behavior get shattered when one party's circumstances change or threaten to change. The lesson is reinforced in shadowy worlds of illicit behavior.

The famed prisoners' dilemma is a striking example. Two partners in crime who vowed never to snitch on each other are caught red-handed in a single robbery. The expected sentence is two years. Each prisoner is told in private that if he confesses to the pair's other robberies and his partner does not, he will get off with one year. Moreover, if his partner confesses and he does not, he can expect a five-year sentence. If both confess, there is some credit for coming clean; they both get three years. Note that whatever your partner does, it is better to confess. You get one year rather than two if your partner is mute, and three years rather than five if he squeals. If both players reason this way and confess, each gets three years. Yet silence by both would bring two years each.

Large crime syndicates have recognized this problem and implemented a strategic solution. To facilitate trust among syndicate members (enabling each prisoner to keep his lips confidently sealed), it is necessary to deter squealing, and the most obvious way to do that is by altering the payoff schedule. The outcome of the prisoner's dilemma may be quite different when the reward for confessing includes not only a reduced prison sentence but also the promise (admittedly from a different authority) of death or disability.

Third-Party Interests

Robert Klitgaard's chapter 9, "Gifts and Bribes," notes how the innocuous favor, say a laudatory book blurb, may be issued in the hope or expectation of some form of repayment in the future. Exchanges that look like the building of trust in a two-party relationship may be undesirable if third-party interests are affected. Thus country clubs prohibit tipping, and government officials are not allowed to accept honoraria. Corruption—how to identify it and how to fight it—is the focus of this chapter's discussion of bribes. A tribute to Thomas Schelling—an act of love, not a payback—illuminates gifts.

When two players bargain, third parties may have an interest that gets neglected or overridden. That is an argument for giving the third party property rights, though it is hard to establish a property right in many areas, such as fair dealing in awarding contracts. We seek to impose rules against nepotism or side payments as a means of protecting third parties.

The strategy of choice is filled with conundrums and seemingly counterintuitive results. We recognize that third parties may be exploited. Might we bring in a third party to help us secure a better deal when bargaining with another? Jerry Green's chapter 10, "The Strategic Use of Contracts with Third Parties," takes up an issue Schelling raised three decades ago. Under what circumstances can one make a contract, which merely gives a third party money should various contingencies arise, that creates value for oneself in the bargaining process? The rigorous answer to this question provides its own intriguing results. For example, a silent third-party partner is often preferable to one who plays an active role.

The Ideas of Thomas Schelling

This book will have failed if it does not lead its readers to think differently about the world. It should serve as the opening salvo in an intellectual conversation. If so, Thomas Schelling should be a delighted third party, for our readers will be carrying on in the tradition he pioneered. This book seeks to capture elements of his spirit of investigation,[5] and in chapter 11, "Thomas Schelling and the Analysis of Strategic Behavior," Vince Crawford accepts the specific charge of tracing the impact of a broad thinker on a broad field.

Schelling's approach is to extract the central lessons from real-life phenomena and capture them in simple formulations. In an exercise designed to explore and explain segregation, he placed pennies on a checkerboard, heads and tails for blacks and whites. One's neighborhood consists of the eight surrounding pennies. People differ in their preferences for the color composition of their neighborhood and move when dissatisfied. His startling result is that extreme segregation can result from preferences for residing in neighborhoods where one's own type predominates only slightly.

If there are regularities in the strategic universe, they will be found in the activities of children, parlor-game-type experiments, and everyday social occurrences. In these contexts external influences may be more controllable and more comprehensible, allowing the detection of strategic principles that also apply in grander contexts, but there under heavier camouflage. Schelling sweeps aside conventional wisdom as he reveals parallels between the mundane and the profound.

An economist by training, a policy analyst by demand, a teacher by inclination—Schelling is the world's foremost strategic thinker about social situations and human behavior. He is an acknowledged expert in such areas as global warming (which involves many players), arms control and deterrence (few players), and smoking behavior (one player). Though specialists in such fields may recognize his creativity and his insight, they may well miss the subtle common threads in his analysis: incentives and externalities, information flow and credibility, self-control and a full accounting of costs and benefits. We, his students, have learned that important strategic insights are to be found primarily at the juncture of theory and application. Most important interactive situations mix elements of conflict and cooperation. Although many strategic elements are common to disparate economic and social phenomena, minor differences in structure or parameters within any particular situation can often lead to dramatically different outcomes.

Part III. Choice and Consequence: Just Oneself

In democratic societies, individual welfare is traditionally seen as the basic criterion for judging overall performance and well-being. A classic challenge to philosophers and economists is to define ways to aggregate measures of well-being for different individuals. The attempt to design effective institutions or a just society usually starts from the assumption that individuals know and will choose what they want.

The chapters in the third part of our book demonstrate that we cannot assume that human beings will make choices that accord with the well-developed theory of rational decision. Individuals do not assess their welfare today on any absolute basis, but compare it with yesterday's. Frequently they make choices on the basis of principles, having preferences as a secondary consideration. Where uncertainty is involved (alas the norm in most important choices), decision making may stray further from rational prescription. Our final chapter considers human choices in a particularly troubling area, the valuation of human life. These chapters pose a challenge to those who describe decision-making behavior, to those who would like to train individuals to improve their choices, and to those who would prescribe for society.

Outcomes Not Known

For most important lifetime choices, the long-term consequences of the decision cannot be known at the outset. It is impossible to know exactly how one's relationship will evolve with an intended spouse, or whether ingesting animal fats today will induce cancer forty years later. In contemplating such choices, we should distinguish *risk, uncertainty,* and *ignorance.* With risk, we know the states of the world that may occur and the probability of each state (a flipped coin is 50 percent likely to come up heads, and 50 percent tails). With uncertainty, the probabilities can only be estimated statistically, as in the fats-and-cancer example.

All too often we must choose despite ignorance; we do not even know all possible states of the world, let alone their probabilities. Choices made in the realm of manufacturing determine the chemicals that spew upward, yet we are quite uncertain how the receiving atmosphere will respond. And even if we could predict that, say, a one-degree warming would result, we have little idea what that implies for activity back on earth. In sum, when we choose in ignorance, there is a reasonable probability of a significant surprise, which makes choosing very difficult indeed. (The surprise may be pleasant, as with the brevity of the coalition's ground war with Iraq.)

Externalities among Decisions

Parents know they should not take apparent physical risks when their children are present, even if they would otherwise feel justified in doing so. We tell our child not to dash across the street without looking each way, and offer no cost-benefit-based exception for quiet streets on which one could certainly hear an approaching automobile.

Interrelationships among decisions can affect not only our approach to making choices, but our assessment of the outcomes. Teachers know they should grade more leniently as the term comes to the end, as a way to keep students from becoming discouraged by chance downticks, indeed to make them believe they are gaining momentum. Sometimes our penchant for comparisons poses a strategic conundrum. If one prepares a spectacular dinner for a new romantic interest, does that create a pleasant eternal memory, or an unrealistic expectation leading to disappointment in future meals? One may also manage oneself. If theater is our favorite recreation, should we not end our European trip in London, thus on a high note? But why then should honeymoons be a big splurge, and not third anniversaries? The way past outcomes affect present enjoyments is the theme of chapter 12, "Endowment and Contrast in Judgments of Well-Being," by Amos Tversky and Dale Griffin.

Decision theorists have carved out a distinctive niche for themselves by focusing on rational choice processes. Such processes, they and I believe, lead to outcomes that are superior in terms of satisfying preferences. But more may be involved. Welfare may depend on the choice process itself. If I wish to conceive of myself as a consistently prudent person, or indeed to have any particular view of myself, I may be concerned with how I approach decisions. When ordinary mortals are asked how one should make decisions in life, they are likely to offer answers such as "Develop a philosophy to live by," or"Rely on strong moral principles," or "Do what is right." These prescriptions are not necessarily antagonistic to rational choice, but neither do they give it prominence. The rational choice approach, though yielding more in the way in substantive rewards, may be repellent to many real-world decision makers because it is emotionally less satisfying, subject to individuals' perceptual biases, and devoid of moral content. As a result, individuals may act on principles instead. Drazen Prelec and Richard Herrnstein examine the alternative bases for decision in chapter 13, "Preferences or Principles: Alternative Guidelines for Choice."

Pursuit of Rationality

No debate is more fundamental for strategic choice than the potential for rationality. Even when risks—possible outcomes and probabilities—are well defined, we may have trouble making decisions. If the consequences are not merely financial, as with life-and-dollar decisions, or if the relevant probabilities are exceedingly small, the difficulties may be severe.

Consider for yourself an uncomfortable life-and-dollar problem involving Russian roulette. In the first scenario there are three bullets in the six chambers of the gun. How much would you pay to be allowed to remove one? (Assume that you have no dependents.) In the second scenario there is only one bullet in the gun. How much would you pay to get rid of this bullet? Most people say they would pay more in the second scenario, although rational decision theory would suggest the opposite. Each purchase removes a one-in-six probability of death. In the first situation, however, there is some chance that you will be killed by one of the other bullets, in which case any money you have not spent is worthless (or worth less). People make an "irrational" choice because they give excessive weight to achieving certainty in comparison with merely improving a chance.

Human beings find small probabilities almost impossible to assess, even if they are directly specified. Suppose you are considering investing in partnership A, which in merely two years will double your money. There is unfortunately one chance in 100 that you will be sued successfully. If so, you will lose ten times your initial investment. After wrestling with the decision, you decline the partnership.

Now suppose a new investment opportunity, partnership B, comes along, similar in all respects to A except the chance of the ten-times-investment loss is only 1 in 1,000. Now your expected loss is only 1 percent of your initial investment rather than 10 percent. If you were torn with indecision before, you should surely take B. However, we suspect that many reluctant decliners of A would also reluctantly decline B.

The two situations just described could be explored in a laboratory. In the real world, decision making is still more difficult, because additional factors intrude on rationality. To begin, individuals must make decisions over long periods of time and may wish to be consistent in their approaches, both to reduce internal conflict and to send signals to others. Rational choice theory suggests that we should weigh risks and benefits, at some times taking the risky option, at others opting for the certainty. Howard Raiffa's chapter 14, "Coping with Common Errors in Rational Decision Making," focuses on the obstacles encountered in assessing and valuing outcomes. It provides a short course, complete with pragmatic recommendations, on how we as a society, as organized entities such as corporations, and as individuals should contend with real decision problems.

The most challenging decision arena of all is the one where lives and dollars compete. Our society has not done well in these decisions. Far from relying on rationality, principles, or any other organized approach to decision, we struggle with a haphazard process of litigation, ill-informed legislation, and market processes crippled not just by obstructed information flow but by the institutional arrangements that have developed to compensate for such shortcomings. The result is that we spend substantially more than we should to save fewer lives than we should, employing methods that promote dissatisfaction, not legitimacy. In chapter 15, "Strategic and Ethical Issues in the Valuation of Life," Kip Viscusi strides into this debate. While acknowledging the difficulties, he urges us to take seriously our responsibility to value lives at risk.

Conclusion

The number of players in a game, the criterion that provides the organizing principle for this volume, defines many but hardly all of the strategic features of decision situations. A variety of themes are essentially universal. The following list illustrates the kind of injunctions that might prove helpful to a participant in any strategic situation.

1. Put yourself in the other person's shoes. Whether you are struggling with your procrastinating alter ego or a mugger, it helps to consider how the world looks to him.

2. Think explicitly about the strategies available to all players, and about the payoffs they will receive. This principle might have helped the Soviet putsch plotters recognize that through mere delay their tank crews would be tacitly fostering the "don't attack" equilibrium.

3. Beware of externalities of valuation, and consider which way they run. Am I better off to work in a setting where my colleagues are more or less able than I am? What will be the consequence of breaking all records in your first quarter as a salesperson: will you have established a strong reputation that will carry you through periods of more disappointing results, or set a standard that you will be routinely expected to better?

4. Understand what you really value. Do you want to earn enough to have a comfortable life, or to outdo the Joneses? And how much stress should you put on making decisions according to the rules of rational choice? What advantages would you reap if you proceeded on the basis of principle?

5. Recognize your own feelings about strategic behavior. When is it desirable or acceptable to exaggerate or hide information? Would you overstate a preference in a committee meeting if you expected it to be discounted, or vote against an amendment you favored because its passage might hurt the chances of an original motion you supported? If you were uncertain about your ability to perform well in your new position, would you acknowledge your doubts to your superior when she asked?

6. In sharpening your strategic thinking, try proceeding from the abstract to the particular, but also from the everyday to the cosmic, from the local to the global. If you think first about strategies for getting your son to clean up his room, you may get ideas that will be helpful as you contemplate what can really be accomplished on the West Bank.

This book will have been a success if its readers see the world with new richness. Strategic choice behavior is everywhere, though it often goes unremarked, and its outcomes may be far from straightforward. When each driver slows down almost imperceptibly for a look at a minor roadside distraction, as Schelling pointed out, the result can be a massive traffic tie-up. The college student seeking to curtail his alcohol consumption can impose strict or moderate limits on himself; the latter may be more resilient when temptation triumphs. Every parent has threatened a child with punishment at a time when he knew (and the child knew) he would have neither the incentive nor the will to carry out the threat.

This volume is in some ways a "how-to" book. Were we to follow the conventions of the self-help literature, we might suggest that readers will end up with better marriages, smaller waistlines, or more cooperative work environments. We make a less precise but more credible promise. Acquaint yourself with the strategy of choice. Your successes should be more frequent, and your failures better understood.

Notes

1. When uncertainty plays a role, the setter-decider formulation no longer assures a trade when it will be desirable. The setter has a more complex objective: to pick a price that maximizes the probability of acceptance (i.e., below buyer's reservation price) times the gain on the transaction (price less setter's reservation price).

2. This diagram, to my knowledge, first appeared in Thomas Schelling's *Micromotives and Macrobehavior*, W. W. Norton and Company, 1978.

3. Big prizes may be necessary for any of a variety of reasons. The position of vice-president or boyfriend, for example, may be indivisible. Moreover, if performance is somewhat random and difficult to measure, big prize differentials may be necessary for adequate incentives.

4. To cast ahead in our volume, chapter 12 addresses welfare comparisons when one's own successful past may be not only an object of warm reflection, but also a landmark for unfavorable comparisons that generate future dissatisfaction.

5. For a fuller description of these thoughts, see my article "Distinguished Fellow, Reflections on Thomas Schelling," *Journal of Economic Perspectives*, Spring 1989, pp. 153–164.

I

Micromotives and Macrobehavior: Many Players

2

Positional Externalities

Robert H. Frank

In *Micromotives and Macrobehavior*, Thomas Schelling observes that hockey players, left to their own devices, almost never wear helmets, even though almost all of them would vote for helmet rules in secret ballots. Not wearing a helmet increases the odds of winning, perhaps by making it slightly easier to see and hear, or perhaps by intimidating opposing players (on the view that it is not safe to challenge someone who is crazy enough to play without a helmet). At the same time, not wearing a helmet increases the odds of getting hurt. If players value the higher odds of winning more than they value the extra safety, it is rational not to wear helmets. The irony, Schelling observes, is that when all discard their helmets, the competitive balance is the same as if all had worn them.

The helmet problem is an example of what we may call a *positional externality*. The decision to wear a helmet has important effects not only for the person who wears it, but also for the frame of reference in which he and others operate. In such situations, the payoffs to individuals depend in part on their positions within this frame of reference. With hockey players, what counts is not their playing ability in any absolute sense, but how they perform relative to their opponents. Where positional externalities (or indeed, externalities of any other sort) are present, Schelling has taught us, individually rational behavior often adds up to a result that none would have chosen.

Positional externalities frequently take the form of the familiar prisoner's dilemma. Consider two hockey teams—say, the Bruins and Rangers—each of which can choose to wear helmets or not. The four possible combinations of choices and the assumed rankings of each for the two teams are shown in table 2.1. The key assumption implicit in these rankings is that members of each team value an increase in their odds of winning more than they value the safety increment pro-

Table 2.1
The helmet decision as prisoner's dilemma

		Bruins	
		Wear helmets	Don't wear helmets
Rangers	Wear helmets	Second best for each	Best for Bruins Worst for Rangers
	Don't wear helmets	Best for Rangers Worst for Bruins	Third best for each

vided by helmets. Given these rankings, the dominant strategy for each team is to go without helmets. Yet this combination of choices is worse for both teams than the alternative in which each team wears helmets. And hence the attraction of a helmet rule.

As Schelling demonstrated in *Micromotives*, positional externalities cast a broad net. They affect how we choose seats in auditoriums, how we sort ourselves by race and sex, how we choose mates, even how we might choose genes for our children. In this essay, I augment Schelling's list. My additions are organized into two parts. First I discuss actions that alter some important frame of reference affecting other people or organizations, which I call "positional externalities between agents." Then I examine actions that alter a frame of reference important for the actor himself in the future ("positional externalities within agents"). Positional externalities of both types seem to play some part in explaining a variety of behavior, norms, laws, and institutions. To forestall unnecessary quarrels, I emphasize at the outset that positional externalities need not be the only, or even the most important, explanation for these phenomena.

Positional Externalities between Agents

Twenty-Four-Hour Grocery Stores

Ithaca, a town of 30,000 people in central New York, has seven large supermarkets. Five of them are open twenty-four hours a day. On the rare occasions when I have patronized one of these stores in the middle of the night, I have been almost the only shopper. The convenience of an all-night shopping option could be maintained at lower cost if all but one of these stores were to close during the late-night hours.[1] But the stores, acting individually, apparently do not find it profitable to take such a course.

A simple positional externality helps explain the divergence between private and collective interests. Most people do the bulk of their shopping at a single store. Grocery shopping, after all, is largely a matter of habit, and going to a store with even a slightly unfamiliar layout can upset the normal routine. In choosing which store to patronize, people look for the most convenient package of price, variety, location, hours, and other service features. In communities where most people have cars, physical location is less important than other features. Of course, if nonlocational elements of the service package are essentially the same, the consumer will shop at the store closest to home. But if one store offers a better value along some other service dimension, consumers will freely switch to it. For example, if all stores are equally attractive except for their hours of business, many people will choose the one with the longest hours. Having convenient hours may not be the most important service feature, but even small advantages often tip the balance in close decisions.

Now imagine an initial situation in which all stores close at the same hour—say, 9 P.M. If any one store extends its hours until 10 P.M., it will enlarge its market share. And it may then pay the remaining stores to match the first store's move. If the cost of extended hours is not prohibitive, the only stable equilibrium may be for each store to remain open twenty-four hours. In such situations, the public might be well served by amending the antitrust laws to permit stores to limit hours, perhaps through an agreement whereby each store serves in turn as the only all-night grocery. Alternatively, local statutes might achieve a similar purpose by limiting business hours. Such statutes are often called "blue laws" and remain on the books in many jurisdictions.

Excessive Formalism in Economics

The same forces that help produce the twenty-four-hour grocery store may also help explain the phenomenon of excessive formalism in the economics profession. Several years ago, I submitted a paper to the *American Economic Review* in which I outlined my argument verbally in the main body of the paper, then explored its technical details in an appendix. I was asked to revise the paper by eliminating the verbal development of the argument and the discussion of its implications, and focusing instead on the appendix model. Reluctantly I complied, and the paper that was eventually published forces readers to wade through a tangle of idiosyncratic notation to follow what had originally been an easily accessible argument.

The precision of formalism has obvious advantages. Yet most economists believe that our profession would be better off if more technical material were relegated to appendices. If this belief is valid, why does formalism persist so stubbornly?

Again, positional externalities suggest a possible answer. Of the many qualities of mind a scholar might have, economists rightly prize rigorous thinking above most others. Each candidate for a job thus wants to be perceived as more rigorous than the competing candidates.[2] While highly complex mathematical analysis is not the only way to certify oneself as a rigorous thinker, it is almost surely the most *efficient* way. Its inherent complexity throws up a barrier that only nimble minds can scale. By contrast, many more people can construct verbal arguments, which by their nature leave greater room for subjective debate about level of rigor.

It is thus perfectly rational for an individual job candidate to employ a level of formalism just slightly higher than that of others. But like grocery store managers deciding how long to stay open, competing candidates face compelling pressure to match any escalation in formalism. The result is a shifting frame of reference. In the current environment, many people feel compelled to use tools more formidable than necessary for the problem at hand. Collectively, we would communicate more effectively if we relegated more of our formal analysis to appendices. But it is not necessarily rational for any individual to take this step.

How might excessive formalism be mitigated? As with the hockey helmet rule, the most direct approach would be to build collective input into decisions about the level of formalism. Editors could encourage the relegation of technical details to appendices, or certain journals could pledge themselves to presenting ideas in nontechnical language. (The American Economic Association's *Journal of Economic Perspectives* was launched on this premise.)

If excessive formalism is a form of positional signaling, we should see less of it among scholars of established reputation, who are in effect free to choose their own level of discourse. Seminars by theorists like Gerard Debreu and Roy Radner are typically filled with intuitive examples and a minimum of algebraic manipulation. But less established scholars often feel they must fill several blackboards with algebra, lest their audience mistakenly conclude that they are unable to do so. At the local level, the sponsors of seminars have some power to alter this outcome. If the audience knew that speakers had been *instructed* to adopt a less formal mode, speakers could do so without fear of signaling weakness of mind.

Cycles of Fashion

People today look back with amusement to the ridiculously high tailfins of the 1957 Plymouth and the short hemlines of the late 1960s. Positional externalities suggest how people with a normal sense of esthetics could once have found those designs palatable; and indeed why those same designs may again cycle back into fashion.

For a design to appear innovative or fresh, it must differ somehow from existing designs. If existing cars lack tailfins, the addition of even a very small fin creates an eye-catching profile. And because having such a profile confers a marketing advantage, competitors are quick to add small tailfins of their own. An arms race ensues, and within a few years cars have fins so large that they would surely violate an absolute esthetic standard (assuming such a standard exists). At this point, the stage is set for designers to achieve a bold new look by offering a car without any tailfins, as in fact happened in the early 1960s. Similar dynamics appear to govern the hem length of dresses, the cut of men's suits, the width of neckties and lapels, the size of shoulder pads, and a host of other fashion details. In most cases, the evolutionary design progression seems to reach almost grotesque proportions before individual designers can profit by retreating to an earlier stage in the cycle.

Whether positional externalities lead to cycles or not depends in part on whether there are natural limits on the positional arms race in question. Grocery stores cannot stay open more than twenty-four hours a day, and if continuous operation is not forbiddingly costly, there may be no tendency for individual stores to break ranks. But there are no similar limits on the length of tailfins or the width of lapels. In these cases, the positional arms race is likely to continue until it reaches a breaking point.

Cycles of Public Spiritedness

In his splendid book *Shifting Involvements*, Albert Hirschman observes that the "public mood" of the United States oscillates between private acquisitiveness and public spiritedness. The length of the cycle varies considerably but averages about two decades. In the late 1940s and 1950s, people were primarily concerned with personal material advancement, a mood that gave way to greater community orientation with the New Frontier and Great Society movements of the 1960s. Similarly, after the egoistic emphasis of the last two decades, there is now at least talk of a kinder, gentler orientation.

Positional externalities appear to play a role in these movements. Most people like to think of themselves as being socially responsible, but the criteria that define this quality are strongly dependent on local frames of reference. Thus, for example, the standards of behavior for used car salesmen are considerably more lenient than those for bishops. The role of context in personal evaluation is especially important when standards of behavior in the population change systematically. Suppose, for example, that society is currently in an egoistic mode, with relatively undemanding standards of virtuous conduct. Now if, as Hirschman suggests, people become concerned about the problems generated by their egoism—pollution, inequality, criminal activity, and so on—they may begin to behave more altruistically. The aggregate effect of this change is to raise the standard each person must meet before he or she can take satisfaction from being a virtuous person. And this, in turn, causes the level of virtuous behavior to rise still further. In the process, it becomes increasingly difficult, in absolute terms, for a person to command approval. Eventually, it pays some people to retreat, just as eventually it paid some designers to reintroduce cars without tailfins. The retreat from virtuous conduct sets in motion a downward escalation; eventually a floor is reached, and the cycle is ready to renew.

Bureaucratic Language

Positional externalities also seem to shed light on the standards of language used by federal bureaucrats. While chairman of the Civil Aeronautics Board, Alfred Kahn wrote a memorandum lampooning the bureaucratic language then typical of the board's regulatory orders. His favorite targets were circumlocutions and pomposities like the ones in the following paragraph taken from a board order:

The holder [of a CAB certificate] may continue to serve regularly any point named herein through the airport last regularly used by the holder to serve such point prior to the effective date of the certificate. Upon compliance with such procedures relating thereto as may be prescribed by the Board, the holder may, in addition to the services hereinabove expressly prescribed, regularly serve a point named herein through any airport convenient thereto.[3]

When Kahn's memo found its way into the press, the responses included a marriage proposal from a *Boston Globe* columnist, a nomination for the Nobel Prize from a Singapore newspaper, and an editorial endorsement from the *Washington Post*. In the wake of this publicity, at least some board bureaucrats scurried to employ more direct language.

Suppose, for the sake of argument, that all bureaucrats adopted the clear, direct language Kahn advocated. A look at the incentives facing bureaucrats suggests that this new position would not be stable. In their choice of language, bureaucrats face a delicate balancing act. On one hand, they want to avoid the embarrassment of writing in a noticeably more muddled way than their peers. On the other hand, they are rewarded for choosing indirect forms of speech over more direct ones. After all, language that makes regulatory orders appear to have arisen from thin air helps camouflage the bureaucrat's personal responsibility for making people do things they don't want to do. As Kahn observed, "One is less likely to be jailed if one says 'he was hit by a stone,' than 'I hit him with a stone.'"

The bureaucrat's maximization rule is thus to be as unclear as possible without sounding conspicuously muddled. From a starting point at which all bureaucrats use clear, direct language, any individual could use marginally less direct language without appearing conspicuously clumsy, and doing this would be an advantage. Others would find similar marginal adjustments attractive, and soon the standard of clarity would fall a notch. This shift would enable bureaucrats to muddy their language still further without calling attention to themselves. Only when the standard of communication again fell to an absurdly low level might it pay an individual bureaucrat to break ranks and speak more plainly. The praise he would get for providing a breath of fresh air might be just enough to compensate for the cost of his greater accountability. But if emulation then raised the standard of clarity of bureaucratic communication, the unraveling would be set to begin anew.

Cosmetic Surgery

Cosmetic surgery has produced dramatic benefits for many people. It has enabled badly disfigured accident victims to recover their original appearance and so to continue with their lives. Reconstructive surgery has also eliminated the extreme self-consciousness felt by people born with strikingly unusual or unattractive features.

But cosmetic surgery is not confined to the conspicuously disfigured. "Normal" people are increasingly seeking surgical improvements in their appearance. In individual cases, these interventions may be just as beneficial as they are for accident victims. Buoyed by the confidence of having a straight nose or a wrinkle-free complexion, patients sometimes go on to achieve much more than they ever hoped possible.

This growing use of cosmetic surgery has an unintended side effect: it alters our standards for normal appearance. Thus, for example, a nose that once would have seemed only slightly larger than average may now seem jarringly big; the same person who once would have looked like an average fifty-five-year-old may now look nearly seventy; and someone who once would have been described as having slightly thinning hair, or an average amount of cellulite, may now feel compelled to use minoxidil, or undergo liposuction. Because such procedures shift our frame of reference, their payoffs to individuals are misleadingly large. From a social perspective, reliance on them is therefore likely to be excessive.

It is difficult to imagine legal sanctions against cosmetic surgery as a remedy for this problem. But at least some communities embrace powerful social norms against cosmetic surgery, heaping scorn and ridicule on the consumers of face lifts and tummy tucks. In individual cases, these norms may seem cruel. And yet, without them, many more people might feel compelled to bear the risk and expense of cosmetic surgery.

Human Growth Hormones and Eighth-Grade Redshirts

In many sports, especially contact sports like football and hockey, it is advantageous to be large. An adolescent athlete who wants to grow has several options. He can lift weights; he can allow the natural growth process to continue with the passage of time; and he can take anabolic steroids, human growth hormone, or some other growth-enhancing medication.

Within any given cohort of athletes, the natural growth process creates no positional externalities. Because athletes of a given age tend to grow at roughly the same rate, this process does little to alter the relative size distribution within the cohort. The only way to exploit the natural growth process for individual advantage is to shift from one cohort to a younger one. In college football, the practice of "redshirting" holds athletes out of competition for a year, thus extending their eligibility for an extra season when they will be larger and more experienced.

The advantage gained by individual players who are redshirted does not carry over to the population of athletes as a whole. The forward movement of redshirts in the size distribution is offset by backward movements of those athletes who were not held back. Assuming that being held back has costs, athletes as a group would fare better if redshirting were discouraged. Regrettably, however, there seems to be little movement in this direction. On the contrary, a growing number of parents hold their eighth-grade sons back a year in school to enhance their competitive position.

Consumption of anabolic steroids and human growth hormones creates positional externalities of a parallel sort. And because ingestion of these substances also involves costs (potentially serious long-term health effects), here too it makes sense to curtail their use.

Positional Externalities in the Income Domain

In the examples already considered, the externalities caused by individual attempts to move forward in a variety of specific hierarchies often give rise to positional arms races. Positional externalities also operate with particular force with respect to activities that change the distributions of income and consumption.[4] In the next sections, I discuss how concern about relative position in these distributions might lead us to regulate a variety of activities related to work and consumption.[5]

Occupational Safety Regulation

Occupational safety legislation has often been explained as a means of protecting workers from being exploited by their employers. On this view, competition in the labor market is insufficient to force employers to provide adequate safety measures. The exploitation argument has at least superficial appeal in the context of company towns in which a single employer can dictate the terms of the compensation package. But in view of the high mobility of both workers and firms, monopsony labor markets are increasingly rare; and even in labor markets that are fiercely competitive, the demand for safety regulation is intense.

Many contemporary economists have argued on theoretical grounds that government safety regulations reduce the worker's welfare. The argument, which flows from Adam Smith, is that an employer will (and should) install a safety device if and only if workers are willing to bear its cost. If workers value the safety device at $75 per week, for example, and it costs only $50 per week to install and operate, any firm that does not install the device will lose its workers to a competing firm. Alternatively, if workers value the device at only $40 per week, then they would be made worse off (by $10 per week) if it were installed. Competitive forces, in short, should lead to the optimal level of workplace safety. And yet, as noted, the demand for safety regulation is intense, even in the most bitterly competitive labor markets.

This pattern is intelligible if we see safety regulation as a way to internalize positional externalities. Consider a simple labor market that consists of two workers, Smith and Jones, who face a choice of working in a safe factory or an unsafe factory. The only difference between the factories is that the safe one has filters that eliminate toxic dust from the air. The sole health consequence of working in the unsafe factory is that life expectancy is reduced by ten years. The weekly wage in the safe factory is $200, in the unsafe factory, $250. The $50 difference reflects the cost of installing and operating the air filters.

In the traditional theory of competitive labor markets, the choice between the two factories is straightforward. If the workers value the

Table 2.2
Job safety choices when relative income matters

		Jones's choice	
		Safe factory @ $200/wk	Unsafe factory @ $250/wk
Smith's choice	Safe factory @ $200/wk	Second best for each	Best for Jones Worst for Smith
	Unsafe factory @ $250/wk	Best for Smith Worst for Jones	Third best for each

extra safety at more than $50 per week, they should, and will, choose the safe factory; otherwise, they will choose the unsafe one. But suppose that workers care not only about their safety and the absolute levels of income they have but also about how their incomes compare with others'.[6] If relative income matters, it is no longer legitimate to view each worker's choice in isolation, for the attractiveness of each alternative will depend also on the particular choice taken by his neighbor. If workers' concerns about both safety and relative position are sufficiently strong, we get a decision matrix like the one in table 2.2.

The rankings assumed in table 2.2 tell us that, positional concerns aside, the additional safety is worth more than $50 per week to each worker. To see this, note how the two jobs compare when both workers choose the same type of job. The upper left cell of table 2.2 corresponds to both workers choosing the safe factory, and this alternative is rated higher (second best for each) than the lower right cell, which corresponds to both choosing the unsafe factory (third best for each).

As with the positional externalities we saw earlier, there is no reason to expect individually rational choices to lead to a socially optimal outcome. Suppose, for example, that Jones chooses a job in the safe factory. The best outcome available to Smith will then be to work in the unsafe factory. By so doing, he gives up safety that is worth more than $50 per week to him for a reward of only $50 per week. In the process, however, he also gains a positional advantage over Jones, which (under the assumed rankings) more than compensates for the loss in safety. Alternatively, suppose that Jones had chosen the unsafe factory. Smith again does better to choose the unsafe factory. By so doing, he gets his third-best alternative, whereas the safe factory would have led to the worst possible combination. In short, no matter what Jones does, Smith gets a better outcome by choosing the unsafe factory.

The incentives confronting Jones are exactly the same. He too does better by picking the unsafe factory, no matter what Smith does. Consequently, each person picks the unsafe factory, and this result is worse than if each had chosen the safe factory. The difficulty, as in all prisoner's dilemmas, is that it does not pay either player, acting alone, to choose the alternative that would be better for both. In this situation, it is easy to see why Smith and Jones would favor a binding agreement to work in the safe factory.

It is also easy to see why critics who ignore positional externalities might conclude that a workplace safety regulation makes each person worse off. Before the regulation, they would argue, each person freely chose to work in the unsafe factory. From that choice it seems to follow that additional safety was worth less than $50/week to each worker. The apparent conclusion, finally, is that a safety regulation harms the workers by making them purchase safety that is worth less to them than its cost.

The flaw in this argument lies in the assumption that individual choices always reveal underlying preferences. When positional externalities matter, individual choices simply do not tell us how people feel about the aggregate results of their choices.

Is it plausible that workers would risk their lives to improve their relative economic position? Clearly most people desire to avoid illness and injury. Yet they also want their children to keep up with (or exceed) community standards with respect to education and other important advantages. People are also strongly motivated to emulate the consumption habits of their neighbors. Taking a riskier job will often mean being able to come up with a down payment for a house in a better school district, or not having to drive the oldest car on the block.

Workers' willingness to trade risk for extra pay is vividly illustrated by practices in the nuclear power industry, where it is occasionally necessary to clean up radiation spills. This task commands a significant pay premium—and significant exposure to hazardous ionizing radiation. Even so, there is a ready supply of applicants eager to perform these tasks. Federal regulations limit the amount of radiation exposure, and workers get a bonus if they "burn out," or exceed those limits. The cleanup workers, who are known in the industry as "glow worms," invariably do burn out and, except for the federal limits, would willingly expose themselves to even higher doses of radiation. By their own account, the risks are worth taking in return for the additional advantages they are able to provide for their families. To the extent that many of these advantages are positional in nature, the individual payoffs to risk taking are spuriously inflated.

Seeing our children do well is a source of deep satisfaction. So, of course, is living to a ripe old age. Everyone would like to achieve both of these goals. When people can obtain higher wages by taking health and safety risks, however, the two are squarely in conflict. This conflict is attenuated by collective agreements that limit the risks we can take.

Limiting the Work Week
Positional externalities provide a more plausible rationale than monopsony exploitation for a variety of other regulations of the labor contract. A case in point is the length of the work week. The Fair Labor Standards Act requires that employers pay a 50 percent wage premium whenever people work more than eight hours per day or forty hours per week. This regulation sharply discourages overtime work.

In traditional economic models, which assume that workers do not care about relative position, it is not clear why anyone would favor such a regulation. If workers disliked working long hours, competition would result in an overtime premium even without a regulation. Alternatively, if workers wanted to work long hours, they would presumably not support a law that discourages employers from having them do so. Thus, in conventional economic models of the labor market, an overtime law is either harmful or irrelevant.

Once positional concerns are granted, however, a clear motive emerges for limiting the work week. Someone who stays a few extra hours at work will increase his or her earnings, both in absolute and in relative terms. But one person's forward movement means a backward movement in relative terms for others. Rather than fall behind, others will feel pressure to work longer hours themselves. In the end, these efforts are largely offsetting. After all, the laws of simple arithmetic make it impossible for more than 10 percent of us to be in the top tenth of the earnings distribution.

People who work until 9 P.M. each day can produce and consume more than those who work only until 5 P.M. But the former group has much less time to spend with family and friends. Because many of the individual payoffs to having more goods are positional, the collective payoff to working longer hours is smaller than it appears to each individual. It is thus easy to see why people might prefer institutional arrangements that induce people to quit at 5:00.

Savings
Conservatives were once fond of complaining that the Social Security system deprives people of the option of deciding for themselves when and how much to save for retirement. This is a valid complaint and, on the economist's view that having more options is better than having fewer, it might appear that participation in Social Security should be purely voluntary. Yet this conclusion seems to have been rejected by virtually every society in favor of mandatory programs to supplement retirement incomes. Positional externalities may again help us to understand why.

The argument is essentially the same as in the cases just considered. Parents have the choice of saving some of their current income for retirement or spending that income now on a house in a better school district or on some other form of current consumption. As with decisions involving safety or the length of the work week, positional pressures often make the second option compelling. The aggregate effects of such choices, however, often turn out to be far from what people intend. When everyone spends more on a house in a better school district, for example, the result is merely to bid up the prices of those houses. In the process, no one moves forward in the educational hierarchy, and yet parents end up having smaller savings for retirement. Acting as individuals, however, they have no real alternative except to send their children to less desirable schools.

The Social Security system mitigates this dilemma by keeping a portion of each person's income unavailable for spending. It helps solve a related set of prisoner's dilemmas as well. Job seekers, for example, know they should "look good" for interviews. Like a good education, however, a tasteful appearance is a relative concept. To look good means to look better than others, and the easiest means to this end is to spend more than most others do on clothing. The catch is that this same calculus operates for everyone. The result is a fruitless escalation in the amount people have to spend merely to avoid looking shabby. From a collective perspective, it would make sense to save more and spend less on clothing. But it would not pay any individual, acting alone, to take this step. The Social Security system, by sheltering a portion of our incomes, keeps people from spending too much in this and a variety of analogous situations.

Positional Externalities within Subjects

In the examples considered so far, one agent's behavior affects a frame of reference important for some other agent or organization. Now we turn to cases in which the behavior of an agent affects a frame of reference important for himself at a later point in time. The enjoyment of food, for example, depends on a physiological and psychological frame of reference that in turn is strongly dependent on behavior during the preceding hours. When a person's "current self" eats a whole can of honey-roasted cashew nuts an hour before dinner, he creates a positional externality by spoiling his "future self's" appetite.

Why call such an effect an externality? If the same person owns both a beehive and an apple orchard, he or she can take direct account of the "external" effect that adding more bees will have on the output of the orchard. Similarly, if our current actions affect what happens to us tomorrow, why can't we factor that into our decisions about what to do today? One answer is that we may not always *know* how our current actions affect future opportunities. Before word got around that tropical oils contribute to heart disease, for example, the eating behavior of many current selves unwittingly imposed external costs on their future selves. But even when we know all relevant future costs, we often give them too little weight. That is, we often choose small rewards in the present over much larger rewards available in the future, and later bitterly regret those choices. Both types of problem—ignorance and self-control—arise in connection with the decision of how to spread a given total amount of consumption across time.

The Optimal Timing of Lifetime Consumption

Traditional economic models hold that current utility depends on the current level of consumption. Permanent income and life-cycle theories conclude on this basis that the optimal consumption stream is roughly constant over time. But compelling psychological evidence tells us that current utility depends not only on current consumption

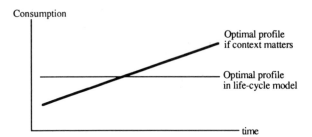

Consumption

Optimal profile
if context matters

Optimal profile
in life-cycle model

time

Figure 2.1
The optimal consumption profile when context matters

but also on the temporal frame of reference in which it occurs. Thus, for example, a person accustomed to consuming $50,000 per year is more likely to be dissatisfied with $30,000 than is someone accustomed to only $20,000.[7]

If utility depends in part on comparisons with past consumption, then current consumption levels may be said to impose positional externalities on the future self. A low level of current consumption will make a given level of future consumption more enjoyable; and conversely, high current consumption will make a given level of future consumption less enjoyable. Under these circumstances, the optimal consumption profile will be upward sloping, not horizontal (see figure 2.1).

People who follow the horizontal consumption profile enjoy greater utility in the early years, but in the process create a consumption context that diminishes their enjoyment of future consumption. As the examples that follow illustrate, this externality may sometimes be eliminated merely by calling attention to it.

Choosing the Right Quality Level

Imagine yourself faced with a choice among three pairs of stereo loudspeakers, which in ascending order of quality are called A, B, and C. A is the quality level you currently own, and you are considering upgrading to B or C. As with any economic choice, the optimal procedure is to keep moving up the quality ladder as long as the additional satisfaction per dollar spent compares favorably with other consumption opportunities. Confronted with the choice described, most people would find it natural to estimate the relevant satisfaction increments by listening carefully to the three pairs of loudspeakers. For the sake of illustration, suppose that the optimal choice by this measure turns out to be C, the highest-quality version.

This procedure seems sensible, yet it overlooks the positional externality at issue. Much of the initial satisfaction from consuming the C system stems from the contrast between its quality level and A's. But once C has been consumed for some period of time, its quality level becomes the norm, and this source of satisfaction vanishes. With the dynamics of this process in mind, a rational consumer might prefer to settle initially for a switch to B, saving the move to C for some future period. Thus, for example, even if your tastes and income are such that a $5,000 pair of stereo loudspeakers is the best choice for you ultimately, your lifetime satisfaction may be higher if you move to that quality level only in stages, rather than all at once.

Similar issues arise with respect to quality choices involving a host of other goods. Suppose that you are ignorant of the nuances of consuming fine wines when a friend invites you to attend a class that will remedy this deficit. Should you accept? You know that people who attend these classes often say they experience great satisfaction from consuming the higher-quality wines they are now able to appreciate. But another consequence of becoming more educated is that these higher-quality wines become the norm. In your current state, you can still enjoy sharing a $5 bottle of wine with your evening meal. Depending on your income level and the value you assign to alternative consumption opportunities, you may be prepared to sacrifice this capacity. But many consumers who confront such decisions are simply unmindful of this dimension of the problem. Learning to think in terms of intertemporal positional externalities may lead to better decisions for at least some of these consumers.

A General Strategy for Deferring Consumption

Merely knowing how current consumption affects the enjoyment possible from future consumption will not necessarily lead to an optimal intertemporal consumption profile. Many consumers already know they would be better off if they could defer current consumption, yet lack sufficient self-discipline to do so.

Within the last decade, Schelling and others have forged a substantial scholarly literature on the topic of self-control.[8] The difficulties they discuss are familiar. Many of us, for example, find it difficult to put down a suspense novel, even though we know that tomorrow we will regret having stayed up late to finish it.

Solutions to self-control problems often involve commitment devices of the sort discussed by Schelling in *The Strategy of Conflict*. Almost every author cites the example of Homer's Ulysses, who realized that once he was within earshot of the sirens' cries, he would be drawn irresistibly toward them and sail to his doom on the reefs. Ulysses' commitment device was to seal the ears of his crewmen and instruct them to strap him tightly to the mast and not to release him, even though he might beg them to, until they had sailed safely past.

Similar commitment devices are familiar in modern life. Fearing we will spoil our dinners, we put the salted nuts out of easy reach. Fearing we will gamble too much, we limit the amount of cash we take to Atlantic City. Fearing we will stay up too late, we move the television set out of the bedroom. In the section that follows, I discuss a more general commitment device that helps solve a variety of within-subject positional externalities.

Deferring Consumption by Deferring Income

For workers in many occupations, productivity increases steadily over time, resulting in upward-sloping wage profiles. To the extent that capital markets do not permit full borrowing against future income, such terms of employment virtually assure a rising consumption profile. But for many other workers, such as commercial airline pilots, productivity is relatively constant over the life cycle. If wages varied strictly in accordance with productivity, as predicted by conventional labor market models, income streams should also tend to be constant over the life cycle. To achieve a rising consumption profile, these workers would have to save during the early years and dissave during later years. The difficulty, as noted, is that saving requires self-control.[9]

One way to insulate oneself from the temptation to consume too much too soon is to form collective agreements with others of like mind. For at least two reasons, a person's coworkers make up a particularly important reference group for such agreements. First, most people have closer and more extensive interactions with their coworkers than they do with any other group, and spatial proximity and degree of interaction are the most important determinants of

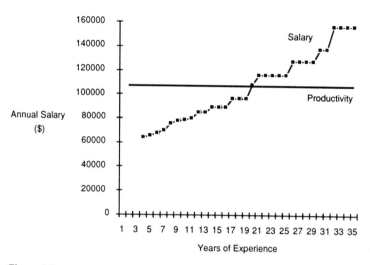

Figure 2.2
The wage profile for commercial airline pilots

reference group membership.[10] Second, the transactions costs of implementing collective consumption agreements are much lower for coworkers than for friends, neighbors, or other less formal associations. If coworkers want to restrict their ability to consume in the present, they can do so by simply accepting employment under an upward-sloping wage profile like the one depicted for commercial airline pilots in figure 2.2.

Naturally, upward-sloping wage profiles will appeal most strongly to workers who expect to remain on the job for extended periods. Workers in short-term jobs will see no advantage in trading current compensation for the promise of higher future earnings that they will not be around to collect. But where long-term commitments exist, this type of contract may be very attractive indeed.

On the assumption that positional consumption externalities are relatively more important in close-knit groups, wage growth over the worker's life cycle should be largest in occupations with the most extensive interaction among coworkers. The consumption standards maintained by a person's coworkers are of course not the only ones that matter. One may also be tempted to match the higher consumption standards maintained by people outside the coworker reference group. As Duesenberry (1949) emphasized, the higher one stands in the overall distribution of income, the less often one is exposed to such temptations. On the plausible assumption that positional externalities from outside the coworker group weigh more heavily for low-income workers, wage growth over the worker's life cycle should be greatest in occupations with the highest incomes. Both relationships—steeper wage profiles among more close-knit groups, and steeper profiles among high income groups—are observed in U.S. data.[12]

Note that having a rising income profile helps solve not only those within-subject positional externalities that result from self-control problems, but also those that result from ignorance. A young person who simply cannot yet afford the most expensive loudspeakers will postpone purchasing them even if he is unaware that this is an optimal consumption strategy.

Concluding Remarks

Positional externalities are a particularly important form of externality. They arise between subjects when one person's action alters an important frame of reference for others. Such externalities may help explain twenty-four-hour supermarkets, excessive formalism in economics, cycles of fashion and public spiritedness, muddled bureaucratic language, excessive cosmetic surgery, and pressures to consume growth hormones. They may also help explain why we regulate safety, working hours, savings, and a variety of actions that affect relative position in the current consumption distribution.

Positional externalities within subjects occur when actions taken by a person's current self affect some important frame of reference for his future self. Knowing about such externalities will sometimes lead people to adopt consumption profiles that rise over time. Rising income profiles are one practical way of assuring rising consumption profiles when limits on self-discipline might otherwise result in excessive early consumption.

Externalities are discussed in many economics texts as though they were an isolated exception to a normal state of affairs in which choices affect only the agents directly involved. In *Micromotives and Macrobehavior*, Schelling has persuaded many of us that external effects are by no means isolated. Indeed, the more we learn about them, the more likely it seems that actions *without* external effects may be the real exceptions.

Notes

I thank Arthur Applbaum, Glenn Blackmon, Darryll Hendricks, Avon Leong, Jay Patel, Harold Pollack, Han Shi, Alan Wertheimer, and Richard Zeckhauser for helpful comments on an earlier draft.

1. Of course, staying open all night is not completely wasteful. Clerks require slack time to restock shelves, clean up, and perform routine maintenance, tasks that are now performed during the night shift. But there are also many other slack hours during the week (notably weekday mornings), and day-shift labor is less expensive than night-shift labor.

2. My colleague John Abowd notes that almost every economist is *continuously* a job candidate.

3. From a CAB certificate of public convenience and necessity, quoted by Kahn in his June 16, 1977, memorandum to the staff of the Civil Aeronautics Board.

4. Early versions of this claim may be found in Smith 1937 (1776) and Veblen 1899.

5. The material in these sections is discussed in greater detail in Frank 1985b.

6. Workers might also care about safety in relative terms. But I have argued elsewhere that relative comparisons along the safety dimension carry less weight than do those along more easily observable dimensions of consumption (see Frank 1985a).

7. For a discussion, see Duesenberry 1949.

8. Ainslie 1975; Elster 1979; Schelling 1980; Thaler and Shefrin 1981; Herrnstein 1981; Winston 1980.

9. See Thaler and Shefrin 1987.

10. Merton and Kitt 1950; Festinger 1954; Homans 1961; Williams 1975.

11. For a detailed discussion of the wage profile of commercial pilots, see Frank and Hutchens 1989.

12. See Frank and Hutchens 1989.

References

Ainslie, George. 1975. "Specious Reward: A Behavioral Theory of Impulsiveness and Impulse Control," *Psychological Bulletin*, 82, July: 463–496.

Duesenberry, James. 1949. *Income, Saving, and the Theory of Consumer Behavior*, Cambridge, MA: Harvard University Press.

Elster, Jon. 1979. *Ulysses and the Sirens*, Cambridge: Cambridge University Press.

Festinger, Leon. 1954. "A Theory of Social Comparison Processes," *Human Relations*, VII: 117–140.

Frank, Robert H. 1985a. "The Demand for Unobservable and Other Nonpositional Goods," *American Economic Review*, 74, March: 101–116.

Frank, Robert H. 1985b. *Choosing the Right Pond*, New York: Oxford University Press.

Frank, Robert H., and Robert Hutchens. 1989. "Feeling Good vs. Feeling Better: A Life-Cycle Theory of Wages," Cornell University, Department of Economics Working Paper.

Friedman, Milton. 1957. *A Theory of the Consumption Function*, Princeton, NJ: Princeton University Press.

Friedman, Milton, and Rose Friedman. 1979. *Free to Choose*, New York: Harcourt Brace Jovanovich.

Herrnstein, Richard J. 1981. "Self-Control as Response Strength," in *Quantification of Steady-State Operant Behaviour*, C. M. Bradshaw, E. Szabadi, and C. F. Lowe, eds., Amsterdam: Elsevier/North Holland Biomedical Press.

Hirschman, Albert O. 1982. *Shifting Involvements*, Princeton, NJ: Princeton University Press.

Homans, George. 1961. *Social Behavior*, New York: Harcourt Brace and World.

Merton, Robert K., and Alice Kitt. 1950. "Contributions to the Theory of Reference Group Behavior," in *Continuities in Social Research: Studies in the Scope and Method of Reference Group Behavior*, Robert Merton and Paul Lazarsfeld, eds., Glencoe, IL: The Free Press.

Modigliani, Franco, and R. Brumberg. 1953. "Utility Analysis and the Consumption Function: An Interpretation of Cross-Section Data," in *Post-Keynesian Economics*, K. Kurihara, ed., London: Allen and Unwin.

Schelling, Thomas. 1960. *The Strategy of Conflict*, Cambridge, MA: Harvard University Press.

Schelling, Thomas. 1978. *Micromotives and Macrobehavior*, New York: W. W. Norton.

Schelling, Thomas. 1980. "The Intimate Contest for Self-Command," *The Public Interest*, Summer: 94–118.

Smith, Adam. 1937 (1776). *The Wealth of Nations*, New York: Modern Library.

Thaler, R., and H. Shefrin. 1981. "An Economic Theory of Self-Control," *Journal of Political Economy*, 89: 392–405.

Thaler, R., and H. Shefrin. 1987. "A Self-Control Theory of Savings," *Economic Inquiry*, XXVI: 609–643.

Veblen, Thorstein. 1899. *The Theory of the Leisure Class*, New York: Macmillan.

Williams, Robin. 1975. "Relative Deprivation," in *The Ideal Social Structure: Papers in Honor of Robert K. Merton*, Lewis A. Coser, ed., New York: Harcourt Brace Jovanovich.

Winston, Gordon. 1980. "Addiction and Backsliding: A Theory of Compulsive Consumption," *Journal of Economic Behavior and Organization*, 1: 295–394.

3

Envy in Social Life

Jon Elster

What is envy? We feel it when we observe another person who has something we want, but lack. As I shall use the term, envy has another distinctive feature. The first urge of envy is not "I, too, must have what he has," but "I want him not to have what he has, because it makes me feel that I am less." For the envious, there is no such thing as another's "innocent utility" (Grua 1956, pp. 323–336). Thus I distinguish envy both from emulation (obtaining a thing similar to what another has) and from competition (obtaining the very thing the other has). Some of the following discussion, however—particularly the remarks about envy-enjoyment—are more plausible if envy is taken in a broader sense that also includes emulation and competition. Although I may enjoy knowing that others wish for the destruction of my assets, it is easier to take pleasure from knowing they wish they had them. Envy must also be distinguished from the feeling of being treated unfairly, although in practice it may be difficult to tell these feelings apart.

Envy is the core of a cluster of attitudes and behaviors that include envy-enjoyment, envy-preemption, envy-reduction, envy-provocation, and envy-avoidance. The feeling of envy is inherently unpleasant.[1] Hence it naturally triggers psychic mechanisms or overt actions to eliminate the feeling or its cause. Being envied is inherently pleasant. Hence it spontaneously suggests actions to create or reinforce that feeling in others. The experience of being envied may nevertheless be an unwanted one. The envied may fear that the envious will try to attenuate the feeling of envy by destroying the assets that gave rise to it. Instead of provoking envy, he may deliberately avoid behavior that could cause it. Third parties may also intervene to reduce or, more rarely, to cause envy.

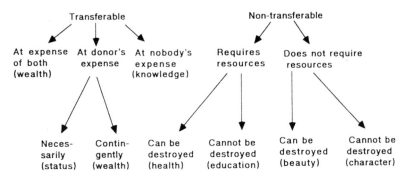

Figure 3.1

The envious urge is more than a wish, yet less than an action; it is a virtual action (Aquinas; *Summa*. IIae, qu.36, third article). According to Kant (1964, part II, §36), "The impulse for envy is . . . inherent in the nature of man, and only its manifestation makes of it an abominable vice." I shall discuss both the destructive impulse itself, its suppression or preemption, and its translation into action, in the forms of envy-provocation, envy-avoidance, and envy-reduction. In conclusion, I offer some comments on the relation between envy and honor and consider the welfare consequences of envy.

Objects of Envy

The objects of envy are the features we envy in others. We may envy another person's success, happiness, intelligence, health, good looks, sunny disposition, character, knowledge, wealth, before-tax income, after-tax income, material possessions, power, title, job, or status—or even his freedom from enviousness.[2] Objects of envy can be classified by the scheme shown in figure 3.1 (see Elster 1989, pp. 252–263).

There are two main categories, transferable and nontransferable goods. Some goods can be transferred and shared without loss to anyone. Abstention from giving such goods shows a mean, spiteful attitude. Knowledge is the classic example. Suppose I am about to go out, not knowing rain is forecast. An acquaintance who knows nevertheless doesn't tell me, relishing the idea that I'll get wet. Most transfers of goods make one or both parties worse off, however. Both can be made worse off when distribution has a negative impact on production, as in strongly progressive taxation. This case is the converse of the previous one. The demand for a transfer that would hurt both parties can only be explained by what I shall call *strong envy*: "cutting off one's nose to spite one's face." In other cases, transfers of goods benefit the recipient at the expense of the donor. This contingent conflict of interest, however, is avoided if the good makes the recipient so much more productive that both donor and recipient end up gaining. If a master feeds his slave better, both may be better off. A necessary conflict of interest arises if the good is a positional one, such as arriving first in a race.

People are envied both for what they *are* and for what they *have*. Even though health, beauty, education, and character cannot be transferred, they can be objects of envy. Sometimes the development of one person's qualities requires resources that might have been spent on developing similar qualities in another. I might have had your glowing health or your cultural skills if my parents had been as wealthy or well educated as yours. Such cases might give rise to *weak envy*: "If I can't have it, nobody shall." Other qualities—beauty or personal integrity—are inborn or acquired in a way that carries no opportunity costs for others. While the envious one would welcome their destruction, their innocent pedigree makes it difficult for envy to come into the open. Instead, it may be sublimated. Freud (1955, p. 121) interpreted the syphilitic's fear of infecting other people in this way: "The dread exhibited by these poor wretches corresponds to their violent struggles against the unconscious wish to spread their infection on to other people; for why should they alone be infected and cut off from so much? Why not other people as well?"

Another distinction is between the nontransferable properties that can be destroyed and those that are indestructible, roughly corresponding to bodily and mental properties respectively. Health and beauty destroy themselves with time, which can be some consolation for the envious, who may feel it must be even worse to lose these properties than to lack them. If natural decay is too slow, the envious might decide to lend nature a hand. An athlete might cripple a rival rather than wait for his powers to subside by themselves. An educated mind and integrity of character, by contrast, are less subject to decay or to destruction. Complete integrity can be destroyed only by destroying the body. "Therefore when they were gathered together, Pilate said unto them, Whom will ye that I release unto you? Barabbas, or Jesus which is called Christ? For he knew that for envy they had delivered him" (Matt.27: 17–18).

As I said, the experience of envy is inherently unpleasant. If the object of envy is another's happiness, a vicious spiral can be set up. Assume that A is stagnating and B is flourishing, but that A is unaware of B's existence. Stipulate that A's level of well-being is 4 and that of B is 7. Assume now that A becomes painfully aware of B's existence and his higher level of well-being, and that the envious awareness of B's prosperity reduces A's well-being from 4 to, say, 3. In other words, when A compares his well-being with that of B, his well-being falls as a result of the comparison. But then, A will presumably carry out another comparison, between B's level and the level to which he, A, is reduced after the first comparison. Depending on further assumptions, the process could converge to a positive level of well-being for A or drive him to suicide.

Targets and Strength of Envy

As Aristotle (*Rhetoric*, 1388a) pointed out, not all persons with enviable attributes are equally envied: "We envy those who are near us in time, place, age, or reputation." Only princes and starlets envy kings and movie stars. This is a matter of qualitative similarity or dissimilarity. Moreover, within the group of qualitatively similar individuals (e.g., people in the same occupational category), we do not envy those who are far above us. The professor without tenure envies one who just got tenure, not the full professor who had tenure long before he arrived on campus. In *The Red and the Black*, Julien Sorel is heartily envied by his fellow students at the religious seminary in Besançon, but as soon as he is made a tutor, he is surprised to find that they hate him less. This local character of envy has been described as "neighborhood-envy": each person in the income hierarchy envies only the person immediately above himself (Bös and Tilman 1985). More plausibly, the income of others earning more than oneself has decreasing marginal disutility up to a certain point, beyond which the envious experiences a release from envy and a gain in welfare. In the immediate neighborhood of the agent there may be an interval in which others' income has increasing marginal disutility, but this is not the case throughout the whole income range.[3]

Which individuals become targets of envy depends on the causal and moral aspects of the situation. The envious urge may arise in innumerable cases, but in most it is almost immediately suppressed as irrelevant or illegitimate. If we can tell ourselves, plausibly,[4] "it could have been me," the predisposition to envy is enhanced. Why should *he* be promoted while I am not? The envy may be allowed to come out in the open if, in addition, we can say "it should have been me." Why should a newly hired worker be promoted over my head? Often feelings of envy arise from a sense of injustice. Much of the literature, however, stresses the opposite causal link: judgments of justice are little more than rationalizations of envy.[5] In reality, both links undoubtedly exist.

The role of *luck* in triggering envy is similarly ambiguous. On the one hand, another's ability to obtain a scarce good by sheer luck encourages the thought that "it could have been me." On the other hand, it does not favor the thought that "it should have been me." One cannot claim an entitlement to luck. Imputation of luck, however, is flexible and manipulable. Rather than causing feelings of envy, it may arise to justify or assuage them. One may envy one's neighbor's good luck if it can be understood as the exercise of occult powers. "Among the Bemba of Northern Rhodesia, for example, it is said that to find a beehive with honey in the woods is good luck; to find two beehives is very good luck; to find three is witchcraft" (Thomas 1973, p. 643). Similarly, one may find comforting excuses for one's own misfortune by attributing it, falsely, to bad luck.

The definition of targets of envy can be governed by either of two mechanisms.[6] On the one hand there is a *spillover effect* by which the habit of envy tends to spread. According to Plutarch, once the habit of envying enemies is established, "it sticks; then from habit we start hating and envying friends" (Walcot 1978, p. 36). On the other hand there is a *zero-sum effect*: if envy is denied one outlet, it will seek another. Plutarch, again, argues that to the extent that "envy is a fact of life, unload it on enemies, who will render you pleasanter to your friends in their prosperity by draining your potential for envy" (ibid.). Instead of concluding that Plutarch was contradicting himself, we may interpret him, more charitably, as implying that in any given case the context will determine which of the two mechanisms operates.

I have been considering only individuals as the carriers and targets of envy. Could there also be envy among collectivities? Tocqueville, for one, thought so. In his American travels he found that the Southern states were permeated by "envy and distrust" towards the North (Tocqueville 1969, p. 381). Some states "feel that they are getting poor because they are not getting rich as quickly as their neighbors, and

Table 3.1

	I	II	III	IV	V
A has	5	3	4	4	4
B has	5	3	5	4	3

they think they are losing their power because they have suddenly come in contact with a power greater than theirs" (ibid., p. 383). West Germany's chancellor, Helmut Kohl, suggested that other nations' fear of a united Germany may really be "economic jealousy" (*International Herald Tribune*, 5 February 1990). Mercantilist policies of seeking relative rather than absolute gain could also be cited, although in this case relative gains in "plenty" were usually sought to obtain absolute gains in "power" (Wilson 1967). In any case, methodological individualism precludes literal talk about collectivities as the carriers of envy.[7] If anyone envied the Northern American states, it must have been the individual Southern citizen. Collectivities can be targets of envy, however. In philosophical language, the substitution, *salva veritate*, of individuals for collectivities cannot be carried out in intensional contexts. Southern envy may well have been directed against "the North" rather than against individual Northerners.

Envy and Its Cognates

I shall now consider the main varieties of envy and its cognates. First, let me spell out more precisely the distinction between weak and strong envy. Consider the five situations depicted in table 3.1. In my terminology, a weakly envious A would prefer IV to III. If strongly envious, A would prefer II to III. A spiteful person derives pleasure from observing a less fortunately endowed person. Tertullian, for instance, said that on the day of the last judgment, he would "rejoice and be happy at the sight of so many great monarchs of whom it was said that they had made it to heaven, to see them crying in deep darkness" (cited after Mora 1987, p. 22). If spiteful, A would prefer V to IV and even to I. Like envy, spite makes us wish for the destruction of the goods of others, at no benefit (weak spite) or even at some cost (strong spite) to ourselves. In weak envy and spite, my welfare is lexicographically prior to the illfare of other people: I may wish for the destruction of their assets, but only when it does not hurt me. In strong envy and spite, there are trade-offs: I am willing to give up some of my welfare for an increase in another's illfare. Whereas envy wishes for a situation in which the other's superiority is eliminated, spite wishes for his inferiority. A more general formulation, covering all four cases, would make my utility a function of (i) the quantity of desired goods possessed by myself and (ii) the quantity possessed by the other. This would allow for lexicographic ordering of (i) and (ii) as well as for trade-offs. Also, (ii) could affect my utility only when I have less than the other, or both when I have less and when I have more. Whenever there is envy, we usually find both strong envy and strong spite: lexicographic preferences are rarely found in reality and envy tends to bring spite in its wake. Nevertheless, in some cases the trade-offs may be so steep that the notion of weak envy is useful; and sometimes people may be willing to acknowledge envy as an egalitarian motive and more reluctant to admit the purely destructive motives of spite. In fact, envy toward those who are better off may go together with compassion for those who are worse off (Scott 1972). In that case, A's welfare is reduced both when B has more and when he has less. One should keep in mind, however, that what looks like downward altruism may in reality be a form of self-interested envy-avoidance or envy-reduction.

Contemplating the fortune of another highlights our own misery. The spectacle of one who is worse off brings out our own happiness. Hume believed, wrongly in my opinion, that envy and malice are mere contrast effects of this kind: "The misery of another gives us a more lively idea of our happiness, and his happiness of our misery. The former, therefore, produces delight; and the latter uneasiness" (Hume 1960, p. 375). Although this explanation of envy cannot satisfactorily account for its destructive, malevolent character, it is true that envy, spite, and the contrast effects have some things in common. If our happiness depends, inter alia, on the contextual range of experience (Tversky and Griffin, this volume; Elster and Loewenstein, forthcoming), then observing the state of another person may extend the range upward or downward so as to decrease or increase our welfare. For the state to become part of our subjective range, we must be able to tell ourselves, "it could have been me." In that respect the contrast effect is similar to envy and spite. Like envy, spite is limited to those with whom we can in some sense identify. We do not want to spite the beggar in the street. This creates a built-in limitation to how far we are willing to go to satisfy our spiteful emotions: we do not want the target of spite to be too badly off.

Spite is related to what Abram de Swaan (1989) calls downward jealousy: "X has or is something which (s)he does not want Y to have or be too (even if X would not have or be less for the fact)." Spite differs from downward jealousy, however, in its urge for active destruction of the goods of others. The "endowment effect" that makes people value goods they have acquired more highly than identical goods not in their possession (Thaler 1980) may also make spite less acceptable to ourselves and others than downward jealousy. The petty bourgeoisie, Swaan claims, has often opposed universal social security, which would give workers a good that the petty bourgeoisie itself has obtained only by hard work and saving. Rich Egyptian fellahins, having made sacrifices to get rich, feel jealousy toward the poor: "The owner of a camel envies the owner of a goat" (Ghosh 1983, p. 221). A child who is given a toy as a reward for going to the dentist will be angry if siblings are given a similar toy without having done anything to deserve it. In these examples, downward jealousy is linked to the notion of desert. In other cases it is due to sheer desire to stand out among others. The Greeks' gods were thought to feel downward jealousy toward powerful mortals (Ranulf 1933, ch. V). Risë Stevens refused to sing at the San Francisco opera house because management would not accept her demand that no other star be paid as much (Schoeck 1987, p. 281).

Spite and downward jealousy differ from envy-enjoyment. Even if I derive no pleasure from the fact that you have little compared with me and would not suffer were you to get more, I may savor your obsessional preoccupation with my fortune. Indirectly, therefore, I may be induced to keep you down.[8] Relations between siblings can illustrate this pattern, with the older sibling actively sabotaging the effort of the younger to obtain the same privileges from the parents. Note that the nonenvious fare better in this respect. Thus envy can be multiply harmful to the envious. First, it is a source of pointless suffering. That my welfare should drop when and because I discover that another has more of the goods I value, and rise again if he loses some of his possessions, is surely a perverse state of affairs. Because of this very perversity, envy is also a source of painful shame when acknowledged. In contrast, the acknowledgment of other painful emotions, like grief, does not create additional pain. Moreover, my envy may induce those whom I envy to perpetuate the state that causes the suffering. These and other welfare effects of envy are further considered in the final section.

Envy-enjoyment, though, is a murky emotion, similar in that respect to the emotion on which it is parasitic. Envy, to be sure, is a form of esteem; like hypocrisy, it is a homage paid by vice to virtue. It is also, indeed, a vicious emotion. The question is whether the envied can really gain *durable* satisfaction through esteem coming from such a vicious source. Compared with "praise of the good by the good,"[9] the enjoyment of envy is like ashes in the mouth.

Envy of others ought to be distinguished from fear of the spite and envy-enjoyment of others. In keeping up with the Joneses, Smith's main worry may be that they will enjoy his inferiority or his envy of their superiority. Smith's actual envy may be mild, that is, but the thought that the Joneses delight in his misery could be insufferable. At this point, envy shades over into a feeling of humiliation, and the rat race for consumption goods takes on some of the aspects of the duel (see "Envy and honor" below).

Contrary to some views,[10] envy does not presuppose a zero-sum image of worldly goods. I may wish for the destruction of another's good even if I know it will not make me better off in material terms.[11] In an Egyptian village, land (a limited good) was never the object of envy. Instead, envy centered on livestock, the amounts of which were subject to uncorrelated fluctuations.[12] The zero-sum view is more plausible if stated in terms of welfare, since the loss of the assets of the envied does create a preferred state for the envious. Although I may recognize that others find pleasure rather than pain in the pleasure of others, that knowledge itself tends to make me even more miserable. But many altruistic interactions take place unobserved by any envious individuals and hence are net creators of happiness.

The calculus of envy and spite should be distinguished from the calculus of inferiority and superiority. The knowledge that one is near the bottom of the prestige hierarchy is painful in itself, whether or not it is also accompanied by envy of one's superiors. Conversely, one's pleasure in being at the top need not be tainted by spite or envy-enjoyment. Prestige or deference stems from the esteem of others (Shils 1968) and is valued because we desire to be esteemed (Lovejoy 1961, ch. IV). Because prestige is largely attached to occupations or social positions rather than to individuals, it cannot be made or unmade by spiteful or envious behavior.[13] A society must have doctors and garbage collectors, but it need not have millionaires or starving poor. Now, what counts above all for many is not to be at the bottom (ibid., p. 114). In the individual prestige rankings that are used to construct indices of aggregate prestige, respondents tend to rank their own occupation higher than the place it is given in the aggregate ranking. In particular, believing that one is not at the bottom can give sorely needed peace of mind, as when slaves and poor whites despise each other. The discrepancy has cognitive as well as motivational causes (Shils 1968, pp. 121–122; Nisbett and Ross 1980, pp. 231–337).

Preemption of Envy

The subjective experience of envy is painful. Sometimes, as I discuss under "Envy-Reduction," the envious try to get rid of their feeling by destroying the objects of envy. Frequently, however, things do not get that far. Indeed, people use or are subject to a variety of mechanisms to preempt envy formation. Most are purely psychic mechanisms and do not involve overt action.

Consciously or unconsciously, people choose friends and acquaintances to avoid those of whom one would be envious (Goldthorpe 1969, pp. 109, 141). Anticipating the undesirable feelings of dissonance that might arise from associating with those who are better off, one seeks out instead individuals less likely to induce feelings of inferiority.

A psychic analogue of this mechanism is the choice of reference group. Many groups may be similar enough to a given individual to play this role. The choice of one group may be made on various grounds. Anticipatory socialization (Merton 1957, pp. 265ff.), induced by the desire to become a member of a higher group, need not lead to envy if one believes that one's turn will come eventually (Hirschman 1973). In this case the choice of reference group is not made for the sake of its envy-reducing effects. People with little hope of upward mobility may be governed entirely by the pleasure principle as they choose a reference group (Hyman 1968). The individual shops around, as it were, until he finds a group that minimizes felt envy, subject to the similarity constraint. A badly paid unskilled worker may to some extent preempt the envy of his colleagues by making neighborhood life the axis of his existence.

Envy can also be preempted by the mechanism of "sour grapes," or adaptive preference formation.[14] Instead of acknowledging envy of another's assets, one may persuade oneself that they are not worth having. The top job is too stressful; good-looking people are more miserable than others when they lose their bloom. Or one may drive envy away by the thought that possession would trigger envy: great wealth would only arouse a destructive urge in others. Of course, if all entertained this thought it would ipso facto not be true: some have to be envious for others to believe that envied objects are not worth having.[15]

A related mechanism is to devalue other aspects of the person who has an envied attribute (Schalin 1979, pp. 134–135). Thus the stereotype that beautiful blondes are dumb may be due as much to other women's envy as to male chauvinism. Among the strategies for "restoring equality" found in a French village, that of introducing additional criteria of evaluation was prominent. "It is possible for a villager to reject or annul almost any bid for prestige or accusation of low status because of the diversity of ranking criteria" (Hutson 1971, p. 47). It has been argued that in classical antiquity there was a presumption that whoever excels in one respect excels in all (Veyne 1976, pp. 114, 773). In other societies, envy may give rise to the opposite presumption.

Finally, envy can lose its sting through cognitive framing. Like an appeal to luck, the religious belief in providence can make one's misfortune more palatable. Keith Thomas notes that in seventeenth-century England this belief "was extraordinarily elastic. In a good year Robert Loder praised the lord for his assistance; in a bad one he stoically reflected that God distributed his mercies as he pleased" (Thomas 1973, p. 95). Astrology could also provide a modicum of peace of mind (ibid., p. 390). Explaining one's misfortune by one's own lack of desert may force envy underground, but will not make it disappear. Explaining it by the malicious intervention of others will bring it out in the open and strengthen it. By contrast, an explanation in terms of impersonal cosmic forces will allow the mind to cleanse itself of envy.

Social Conditions of Envy

Tocqueville (1969, p. 310) refers to envy as a "democratic sentiment," arguing that it is encouraged by equality and mobility:

Men's hatred of privilege increases as privileges become rarer and less important, the flame of democratic passion apparently blazing the brighter the less fuel there is to feed it. . . . When conditions are unequal, no inequality, however great, offends the eye. But amid general uniformity, the slightest dissimilarity seems shocking, and the completer the uniformity, the more unbearable it seems. (Tocqueville 1969, pp. 672–673)

The view that envy increases with equality can be understood in several ways. Is Tocqueville asserting that envy is negatively correlated with the income gap or that, for a given income gap, envy is negatively correlated with the overall amount of inequality in society? (Or does he hold both views, which are perfectly consistent with each other?) The second view can in turn be taken in two ways, as asserting that overall equality is either a cause of the envy function or an argument in it.[16] Of these readings, only the view that the degree of felt envy is causally affected by the social environment is, properly speaking, a sociological explanation. The others are consistent with the idea of an unchanging human nature (or utility function), which induces people to feel and behave differently only when they are faced with different external circumstances (or arguments in the utility function). There is less envy in aristocracies simply because there is more inequality, not because people feel differently about it.

Tocqueville's notion of the "democratic social state" is also ambiguous. Sometimes it means equality of income or wealth at a given time—as in the image of a uniform surface on which the slightest unevenness will stand out. At other times it means the absence of legal privilege together with high rates of de facto mobility. Mobility is vital in ensuring an important condition for envy, the perception that "it could have been me." (With *very* high rates of mobility, however, the target of envy may be moving too fast for the emotion to have time to arise.) Privilege, however, is also important in ensuring another condition of envy, the perception that "it should have been me." These apparently conflicting arguments suggest that envy is likely to be especially acute in transitional periods, when there is both enough mobility to allow the thought that one could have had another's place and enough unjust privilege to allow the thought that one should have had it (see also Tocqueville 1969, pp. 579–580).

A related argument is that envy is stimulated by status incongruence. When I am the equal of another in one respect but his inferior in another, the equality may encourage the thought "it could and should have been me" and thus turn the inequality into a source of envy. To reduce envy, there has to be equality across the board, as in Sparta. Political equality without equality in birth or wealth, as in Athens, tends rather to exacerbate envy (Walcot 1978, p. 64).

The relation between group size and envy is not quite clear. It has been argued on a priori grounds that feelings of inferiority and envy are less intense in small than in large groups, because a large group is more likely to have some high outliers that will induce more envy (Brickman and Bullman 1977, p. 175 and Kagan 1984, p. 65). However, because envy comes from comparisons with similar individuals, this argument ceases to apply beyond a certain point. Also, in a large group one's envy is less likely to become visible to the superior person, and hence is less likely to be reinforced by the fear that he is enjoying it.

The impact of mobility, equality, and group size on the prevalence and strength of envy is somewhat indeterminate. Perhaps the best hypothesis is that envy reaches a maximum in imperfectly mobile, imperfectly equal, and intermediate-size groups.

Envy and Action

Envy presents a paradox: unique among the emotions in its smoldering, subterranean character, it is a strong feeling that often induces no action. To acknowledge one's envy to oneself is painful. To act out of envy makes it hard not to acknowledge the emotion, unless some rationalization is handy. (*Inaction* is easier in this respect, especially when it can be dressed up as sturdy self-reliance: I don't ask for any help, nor do I give any.) Consider, for instance, envy of other people's excellence. In itself, another's superior wealth or gifts cannot harm me, but I might fear that he will put his wealth and talents to dangerous use. What looks like a Pareto-improvement might, on further inspection, have the potential for making some worse off (Morgenstern 1973, pp. 1169–1170; see also Aquinas, *Summa*, IIae, qu.36, first article). The debate over the Greek practice of ostracism illustrates the point. Plutarch refers to ostracism as a device "by which they cut down and expel from time to time whoever of the citizens excels in reputation or power, relieving their envy rather than their fear" (Walcot 1978, p. 58). Ranulf (1934, p. 282; 1938, p. 282) also asserts that the basic root of ostracism was envy, viewed as a general propensity of the lower middle class. Others (see Ranulf 1933, pp. 136–138) have explained ostracism by supposing that the Greeks had a justified fear of demagoguery, oligarchy, and tyranny. Most probably, there is an element of truth in both views. The inadmissible feeling of envy must attach itself to more acceptable arguments, which may indeed have some foundation.

To what kinds of action may envy give rise? In many societies, there has been a belief that envy works magically through the "evil eye," not by overt, destructive behavior. In an Egyptian village "people believe that envy, working through the agency of the glance, has efficient action and can destroy or harm the objects or people against which it is directed."[17] Among the nomads of Southern Iran, the link is even more tenuous: "since it is the unconscious envy that harms, only friends, acquaintances and relatives cast the evil eye, while declared enemies are impotent to do so" (Barth 1964, p. 145). Although envy cannot actually work in this way, the fact that people believe it can is sufficient to trigger envy-avoidance and envy-reduction.

A cautious approach is important as we seek evidence of envy-related behavior. That an action or behavioral pattern reduces or provokes envy does not by itself show that it can be explained through that effect. A society that equalizes incomes might reduce envy, without having sought that goal. An individual who achieves success might provoke his neighbor's envy as an unintended (or at least nonexplanatory) by-product. A's envy of B may benefit C even if C did nothing to cause the invidious comparison. This general problem takes on an added twist in the case of envy, since the agents involved are themselves likely to indulge in such fallacious explanations.[18] B may falsely believe that A's striving for success was motivated by a desire to make him feel inferior and envious, a belief that will provide more acceptable grounds for resentment than the mere fact of A's success. Thus according to Scheler (1972, p. 52), envy arises when "our factual inability to acquire a good is wrongly interpreted as a positive action against our desire."

Envy-Provocation

Given that those who have less tend to envy those who have more, and that people tend to enjoy other people's envy, those who are better off may be expected to take actions designed to provoke or maintain the envy of the worse off. Francisco de Quevodo said that "whoever does not want to be envied, he does not want to be a man" (Mora 1987, p. 37). People can provoke envy in at least four ways: by acquiring more of the envied good; by making one's own superiority more visible; by ensuring that the worse-off remain badly off (or are made even worse off); and, paradoxically, by making them better off.

Veblen—the central writer on envy-provocation—emphasizes the first two strategies. He argues that among the "incentives to acquisition and accumulation," a central component is "the desire to excel in pecuniary standing and so gain the esteem *and envy* of one's fellow-men" (Veblen 1965, p. 32; my italics). Similarly, Hesiod writes (*Works and Days*, verses 312–313), "if you work, soon will the work-shy be jealous of your wealth," offered as reason for working more, not—as in envy-avoidance—for working less. Conspicuous consumption is an instance of the second strategy: "Costly entertainments, such as the potlatch or the ball, are peculiarly adapted to serve this end. The competitor with whom the entertainer wishes to institute a comparison is, by this method, made to serve as a means to the end. He consumes vicariously for his host at the same time that he is a witness to the consumption of that excess of good things which his host is unable to dispose of single-handedly, and he is also made to witness his host's facility in etiquette" (Veblen 1965, p. 75). Here the envy-inducing display of superiority is exquisitely combined with a humiliating show of hospitality.

Siblings and spouses often follow the third strategy of envy-provocation. Husbands who do not want their wives to hold jobs may be motivated partly by enjoyment of their spouses' envy. Now, if envy in general is a tainted form of esteem, the envy of those whom one has deliberately held down is an especially debased form. The pleasures it provides are not likely to prove very robust. In this respect the fourth strategy is more satisfying. Attempts by the envied to restore equality by sharing some of their goods with the envious stimulates envy rather than assuaging it (see the numerous examples in Schoeck 1987 and Mora 1987). The more you give, the greater my resentment at the superior character manifested in your giving. Ordinarily such humiliation is an unintended and unwelcome effect of attempts to reduce envy; occasionally, however, it may provide the very motive for the assistance.

Envy can also be provoked by a third party, as part of a divide-and-conquer strategy. Thus, "One of the deadliest weapons in the arsenal of psychological warfare is propaganda aimed at convincing some segments of the enemy group that they are suffering more hardships or are gaining fewer benefits than other segments of the group" (Kreech and Crutchfield 1948, p. 411). Here, as always, it is important to distinguish genuine cases of divide-and-conquer from the superficially similar phenomenon of third-party benefits or *tertius gaudens* (Simmel 1908, pp. 82ff.). If A's envy of B happens to work to the benefit of C, we should not jump to the conclusion that C has helped to create the envy.

Envy-Avoidance

Envy-avoidance is the deliberate abstention from behavior that would provoke the envy of others. Assume that A contemplates an action that is likely to provoke B's envy. Against the benefits of the action itself and of envy-enjoyment, A must weigh the direct costs of achieving the goal and the risk that an envious B may do something to destroy A's assets. On balance, A might find it best to abstain. Conceivably, "the marginal utility of being superior decreases as the number of persons one is already superior to increases. . . , while the interpersonal costs of superiority remain constant" (Brickman and Bullman 1977, p. 175).[19] Then there may be an optimal degree of superiority, beyond which it is unwise to trespass.

Here, envy reduces welfare indirectly. Instead of destroying assets, it ensures that they are never produced in the first place. In many traditional societies, the anticipation of envy is a dead hand that stifles innovation and progress. The fear of being branded as a witch is especially potent. Accusations of witchcraft against the rich and successful are common in many societies (Kluckhohn 1944, pp. 56, 63, 68; Thomas 1973, pp. 643–644). Success is also seen as inviting victimization by witches, who are thought to envy good fortune (Mayer 1954, p. 65). There is also a social norm that the poor must be treated kindly lest they turn into witches (Kluckhohn 1944, p. 67). Finally, witchcraft is frequently invoked to explain failure as well as success. In the words of a seventeenth-century English writer, "We think them bewitched that wax suddenly poor, not them that grow hastily rich" (Thomas 1973, p. 644). In other words, both rich and poor can be considered especially likely to be either witches or victims of witchcraft. All four mechanisms conspire to bring about egalitarianism. People hesitate to become rich lest they be accused of witchcraft or become the targets of witchcraft. The poor are prevented from getting too poor by the fear that they may be provoked into witchcraft. The idea that the poor are victims of witchcraft can sustain a relatively sympathetic attitude toward them. (This argument is more speculative than the three others.) In these societies, egalitarianism results from a combination of envy and apparent altruism, but the altruism is largely an effect of envy-avoidance.

During a recent visit to China, I was told that envious motives and egalitarian ideology are inextricably intertwined in the workplace. To avoid harassment by their fellow employees, model workers spend their bonus on a good meal for everybody. The manager keeps his bonus down not only because he fears the workers, but also because he wants to avoid the envy of the other executive officers. In the West, too, social norms against rate-busting may owe some of their force to weak envy (Elster 1989, pp. 122, 145–146).

In an entirely different sense, envy-avoidance could also denote the deliberate abstention from behavior that would make others believe that one is envious. It is mainly important when a person thought to have the evil eye may be pursued as a witch or otherwise persecuted. Just as people may abstain from putting glass windows in their house so as not to provoke envy, those who walk by may be "careful to keep their eyes averted from the interiors of other houses, lest they be thought envious" (Ghosh 1983, pp. 213–214). Just as people do not like to be seen while eating, others may retire in haste if they come across a person eating, "an act of good manners calculated to assure the diner that he is not envied his food" (Foster 1972, p. 184).

Envy-Reduction

The envious, the envied, and third parties may all take actions to reduce envy. I begin with actions taken by the weakly envious. In *Amadeus*, Salieri's envy inspires him to undermine Mozart's fame and ultimately his health. A child may take a sudden interest in a toy when and because another child picks it up.[20] Many crimes have been committed out of envy, ranging from arson prompted by envy of more gifted fellow students to a schoolboy killing a friend's mother because, unlike that friend, he could not afford summer camp (Schoeck 1987, ch.8). If Freud is right in believing that syphilitics have a wish to infect others, some might translate it into action.

Weak envy can affect wage bargaining. Often, what matters to a union is to preserve and if possible to improve wage differentials, or to achieve parity with another group. These goals can be achieved by improving one's own position, but also by preventing others from getting ahead. In Sweden, the central labor union (LO) has often tried to reduce the degree to which other groups are compensated for wage drift. Here, it may be difficult to distinguish fear of inflation from relative wage goals. But in 1983 LO economists proposed that reductions in progressive taxation for high-income groups be given up, to forestall compensation demands from low-income groups that wanted to preserve relativities. In such cases, envy seems to be the appropriate characterization of union behavior.

Consider next strong envy (and strong spite),[21] cutting off one's nose to spite one's face.[22] Early German law had statutes forbidding "envious building" (Neidbau), defined as "when a prospective building is planned clearly to the detriment of a neighbour and without pressing need, or where such building has little or no purpose, while representing great damage, and loss of light and air, to the neighbour" (Schoeck 1987, pp. 137–138). In English and especially in American common law, we find similar bans on "spite fences" (Liebermann and Syrquin 1983, p. 31). The existence of such laws suggests that the prohibited practices were not uncommon. It has been said about the Athenian (Ranulf 1933) and early American (Tocqueville 1969, p. 198) democracies that popular envy ensured the defeat of the most competent whenever they sought office. The implication is that the electorate was assuaging its envy at the expense of its substantial interests, which were presumably best served by good leaders. Strong envy may also motivate efforts to increase tax rates even if disincentive effects actually decrease tax revenues (Boskin and Sheshinski 1978, p. 590).

There is experimental evidence for behavior that amounts to cutting off one's nose to spite one's face. One person is asked to propose a division of a certain sum of money between himself and another, who will accept or reject the proposal. If he accepts it, both get what the first proposed; if he rejects it, neither gets anything. Under these circumstances, many individuals who are placed in the second position reject the proposal if it deviates too much from an equal-split solution. Although the motivation behind such refusals is characterized as "fairness" (Kahneman, Knetsch, and Thaler 1986), "envy" would sometimes be more appropriate for analogous behavior in real life (Ranulf 1938).

Envy-reduction by the envied is an attempt to preempt envy-reduction by the envious. It can take two forms: divesting oneself of one's assets or hiding them. As noted above, divestiture may be self-defeating if it takes the form of a transfer to the envious.[22] Outright destruction of assets might not achieve the goal either, since it suggests an enviable lack of concern for the envied goods. The envious will not be content until he sees the envied person being stripped of his assets against his will, a feat that is hard to achieve at will. One may, however, try to create the appearance that the assets were destroyed nonvoluntarily. Much more frequent is the attempt to reduce envy by hiding one's assets from the sight of the envious (Foster 1972, pp. 175–176). Haitian peasants sometimes tried to disguise their true economic position, and so ward off envious black magic, by purchasing several smaller fields rather than one larger piece of land (Simpson 1941). (In other societies, this behavior is usually explained by the need to hide from the tax collector—to preempt, that is, another form of envy-reducing behavior.) In Ghana, a rich man reduced his relatives' envy by purposively leaving unfinished a house he was building, to substantiate his claims to poverty (Schoeck 1987, p. 74). In Mexico, fear of envy rather then fear of robbery was the main reason for the refusal to install glass windows in houses (Foster 1965, p. 154).

Envy-reduction by third parties can stem from two motives: the desire to create social justice and the desire to avoid social unrest. (Needless to say, one may act on both motives at the same time.) The second motive may be interpreted as an attempt to preempt direct envy-reducing behavior by the envious. The first, on which I concentrate, can be spelled out in several distinct ways. The absence of envy may itself be used as a definition of fairness. A utilitarian argument could be that transfers to the envious are needed to maximize total utility. An egalitarian argument is that envy-reducing transfers are needed to equalize welfare, income, or some other egalisandum. This strategy need not be motivated by envy-reduction; one could advocate equalizing incomes even were there no envy. Some egalitarian arguments do, however, refer to the need to reduce envy. John Rawls's theory of justice is egalitarianism tempered by the need to take account of the incentive effects of equalization. This modification of pure egalitarianism is itself modified or curtailed by the need to reduce the "excusable envy" that might arise in a society with large inequalities. Rawls's argument is that envy may affect one's self-esteem, which as a "primary good" is to be equalized (Rawls 1971, p. 534).

Two simple examples will illustrate envy-reduction by third parties. In China during the Cultural Revolution, farmers with fruit trees were ordered to cut them down (Zhang and Sang 1987, pp. 121, 126). No one was allowed to have what not all could have. In a similar spirit, school teachers sometimes ask parents not to pack special (even if inexpensive) treats in their children's lunches, lest classmates become envious.

Similar, if more complex issues arise in the allocation of scarce indivisible goods, such as organs for transplantation, exemption from military service, or custody of a child (Elster, forthcoming). Here, the all-or-none principle has considerable appeal. Solomon's first judgment is one example. According to Tocqueville, universal military service is an expression of the democratic sentiment of envy: "It is the inequality of a burden, not its weight, which usually provokes resistance" (Tocqueville 1969, pp. 651–652). The recent Oregon moratorium on nonrenal transplantations provides another example of all-or-none reasoning; however, it was probably based more on fear of litigation than on a desire to reduce envy (Gilbert and Larson 1988). It has been argued that the early Massachusetts policy on liver transplants was more directly inspired by envious-egalitarian motives, since it did not allow the rich to buy transplant operations even if they paid the full social cost (Havighurst and King 1986). The example suggests that envy, instead of destroying another's assets, may take the form of making them less convertible into other goods. The rich should not be allowed to buy organ transplants or exemption from military service, even if they offer terms that would appear to make everyone better off (Walzer 1983, pp. 97ff.). Blocking such transactions can often be justified by the tendency of the rich to use their political power to get the goods at less than the full social cost, or the tendency of the poor to accept deals that they would not have made had they been better informed. But the motive could also be sheer envy.

There is a considerable economic literature on envy and on envy-reducing measures that governments can take.[23] Foley (1967) defines a fair or *envy-free* allocation of goods as one in which nobody would rather have anyone else's bundle of goods than his own. (As I argue later, violation of this condition does not imply that anyone actually envies anyone else.) Such allocations always exist (the equal allocation is one example), but they are not always Pareto-efficient in an economy with production. (In a pure exchange economy, efficient envy-free allocations can be realized by endowing all agents with the same bundle and letting them trade to equilibrium.) Suppose fairness were defined as balanced envy, realized when for each person the number of people who envy him is equal to the number of people that he envies. Under this definition it has been shown that efficient balanced allocations always exist (Daniel 1975). Since the ethical appeal of balanced envy is dubious, the result has no particular significance.

A goal of envy-freeness is vulnerable to two objections. First, it may not be possible to achieve the goal if we also insist on efficiency. Second, it fails to capture the idea that one may envy another person his happiness and not just his consumption bundle. A handicapped person might not prefer anyone else's bundle to his own; yet all might think it fair that he should get a larger bundle. To respond to the first objection, one might define the overall degree of envy in a society by the number of pairs (i,j) such that i would rather have j's bundle than his own. Government policy might then be set to minimize overall envy subject to some efficiency constraint (Feldman and Kierman 1974; Bös and Tillman 1985). I shall not here pursue this line of reasoning, because it ignores two crucial aspects of the situation: (1) intrapersonal differences of intensity: individual i might envy j much less than he envies k, yet the two relationships count equally in the minimand; (2) interpersonal differences: individual i's envy of k might be much less virulent than j's envy of m, but again the two count equally.

The last comment, as well as the idea that we may envy another person his happiness, assumes the possibility of interpersonal comparisons of utility. It is, notoriously, as hard to defend this assumption as it is to reject it (Elster and Roemer, eds., forthcoming). Here, I shall just take it for granted and explore the implications for envy-reduction.

Assuming interpersonal comparability, we may redefine the notion of overall envy, summing over all pairs (i,j) the difference between i's utility when he retains his own bundle and what he would achieve given j's bundle. Once again, government policy could be set to minimize envy, subject to efficiency constraints (Feldman and Kierman 1974, pp. 1003–1004). To my mind, this proposal raises two conceptual problems. First, if we assume that the government can compare utilities across persons, why should we not impute the same ability to the individuals themselves? In that case, and denoting utility functions by u and bundles by x, the relevant utility difference would seem to be $u_i(x_i)-u_i(x_j)$ rather than $u_j(x_j)-u_j(x_j)$ (Hammond 1987). Second, before the government decides to minimize envy in one of these utility-difference senses, it must ascertain that utility differences are good proxies for felt envy. The individuals concerned must actually experience envy and, moreover, the envy should be proportional to the utility differences. I have argued that the proportionality assumption is highly implausible, as people tend to envy only those near them in the hierarchy.

Now, envy could of course be *defined* simply as some sort of utility difference and dissociated from any disutility created by the difference itself. (As indicated under "Objects of envy," we have to assume that the infinite regress raised by this phrase converges to some positive level of utility.) In that case, the policy proposal reduces to a somewhat convoluted form of egalitarianism (see also Sussangkarn and Goldman 1983). If, however, one wants to retain the everyday connotations of "envy," some alternative to the proportionality assumption must be found. In the literature, this is done in one of two ways. Some writers assign weights to individuals or to social positions that reflect the government's willingness to take account of their envy, higher weights being typically assigned to individuals at the bottom of the hierarchy. The idea is discussed in Feldman and Kierman 1974 and in Bös and Tillman 1985. It is clearly related to Rawls's idea of excusable envy. This proposal is really a solution to another problem, however. Others introduce a behavioral assumption, such as the postulate of "neighborhood envy" or one of the more complicated relations discussed above. For purposes of public policy making one should do both. First, that is, one should try to assess empirically degrees of pairwise envy between individuals in different positions. In general, one would not find that perceived envy is proportional to utility differences. Next, one should try to assess normatively how much weight to assign to the perceived envy of different individuals. Once again, a proportionality assumption of equal weights for all would be inadequate.

One final twist on the theme of third-party reduction of envy: the Greek gods reputedly struck down those who rose above the average. We who do not believe that there were any Greek gods cannot describe this police action as a third-party reduction of envy. Yet although they may have been only projections of the Greeks' own envy, the gods' supposed vengefulness may have had the effect of relieving human envy (Ranulf 1933, p. 69). There may have been less need for first-party action to reduce envy: Why should I destroy envied assets if the gods will do it for me? Alternatively, a Greek might reason: Because the gods do it, I am allowed to do so as well. Note that these two reactions represent an interpersonal version of the distinction between spillover effects and zero-sum effects.

Envy and Honor

The urge to be superior and to be seen as superior is universal. Envy—more precisely, the inducement of envy in others—is one aspect of this urge. Another is related to *honor*, in the sense of proving one's worth at the expense of another's. These forms of behavior need not have the same causal origin, for example, a tendency for evolution to produce spiteful behavior (Hamilton 1970). They may stem from distinct causes and share only a general description, as do birds and bats or sharks and killer whales. But it seems worthwhile to explore some of the similarities and differences between envy and honor.

As I shall define it, honor is achieved by challenging and humiliating another person in the presence of a third party. Unlike the dyadic phenomena of envy and its correlates,[24] honor is a triadic relation, regulated by a rich set of social norms. The strong emotions involved in the pursuit of honor may be prompted by actions that would have no significance in the absence of these norms, such as the Albanian practice of passing a cup of tea under one's left arm to show disrespect. Envy and envy-enjoyment, by contrast, are presocial emotions that arise spontaneously in the mind. Their proximate or ultimate cause is the possession of objects that are desired for their own sake.[25] Honor also differs from envy in being interactive, involving face-to-face confrontations. Envy is outcome-dependent and action-independent; honor is action-dependent (Hirshleifer 1987).

Let me first define a dyadic relation that we may call *proto-honor*. This is the relation of domination and subordination described in Hegel's master-slave dialectic (Hegel 1982, pp. 112–116). In a struggle for life and death, one of the protagonists surrenders to the other, thereby showing himself more attached to the material side of existence. He becomes the slave of the other, who emerges as the master. By risking his life, the master showed that he was more concerned with proto-honor—the recognition (*Anerkennung*) by the other of his superiority—than with material security and well-being. As a by-product of the quest for proto-honor, he also achieves material riches, however, as he can now set the slave to work for him. Yet the master's satisfaction proves illusory, for who can gain honor from being recognized by a slave? The lack of worth of the slave also devalues any deference he confers on the master.

The search for proto-honor, then, is inherently self-defeating. Not so the search for honor. By exposing oneself to the risk of death in the presence of a third party, one gains stature in the eyes of the onlooker. To be sure, a triumph over a known coward does not confer honor. But if the challenged person backs down and only thereby shows himself to be a coward, the challenger's honor is nevertheless enhanced, since for all he knew the challenge might have been taken up. The action has to be both courageous ex ante and recognized ex post by a party capable of conferring honor. Only a triadic relation satisfies both conditions.

The ultimate guarantee of honor is violence, as in a murderous act of revenge (Elster 1990b) or a duel. In Montenegro until quite recent times, many feuds were caused by acts undertaken with the knowledge that a feud might ensue, and undertaken only because a feud might ensue, although not for the purpose of causing a feud. These were acts of brinkmanship—insults carried to the point at which there was a real risk that the offended party might retaliate. "The exchanging of insults, then, was a very delicate art that involved ultimate risk taking. Decisions as to what to say next were potentially matters of life and death, since simply to maintain one's honor one had to take at least some small risks of being killed" (Boehm 1984, p. 146). The same observation would have applied to actions that might lead to a duel in sixteenth-century Italy. According to a contemporary writer, "giving [insults] pertains to the nature of man; because everyone seeks distinction, one mark of which is to offend fearlessly" (Bryson 1935, p. 28). An honorable man, when offended, had to seek redress to preserve his honor. Not doing so would show that he valued his life higher than his honor. Not all persons, however, have the capacity to insult or to confer honor by backing down from a challenge. Persons incapable of honor have regularly included women, children, slaves, and servants. In some societies, they have also included members of stigmatized social groups, such as Jews. To go out of one's way to insult a person of one of these categories would detract from one's honor, not add to it. If offended by such a person, the proper response was to punish him rather than challenge him to a duel.

Frederick Bryson observes that in sixteenth-century Italy it made a great difference whether one insulted by word or by act (Bryson 1935, pp. 39ff.). To an insult by word (e.g., "You are a traitor") the proper response usually was to accuse the other person of lying. To redress his honor, the latter might then issue a challenge to duel, in which the insulted party would then have the choice of arms. To an insult by an act (a kick, blow, or slap) the proper response often was a challenge to duel, in which the insulting party would have the choice of arms. A further complication arose if the accusation by word was known to be true. The insulted could then not give the lie, "but one might answer, 'In saying so-and-so you have acted unjustly', whereupon the first speaker could reply, 'In saying that I have acted unjustly, you lie'. The other party would then, in case of a duel, become the challenger and so lose the choice of arms" (Bryson 1935, pp. 57–58). Presumably the same reply could be given to untrue accusations. Now, to have the choice of arms was obviously an advantage if one's goal was to survive the duel. Bryson suggests, without saying so explicitly,[26] that this fact created an incentive to strategic behavior—that is, to choose the mode of insult and of response that would give oneself an edge. The logic of honor, however, points to the opposite conclusion. To use a specific form of insult for the purpose of getting the choice of arms would show a dishonorable attachment to mere survival.

Envy-provocation, the search for proto-honor, and the quest for honor are all instances of the urge to be superior. I have argued, however, that the first two have inherent limitations. The baseness of the feeling of envy also makes the envious one too base for his envy to be of much value. The slave who yields to the master shows ipso facto that he is too cowardly to be capable of conferring status. Full-blown honor, acquired by the humiliation of another in the presence of a third party, is more likely to provide satisfaction.[27]

Welfare Implications of Envy

Envy is one of several emotional dispositions that either make us worse off directly or make us behave in ways that make us worse off. Regret, extreme risk-aversion, and impulsiveness are other examples. As parents, we teach our children not to be envious; not to focus their attention on worst-case assumptions; not to cry over spilled milk; and not to give in to impulses for immediate gratification. One reason we do so is surely that we believe they will be happier without these tendencies. (In the case of envy, there is also the reason that envy can make us undertake actions that are morally wrong, rather than simply imprudent.) There are instructive differences and similarities among the four cases. Impulsiveness can lower welfare because of the long-term effects of myopic behavior. Risk-aversion can harm us if it keeps us from engaging in highly pleasurable activities that carry a small risk of a small accident. In addition, risk-aversion can lower welfare directly, if it makes us anxious about low-probability disasters outside our control. Regret and envy are, in the first place, direct sources of suffering. In addition, they may induce us to take actions that in the long run lower our welfare.

Economists are accustomed to treating risk-aversion and time discounting (Becker and Murphy 1988) on a par with more substantive preferences, such as the desire for bread, butter, or caviar. There is no reason to think of these attitudes as in any way irrational. Some take this view of regret as well (Loomes and Sugden 1982). Although envy is less frequently discussed in the economic literature, it is sometimes treated as just another source of utility or disutility (Sussangkarn and Goldman 1983). People with envious preferences are simply better off if others have less. But even if the envious preferences are taken for given, envy can make the envious worse off. Moreover, we should tally the impact of envy on the welfare of others. Finally I assert—it is not really an argument—that the envious would be better off with non-envious preferences.

Consider the individual envious person, whose utility function includes as arguments both his own consumption and that of others. To assess the impact of his envy on his welfare, we may distinguish four effects. (i) I assume (plausibly, I think) that the envious is unable to hide his envy from others. Even if he does not act out of envy to destroy the assets of others, he cannot hide it from the world. As a result, he will be shunned and ostracized, ending up with fewer consumption goods. (ii) Other people's envy-enjoyment may induce them to keep the envious down. (iii) The mechanism of envy-avoidance may deter others from innovative activities that would have increased everybody's consumption, including that of the envious. This effect might raise the welfare of the envious or decrease it, depending on the distribution of the benefits and on the shape of the envious person's utility function. Usually, one person's envy will not deter others so much that he suffers substantial consequences, but in small groups the effect might be noticeable. (iv) The welfare of the envious will increase if he succeeds in destroying some of the envy-causing assets of others, even at some asset-cost to himself. The first three mechanisms reflect the fact that envy, like other emotions, affects both the pleasure we get from the inputs to our senses and the amount of these inputs themselves (Elster 1985). Taking account of all four effects, the final bundle of one's own goods and others' goods might well be inferior, *in terms of the envious preferences*, to the bundle that would have obtained if he had not been envious. I strongly suspect, but cannot prove, that in the vast majority of cases the net effect of envy is negative.

Consider next the impact of envy on the welfare of others—envied or third parties. The costs are obvious. Because others will be reluctant to enter into otherwise mutually profitable deals with the envious individual, his envy can detract from their welfare. By destroying or causing third-party destruction of the assets of the envied, he can reduce it still further. By discouraging them from innovation, he harms them no less than himself. The envious may also benefit others, however, by offering an opportunity for envy-enjoyment. More important, the fear of envy-enjoyment can motivate people to excel in ways that also benefit others. When everyone takes one more year of education, in the spirit of keeping up with the Joneses, nobody gets ahead in the rat race, but all contribute to a more skilled work force and a more productive and efficient economy. (I am assuming that education does not merely act as a screening device, but actually improves performance.) When all are motivated by relative levels of welfare, they end up being better off, not because they make an extra effort but because they benefit from the extra effort of others. The erroneous belief that education will make one better off than others induces, if universally shared, behavior that makes all better off than they would otherwise have been.[28] Again, the net effect of these various tendencies on welfare is likely to be negative, at least if envy is taken in the narrow sense defined early in this chapter. Although the last-mentioned effect might be thought to count heavily on the positive side, I believe that the attempt to get ahead in the rat race is more frequently induced by a less complicated motive, viz. the wish to equal others rather than the wish not to be thought inferior by them.

Many will feel, and I believe correctly, that the argument of the two last paragraphs is beside the point. The central fact about envy is that it debases the envious. From his tortuous and distorted perspective, he may be better off when the assets of others are destroyed, but this gain is nothing compared with his inability to live in peace with himself. The tendency to feel a pang of envy at another's fortune is universal. Usually, the feeling is fleeting. It is not a spur to action, not even a source of lasting unhappiness. When it is, it has crossed the border between the normal and the pathological. In such cases, envy is not a preference; it is a disease.[29]

Notes

I am indebted to Natalie Rogoff Ramsøy for penetrating and constructive remarks on a draft of this article and to Sissel Reichelt for valuable suggestions. Comments by Fredrik Engelstad and Aanund Hylland forced me to clarify several key issues. Comments by the editors of the volume and members of the discussion group they had organized around it were extremely useful in forcing me to focus on the important issues. Sven Lindblad provided invaluable bibliographic assistance.

1. Comparisons may prompt other emotions besides envy. My neighbor's poverty may inspire malicious glee or a pang of compassion (or, frequently, both). His prosperity may induce a pang of envy or a glow of pleasure at his good luck (or, frequently, both). When I observe his envy of my prosperity, I may feel smugly self-satisfied or deeply embarrassed. In this article, I consistently assume the baser motives.

2. "The negative capability of tolerating ignorance and/or frustration awakes the bitterest envy" (Etchegoyen, Lopez, and Rabid 1987, p. 50).

3. Brennan 1973 assumes increasing marginal disutility of others' income for the whole income range. I believe this goes in the face of all we know about the psychology of envy.

4. For the relevant notion of plausibility, see Kahneman and Tversky 1982.

5. This is the central theme in the two main book-length treatments of envy, Schoeck 1987 and Mora 1987. While useful, both books are tainted by smugness and ideological bias.

6. For details about these two mechanisms, see ch. IV of Elster 1990a.

7. Contrary to Foster 1972, p. 170: "Individuals envy individuals and groups envy groups."

8. I might also, however, be induced to hold you up. Your envy would not really be worth having, and might not even be forthcoming, if you were too great a failure. Hence it is in my interest to keep you from slipping down too far. As Stephen Holmes has pointed out to me, this was the attitude of the Athenians to their vassal states. Compare also the remarks above on the built-in limitations on spite.

9. Bryson 1935, p. 9.

10. Notably in Foster 1972; see also Foster 1965, ch. 6.

11. Foster 1972, p. 169 tacitly recognizes as much when he cites as an instance of envy the wish of the tuberculous that others should have the ill-

ness too. For criticisms of the zero-sum hypothesis, see also Dow 1981 and Ghosh 1983, p. 218.

12. Ibid.

13. Prestige may no doubt be transferred from one occupation to another, but it cannot be destroyed. Professions guard their privileges jealously because they might be acquired by others, not because they might be destroyed.

14. See ch. III of Elster 1983a. Deciding that "it isn't so important" was one of three reactions found in Salovev and Rodin 1988. The other two reactions, self-reliance and self-bolstering, seem less central.

15. According to Mora (1987, p. 72), adaptation tends to overshoot: "The autonomous dynamism of such an energetic psychic position and the powerful mental inertia of the effort already carried out to negate some value propel resentment towards a final movement consisting of the affirmation that *that* is a counter-value." I may begin envying you a promotion; then I decide that a promotion is not worth having; and I end up thinking that a promotion can be attained only through disreputable means. For the idea that adaptation tends to overshoot, see also Veyne 1976, p. 312 and ch. I of Elster 1990a.

16. The distinction is analogous to that between conformism and altruism. In conformism, other people's behavior changes my preferences. In altruism, it affects the extent to which they are satisfied.

17. Ghosh 1983, p. 211. For discussions of the evil eye, see also Walcot 1978, ch. 7 and Maloney 1976.

18. See for instance ch. 2 of Elster 1983b. In the literature on envy, Foster 1965 and 1972 abound with examples of speculative and implausible functional explanations, often combined with equally conjectural references to the unconscious.

19. These costs are supposed to stem from the dangerous malevolence of the inferior. A more adequate formulation would have to take account of degrees of inferiority and superiority, and not merely the absolute number of inferiors and superiors. Both the pleasures and the dangers created by another's inferiority fall to zero beyond a certain degree of inferiority.

20. In referring to this phenomenon, Simmel (1908, p. 211) asserts that "approximately halfway between the clearly defined phenomena of envy and jealousy there is a third, belonging to the same scale, which might be termed begrudging: the envious desire for an object, not because it is of itself especially desirable to the subject, but only because others possess it." In my opinion, it *is* a form of envy: one envies the other person's happiness, while being indifferent toward the object that has caused him to be happy.

21. Many of the cases I have listed as actions taken out of weak envy could also be classified as acting on strong envy, since the destruction of another's assets usually involves some risk or cost. At the level of preferences, the distinction remains clear enough, however.

22. Walcot (1978, p. 59) sees the Greek liturgies as a form of "sop expenditure" designed to assuage envy. I am more persuaded by the argument in Veyne 1976 that envy-reduction was neither the motive nor the effect of the liturgies. See also ch. I of Elster 1990a.

23. Under majority rule, it may be misleading to refer to these measures as envy-reduction by third parties. They should perhaps be considered direct forms of envy-reduction by the envious themselves, a nonviolent alternative to plundering rather than a preemption of it.

24. Strictly speaking, envy, too, is triadic. Its basic form is "A envies B his possession of C" (Joseph 1976). However, only two *persons* are involved. If C is a person, we are dealing with jealousy, not envy. Similarly, we might define the quadrilateral relation "A challenges B for possession of C in the presence of D," where C and D might or might not be the same person. Fights over women take this form in many societies (Elster 1990b).

25. The identification of objects of envy may also owe something to social norms, however. We may not envy a woman who flaunts her wealth by wearing an expensive fur in the bus queue, but we may resent it if she tries to buy her way into the head of the queue.

26. In his unpublished dissertation he states, however, that "the effect of the rule as to the choice of arms was that each party sought to exceed the other in giving offense" (Bryson 1933, p. 205). I find it puzzling that in his extensive survey of the literature he cites no authority to the opposite effect.

27. Honor may itself be the object of envy. A may try to prevent B from challenging C in order to remove an opportunity for B to increase his honor. Demosthenes said that King Philip of Macedon was so jealous that he wanted his generals to fail rather than succeed (Walcot 1978, p. 18). In *The Frogs* by Aristophanes, Heracles tries to deter Dionysus from venturing into the underground: "Heracles had already visited the nether regions and acquired reputation and honour by this exploit; his honour would inevitably be curtailed if another son of Zeus followed him in this exploit" (ibid., p. 19). Thus one might seek honor not only to be admired by third parties, but to provoke their envy.

28. This statement does not turn upon an ambiguity as to what counts as "better off." People have an interest in both relative and absolute levels of welfare. Each person acts on the assumption that the sum of the absolute and relative benefits conferred by an extra year of education exceeds the costs of education. When all act in this way, two things happen. First, nobody gets the relative benefits. Second, everybody gets greater absolute benefits than he expected, because he benefits from the investment of others.

29. The most famous literary description of envy, in Ovid's *Metamorphoses* (II, 760ff.), brings out well the pathological aspects of envy. Even more poignant is a text by a medieval French writer, Guillaume de Digulleville, cited in Vincentcassy 1980, p. 256.

References

Barth, F. 1964. *The Nomads of South Persia*, Oslo: Universitetsforlaget.

Becker, G., and K. Murphy. 1988. "A Theory of Rational Addiction," *Journal of Political Economy*, 96, 675–700.

Boehm, C. 1984. *Blood Revenge: The Anthropology of Feuding in Montenegro and Other Tribal Societies*, Lawrence, KA: University of Kansas Press.

Bös, D., and G. Tillman. 1985. "An 'Envy Tax': Theoretical Principles and Applications to the German Surcharge on the Rich," *Public Finance/Finances Publiques*, 40: 35–63.

Boskin, M. J., and M. E. Sheshinski. 1978. "Optimal Redistributive Taxation When Individual Welfare Depends on Relative Income," *Quarterly Journal of Economics*, 92: 589–602.

Brennan, G. 1973. "Pareto Desirable Redistribution: The Case of Malice and Envy," *Journal of Public Economics*, 2: 173–183.

Brickman, P., and R. J. Bullman. 1977. "Pleasure and Pain in Social Comparison," in *Social Comparison Processes*, J. M. Suls and R. L. Miller, eds., pp. 149–186, Washington, D.C.: Hemisphere.

Bryson, F. R. 1933. *Honor and Duel in Sixteenth-Century Italy*, Ph.D. dissertation, Department of Romance Languages and Literature, University of Chicago.

Bryson, F. R. 1935. *The Point of Honor in Sixteenth-Century Italy*, New York: Publications of the Institute of French Studies, Columbia University.

Daniel, T. E. 1975. "A Revised Concept of Distributional Equity," *Journal of Economic Theory*, 11: 94–109.

Dow, J. 1981. "The Image of Limited Production," *Human Organization*, 40: 360–363.

Elster, J. 1983a. *Sour Grapes*, Cambridge: Cambridge University Press.

Elster, J. 1983b. *Explaining Technical Change*, Cambridge: Cambridge University Press.

Elster, J. 1985. "Sadder But Wiser? Rationality and the Emotions," *Social Science Information*, 24: 375–406.

Elster, J. 1989. *The Cement of Society*, Cambridge: Cambridge University Press.

Elster, J. 1990a. *Psychologie politique*, Paris: Editions de Minuit.

Elster, J. 1990b. "Norms of Revenge," *Ethics*, 100: 862–885.

Elster, J. Forthcoming. *Local Justice*.

Elster, J., and G. Loewenstein. Forthcoming. "Utility from memory and anticipation," in *Choice over Time*, G. Loewenstein and J. Elster, eds.

Elster J., and J. Roemer, eds. Forthcoming. *Interpersonal Comparisons of Well-Being*, Cambridge: Cambridge University Press.

Etchegoyen, R., B. Lopez, and M. Rabid. 1987. "On Envy and How to Interpret It," *International Journal of Psychoanalysis*, 68: 49–61.

Feldman, A., and A. Kierman. 1974. "Fairness and Envy," *American Economic Review*, 64: 995–1005.

Foley, D. K. 1967. "Resource Allocation and the Public Sector," *Yale Economic Essays*, 7: 45–198.

Foster, G. 1965. *Tzinkuntzan: Mexican Peasants in a Changing World*, Boston: Little, Brown.

Foster, G. 1972. "The Anatomy of Envy," *Current Anthropology*, 13: 165–86.

Freud, S. 1955. "Group Psychology and Analysis of the Ego," *The Standard Edition of the Complete Psychological Works of Sigmund Freud*, vol. XVIII, London: The Hogarth Press.

Ghosh, A. 1983. "The Relations of Envy in an Egyptian Village," *Ethnology*, 22: 211–223.

Gilbert, H., and E. B. Larsons. 1988. "Dealing with Limited Resources: The Oregon Decision to Curtail Funding for Organ Transplantation," *The New England Journal of Medicine*, July 21: 171–173.

Goldthorpe, J. H. 1969. *The Affluent Worker*, Cambridge: Cambridge University Press.

Grua, G. 1956. *La justice humaine selon Leibniz*, Paris: Presses Universitaires de France.

Hamilton, W. B. 1970. "Selfish and spiteful behavior in an evolutionary model," *Nature*, 228: 1218–1220.

Hammond, P. 1987. "Envy," in *The New Palgrave*, London: Macmillan.

Havighurst, C. M., and N. M. King. 1986. "Liver Transplantation in Massachusetts: Public Policymaking as a Morality Play," *Indiana Law Review*, 19: 955–987.

Hegel, G. W. F. 1982. *The Phenomenology of Spirit*, Oxford: Oxford University Press.

Hirschman, A. 1973. "The Changing Tolerance for Income Inequality in the Course of Economic Development," *Quarterly Journal of Economics*, 87: 544–565.

Hirshleifer, J. 1987. "On the Emotions as Guarantors of Threats and Promises," in *The Latest on the Best*, J. Dupré, ed., pp. 307–326, Cambridge, MA: MIT Press.

Hume, D. 1960. *A Treatise of Human Nature*, Selby-Bigge, ed., Oxford: Oxford University Press.

Hutson, S. 1971. "Social Ranking in a French Alpine Community," in *Gifts and Poison*, F. Bailey, ed., pp. 41–68, Oxford: Blackwell.

Hyman, H. 1968. "Reference Groups," in *The International Encyclopedia of the Social Sciences*, vol. 13, pp. 353–361, New York: Macmillan.

Joseph, J. 1976. "Envy: A Functional Analysis," *Linguistic Theory*, 7: 503–508.

Kagan, J. 1984. "The Idea of Emotion in Human Development," in *Emotions, Cognitions and Behavior*, C. E. Izard, J. Kagan, and R. Zajonc, eds., pp. 38–72, Cambridge: Cambridge University Press.

Kahneman, D., J. Knetsch, and R. Thaler. 1986. "Fairness and the Assumptions of Economics," *Journal of Business*, 59, supplementary volume: 101–116.

Kahneman, D., and A. Tversky. 1982. "The Simulation Heuristic," in *Judgment under Uncertainty*, D. Kahneman, P. Slovic, and A. Tversky, eds., pp. 201–208. Cambridge: Cambridge University Press.

Kant, I. 1964 (1785). *The Metaphysic of Morals*, New York: Harper and Row.

Kluckhohn, C. 1944. *Navaho Witchcraft*, Cambridge, MA: Papers of the Peabody Museum, Harvard University.

Kreech, D., and R. S. Crutchfield. 1948. *Theory and Problems of Social Psychology*, New York: McGraw-Hill.

Liebermann, Y., and M. Syrquin. 1983. "On the Use and Abuse of Rights," *Journal of Economic Behavior and Organization*, 4: 25–40.

Loomes, G., and R. Sugden. 1982. "Regret Theory," *Economic Journal*, 92: 805–824.

Lovejoy, A. O. 1961. *Reflections on Human Nature*, Baltimore: Johns Hopkins University Press.

Maloney, C., ed. 1976. *The Evil Eye*, New York: Columbia University Press.

Mayer, P. 1954. "Witches," in *Witchcraft and Sorcery*, M. Warwick, ed., pp. 54–70. Harmondsworth: Penguin.

Merton, R. 1957. *Social Theory and Social Structure*, Glencoe, IL: The Free Press.

de la Mora, G. F. 1987. *Egalitarian Envy*, New York: Paragon House Publishers.

Morgenstern, O. 1973. "Thirteen Critical Points in Contemporary Economic Theory," *Journal of Economic Literature*, 10: 1163–1189.

Nisbett, R., and L. Ross. 1980. *Human Inference*, Englewood Cliffs, NJ: Prentice Hall.

Ranulf, S. 1933. *The Jealousy of the Gods and Criminal Law at Athens*, vol. I, London: Williams and Norgate.

Ranulf, S. 1934. *The Jealousy of the Gods and Criminal Law at Athens*, vol. II, London: Williams and Norgate.

Ranulf, S. 1938. *Moral Indignation and Middle Class Psychology*, Copenhagen: Munksgaard.

Rawls, J. 1971. *A Theory of Justice*, Cambridge, MA: Harvard University Press.

Salovev, P., and J. Rodin. 1988. "Coping with Envy and Jealousy," *Journal of Social and Clinical Psychology*, 7: 15–33.

Schalin, L. 1979. "On the Problem of Envy," *Scandinavian Psychoanalytical Review*, 2: 133–158.

Scheler, M. 1972. *Ressentiment*, New York: Schocken Books.

Schoeck, H. 1987. *Envy*, Indianapolis: Liberty Press.

Scott, R. 1972. "Avarice, Altruism and Second Party Preferences," *Quarterly Journal of Economics*, 86: 1–18.

Shils, E. 1968. "Deference," in *Social Stratification*, J. A. Jackson, ed., pp. 104–132, Cambridge: Cambridge University Press.

Simmel, G. 1908. *Soziologie*, Berlin: Dunker und Humblot.

Simpson, G. E. 1941. "Haiti's Social Structure," *American Sociological Review*, 6: 640–649.

Sussangkarn, C., and S. Goldman. 1983. "Dealing with Envy," *Journal of Public Economics*, 22: 103–112.

de Swaan, A. 1989. "Jealousy as a Class Phenomenon: The Petite Bourgeoisie and Social Security," *International Sociology*, 4: 259–271.

Thaler, R. 1980. "Towards a Positive Theory of Consumer Behavior," *Journal of Economic Behavior and Organization*, 1: 39–60.

Thomas, K. 1973. *Religion and the Decline of Magic*, Harmondsworth: Penguin.

de Tocqueville, A. 1969. *Democracy in America*, New York: Anchor Books.

Veblen, T. 1965. *The Theory of the Leisure Class*, New York: Augustus Kelley.

Veyne, P. 1976. *Le pain et le cirque*, Paris: Editions du Seuil.

Vincentcassy, M. 1980. "L'envie au Moyen Âge," *Annales: Economies, Société, Civilisations*, 35: 253–271.

Walcot, P. 1978. *Envy and the Greeks*, Warminster: Aris and Phillips.

Walzer, M. 1983. *Spheres of Justice*, New York: Basic Books.

Wilson, C. 1967. "Trade, Society and the State," in *The Cambridge Economic History of Europe*, vol. IV, Cambridge: Cambridge University Press.

Zhang, X., and Y. Sang. 1987. *Chinese Lives*, New York: Pantheon.

4

Free Riding versus Cooperation

Howard Margolis

We are better off with a government that collects taxes and provides public services than with no government and no services. But individually I would be even better off if the government collected taxes from everyone else, but somehow neglected to collect from me. The overall level of public services would look the same whether I paid or not (provided the rest of you continue to pay), but what I could spend on myself would be noticeably larger. So why pay?

The answer is not so obvious as might first be supposed. Of course, I can get into serious trouble by not paying. Yet the tax system depends on a very significant measure of "voluntary compliance" (Roth et al. 1988). More broadly, no society could survive if its citizens violated its rules whenever a favorable opportunity arose: that is, whenever the risk of punishment was small enough to make the gamble tempting as a matter of narrow self-interest. On the other hand, no society elicits such a high degree of voluntary compliance that it can get along without police and tax audits.

In general, understanding how societies function depends a great deal on how compliance with social rules is sustained and at what cost that compliance is secured. How that works will vary across sorts of rules and across conditions under which individuals might be tempted to violate the rules. Under some circumstances, normal levels of compliance can break down, although calamities (such as earthquakes) that produce social disorder in one community may elicit exceptionally cooperative behavior in another. There is always tension between forces favoring compliance with social norms and forces favoring narrowly self-interested behavior. Somehow a balance ordinarily prevails that allows a stable basis for social life. But that stability is not automatic or unchallengeable. Sometimes the balance is upset.

We are going to attempt some steps toward exploring all that by way of an analogue to the trading equilibrium of a market. In the market context, the equilibrium that emerges at the social level (a set of prices, for example) is contingent on and interacts with the equilibrium personal spending choices of individuals. So the analysis of market equilibrium is built up from the properties of equilibrium individual allocations of resources (budgets) across feasible bundles of economic goods. We want to consider an analogous dual equilibrium, with individuals allocating between social and self-interested use of their resources, yielding a social equilibrium contingent on those individual allocations.

Suppose that human beings are motivated to some extent by social concerns, not solely by self-interest.[1] Then efficient social institutions would certainly take account of that—most obviously, though not only, because in many commonplace situations it would be prohibitively costly or unreliable to try to govern social behavior through incentives tied only to self-interest. A generalized evolutionary argument suggests that firms must be at least reasonable approximations of profit maximizers (because otherwise, how would they survive?). A variant of that argument suggests that social institutions should be reasonably effective exploiters of social motivation.[2]

Some version of this argument seems essential to understanding how societies work. I will try to set out the basic lines of such an analysis. The main analytical device I will use is Schelling's (1978) simple but very rich diagrammatic treatment of the relation between individual and social choice, as presented in the concluding chapter of *Micromotives and Macrobehavior*. Although we can deal with only the simplest cases, we reach a provocative result, opening a line of analysis that might be taken quite a long way.[3]

The Basic Schelling Diagram

Although the point of the paper is to consider how social motivation interacts with self-interest, it is convenient to start from the far end of the range of possibilities. We start from the case of strictly voluntary choices made by strictly self-interested individuals.

The horizontal axis in figure 4.1 measures the extent of cooperative behavior. At the left (marked 0), no one is cooperating; at the other extreme, on the right, everyone is.[4] The vertical distance from the axis measures value to the individual, who must choose between free riding (the *FR* curve) and cooperation (the *C* curve). Figure 4.1 is drawn with the payoffs for free riding and for cooperation as parallel straight lines. Ordinarily that could not hold, because as we move across the figure, different individuals are choosing under different conditions. But to provide a clear baseline for the more complicated situations that are our main concern, it is convenient (and harmless) to start from that simplest possible configuration.

The context that concerns us could be one of seeking voluntary monetary donations to some public function (say to a July 4 fireworks display or a public television station), or seeking donations of time (say, to clean up a neighborhood), or any other activity that provides benefits to everyone in a community, whether or not they have helped provide the benefits. As with markets, the analytics are simplest for cases with large numbers of actors, no single one of whom alone has a perceptible effect on the social outcome: in the set just mentioned, the public television context is an example.

On almost any such matter there will be some temptation to go along for the ride, letting other people handle the costs. But if we all do that, nothing gets done, and we are all worse off. If the group is small, and everyone pretty well knows what everyone else is doing, then the free-rider temptation may be small even if choice is strictly voluntary and self-interested. But as numbers grow large (the case that concerns us here), anonymity becomes more pronounced, and the advantage to self-interest of free riding becomes increasingly unambiguous.

Figures 4.1 through 4.6 all show the incentives facing the marginal chooser, contingent on how everyone else is choosing. Figure 4.1 is for the initial (strictly voluntary, strictly self-interested) context; the balance of the figures are for various conditions that depart from strictly voluntary and self-interested motivation. At each point across any diagram we are considering the person most easily tempted to change his or her choice (switch from cooperation to free riding, or the reverse), given any particular level of cooperation by others.

For this large-numbers case, the only effect on self-interest perceptible to the marginal chooser (if he should choose to contribute) would be that he has lost the cost of his contribution, but avoided whatever risk of punishment for free riding may be present. But for the strictly voluntary, self-interested case of figure 4.1, there is no such risk, so that the cooperate curve *C* is just the free-ride curve *FR* minus the cost of cooperating.[5]

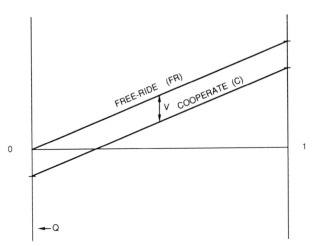

Figure 4.1

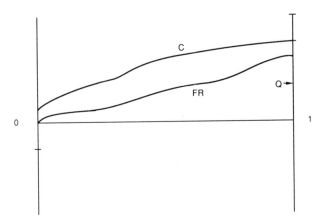

Figure 4.2

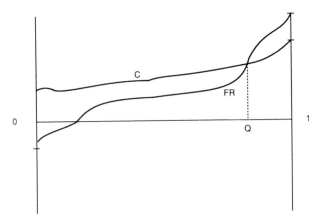

Figure 4.3

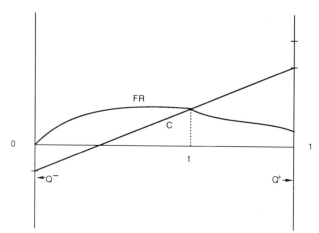

Figure 4.4

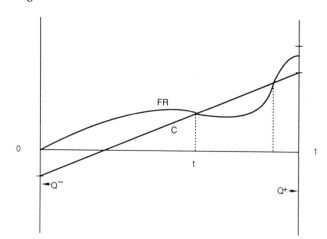

Figure 4.5

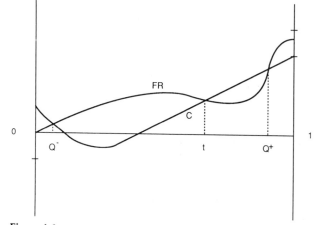

Figure 4.6

The only equilibrium in figure 4.1 is at the extreme left, where no one is cooperating. For at every point in the figure, the free-ride curve lies above the cooperate curve. As we move across the horizontal axis, everyone at some point becomes the marginal chooser, and whatever we might assume about the prevailing level of cooperation, that marginal chooser always does better to free ride. The prevailing level consequently would move a bit to the left, where another person is the marginal chooser: and that person also will choose to free ride.[6] This unraveling continues until we reach the familiar result (Samuelson 1954, Olson 1965) that although everyone would be better off if the social choice were at 1 (100 percent cooperation), the only equilibrium outcome for strictly voluntary self-interested choice would be at 0.

But actual communities commonly manage to avoid this dismal result. Somehow, apparently, there are ordinarily incentives present (beyond what can be accounted for in terms of strictly voluntary self-interest) whose sum is sufficient to offset the cost of cooperating.

Tipping Points and Equilibria

Now consider the simplest conceptually possible ways in which the incentive curves of figure 4.1 might be shifted to allow a non-zero level of cooperation. Figures 4.2–4.6 show various possibilities, with the horizontal ticks on the vertical axes of those figures marking the location of the endpoints of the original FR and C lines of figure 4.1. Calling the cost of cooperating V, we want to consider the basic possibilities that arise when incentives favoring cooperation exist to offset V.[7]

In the simplest case, the ordinal positions of the free-ride and cooperate curves would be completely reversed (as in figure 4.2), so that the C curve always lies above the FR curve. Then we would get the particularly simple outcome in which the advantage to free riding of figure 4.1 completely disappears. The unique equilibrium is at the far right, with 100 percent cooperation.[8,9]

But a complete reversal (as in figure 4.2) would rarely be seen, reflecting the reality that ordinarily it costs the society something to provide incentives that offset the advantage to free riding. This might occur with diminishing marginal effectiveness as we move toward higher cooperation, or (conceivably) with increasing marginal effectiveness.

Figure 4.3 shows a case in which the offsetting incentives are most effective when cooperation is low, with diminishing marginal effectiveness with increasing cooperation. The net advantage favors cooperation at the far left of figure 4.3, but the advantage shifts toward free riding as the fraction induced to cooperate increases. The advantage falls to 0 at the crossover point and becomes increasingly adverse to cooperation as we move beyond the crossover point to still higher levels of cooperation.

Figure 4.4 shows the opposite case, in which the offsetting incentives are most effective when cooperation is high, so that the strong free-rider advantage when cooperation is low decreases as we move to the right, reaches 0 at the crossover, and thereafter the net advantage increasingly *favors* cooperation.

As Schelling pointed out, the situations of figures 4.3 and 4.4 have strikingly different consequences for the evolution of the social situation. In figure 4.3, where the cooperate curve crosses the free-ride curve from above, the crossover identifies an *equilibrium* (Q). In figure 4.4, where the cooperate curve crosses the free-ride curve from below, the crossover identifies a *tipping point* (t), with two possible equilibria, one with zero cooperation, the other at 100 percent cooperation. To follow the balance of the argument, it is essential to see why in figure 4.3 the crossover is an equilibrium, but in figure 4.4 it is a tipping point.

Starting from any point in figure 4.3, the social process would always move toward Q. Anywhere to the left of Q the net advantage is always to cooperate (the marginal individual would always find it in his interest to choose C), which moves us further right in the figure (toward higher cooperation) until we get to Q. Starting from any point to the right of Q, the opposite net advantage prevails, and again we would always move toward, never away from, the crossover point at Q. But for figure 4.4, the opposite holds. We would always move away from t until we reached equilibrium, which here would be at the extreme possibilities: either 0 cooperation or 100 percent cooperation. So in contrast to the case of figure 4.3, where social evolution is always moving toward the stable equilibrium, the result could vary radically, contingent on how events leading to the eventual equilibrium had unfolded.[10]

Strictly speaking, it is possible that we are *exactly* at t, like a pole balanced exactly on its end. But the pole would not stay put very long, because the slightest perturbation would set things moving away from perfect balance, and the same would hold for the social analogue.

Finally, there is no reason that the situation should be as simple as the cases considered so far. Rather, we could get more than one crossover. Then (by applying the preceding argument to cases like those of figures 4.5 or 4.6) we could have at least one tipping point and at least one interior (not 0 or 1) equilibrium point. As will be seen next, possibilities of that sort are what we can usually expect to find in the world.

Rewards and Punishment

Additional incentives to individual choosers (Olson's "selective incentives") or social (rather than only private, self-interested) motivation, or some combination of both, might serve to offset the free-rider advantage. The availability and effectiveness of either selective incentives or social motivation vary from issue to issue within a society and across societies on any particular issue. But on the account here, all three (positive incentives, negative incentives, social as well as self-interested motivation) will ordinarily play a role in every choice.

Setting aside social motivation until the next section (so that we are still allowing for only strictly self-interested motivation), the possibilities for shifting the free-rider advantage could come either from imposing a risk of punishment on those who fail to cooperate or offering a promise of reward for those who do. We want to consider how the effectiveness of such negative or positive incentives might vary as we move from low toward high compliance. Or put another way, we want to consider varying returns to scale of incentives.

Positive incentives (rewarding cooperation) would raise the cooperate (C) curve of figure 4.1. Negative incentives would lower the free-ride (FR) curve. So there would be several ways in which some combination of shifts in the original curves might be sufficient to reverse the vertical position of the curves over at least some range of cooperation. The effects at issue here are really just those that Schelling (1960) discusses in another way in his analysis of deterrence.

Workable positive incentives (rewards) must offer something analogous to gains from trade. Society (more precisely, some agent with authority to act for the society) must have access to resources that cost little to give away compared with their value to potential compliers. The social value of the incremental cooperation elicited must be higher than the cost of providing the incentive.[11] An outstanding example is the honorary award, which may be highly valued by individuals, and which indeed may have substantial economic as well as psychic value (hence may be capable of eliciting substantial resources from potential cooperators), but which costs the agent almost nothing to provide. Other familiar examples of positive incentives are premiums given to donors by a fundraising drive, or invitations to social events.

Positive incentives typically will exhibit either increasing unit costs to the agent or decreasing value to marginal compliers, or both. So marginal effectiveness (the ratio between the gain perceived by the chooser and the cost to the agent of providing that incentive) will ordinarily decline as we move toward high levels of cooperation. There will be exceptions, especially for Olson's context of selective incentives within interest groups, as when information is provided to members of a professional association. But for the society at large, positive incentives with increasing or even constant marginal effectiveness must be rare. Rather, the positive incentive to a marginal complier that can be provided at some fixed cost to the agent almost always diminishes. This implies that, considering positive incentives only, net incentives would have the general shape of figure 4.3, with a unique equilibrium at Q.[12]

The situation is less clear for negative incentives. With exceptions (such as honorary awards), which can usually be offered to only a few individuals, providing positive incentives is costly, but the administrative costs are low. People who have earned a reward will not ordinarily conceal their behavior or evade attempts to supply the promised consequences. But the opposite applies for penalties. If penalties for noncooperation take the form of fines, or of denying ordinarily available benefits, then costs (for the agent) are negative.[13] But the various components of policing—surveillance, apprehension, adjudication—all involve positive costs for the agent. So for negative incentives, the "delivered" incentive may actually be profitable for the agent, but it costs to detect noncompliance, identify noncompliers, and bring them to the point at which penalties can be imposed.[14]

But since penalties to an apprehended noncooperator can be made large compared with V, an effective negative incentive requires only some sufficient risk of detection to deter free riding. That risk might be small enough that it could be reasonably cheap to create. So it is more plausible for negative incentives than for positive that some substantial measure of cooperation could be achieved by incentives alone (excluding any effect of social motivation).

But the effect of negative incentives also could vary sharply depending on whether those incentives—in particular, as just mentioned, the costs of imposing some sufficient risk of punishment—are mainly "wholesale" or "retail."

At one extreme ("wholesale"), there is the case in which setup costs (arranging for surveillance, for example) are substantial, but the marginal costs of imposing risks on noncompliers are small. A physical analogy would be the building of a fence. Until the fence is complete, it is easily evaded; but thereafter modest costs for patrolling assure high levels of compliance. At the other extreme, wholesale surveillance is infeasible, and free riding must be deterred "retail." The agent can start by choosing particularly favorable targets (people who are particularly easy to watch, or particularly risk-averse, or both), after which marginal costs rise as less and less vulnerable individuals must be covered.

For the retail case, we would get a direct analogue of the figure 4.3 situation—except that here (in contrast to the case of positive incentives), the incentives would push the free-ride curve down instead of moving the cooperate curve up. But for the wholesale case, we would get something like the figure 4.4 situation, in which free riding becomes less attractive relative to cooperation as compliance increases. More realistically, we must suppose that at some sufficiently high level of compliance we would run into decreasing returns even with the fence. So we could expect a curve like figure 4.5, which exhibits the multiple crossovers mentioned at the end of the previous section.

But a puzzle now emerges. For the cost of deterring free-riding behavior (per capita) is ordinarily lower in a community where compliance is high than where compliance is low. A fortiori, then, the marginal cost of deterrence must be falling as compliance increases, at least up to some high level of compliance. This effect is particularly striking for cases in which the behavior to be deterred includes offenses against private individuals, so that the total costs to the community should include the defensive measures of individuals as well as the policing costs of the central authority. But even setting that aside, the puzzle arises, because it is hard to believe that in fact policing (even considering only costs to the central authority) always or even ordinarily yields increasing returns.

To sum up: when we consider negative and positive incentives separately, we get incentive curves with relative slopes like those of figure 4.3 for either positive incentives or for retail (decreasing returns) negative incentives. But for wholesale (increasing returns) negative incentives we get instead the figure 4.4 configuration, or more realistically, figure 4.5. In both figures 4.4 and 4.5, the relation between the free-ride and cooperate curves becomes increasingly favorable to cooperation over most of the range of possibilities. For a combination of positive incentives and wholesale negative incentives, we would get the figure 4.6 situation, with a low compliance equilibrium at $Q-$ and a high compliance equilibrium at $Q+$.[15]

These two basic possibilities (figure 4.3 vs. figure 4.6—or 4.5 or 4.4, but I want to focus on 4.6) yield qualitatively different pictures of the problem of social organization. If the usual situation were that of decreasing returns to incentives (figure 4.3), then it seems likely that the higher the level of cooperation sought, the less likely there will be a feasible set of incentives sufficient to overcome the free-rider temptation to the marginal chooser. Consequently, compliance could be expected to reveal a distribution across issues that is largest at levels not far from 0 and tends downward as we move across the range from low values of Q toward $Q = 1$ on the right tail of the distribution.

But if the usual situation combines positive incentives with decreasing returns and negative incentives with increasing returns, then we ought to see a bimodal distribution as in figure 4.6. We would have a peak well to the left, with compliance encouraged by positive incentives; and a second piling up of the distribution on the right, with high compliance elicited by negative incentives.

The dynamics of these two salient possibilities would be very different (recall the earlier discussion of tipping points and their relation to equilibria). If the actual situation is commonly like that of figure 4.3, the process of reaching the unique equilibrium would not ordinarily exhibit interesting path-dependent properties. But if the typical situation is like that of figure 4.6, then the dynamics are very important. If somehow the community can get to the right of the tipping point (t) it will reach the favorable equilibrium at $Q+$; otherwise (if nothing else intervenes) it will reach the perverse equilibrium at $Q-$.

Further, if the curves go as in figure 4.6, a disturbance that pushes compliance down to the left of t will lead to unraveling. Unless some further consideration intervenes (for example, imposition of martial law) compliance would fall all the way back to the inferior equilibrium at $Q-$. So for the case of figure 4.3—decreasing returns from resources devoted to creating negative incentives—once incentives are in place, the unique equilibrium appears spontaneously, like the equilibrium price in a market, though that equilibrium may not be far above 0 compliance. But in the increasing returns case, some further social process appears to be essential if the society is ever to reach the high compliance equilibrium at $Q+$ in figure 4.6. Then, if reached, that favorable equilibrium could be vulnerable to social disturbances with potentially radical consequences for the society.

And indeed, although compliance with the social order is ordinarily high, we do occasionally see striking shifts. Apparently something like the unraveling implicit in the existence of tipping points actually occurs. Sometimes (as in Iran at the time of the fall of the Shah, or more recently throughout Eastern Europe) these shifts in compliance with the social order develop suddenly enough to surprise knowledgeable observers inside and outside the country (Kuran 1989).

Thus certain features of observed social processes suggest that Schelling diagrams for real social situations might often take the form of figure 4.6. Yet it is not very credible that negative incentives ordinarily yield increasing marginal returns. And even if they did, there would remain the further puzzle of how the society could ever get beyond the tipping point.[16]

Social Motivation

So far we have considered only strictly self-interested choice. But now consider the possibility of social motivation, starting again from the case of purely voluntary action. In any actual situation, we would expect people to vary in their commitment to the social value of the choice at issue, as revealed by their willingness-to-pay to advance those social values. Lining up people in declining order of this commitment, it is tautological that we would see a negative slope for the social incentive. But in contrast to rewards and penalties, where the presence of the incentive would never make its target *less* likely to cooperate than its absence, for social motivation counterexamples are of deep importance. An individual—and more significantly, on some occasions a substantial fraction of all individuals—may see social value in defying a policy, hence a social loss in compliance. We then see the atypical but familiar and important case of principled civil disobedience. Then treating noncompliance as just another form of free riding would miss the point, though the analytics are just those already sketched. On the other hand, it is much more plausible for social motivation than for positive or negative incentives that the effect would remain nearly constant all across, or almost all across, the population.

Treating social motivation as a simple "warm glow" add-on to the cooperate curve would not change the qualitative picture already discussed in the strict self-interest context. Without social motivation, positive and negative incentives must be sufficient to offset the free-rider incentive (in figure 4.1, the vertical distance between the FR and C curves). Obviously, to the extent that social motivation is simply added to the cooperate curve, the free-rider advantage is diminished. A nonzero equilibrium could appear even though Olsonian selective incentives are not sufficient to make the net advantage to self-interest favor compliance. And given any set of positive and negative incentives sufficient by themselves to yield a nonzero equilibrium, that equilibrium will be pushed to the right (to higher compliance) by the warm glow. But the qualitative remarks at the conclusion of the previous section would require no amendment. More generally, it is not clear that a mere warm glow add-on would play any analytically useful role: ex post it lets us fill up any empirically awkward gap between theory and behavior, but ex ante it does not tell us anything.

However, providing more structure to the notion of social motivation leads to sharper results.

"Neither Selfish nor Exploited"

In recent years many papers and quite a number of books have attempted to account for compliance by invoking social norms or some other formulation of what I am here calling social motivation.[17] Naturally I am partial to my own account (Margolis 1982), and what follows is a much-condensed version of that argument. The basic intuition is that what makes a person feel comfortable about his self-interested and social use of resources—what gives a person a sense of having done his "fair share"—is a certain balance that can be captured by the slogan: "neither selfish nor exploited." I call this, for short, the NSNX principle (pronounced "niz-nex").

A pair of rules for choice transform the NSNX intuition into a form that can be developed analytically. The rules are framed in terms of the marginal use of resources. They yield the analogue of a first-order condition for a "neither selfish nor exploited" equilibrium allocation between self-interest and social motivation:

1. (Efficiency) Other things equal, the more good a bit of resources would do if used socially (compared with what it could do if used for my private interests), the more likely I will use that bit of resources socially.

2. (Equity) Other things equal, the more I have already used resources socially relative to what others are doing, the more inclined I am to spend the next bit of resources on myself.

Rule 1 would make a person willing to consider cooperation if his contribution would be socially useful. The more socially useful the behavior seems to be, the more willing he would be to do more. But the greater the private cost of that contribution, the less willing he would be. It is hard to believe that any effective account of social behavior could fail to incorporate some such rule, turning on the ratio between the perceived social value and the private cost of a contribution to social goals. But Rule 2 says that an individual response to social concerns will also depend on how his sacrifice of private for social values compares with what others are doing.

Although the rules characteristically produce joint effects, so that it is artificial and easily misleading to treat the effects separately, roughly speaking Rule 1 captures the "not selfish" half of the NSNX slogan, and Rule 2 captures the "nor exploited" half.

In terms of the NSNX analysis, the private incentives discussed earlier would work through their effect on the ratio that governs Rule 1. The denominator of that ratio between social gain and private cost depends on how much a person could gain by evading cooperation. In the language of economics, both positive and negative incentives shrink the opportunity cost of cooperation, hence increase the ratio of social gain to private cost, hence (by Rule 1) increase the likelihood of cooperation.

Rule 2 plays a more explicit role in the analysis here. An immediate consequence is that, other things equal, social motivation will increase with an increase in the cooperation of others. For exactly what would give a person a sense that he is being exploited is that he is doing conspicuously more than others in his situation. Similarly, what would give a person a feeling (other things equal) that he is not doing his fair share is that others are doing conspicuously more than he is. So from Rule 2, social motivation would tend to increase as we move across a Schelling diagram from zero to high compliance. Therefore a Schelling diagram that allows for NSNX motivation would tend to have the general form of figure 4.6 (though not necessarily the highly favorable $Q+$ equilibrium of that figure), whether or not "wholesale" (increasing returns) negative incentives are realistically available. So Rule 2 gives an explanation of why we almost always see a favorable correlation between high compliance and low average cost of policing that is independent of the doubtful claim that deterrence per se commonly yields increasing returns.[18]

It is possible to argue that the tendency of social compliance to exhibit the positive feedback implicit in Rule 2 reflects not social motivation but only a general propensity toward conformity. But if so, changes in prevailing norms of compliance (both in the statistical sense of norms and in the normative sense) could only be explained in terms that go no deeper than our ability to account for changing fashions. Since nothing of great consequence is at stake in changes of fashion, it is not surprising that fashion should be subject to trivial, vague, hard-to-pin-down influences. Why not? But here we are concerned with behavior that often has substantial costs to individuals and substantial consequences for society. If our propensities to social conformity have deeper underpinnings, this is where we would expect them to show their effects. So one might expect habit and fashion and conformism to contribute to an explanation of observed compliance, but not to be a sufficient explanation.

A related but distinguishable factor—again important but not sufficient—is the strong propensity we all share for our own judgment to be powerfully influenced by what "everyone knows." The coordination of intuitions across a community of course is not automatic or invariable, but a powerful tendency of that sort is empirically apparent. Coordination would shape intuitions about such matters as the social value of compliance and the tolerability of the private costs. The effect would become increasingly favorable to compliance as prevailing behavior increasingly favors compliance. But there is no reason why the coordination of intuitions would have generally benign rather than random social consequences unless the underlying innate propensities favored social motivation.

Schelling Dynamics

A more general consequence of this argument must be to strengthen the significance of the earlier comments on path dependence, hence emphasizing the associated problem of how a society gets beyond the tipping point. The first thing to notice is that although I have treated compliance as dichotomous (either a person cooperates or he doesn't), compliance is not in fact dichotomous. Very clearly, it can vary continuously, in terms of both level of effort on a particular occasion and reliability of that effort across occasions. I will use the label "intensity" (of compliance) to include both dimensions. I'll use the term "prevalence" to refer to the extent to which what emerges as the average intensity of compliance is in fact widely observed. So prevalence is high when almost everyone is doing some usual thing, though the usual thing need not demand much of any individual complier. In these terms what we are measuring as we move from left to right in the Schelling diagram is increasing prevalence for some given level of intensity.

Holding positive and negative incentives fixed, the equilibria that emerge would reflect the three-way interactions among intensity, prevalence, and perceptions of the social value of compliance. High prevalence alone does not imply a high level of social commitment (high intensity). It only requires that, whatever the standard, it is widely adhered to. But to the extent that the standard is low, the private cost of complying is small. If the perceived social value of this modest social commitment is fairly high (society is not perceived as already having more than enough of whatever is at stake), then from Rule 1 individuals will be moved to do more, though (from Rule 2) ordinarily not much more than seems the usual behavior. But if many people are so moved, cooperation at a higher level of intensity becomes more prevalent.

In general, the consequence under Rules 1 and 2 would be that intensity would increase until an equilibrium that involved both intensity and prevalence was reached. Under other conditions an erosion of overall cooperative behavior would occur. In a companion paper (Margolis 1990), I have provided some further details of how the equilibrium process might operate.

Suppose that the argument here were empirically correct. Then in a society not visibly in crisis, we would expect to see a widely shared (and largely tacit[19]) sense of "reasonable compliance" with various norms and rules.[20] By and large people will abide by that standard, even when there is not an immediately visible threat of negative sanctions if they fail to do so. The configuration of figure 6.6 would remain a good characterization of the situation.

Very often the process by which this equilibrium is reached will be quite simple, because for the most part new modes of cooperation are sufficiently like modes of cooperation already in place that expectations of usual behavior are immediately available. Sometimes this is by design, but more often it is because social intuitions lead things that way even without explicit planning.

More complicated situations arise in the case of new behavior that doesn't readily analogize to what is already done or isn't immediately covered by generalized incentives to obey the law. Crises may be prompted by severe shocks to the system, but also can occur when the underpinnings of a mode of social interaction have been eroded, with social inertia maintaining a veneer of stability until some mild shock triggers a collapse. We thus see social phenomena akin to speculative bubbles in the dynamics of collapse.

Since on this analysis, high prevalence (so that cooperation is well beyond the tipping point) does not mean that social cooperation is necessarily at or even near a level that would be socially efficient, even an equilibrium safely beyond t can be very inefficient. "Reasonable compliance" might be very prevalent, but the society is functioning poorly. Should not the social agent then institute more stringent rules and more stringent negative incentives to secure compliance with those rules? But that may not be easily provided, and perhaps not even prudently attempted. For what is keeping the society at least superficially functioning is some at least minimally viable but widely shared sense of "reasonable compliance." Pushing harder could lead to collapse, not improvement.

Further, social motivation can take forms that would be considered perverse by an outsider, and perhaps eventually even by the children of those involved, as in the intense subloyalties that divide societies like those of Lebanon or Northern Ireland. Even when gross social pathologies are not present, subgroup loyalties can crowd out larger concerns.

There is much more to be said. Societies, for example, are segmented, and subgroups often are guided by what can be called subnorms, which are commonly but not always directed only at the welfare of the subgroup. But subgroups adhering (with some degree of intensity) to a subnorm useful for the society at large must feel "not exploited." Subgroup dynamics would be expected to play an important role in the process by which new generally prevalent norms appear (in recent years, for example, dealing with the environment), or old norms change (in recent years, for example, dealing with smoking).

Summary

Schelling's elegant diagrams can capture a *very* wide range of social interactions. Like any abstract modeling, even in physics, they make things simpler than reality. But they open fundamental questions to analysis and debate, push us to consider critical issues, help us get a clearer sense of the tangles of interacting considerations that characterize social behavior. Starting with the simplest version of the Schelling diagram, I have tried to show how we might sort out the ways in which social cooperation might be elicited when, as is pervasively the case, what would be good for all of us conflicts with what would be privately tempting to each of us.

We saw, first, how those interactions abstractly raise two contrasting basic possibilities: configurations with a tipping point and two equilibria (one with high levels of cooperation, the other with low), or configurations with a single unique equilibrium. We then considered how incentives aimed at the self-interest of choosers interact with the extent of cooperation, finding that indeed some possible configurations of incentives exist that would yield a unique social equilibrium (as in figure 4.3), whereas others would yield the configuration with high and low equilibria separated by a tipping point (figure 4.6). The latter would allow the possibility of a more favorable social equilibrium; but it would also introduce a potential for instability, and the problem of how the more favorable equilibrium might be reached if it exists. I argued that the world looks like the tipping point configuration in fact is important, but that private incentives alone (which would require generally increasing marginal returns to negative incentives) were unlikely to adequately explain that. We then considered what happens when we take account of social as well as self-interested motivation. The tipping point configuration of figure 4.6 emerged as the characteristic social situation, leading us to a concluding survey of the path dependence and stability problems that then arise.

This paper has focused on the basic analytics, and I have been able to give only a bare sketch of the way the analysis might be developed. Readers will think of further issues I have not touched upon, difficulties I have not discussed, and no doubt difficulties that I have not even noticed. Readers familiar with Schelling's own presentation of the diagrams will remember how wide a range of situations these simple diagrams can capture.

Notes

I am indebted to Richard Zeckhauser and the members of his social theory seminar and to a reviewer for comments on a draft of this chapter.

1. Allowing for social motivation (or something functionally equivalent) within a rational choice framework is noticeably less outside the mainstream than it seems to have been only a few years ago. For examples, see Frank 1988 (for economics), Maynard-Smith 1989 (for evolutionary biology), and Elster 1989 (for political science). For a wide sampling of recent developments, see the collection of papers edited by Jane Mansbridge (Mansbridge 1990).

2. The evolutionary argument is plausible only if we can point to some plausible source of competitive pressure. One possibility is the pressure on political leaders from comparisons with other countries. Recent events in Europe provide spectacular illustrations. But looking at history and the evolution of culture on a larger scale, outright conquest seems to have played a significant role in the shaping of social systems. Over the long span of history, societies that were not reasonably effective in organizing themselves for social action have not survived.

3. Among the issues I will have to leave aside, a particularly critical point is that any complex society will have an intricately overlapping social structure. Each of us is simultaneously a member of many different subcommunities and perhaps also of superordinate communities, reflecting ties (ethnic, professional, and so on) either within or beyond the primary community—in today's world, ordinarily the national state. These different loyalties are sometimes complementary, often competing (in the sense that they would favor alternative uses of scarce resources), and sometimes downright conflicting, though we can expect that individuals will in various ways shield themselves from facing too bluntly that unpleasant or awkward reality.

How a person mediates among these competing loyalties seems essentially a perceptual issue that falls outside the range of rational-actor analysis, though not necessarily outside the range of disciplined inquiry which can complement that analysis. I cannot begin to explore that possibility here. Nor can I consider dichotomous (or more finely structured) contrasts in preference across groups within a society (conservative vs. liberal, Catholic vs. Protestant, and so on). Such divisions must often play a large role in an analysis that goes much beyond my preliminary sketch, because polarization is a very marked feature of politics.

But setting all these complications aside for now is the appropriate tactic. It lets us concentrate on the basic analytics, in the same way that analysis of idealized markets provides a starting point for attempts to make sense of the complexity of actual markets, where information is never perfect and external effects never wholly absent.

4. Both internal and external incentives might motivate behavior. I might go to a party because I expect to enjoy it, or because my wife insists that I must, or perhaps from a mixture of both. Similarly, the social behavior labeled cooperation in figure 4.1 might be either internally or externally motivated and typically arises from a combination of both types of motivation. So we are commonly dealing with the case of what I have called "incomplete coercion" or what Margaret Levi (1988) has called "partially voluntary compliance." But we seem to have no comparably neutral term for the social analogue of "go" (to the party). "Cooperate" suggests that the choice is internally motivated; "comply" suggests that it is externally motivated. Here I will mostly use the verb "cooperate," but from these comments you will understand that the word is intended as shorthand for something like "cooperate/comply."

5. I have so far left out of the discussion a further possibility: some special reward for cooperation. But when we come to consider punishments, we will also consider rewards.

6. Might not a person choose to cooperate, even though his free-ride curve shows a higher payoff than his cooperate curve, just because he prefers to do what he takes to be the right thing? He might indeed. But it is precisely that kind of motivation we want to bring *within* the scope of the formal analysis. So, as will be discussed in more detail later, any such social motivation would be a factor that raises the value of cooperating to the choosing individual, not something from outside the analysis that makes him choose to cooperate whether or not his incentives favor cooperation.

7. As will be seen, it is essential to the analysis (and a persistent feature of the world) that cooperating and free riding are not necessarily or even ordinarily dichotomous choices. So there need not be, and most often in fact there is not, any unique cost of contributing, V. Even when there is a standard contribution, a person may contribute on some occasions but not every time, effectively defining contributions less than V. Someone else may contribute time or money beyond V. But it is convenient to set such complications aside for a while.

8. Is the situation better than the situation of figure 4.1? Not necessarily. Some social policies—and more obviously 100 percent compliance with a policy—might be obtained only by such severe repression that even individuals who judge the policies socially beneficial would regard the net result as unreasonable.

9. I've drawn the curves in figure 4.2 as "curvy" as a reminder that any given incentive must be expected to vary in effect as we look across the figure. So even though we have arbitrarily taken the basic FR and C curves

to be parallel straight lines (figure 4.1), once adjusted for incentives those curves would have some more complicated form.

10. For example, if the situation had been that of figure 4.2, but changes in circumstance had reshaped it to that of figure 4.4, the outcome would be at 1. If somehow the situation had been that of figure 4.4, but right at the tipping point, then otherwise trivial accidents would determine whether the process would unravel to 0 or roll up to full cooperation.

11. Because there must be costs in providing the incentives intended to offset the free-rider advantage, the level and intensity of compliance that makes social sense will represent some compromise between the social value of higher compliance and the social costs of providing the incentives. In a fuller treatment than I can attempt here, therefore, we would need two pairs of curves to characterize a situation: the pairs of incentive curves discussed here (the Schelling diagram) and a pair of policy curves showing (1) the intrinsic value of the policy at issue—as judged by some individual facing a choice about what to do, and (2) the adjusted value, taking account of the cost of providing sufficient incentives to reach a given level of cooperation.

If social motivation plays a role in eliciting cooperation, then these policy curves will be relevant even to choice by a particular individual, since social motivation will surely depend in part on an individual's sense of the social value of his cooperation. The relevant policy curves of course must reflect the social value of cooperation as judged by that individual, which need not co-incide with the judgment of the agent choosing the policy. The two need not even have the same sign, and of course the world offers many examples in which they do not. So choice will be contingent on interactions between the policy curves as judged by individuals and the corresponding individual incentive curves. Those individual choices will have consequences (hence further interactions) for choices about policies and incentives by policymakers. Analysis of these effects obviously goes far beyond what can usefully be attempted here.

12. But if positive incentives alone were operating, the FR curve would remain unchanged from figure 4.1, with all the shift due to the moving up of the C curve. The opposite would hold for the negative incentives case discussed next. Note that although I've drawn the curves showing incentives effective enough to produce a crossover, there may be no such crossover.

13. Significant issues must arise from the distinction between fines and forfeited benefits, mainly connected with the cognitive distinction discussed by Tversky and Kahneman (1981) under the heading of framing effects, especially as those interact with gain/loss asymmetries. But these complications are not essential for the argument here.

14. We can imagine a situation in which the agent uses negative incentives less to elicit compliance than to profit from the penalties incurred. Speed traps are the most familiar example. But the conditions under which they can be maintained are peculiar. Usually, if the agent can turn a profit by levying

fines, he would be able to less offensively collect taxes of the same magnitude.

Ordinarily, fines cannot yield much income when compliance is high, because only a few people are subject to penalties, and not all of them can be caught. But everyone must be subject to surveillance. So the costs of policing are unlikely to be much offset by profits from collecting fines. But the same will usually hold even if compliance is low. For we can expect a moving frontier of effective deterrence. Whatever the equilibrium level of compliance (Q), individuals to the left of Q are deterred (hence not subject to penalties); individuals clearly to the right of Q are those who are not at much risk of being caught in the circumstances in which their violations occur. Such people are neither deterred nor more than rarely apprehended. So it is only in the vicinity of Q that we find people taking a significant risk of apprehended violation, only some of whom lose this gamble.

15. So in a situation where the social agent does not see much chance to get beyond the tipping point, he might choose to rely on positive incentives and settle for the low compliance equilibrium.

16. Meaning here, a pragmatically plausible path. There is no difficulty in suggesting a logically possible path, as illustrated in note 10.

17. Mansbridge 1990 provides a generous sampling of recent approaches.

18. From Rule 2, the social incentive is growing larger as we move to higher compliance. But note that once the society is at high compliance, everyone is choosing *from that situation*, in which an effective deterrent risk can be small (because social motivation is high) compared with that which would have to confront any particular chooser if compliance were low. The inframarginal complier when the level of compliance is at Q does not face the incentive at which he in fact would be the marginal chooser. He chooses from the situation at Q, just as an inframarginal buyer (in the standard market equilibrium diagram) does not pay the premium price he is in fact willing to pay, but only the equilibrium price.

Then, once only a modest risk of penalty is required to deter noncompliance, policing resources need not be spread at all equally across all potential noncompliers. Rather, a light deterrent on most people will be more than enough, and policing resources can be focused on deviant segments of the population.

19. Explaining just how such tacit knowledge works is a tricky task. But that it exists and plays an absolutely essential role in governing belief and behavior is empirically beyond doubt. Any speaker of a language ordinarily can recognize well-formed sentences without being able to articulate rules of grammar. We recognize faces with knowing how we do so. And in what appears to be the same sort of thing, we also have a sense of what looks or feels appropriate or inappropriate in our culture on a vast range of topics, such as how close to stand to a person when talking to him, and so on.

20. Filling out this notion of "reasonable compliance" requires a second spectrum (pure "norms" to pure "rules"), complementing the spectrum of com-

pliance discussed so far. The polar cases would be a purely voluntary *norm*, contrasted with the pure *rule* for which compliance is narrowly a function of the risk of formal punishment. Voting is an example of the former; a 55 mph speed limit on freeways seems to be a good example of the latter. Some behavior is typically governed by (at least legally) voluntary norms, and other behavior—although also normative in character—is strongly backed by police power. Very often, even usually, rules and norms in the particular sense used here interact with each other, with overlapping domains.

References

Elster, J. 1989. "Social Norms and Economic Theory," *Journal of Economic Perspectives*, 3: 99–117.

Frank, R. 1988. *Passions Within Reason*, New York: Norton.

Kuran, T. 1989. "Sparks and Prairie Fires: A Theory of Unanticipated Political Revolution," *Public Choice*, 61: 61–76.

Levi, M. 1988. *Of Rule and Revenue*, Berkeley, CA: University of California Press.

Mansbridge, J., ed., 1990. *Beyond Self-interest*, Chicago: University of Chicago Press.

Margolis, H. 1982, 1984. *Selfishness, Altruism and Rationality*, Cambridge: Cambridge University Press; paper reprint, Chicago: University of Chicago Press.

Margolis, H. 1990. "Equilibrium Norms," *Ethics*, 100: 821–837 (*Symposium on Norms in Moral and Social Theory*).

Margolis, H. 1991. "Incomplete Coercion," in *The Economic Approach to Politics*, K. Monroe, ed., New York: Harper/Collins.

Maynard-Smith, J. 1989. "Origins of Social Behavior," in *Origins*, A. Fabian, ed., Cambridge: Cambridge University Press.

Olson, M. 1965. *The Logic of Collective Action*, Cambridge, MA: Harvard University Press.

Roth, J. A., J. T. Scholz, and A. D. Witte, eds., 1988. *Taxpayer Compliance*, Washington, D.C.: National Academy Press.

Samuelson, P. A. 1954. "Pure Theory of Public Expenditure," *Review of Economics & Statistics*, 36: 386–389.

Schelling, T. C. 1960. *The Strategy of Conflict*, Cambridge, MA: Harvard University Press.

Schelling, T. C. 1978. *Micromotives and Macrobehavior*, New York: Norton.

Tversky, A., and D. Kahneman. 1981. "The Framing of Decisions and the Psychology of Choice," *Science* 211: 453–458.

5   Systems Effects

Robert Jervis

When you pick up one piece of this planet, you find that, one way or another, it's attached to everything else—if you jiggle over here, something is going to wiggle over there. . . . We need this sense of the continuing interconnectedness of the system as part of the common knowledge, so that politicians feel it and believe it, and so that voters feel it and believe it, and so that kids feel it and believe it, so that they will grow up with an ethic. Because what we do—or not do—now will be an inheritance for all time. (Dr. Sylvia Earle, a leading marine biologist and ecologist, quoted in White 1989, p. 56)

[To minimize oil spills] we should . . . mandate double-hulled vessels and compartments in tankers. (Dr. Sylvia Earle, quoted in White 1989, p. 46)

Systems and Interaction Effects

Although they are familiar, the basic ideas of systems and interactions go against the grain of instinctive ways of thinking and so are often ignored.[1] We fail to realize that many outcomes result from complex interactions of forces and behaviors. The world would be easier to understand if its relationships were straightforward, one-way, linear, and additive.

A few definitions are in order before we proceed:

• A straightforward effect is one whose direction accords with common sense. That is, a straightforward effect of giving foreign aid to a country would be to benefit it; providing incentives for a person to behave in a certain way would make her more likely to do so; a policy of deterrence would decrease the probability that the target country would take the proscribed action.

• In a one-way relationship, independent and dependent variables can be clearly distinguished.

• In linear relationships, variable A influences B in direct proportion to the magnitude of A.

• By additive I mean that the combined effect of A and B on C can be estimated by summing the separate impacts of A and B alone. The same method can be used backward to determine the impact of any particular variable on a known outcome. That is, in conformity with the standard scientific method, one can see what role a given variable is playing by comparing situations identical except for the difference in the variable under consideration.

I do not want to suggest that these assumptions and ways of proceeding are always misguided, let alone foolish. But they are not adequate for catching systems effects.

When more than one actor is present, behavior may have consequences that are not linear, additive, and straightforward,[2] hence the existence of *systems effects, interaction effects,* or *perverse effects* (terms that are largely interchangeable as I use them). A force may change the environment in which it operates so that amplifying or counterbalancing forces are called up; the kind as well as the degree of the effect may depend on the magnitude of the stimulus; and the combination of several factors may produce an effect that cannot be deduced from their independent influences. Indeed, the language of independent and dependent variables, actions and responses, and separate factors and forces may be misleading when we are dealing with a system.

Consider the epigraphs at the head of this chapter. It seems obvious that if tankers had double hulls, there would be fewer oil spills. But because of interconnections, the obvious and immediate effect might not be the dominant one. The straightforward argument compares two worlds, one with single-hulled tankers and one with double-hulled ones, holding everything else constant. But while this assumption is analytically simple, and indeed is often necessary, the world is so interconnected that even the most careful study could not predict all the consequences of an action (and the predictions themselves could change some of the effects). Indeed, I would conjecture that no major human endeavor has had all the effects and only the effects that were expected and intended.

What might be the effects of requiring oil tankers to have double hulls? The shipping companies, forced to purchase more expensive tankers, might cut expenditures on other safety measures, perhaps believing such economies were justified by the greater protection supplied by the double hulls. The relative cost of alternative means of transporting oil would decrease, perhaps shifting the incidence of spills from the ocean to the areas traversed by new pipelines. But even tankers' spills might not decrease. Captains, knowing that their ships were safer, might go faster, take more chances, and get into more accidents than they did before. The current trade-off between costs and spills may reflect the preferences of shippers and captains, who might adjust to the new constraints to return to something like the old equilibrium. To take an example from a different context, society might try to compensate for weaknesses in the family by asking schools to provide more support and nurturance for children; this approach would not be effective if parents reacted to the schools' greater efforts to guide their children by reducing their own efforts so that they could use the liberated time and energy for other purposes.

This reasoning may seem farfetched, but it is consistent with the basic insights of economics and systems theories. Studies of automobile safety indicate that laws requiring the use of seat belts and better braking systems did not decrease injuries and deaths. Rather, drivers took advantage of the fact that they were more likely to survive an accident to drive faster or more recklessly. In effect, rather than saving lives, drivers chose to save time spent on the road (Peltzman 1975; Wilde 1982; Perrow 1984, pp. 179–180).

Two Qualifications

Many actions do have straightforward and expected consequences, of course, for not everything in the world is connected to everything else. The way I behave toward my wife has very little impact on the price of cement, and vice versa. Even in the international system, many interconnections are weak enough to be ignored. Furthermore, some cases of apparent systems effects really are instances of actors either reacting to the same objective situation or being driven by internally generated impulses. Thus countries involved in an "arms race" may be responding primarily to domestic pressures rather than to each other.[3]

Furthermore, as Albert Hirschman (1989) has stressed, straightforward effects are common, and unexpected consequences can reinforce rather than undermine the expected ones. Indeed, if unexpected and undesired consequences dominated, it would be hard to see how society or stable human interaction could have developed, let alone how people could have reached their goals. Action often does work: seat belts may not always decrease fatalities, but many safety measures have been effective. Even if it is true—which is highly debatable—that some welfare measures have increased rather than decreased poverty, government food stamps ended most extreme hunger; public health measures have controlled diseases; the federal highways program has vastly increased commerce and travel throughout the United States, albeit at the expense of a number of undesired and at least initially unexpected side effects.

Systems: The Example of Deterrence

Deterrence is built on the fundamental understanding that one side's behavior affects the other and that the latter's responses affects the first side. Nevertheless, many analyses are excessively static: they do not appreciate the alternative possibilities for the other's behavior and assume that the nature of the adversary, its beliefs and its preferences, remain unchanged throughout the encounter. In fact, threats can set off spirals of counterthreats; the state's attempt to increase its security can decrease it; the effort to contain an adversary can create an enemy; the effort to reduce the other side's opportunity to expand can increase the incentives it feels to do so (Herz 1950; Butterfield 1951; Wolfers 1962; Jervis 1976). These processes are well known, although the conditions under which they are likely to occur are less well understood.

Less familiar changes can be at least as disturbing for deterrence. First, deterrent success may make later deterrence more difficult by increasing the challenger's dissatisfaction with the status quo and therefore its desire for change. By blocking the most obvious paths by which the adversary could reach its goal, the state also inadvertently gives the other strong incentives to develop alternative means to reach the desired ends. In the years after the 1967 war, for example, Israel's air superiority kept Egypt from launching attacks across the Suez Canal. But this very fact goaded the Egyptians to discover ways of nullifying this advantage, which they did by developing an effective anti-aircraft system. Second, a challenger can learn and adapt to the tactics that permitted successful deterrence in the past. For example, if the defender prevailed by using the tactic of commitment—that is, staking its reputation on standing firm (Schelling 1960)—the challenger may learn that next time it must act before the defender can become committed. Third, the challenger may change its beliefs about the defender in ways that alter the effect of the latter's policy. For example, it may react to a policy based on the "rationality of irrationality" (Schelling 1960, pp. 16–19) by concluding that the defender is so irrational that a war is inevitable. Or it may come to see the defender as a state that seeks to overturn rather than uphold the status quo.

Systems processes also operate when actors physically clash with each other. When the United States introduced combat forces into Vietnam, its leaders correctly estimated that it would be able to defeat the enemy's large military formations, which were threatening to conquer the country. But they believed that this military victory would defeat the other side. Overlooked was the possibility that the enemy would revert from what Mao had called "stage III" (large-unit warfare) to the preceding phase of insurgency, with which the army was not prepared to cope (Krepinevich 1986, pp. 140–141, 159). A systems approach also questions the standard notion that in the late 1950s the American advisors in South Vietnam erred by worrying about a conventional attack from the North and so trained the South Vietnamese army to meet a fictitious danger (Krepinevich 1986, pp. 19–26). It is at least possible that Diem's enemies turned to guerilla warfare precisely because the South Vietnamese had foreclosed the option of conventional warfare. The American policy was still in error, but it may not have been foolish from the start.

Identification of a System with Its Parts

Common sense suggests that a system must share the characteristics of its parts. If a lawn is to be green, the component blades of grass must be green. But when the units interact rather than accumulate, this may not be true. According to Margaret Thatcher, "You get a responsible society when you get responsible individuals" (quoted in Apple 1979, p. 36). According to Charles Kindleberger, "For the world economy to be stabilized, there has to be a stabilizer" (Kindleberger 1973, p. 305). It is frequently argued that for the balance of power to work, one country must be a balancer, or that restraint in international politics is possible only if the individual nations restrain themselves. But it is a mistake to identify the state of the whole system with that of its parts. A geometrical figure can be symmetrical even though—or because—each of its components is asymmetrical.

As the theory of collective goods makes clear, the fact that all actors desire a certain common goal does not mean that it will be attained. Thus even if everyone wants the system to be stable, no one may have incentives to contribute to that end. To turn Thatcher's quote on its head, even if individuals are responsible, the society might not be. Conversely, the system characteristic could result from the unintended by-products of individual actions taken for other reasons. Thus Thatcher seems to deny the basic argument of the *Wealth of Nations*, although she is a follower of Adam Smith in so many respects. Similarly, while Kindleberger's position is supported by arguments about the illogic of collective action, we cannot dismiss the possibility that stability could arise even if no stabilizer set out to produce this result; the externalities of individual behavior can be positive as well as negative.[4] The balance of power may similarly not require a balancer. Indeed, the mistaken argument (often advanced in international politics texts) that Great Britain stabilized the system by "holding the balance" in the nineteenth century may seem plausible largely because of the tendency to equate the characteristics of systems with those of their parts.

Closely related is the propensity to treat systems as though they could be understood by summing the characteristics of the parts or adding up the bilateral relations between pairs of actors. One student of international politics maintains that "a system of merely growth-seeking actors will obviously be unstable; there would be no provision for balancing or restraint" (Reinken 1968, p. 469). Other scholars have argued that international systems will be moderate when the conflicts of interest between powerful pairs of states are relatively limited (Hoffmann 1965, pp. 88–122; Aron 1966, pp. 99–104, 147–149, 373–403). This commonsense position may be correct for certain historical periods (Schroeder 1986, 1989). But if we are dealing with a system, then immoderation, instability, and conflict can result even if the countries are peaceful and most bilateral relations are relatively good; similarly, stability and perhaps peace can result even if each state is dissatisfied with the status quo and wants to expand.

Indeed, the most careful version of balance-of-power theory argues that stability results, not from the fact that any state desires this outcome, but from the competitive interaction among states' conflicting desires (Waltz, 1979; Claude 1962; Jervis 1982). Each state's attempt to expand can check the expansionist tendencies of others. The other side of this coin is that even if states follow moderate foreign policies and bilateral conflicts are relatively mild, large wars are possible. This is one reading of World War I. The states' goals were generally limited—even Germany did not want to overthrow the system—and the bilateral conflicts were fairly slight. France's desire to regain Alsace-Lorraine was muted to say the least; the Anglo-German trade rivalry was not a strong incentive for armed conflict; even the Russo-Austrian rivalry in the Balkans was much less intense than other conflicts that did not burst into flame. But the concatenation of elements, including other factors such as beliefs about military technology, produced the outcome.

Outcomes Do Not Follow from Intentions—Indirect Effects

The previous paragraphs are linked to the most obvious characteristic of systems: the outcomes may not correspond with the intentions of any of the actors, even the most powerful (Waltz 1979). This point is sufficiently obvious that I bring it up only because people—even those who write about systems dynamics—are prone to ask instinctively of any result of human action: "Who sought that?" Thus a sophisticated reporter analyzed the 1988 elections in these terms: "The electorate covered its bets . . . almost as if they had read their James Madison so carefully that they set off to the polls wearing buttons that read 'Checks and Balances Now!'" (Dionne Jr. 1988). But although many voters split their tickets, none may have wanted divided government. Similarly, in the closing years of World War II many analysts argued that because Stalin needed peace to rebuild his country, he would cultivate good relations with the West. But this commonsense judgment did not take into account the possibility that the way Stalin sought to guarantee peace and his regime's security would greatly increase international conflict. Thus it is not so surprising that the post–World War I system was consciously designed to bring about peace and stability and yet produced war within a generation, whereas the system after World War II was not designed at all, yet endured (Gaddis 1987, pp. 215–216).

Outcomes do not correspond to intentions because effects are often indirect, in two senses of the word. First, outcomes are often produced through a chain of actions and reactions. Second, the result of trying to move directly toward a goal may be movement in the opposite direction. Perhaps best known are examples of diplomatic and military surprise. A state believes that the obstacles to a certain action are so great that the adversary could not undertake it; the state therefore makes no additional efforts to block that action; the adversary therefore works especially hard to see if it can take it. More generally, actors often pursue "he thinks that I think that he thinks" reasoning in an effort to do what the adversary does not expect. One of my graduate school roommates thought he was securing extra protection for his possessions by putting a lock on his bedroom door. In fact I am sure he was increasing his risk: any burglar would assume that the one room with a lock contained what was of most value.

Some indirect effects work through fairly short-run calculations. For example, permitting members of a group to write a minority report could actually increase the chance of eliciting a unified document. The knowledge that a minority report is possible may induce a general spirit of compromise in order to avoid such an open split. The authorities in West Berlin made good use of this kind of dynamic at the beginning of the Berlin blockade. Knowing that much of the water for the city came from the East, West Berliners started to fill their tubs as insurance, thus dangerously depleting the water supply. Rather than urging people to use less water, the authorities assured them that supplies were ample and they could use all they wanted. Demand quickly dropped to manageable levels (Howley 1950, pp. 202–203).

Nonlinear Relationships

More of a good thing is not necessarily a better thing. All physical and social scientists and most of us in our everyday lives know of cases in which the relationship between two variables is curvilinear. Nevertheless, our first impulse is to assume that a linear relationship obtains. Thus statesmen commonly infer that if the adversary is difficult when it is weak, it will be more difficult when it is stronger. Of course, this prediction often is correct. But in other cases the adversary is intransigent because it knows it is weak and believes any concessions will encourage others to push it further. Thus China's leaders apparently believed that others would see the country as weak when it was experiencing domestic unrest and therefore felt it especially important to be unyielding during those periods (Whiting 1975;

Gurtov and Hwang 1980). As such a nation grows stronger, it may become more reasonable. Eventually, however, its greater power will allow it to impose its desires and it will stiffen its bargaining position. Similarly, we might expect a direct and monotonic relationship between the resources an actor controls and his ability to influence others. But often the dynamics of the system defeat this logic: others react adversely to the actor's increase in power and his ability to harm their interests by mobilizing their resources and forming coalitions to contain him (Maoz 1989).

When a policy instrument yields insufficient effects, proponents often call for increased effort. Because a little power, military force, economic aid, antidiscrimination program, or government intervention has made some but insufficient progress against an ill, common sense indicates that more will produce a greater effect. But the use of the instrument may have changed the environment so that continued or increased use will produce perverse effects. In the early 1960s, for example, when the U.S. provision of helicopters to the South Vietnamese army failed to produce continued advantage, attention should have focused on how the Viet Cong had countered the new tactic. Instead, the American military "requested *more* helicopters to conduct similar operations at a higher level of intensity. The new emphasis on air mobile operations also affected the [South Vietnamese army], which became dependent upon helicopters and fire power as a crutch in lieu of sustained patrolling" (Krepinevich 1986, p. 76).

Linear thinking also underlies the common assumption that an ability to cope with the most severe threat or contingency automatically enables us to deal with lesser difficulties. Thus in the 1950s many defense analysts believed the forces that could deter the Russians from starting a nuclear war would also deter limited wars as a lesser included evil—"the dog we have to keep the cat will keep the kittens too" was the saying at the time. But when deterrence of all-out war is mutual, the ability to prevent the worst outcome is not automatically sufficient to cope with lesser threats.

Networks, By-Products, and Complexity

Because system elements are interconnected, a change at one point will have wide-ranging effects. Thus when the European settlers in North America made friends or enemies of a tribe of native inhabitants or gave them modern tools and weapons, they altered relations between that tribe and its neighbors, setting in motion a ripple effect. As one historian has noted,

a tribe whose enemies had the weapons which it lacked had few alternatives, and all of them were unpleasant. It inevitably made war upon the competitor. So quickly did such hostilities arise after the entry of the European, and so fiercely did they continue, that observers were prone to consider war as the usual intertribal relationship, not knowing how they themselves had transformed these relations. . . . [S]o swift was [the transformation], in fact, that it is doubtful whether first-hand [European] observers ever saw intertribal relations exactly as they had been before. (Hunt 1940, p. 19)

Intertribal relations were themselves interrelated through normal alliance dynamics, and so the initial stimulus provided by settlers' good or bad relations with a particular tribe in their immediate vicinity could affect not only the extent of hostilities but also their shape hundreds of miles away.[5]

Ripple effects move through channels established by actors' interests and strategies. Because the strategies are intricate, usually the ramifications are also, and so the results can surprise the actor who initiated the change. Maladroit German diplomacy in the late nineteenth and early twentieth centuries supplies several examples. Dropping the Reinsurance Treaty with Russia in 1890 simplified German diplomacy, as the Kaiser and his advisers had desired. More important, though, was the indirect and delayed consequence—Russia turned to France and signed the Franco-Russian alliance of 1894. This increased Germany's need for Austrian support, thereby making Germany hostage to its weaker and less stable partner. In 1902, the Germans hoped that the Anglo-Japanese Alliance, motivated by Britain's attempt to reduce its isolation and vulnerability to German pressure, would actually have the opposite effect by worsening relations between Britain and Russia (Japan's rival in the Far East) and between Britain and France (which wanted to pressure Britain into making colonial concessions), thereby increasing British dependence on Germany (Rolo 1969, p. 121). There were indeed ramifications, but more to Britain's than to Germany's liking. The British public became less fearful of foreign ties, easing the way for ententes first with France and then with Russia. Furthermore, Japan, assured of Britain's benevolent neutrality, was able to challenge and then fight Russia. This war initially increased Anglo-Russian tensions and then, because Britain thought Germany was egging Russia on when its fleet mistakenly fired on British fishing boats, produced a war scare between Germany and England. The Russian defeat at Japanese hands, coupled with the strengthening of the Anglo-Japanese treaty, effectively ended Russian pressure on Britain in India, making it much easier for these two rivals to cooperate, much against Germany's interests and expectations.

In other cases, the existing network of alliances and interests is strong enough to guide ripple effects in ways that actors should be able to predict, but sometimes fail to. Thus given that "the enemy of my enemy is my friend" and "the friend of my enemy is my enemy," it is not surprising that the American opening to China in 1971 not only distressed the Soviet Union (as it was meant to), but made other adversaries of China, such as India, more hostile to the United States and encouraged them to seek closer ties with the Soviet Union. Even South Korea responded by exchanging secret visits with North Korea (Garthoff 1985, p. 245).

Actors' behavior will be guided by the connections and ramifications they can foresee. Thus American policy in the Indo-Pakistani war of 1971 was based not on the direct issue, but on the expected impact on China. Frequently, a state decides not to intervene in an issue because doing so seems likely to offend a third country whose favors it requires. When Austria argued that the city of Scutari should go to the new Albanian state in 1913, Britain's foreign secretary acknowledged that while this claim had validity in the abstract, Russia would object. "To my mind it is a matter, selfishly speaking, of perfect indifference to us as to who should be the possessor of Scutari, but it is of great importance that we should adopt no line which would in any way weaken or impair our understanding with Russia" (quoted in Crampton 1980, pp. 83–84). In other cases, a state's policies in a local area may be driven by the need to avoid the adversary's trap. Thus in 1915 Secretary of State Lansing wrote in his diary:

Looking at the general situation I have come to the following conclusion: Germany desires to keep up the turmoil in Mexico until the United States is forced to intervene; therefore we must not intervene. Germany does not wish to have any one faction dominant in Mexico; therefore we must recognize one faction as dominant in Mexico.

When we recognize a faction as the government, Germany will undoubtedly seek to cause a quarrel between that government and ours; therefore we must avoid a quarrel regardless of criticism and complaint in Congress and the Press. It comes down to this: our possible relations with Germany must be our first consideration; and all our intercourse with Mexico must be regulated accordingly. (quoted in Katz 1981, p. 302)

But regardless of the form of the dynamics at work, contemporary and later observers will misunderstand the state's policy if they examine it only in local terms. British behavior on India's border issues in the late nineteenth century was largely regulated by policy toward Russia, which was in turn conditioned by general calculations of European politics. Thus when Russia asked Britain to join in putting pressure on Japan to moderate its peace terms in the wake of the Japanese victory over China in 1895, British statesmen were placed in a difficult position. They did not wish to offend Japan, but neither did they wish to sacrifice Russian support. In the event, they compensated for rejecting the Russian request by being conciliatory on Indian issues—a connection that escaped contemporary observers and later historians who examined the border question through the perspective of the seemingly most relevant documents in the India office. As Gordon Martel, to whom I owe this discussion, points out, "Foreign secretaries were not in the habit of explaining their Moroccan policy to the Viceroy of India, nor were they in the habit of showing their Ambassador at Paris how events in the North of India influenced negotiations in Nigeria" (Martel 1980, p. 291).

The propensity to concentrate on bilateral relations is so strong that it can lead us to miss even the relatively manageable complexity produced when three states interact. Thus one scholar has nicely argued that American, British, and Soviet diplomacy in the 1940s has often been misunderstood because we have not appreciated the extent to which one country's policy toward another often had—and sometimes was designed to have—consequences that ramified throughout the triangle (Harbutt 1986).

The effects of one actor's behavior toward another are conditioned by the possible arrangements the other can make with the third party. Winston Churchill understood that such interactions would nullify some of his possible initiatives during the year of Britain's maximum isolation after France fell and before Germany attacked Russia. He saw that one consequence of Britain's successful efforts in the summer of 1940 was not to weaken Germany but to increase the latter's need for French support in what now looked to be a longer struggle. "Owing to our unexpected resistance," Churchill trenchantly remarked, "the Vichy authorities have been able to market their treachery at a slightly higher rate than would otherwise have been possible" (quoted in Colville 1985, p. 283). Similarly, although he wanted to improve relations with Russia, he rejected Foreign Secretary Eden's suggestion that he fly to Moscow: "A mere visit would do no good. They might simply trade it to Germany" (quoted in Harbutt 1986, p. 33). Britain's efforts could then allow others to strike better bargains with Germany, but could do little to actually gain their support.

Coalition formation with as few as three parties may have no determinant solution. Indeed, the problem is not only one of choice and volition: many physical systems with three elements can be modeled only probabilistically. "A system as simple as the sun, the earth, and an asteroid . . . can become chaotic. Although all three bodies act according to Newton's laws of motion, the complex influences of the two larger bodies can make the movement of the asteroid so irregular that its future positions can only be described in terms of probabilities" (Pool 1989, p. 26). As the number of actors increases, the paths of interaction in the natural systems multiply and become extremely intricate. For example, differences in the patterns of eating, aggression, and behavior toward the young in two closely related species of monkeys have been traced to whether the female or the male took the initiative in mating. Through a complex chain of causation, this one difference had far-reaching effects on many other aspects of the species' social structures (Janson 1986). Changes over time also display complex ramifications. It took a close observer seven years to figure out that the sudden shift from a territorial to a nonterritorial mating system among pronghorn antelope in a Montana national park was caused by a change in the age structure of the males stemming from a harsh winter three years before the study began. Furthermore, when the age structure returned to normal, the territorial system was not reestablished because it could not develop incrementally. Even a large male can defend his territory and harem only if many of the other males are tied down to their areas and females. As long as a great many males are free to be intruders, no territory can be defended (Byers 1989).

Implications for Testing and Method

When dealing with systems, static comparisons are not likely to be appropriate. This central implication of economics is sometimes neglected. Thus analysts often conclude that because the United States relies heavily on imports for vital raw materials, it is at the mercy of foreign suppliers. Neglected is the fact that cutting off the primary sources would prompt many other changes as the system adapted to the shock. Generally speaking, the price would increase sharply, leading to conservation, the search for substitutes, and the development of new sources of supply that previously were too expensive to be worth pursuing. Of course these processes do not solve all problems. But one cannot make sense of what will happen without recognizing the interconnections that exist or will be called into being.

Even those who stress the importance of systems dynamics may make this error. Thus economists have been among those who have carried out the misleading studies of American vulnerability, and Kenneth Waltz, the leading analyst of international systems, has argued that the difference between American and European policies toward the Middle East can be explained by the fact that the Europeans are much more dependent on oil from the Persian Gulf (Waltz 1979, pp. 152–158). But the market for oil is an integrated one; in the event of shortages the Europeans would seek oil from countries that now supply the United States, even including, if the market were not subject to political controls, American oil fields. Similarly, during World War I thinking in static terms led the British navy to conclude that convoys would not defeat the German submarine menace. Such tactics were seen as merely defensive, promising temporary relief at best. Only tracking down the German U-boats could put an end to the threat. In fact, convoying merchant ships forced the U-boats either to abandon their attacks or to come to a place where they could be destroyed by the naval escorts.[6]

When elements are interconnected, we cannot confidently probe the system by altering them one at a time. It seems obvious that one could try several tactics in different areas and then adopt the one that works best on a wider scale. But the tactic's success could be attributable to the entire ensemble that had been employed; the ones that had apparently failed might have contributed to the successes. In Vietnam the critics argued that resources should be shifted from the large search-and-destroy operations, which had yielded few results, to the pacification program, which had cleared the enemy from the areas to which it had been applied. But the army's reply may have been valid: pacification worked only because the large conventional offenses engaged and contained the enemy's most effective forces, which would destroy the pacification efforts if American policy changed.

Even in a system of just two actors, processes such as these can escape the notice of those who are not sensitive to them. Thus in the fall of 1940, Winston Churchill believed that the threat of invasion of the British Isles had declined to a low level, but he resisted the suggestion that England should therefore send more troops to other fronts. It was the very presence of these troops that had reduced the threat of invasion, he insisted (Colville 1985, p. 283). Similarly, the effects of changes in one state's policies are often predicated on the assumption that nothing else will change. Thus it is often asserted that an increase in arms will make the state more secure (ignoring adversaries' likely responses), or that if a state increases its contribution to a common venture, the result will be a greater combined effort (overlooking the possibility that the partner will respond by slacking off).

When actors take steps to influence others, they often forget that the change in their behavior will itself be noted and interpreted, perhaps with unintended consequences. A husband may believe that he can please his wife by listening more patiently to her complaints and being more solicitous. But she may find this new behavior suspicious, if not alarming, and react accordingly. To take an international example, when one state moves to commit itself to standing firm in a dispute with another, the latter may *lower* its estimate of the probability that the state will stand firm, rather than increase it as standard bargaining theory argues (Schelling 1960). It may reason that if the state really had sufficient incentives to pay a high price in order to prevail, it would not have needed to resort to the tactic of commitment. Similarly, if a state increases its defense spending, the adversary may infer that the state feels militarily unprepared—and so probably will not fight. It is true that, all things being equal, increasing defense spending or becoming committed to standing firm will increase the chance that the other side will back down. But it can never be the case that "all things are equal" because a very important element is the other side's beliefs, which will be modified by the state's actions.

Our standard techniques for testing the validity of propositions assume independences that are not present in a system. We can see this by looking at commitment from a different perspective. Deterrence theory indicates that in situations resembling the game of "chicken" (in which each side wants to stand firm, but the worst outcome for each arises if both do so and collide), an actor can increase his chance of prevailing by staking his reputation on maintaining his position before the other has actively challenged it (thus the problem of the other side's inferences discussed in the previous paragraph does not arise as strongly) (Schelling 1960). This proposition might be tested by comparing the outcomes of two sets of crises, one in which an actor had committed himself and another in which he had not, and seeing whether the actor prevailed in a higher percentage of the former cases. But this method in fact would be inappropriate. Given a commitment, a challenge will not be issued unless the challenger either does not understand the situation or is extremely strongly motivated to prevail. In either case, the challenger will be difficult to dissuade. Thus commitment might decrease the number of challenges that occur, but not increase the chance of prevailing when a challenge does result because those cases will be a special subset of the crises that would have occurred in the absence of commitments.[7] In other words, the characteristics that lead to a crisis are not independent of the actors' use of the tactic of commitment.

Even if actors are not trying to outwit each other, their interactions can cause changes over time that defeat the methodological assumption that the comparison involves looking at two cases that are the same on all dimensions except one. Many colleges use the yield rate as a measure of their quality: if only 40 percent of the people we accepted actually enroll in our program this year, we must be doing worse than we were five years ago, when 60 percent enrolled. This inference seems especially compelling if the yield rate in competitors' programs did not drop. But perhaps the college's reputation has improved, so that better applicants now apply; because many of these attractive candidates also are admitted to other institutions, the yield may fall. This explanation could hold even if the total number of applicants did not increase, since weaker ones might no longer apply.

More drastic changes can undermine the utility of yardsticks of success that were initially valid. This is especially likely to be the case when two sides each try to defeat the other's tactics. As each alters its behavior in response to the other, many of the standard indicators of success will be drained of meaning. For example, in the early 1960s the United States and South Vietnam established the strategic hamlet program in order to provide security for the rural population. They then used the percentage of the hamlets that were overrun by the Viet Cong as a measure of the program's success and the strength of the adversary. But because many of the initial hamlets were able to withstand direct assault, the Viet Cong were forced to change their tactics and rely more on infiltration, inducements, and intimidation. As a result, while the percentage of hamlets conquered or even attacked decreased, this measure no longer was a good indicator of the program's success (Krepinevich 1986, pp. 87–88). Similarly, Israel's use of air power in the middle of the war of attrition with Egypt in 1969 produced success as measured by a reduction in Egyptian artillery fire, but this impression is misleading because the Egyptians reacted by shifting to small-arms fire (Shimshoni 1988, pp. 154–155).

Simpler dynamics of this type are also possible: if an actor lets it be known that he is drawing inferences from certain aspects of the other's behavior, those inferences may not be valid in the future. For example, when the Soviets asserted that nuclear superiority was possible, many American defense analysts argued that such statements showed that the USSR was aggressive; soon afterward such statements diminished. The Soviets' outlook may have changed; alternately, once they saw the effect of their statements, they may have manipulated this source of information to create a more desired image.[8]

Games against Nature Are Not "Games against Nature"

Many of the errors we have discussed can be summarized in the claim that people often think that they are playing games against nature when in fact they are dealing with actors who will respond to them. But even nature reacts—or, more precisely, the elements in nature compose a system—although natural forces do not scheme to defeat human efforts. While William McNeill may go too far when he talks of "the tendency towards the conservation of catastrophe," he is certainly correct to point out that many attempts to "tame" natural forces have unleashed more or different kinds of disasters (McNeill 1989).

In my lifetime the Army Corps of Engineers began to control Mississippi floods by building an elaborate system of levees along the river's lower course. This had the undesired effect of concentrating sediment on the river bottom between the levees. As a result, the water level now rises each year, and the levees have to be raised higher from time to time. Under this regimen, sooner or later the mighty Mississippi will break its banks and inflict far greater damage on the surrounding landscape than if there were no levees and the river were free to overflow each spring and deposit sediment across the breadth of its natural floodplain, as it did in my childhood. (McNeill 1989, pp. 1–2)

Attempts to control beach erosion provide several examples of
perverse effects. To preserve the sand on his own beach, a property
owner sometimes erects groins that trap sand moving laterally along
the beach. But stopping the flow of sand creates severe erosion
on the other side of the groin, forcing the neighbor to build his own
groin if his area is not to be completely stripped. And so it goes all the
way down the beach. Realizing the dangers of this individualistic
approach, other communities have tried dealing with the problem
frontally—that is, by constructing barriers to weaken the power of
the waves and stabilize the beach. These rarely work: the beach is
indeed prevented from migrating inland as it would have without
intervention, but slow erosion is replaced by periods of temporary
stability broken by catastrophic failures when the waves, no longer
able to dissipate their energy on a beach shaped by natural forces,
break through the barriers (Dolan 1972; Raufman and Pilkey 1983).

Most people's ideas of evolution assume one-way causation. That
is, species compete with one another within the environment, thus
driving evolution by natural selection. In fact, however, there is co-
evolution: plants and animals not only adapt to the environment,
they change it. As a result, it becomes more hospitable to some life
forms and less hospitable to others.[9] Indeed, the very atmosphere
that supports current life was produced by earlier forms of life, some
which could not survive in the new environment. On a smaller scale
as well, most living things alter their environments, rendering them
more suitable for some, less suitable for others, and open to coloniza-
tion by new species. To simplify one example, elephants thrive on
acacia trees. But the latter can develop only in the absence of the
former. After a while, the elephants destroy the trees, drastically
altering the mix of other animals that can live in the area, and even
affecting the physical shape of the land (Lewin 1986). In the process,
they render the area uncongenial to themselves, and they either
move on or die. The land is adapting to the elephants just as they are
to it. The dynamics of a complex system cannot be captured by arbitrarily labeling one set of elements "causes" and others "effects."

Acting in a System

It is not possible to control (or even understand) a system by behaving as though straightforward, one-way, linear processes dominated.
But can knowledge of systems dynamics be used to produce

desired outcomes?[10] This may be possible when others can be out-guessed or are heavily constrained. In some cases, one may be able to reach a desired goal by taking a path that leads directly in the opposite direction. For years, the United States tried to convince its allies to increase their defense spending by increasing its own. It is possible that more favorable results would have been secured had the United States done the opposite and decreased its spending. But such an outcome was not guaranteed, especially if the allies believed they were being manipulated. It is at least possible that if Britain granted citizenship to residents of Hong Kong, a stable and beneficial arrangement might be worked out when China takes control of the colony in 1997. To gain a viable Hong Kong, China would have to come to terms with its citizens, who would have the option of departing. But the residents of Hong Kong might demand too much, either because they miscalculated or because emigration to Britain looked better than any offer China was willing to make. In many of the cases we have noted, decision makers were aware of systems dynamics and tried to manipulate them, yet still ended up with perverse effects due to their limited understanding of the situation or their miscalculations about what others could do.

One interesting possibility is that a state might be better able to protect another by *not* committing to its defense. Although commitment can produce a deterrence, three other effects should not be overlooked. First, it can increase the client's freedom of action, leading it to behave in ways the protector does not want. Second, commitment may reduce the incentives of third parties to promise assistance to the client. Third, commitment may provoke the adversary either by threatening it or by inflating what it will gain if it prevails (because victory would now damage the protector state's reputation). There might have been greater regional opposition to the Soviet invasion of Afghanistan if the United States had not quickly supplied Pakistan with support and arms. Marc Trachtenberg argues that reducing the American commitment to West Germany during the Berlin crisis of 1958–62 might have ameliorated the conflict by moderating Adenauer's behavior and decreasing Soviet fears that German interests might dictate American policy (Trachtenberg, forthcoming). Similarly, Liddell Hart argues that *not* providing a guarantee to Poland in 1939 would have been the best way to prevent World War II, or at least to improve Britain's ability to fight it.

If we had not given that delusory guarantee, Poland would have been forced to accept Russia's help, as the only chance of withstanding German pressure. And Russia would have been forced to give Poland such support, because of her then existing value as a buffer state, and as an auxiliary army. Under these circumstances, it would have been much less likely that Germany would have attacked Poland. (Liddell Hart 1954, p. 39)

This may be too clever by half, however. Stalin may have signed the Nazi-Soviet Pact primarily because he feared the Western powers were maneuvering him into fighting Germany alone, a fear that Britain had reason to believe could have been assuaged only by an unequivocal commitment to Poland.

Being aware of systems dynamics is likely to reduce the incidence of perverse effects somewhat; trying to judge how others will seek to increase their security in reaction to the state's effort to do so will often benefit both sides. In many cases the successful use of systems effects by one actor must mean disadvantage to another. In other instances, however, people can improve their ability to deal with the web of forces within which they must act, and produce not only greater efficiency but mutual or even general advantage.

Notes

1. Studies from cognitive psychology have shown that people much more readily detect additive, linear patterns than interactive ones. See Bruner, Goodnow, and Austin 1956.

2. One obvious question, to which I return later, is what happens when actors are aware of the prevalence of perverse effects. Under what circumstances can they act to avoid them and produce the result they wanted in the first place? Indeed, the whole notion of what is a straightforward effect and what is a perverse one depends on the actors' expectations and knowledge.

3. It is extremely difficult to determine when one element is affecting others and when all of them are responding to the same kind of stimulus. Did Berkeley's free-speech movement lead to student unrest around the country, or were students reacting to similar conditions in different locations?

4. For an argument that this was the case for the operation of the gold standard in the nineteenth century, see Gallarotti (forthcoming).

5. For a discussion of European alliance configurations in these terms, see Jervis 1979, "Systems Theories and Diplomatic History."

6. This was not the most egregious of the navy's miscalculations, most of which were rooted in the desire to preserve its traditional ways of doing things.

7. To use Morgan's terms, commitment may then positively correlate with the success of general deterrence and negatively correlate with the success of immediate deterrence. See Morgan 1977.

8. For further discussion of the manipulation of signals and indices, although in a different framework, see Jervis 1989.

9. Insightful if sometimes polemical is Levins and Lewontin 1985.

10. See Waltz 1979, pp. 197–199; also see the ingenious discussion in Watzlwick, Weakland, and Fisch 1974. A great deal of recent game theory has explored nonmyopic equilibria, but the restrictive conditions may limit the applicability of the conclusions.

References

Aron, Raymond. 1966. *Peace and War*, Garden City, NY: Doubleday.

Apple, R. W., Jr. 1979. "Margaret Thatcher: A Choice, Not an Echo," *New York Times Magazine*, April 29.

Bruner, Jerome, Jacqueline Goodnow, and George Austin. 1956. *A Study of Thinking*, New York: Wiley.

Butterfield, Herbert. 1951. *History and Human Relations*, London: Collins.

Byers, John. 1989. "Pronghorns in—and out of—a Rut," *Natural History*, April: 39–48.

Claude, Inis. 1962. *Power and International Relations*, New York: Random House.

Colville, John. 1985. *The Fringes of Power: 10 Downing Street Diaries, 1939–1955*, New York: Norton.

Crampton, R. J. 1980. *The Hollow Detente: Anglo-German Relations in the Balkans, 1911–1914*, London: George Prior.

Dionne, E. J., Jr. 1988. "Coming Up," *New York Times*, November 13.

Dolan, Robert. 1972. "Barrier Dune System along the Outer Banks of California," *Science*, vol. 176, April 21: 286–288.

Gaddis, John. 1987. *The Long Peace*, New York: Oxford University Press.

Gallarotti, Giulie. Forthcoming. *The Anatomy of Spontaneous Order*, New York: Columbia University Press.

Garthoff, Raymond. 1985. *Detente and Confrontation*, Washington, DC: Brookings Institution.

Gurtov, Melvin, and Byong-Moo Hwang. 1980. *China Under Threat*, Baltimore: Johns Hopkins University Press.

Harbutt, Fraser. 1986. *The Iron Curtain: Churchill, America, and the Origins of the Cold War*, New York: Oxford University Press.

Herz, John. 1950. "Idealist Internationalism and the Security Dilemma," *World Politics*, vol. 2, January: 157–180.

Hirschman, Albert. 1989. "Reactionary Rhetoric," *Atlantic*, May: 63–70.

Hoffmann, Stanley. 1965. *The State of War*, New York: Praeger.

Howley, Frank. 1950. *Berlin Command*, New York: Putnam's.

Hunt, George. 1940. *The Wars of the Iroquois*, Madison, WI: University of Wisconsin Press.

Janson, Charles. 1986. "Capuchin Counterpoint," *Natural History*, February: 45–52.

Jervis, Robert. 1976. *Perception and Misperception in International Politics*, Princeton, NJ: Princeton University Press.

Jervis, Robert. 1979. "Systems Theories and Diplomatic History," in *Diplomacy*, Paul Lauren, ed., New York: Free Press.

Jervis, Robert. 1982. "Security Regimes," *International Organization*, vol. 36, April: 357–378.

Jervis, Robert. 1989. *The Logic of Images in International Relations*, New York: Columbia University Press.

Kaplan, Morton. 1989. "A Poor Boy's Journey," in *Journeys Through World Politics*, Joseph Kruzel, and James Rosenau, eds., Lexington, MA: Lexington Books.

Katz, Friedrich. 1981. *The Secret War in Mexico: Europe, the United States and the Mexican Revolution*, Chicago: University of Chicago Press.

Kaufman, Wallace, and Orrin Pilkey, Jr. 1983. *The Beaches Are Moving*, Durham, NC: Duke University Press.

Kindleberger, Charles. 1973. *The World in Depression*, Berkeley, CA: University of California Press.

Kindleberger, Charles. 1986. "Hierarchy versus Inertial Cooperation," *International Organization*, vol. 40, Autumn: 841–847.

Krepinevich, Andrew, Jr. 1986. *The Army and Vietnam*, Baltimore: Johns Hopkins University Press.

Levins, Richard, and Richard Lewontin. 1985. *The Dialectical Biologist*, Cambridge, MA: Harvard University Press.

Lewin, Roger. 1986. "In Ecology, Change Brings Stability," *Science*, vol. 234, November 28: 1071–1073.

Liddell Hart, Basil. 1954. *Why Don't We Learn From History?* London: Allen & Unwin.

Maoz, Zeev. 1989. "Power, Capabilities, and Paradoxical Conflict Outcomes," *World Politics*, vol. 41, January: 239–266.

Martel, Gordon. 1980. "Documenting the Great Game: 'World Policy' and the 'Turbulent Frontier' in the 1890's," *International History Review*, vol. 2, April: 288–320.

McNeill, William. 1989. "Control and Catastrophe in Human Affairs," *Daedalus*, Winter: 1–12.

Morgan, Patrick. 1977. *Deterrence: A Conceptual Analysis*, Beverly Hills, CA: Sage.

Peltzman, Sam. 1975. "The Effects of Automobile Safety Regulation," *Journal of Political Economy*, vol. 83, August: 677–725.

Perrow, Charles. 1984. *Normal Accidents*, New York: Basic Books.

Pool, Robert. 1989. "Chaos Theory: How Big an Advance?" *Science*, vol. 245, July 9: 26–27.

Reinken, Donald. 1968. "Computer Explorations of the 'Balance of Power'," in *New Approaches to International Relations*, Morton Kaplan, ed., New York: St. Martin's Press.

Rolo, P. J. V. 1969. *Entente Cordiale*, New York: St. Martin's Press.

Schelling, Thomas C. 1960. *Strategy of Conflict*, Cambridge, MA: Harvard University Press.

Schroeder, Paul. 1986. "The Nineteenth-Century International System: Changes in the Structure," *World Politics*, vol. 39, October: 1–26.

Schroeder, Paul. 1989. "The Nineteenth Century System: Balance of Power or Political Equilibrium?" *Review of International Studies*, vol. 15, April: 135–154.

Shimshoni, Jonathan. 1988. *Israel and Conventional Deterrence: Border Warfare from 1953 to 1970*, Ithaca, NY: Cornell University Press.

Trachtenberg, Marc. Forthcoming. "The Berlin Crisis," in Trachtenberg, *History and Strategy*, Princeton, NJ: Princeton University Press.

Wallace, White. 1989. "Profiles (Sylvia Earle)," *New Yorker*, July 3.

Waltz, Kenneth. 1979. *Theory of International Politics*, Reading, MA: Addison-Wesley.

Watzlwick, Paul, John Weakland, and Richard Fisch. 1974. *Change*, New York: Norton.

Whiting, Allen. 1975. *The Chinese Calculus of Deterrence*, Ann Arbor, MI: University of Michigan Press.

Wilde, Gerald S. J. 1982. "The Theory of Risk Homeostasis: Implications for Safety and Health," *Risk Analysis*, vol. 2, December: 209–225.

Wolfers, Arnold. 1962. *Discord and Collaboration*, Baltimore: Johns Hopkins University Press.

6 Autocracy, Democracy, and Prosperity

Mancur Olson

I

What incentives explain the emergence of government? How do the incentives facing the leaders of dictatorial and democratic governments differ? Do the democratic nations of the world have higher per capita incomes, on average, than the nondemocratic countries because of—or in spite of—their democratic governments? In this chapter I shall develop an argument that answers these three questions. The main foundation on which my argument rests is an insight in Thomas Schelling's *Arms and Influence*. It was also because of Schelling that I became aware of Edward Banfield, and it was a quotation in a book by Banfield that happened to start me thinking, quite some time ago, about the questions this chapter addresses.

In *The Moral Basis of a Backward Society*, Banfield reported the results of interviews with the residents of a poor and remote village in southern Italy. One of the interviews was with a man who believed in monarchism—not in a figurehead monarch of the British or Scandinavian type, but absolute monarchy. The village monarchist suggested that "A monarchy is the best kind of government because the King is then owner of the country. Like the owner of a house, when the wiring is wrong, he fixes it."[1]

When I read this quotation in my graduate student days, I had never before come upon such an argument, and the idea jarred my democratic convictions. There was undoubtedly some truth in the monarchist's argument: the owner of a country would indeed have an incentive to make his property as productive and valuable as possible. The monarch's subjects would presumably also gain something from this. Yet I believed that democracy was probably the highest form of government and that absolute monarchy was a totally outdated idea. Thus it was natural to ask, "Can our belief that democracy is a much better form of government than absolute monarchy be reconciled with the obvious germ of truth in the village monarchist's argument?" Some may think this question is silly or trivial, but it bothered or intrigued me so much that I have been thinking about it, off and on, over most of my career. When, more recently, I came upon an answer to this question, it seemed worth developing into a systematic analysis or model of anarchy, autocracy, and democracy.

II

To develop an intellectual framework that does justice to the village monarchist's argument and to the visceral belief in democracy that most of us have, we need to go back to basic questions about why governments are needed and how they came to exist. Because governments are the main custodians of the power to employ violence in modern societies, we have to go back to the even more elemental question of why violence plays such a depressingly large role in human affairs.

This primeval question was best answered by Thomas Schelling:

One of the lamentable principles of human productivity is that it is easier to destroy than to create. A house that takes several man-years to build can be destroyed in an hour by any young delinquent who has the price of a box of matches. Poisoning dogs is cheaper than raising them. And a country can destroy more with twenty billion dollars of nuclear armament than it can create with twenty billion dollars of foreign investment . . .

The power to hurt—to destroy things that somebody treasures, to inflict pain and grief—is a kind of bargaining power, not easy to use but used often. In the underworld it is the basis for blackmail, extortion, and kidnapping, in the commercial world for boycotts, strikes, and lockouts . . . it underlies the humane as well as the corporal punishments that society uses to deter crime and delinquency. . . . It is often the basis for discipline, civilian and military; and gods use it to exact obedience.[2]

Thus there are often incentives to threaten the use of—and sometimes to employ—violence: violence, for the individual person or country, is sometimes rational. If violence were never rational, there would not be so much of it. Because violence normally brings great costs to those on whom it is inflicted and also some risks and other costs to those who use it, but nonetheless produces nothing of value, the use of violence is virtually always inconsistent with social rationality: it is only in the bizarre case of consensual violence between a sadist and a masochist that violence could conceivably be rational from the point of view of society or the human race as a whole.

It is mainly because of the incentive individuals sometimes have to commit violence that anarchy is so terrible. Throughout history, people have fled from anarchic areas and moved even to areas with very bad governments; there have also been many cases of individuals opting for slavery to get protection from anarchy. Hobbes seems to have been right in saying that the life of man in anarchy is "solitary, poor, nasty, brutish, and short." The history books do not recount a single case of successful anarchy.

Since life in anarchy is appallingly inefficient, there are gains from making and carrying out an agreement to maintain peace and order. Indeed, these gains are so colossal that there is a vast variety of ways in which the gains from a peaceful order can be shared that will leave everyone in a society better off than under anarchy. Can we then conclude that, because everyone can gain from it, peaceful order emerges by voluntary agreement?

III

In very small groups whose members have reason to interact over an indefinitely long period, a generally peaceful order should indeed emerge by voluntary agreement. If there are, say, five similar people, each of them will tend to get about a fifth of the gains from the creation of a peaceful order. Though each individual will bear the full costs or risks of what he does to help establish such an order, the advantages of a peaceful order over anarchy are so large that one-fifth of the gains from a peaceful order could easily exceed the total sacrifice needed to establish such an order. Moreover, when there are only a few people in a group, it will be clear that the welfare of each person depends conspicuously on whether each other individual acts in a group-oriented or in an antisocial way. Thus each person, by making clear that cooperation by others will bring forth cooperation from him but that noncooperation will not, can increase the likelihood that others match his behavior. This not only increases the probability of peaceful interaction, but even makes it easily possible that cooperation will reach an ideal or group-optimal extent.[3]

When the gain from peaceful interaction is just a one-time thing or is definitely coming to an end at a given date, there can be an incentive to cheat on agreements to cooperate; someone who steals the fruits of peaceful cooperation as the interaction ends may be better off than if he honored his agreement. Though this possibility does sometimes cause problems, human interaction normally provides benefits indefinitely. In addition to the gains from a continued peaceful order, there are normally also gains from trade and from producing goods in cooperation with others, not only in modern societies but also in the most primitive societies (in the hunting of big game, for example). There are also gains to virtually everyone from sociable companionship (in many societies, solitary confinement is the harshest legal punishment short of death). Because the gains from social cooperation go on through one's entire life, and the date of one's death is normally unknown, there is often no last period in which it pays to renege on an otherwise advantageous agreement to cooperate. In some conditions, an individual may betray one small group yet later enjoy the gains of social participation in another group, but in other conditions (such as sparsely settled primitive societies) this is not possible. Therefore, when the numbers of those involved are small and stable enough for a peaceful order to be established by voluntary cooperation, we know (by the so-called folk theorem of game theory) that this cooperation can be sustained over time. Thus the logic of rational individual behavior leads to the prediction that sufficiently small groups will be able to establish and maintain peaceful order by voluntary agreement.

This theoretical prediction fits the evidence very well. We have not only the general evidence that voluntary cooperation of small groups to achieve common purposes is commonplace,[4] but also the anthropological observation of the most primitive societies. The most primitive food-gathering and hunting societies are normally made up of bands of only about 50, and almost never more than 100, people, including children. In other words, such a band will usually have only a few families that need to cooperate. As the theory predicts, such hunter-gatherer bands tend to maintain peace and order by voluntary agreement. Many readers may assume that primitive tribes are at least as dictatorial and repressive as the monarchies of early modern Europe, but this is not so. Many such hunter-gatherer bands are acephalous and make all important collective decisions by consensus. Those that have chiefs are also fundamentally consensual. When a band gets larger and disagreement is intense, the band may split in two, but the new bands normally also make decisions by consensus. Thus it is voluntary agreement that normally explains the relatively peaceful order in the most primitive and smallest bands. For these small groups, the huge gains from peaceful order rather than anarchy motivate voluntary agreements to maintain the order of the band.

Many less primitive and larger societies are made up of small groups such as extended families, villages, and other communities small enough to maintain order through voluntary consent. Some are even federations of such small groups. Some of the peaceful order in these societies is also explained by the gains of voluntary agreement to keep the peace. It is obvious, however, that only a part of the order in large societies with many thousands or millions of people can be explained in this way. What mainly explains the law and order that normally characterizes larger societies?

IV

The fact that law and order is incomparably better for people than anarchy clearly does *not* explain the emergence of law and order in large societies. A typical individual in a society with a million people will get only about one-millionth of the gain from establishing law and order, but will bear the whole cost and risk of whatever he does to establish it. The typical individual in a population of a million will normally have no significant impact on the likelihood that any other individual will enjoy law and order, so there is also no strategic interaction; it pays an individual to make no voluntary contribution to providing the collective good of law and order, whether others contribute or not. The rewards and punishments of social interaction also do not motivate contributions to collective action when groups are too large for most individuals to interact socially with most of the others. So logic tells us that the collective good of law and order, like other collective goods, can never be obtained through voluntary collective action in really large groups.[5]

This theoretical prediction fits the facts. There have been lots of writings about the desirability of "social contracts" to obtain the benefits of law and order, but no one has ever found a large society that obtained law and order through a voluntary social contract of the individuals in the society. There is no record of any large society that overcame an anarchic situation through any kind of voluntary agreement.

V

Why, then, do virtually all large societies no less than small ones have law and order rather than anarchy? The route to the answer came to me when by chance I was reading a book on a Chinese warlord. In the 1920s China was in large part under the control of various warlords. The warlords were men who had some armed band or small army with which they had conquered some province or set of villages and who then made themselves lords of the territory they had conquered. They usually taxed the population heavily and pocketed the proceeds of this taxation for their own purposes. One warlord, Feng Yu-hsiang, had a reputation for the exceptional extent to which he used his army for suppressing bandits and for his defeat of the relatively substantial army of the famous bandit leader White Wolf. There was evidence that considerable numbers of peasants, merchants, and intellectuals in his domain were sorry to lose him.

This seemed arbitrary to me: why should warlords who were simply stationary bandits be preferred to roving bandits? The warlords had no claim of any kind to legitimacy and were distinguished from leaders of roving bandit armies only because they took their theft in the form of regular taxation rather than episodic plunder. Others have also asked whether " 'warlord' was not simply a euphemism for 'bandit'."[6]

I am now convinced that I was wrong and that the Chinese who preferred settled bandits to roving ones were right. If a roving bandit settles down and decides to steal through regular taxation, and at the same time insists that he has a monopoly on theft in his domain, then those from whom he exacts taxes will, in spite of his exactions, have an incentive to produce and accumulate wealth. The rational stationary bandit will take only a part of income in taxes, because he will be able to exact a larger total amount of income from his subjects if he leaves them with an incentive to have a high level of production.

If the stationary bandit successfully monopolizes the theft in his domain, his victims do not need to worry about theft by others. If he steals only through regular taxation, his subjects know that they can keep whatever proportion of their output is left after they have paid their taxes. Thus the rational monopolization of theft, as compared with an anarchic environment with ubiquitous theft, greatly increases the probability that an individual will be able to retain any capital he accumulates. Once an individual has paid the stipulated tax rates, he has reasonably good odds of hanging on to whatever wealth he has accumulated.[7] This greatly increases the incentive to save and to invest. Since all of the settled bandit's victims are for him a source of tax income, he also has an incentive to prohibit others from killing or maiming his subjects. The monopolization of theft and the protection of tax-generating subjects eliminates anarchy. Since the warlord takes a significant part of total production in the form of tax theft, it will often also pay him to provide some irrigation works and other public goods, because the provision of these goods will normally increase taxable income.

Bandit rationality will also lead bandits who can conquer and hold an area for any considerable period of time to stop roving around and set themselves up as lords of a settled domain: with roving banditry there is little or no incentive for anyone to produce or accumulate anything that may be stolen, and thus little for roving bandits to steal. Thus we have what I call "the first blessing of the invisible hand." The leader of the roving band of bandits is led, as though by an invisible hand, to settle down and set himself up as head of a government; the colossal increase in output that arises from the creation of a peaceful order gives a stationary governing bandit a larger take than he could obtain if no government is provided. The provision of the public goods provided by government to groups that are larger than tribes results from "bandit entrepreneurship" or, more generally, the entrepreneurship of those with superior capacities to wreak violence. By taking Thomas Schelling's analysis of the incentives that account for violence a few steps further, we have accounted for the emergence of government in large as well as small groups.

The emergence of the kings, pharaohs, and emperors who have played such a large role in human history can be better explained in terms of the incentives to replace roving banditry with tax theft than by any other model of similar parsimony. Dictatorial peace also

allows the development of some civilization. To a degree, the civilization that emerged, say, in France of the Old Regime—a civilization
that produced a Voltaire—was due to the superior incentive to produce and create under rational tax theft than under anarchic types of
theft. The peace of a rational self-interested dictator is better than
anarchy.

VI

The main tool of thought that drives my analysis of autocracy, and
that will also drive my account of democracies, is the concept of
the "encompassing interest" from my book *The Rise and Decline of
Nations*.[8] This is the idea that the extent of the concern of an interest
group, office holder, political party, monarch, or any other partial or
total "owner" of the society will vary with the size of the stake in the
society. Other things being equal, the larger or more encompassing
the stake an organization or individual has in a society, the greater
the incentive the organization or individual has to take action to increase the productivity or efficiency of that society, and the greater
the incentive to avoid actions that would damage the society.

   In the case of our stationary bandit or king, we can see the extent of
his encompassing interest most simply by temporarily assuming that
the marginal tax rate is the same as the average tax rate, so that the
autocrat always gets a constant fraction, F, of any increase in the
national income in tax revenues. If F is one-third, the monarch gets a
third of any increase in the national income in tax collections, and he
will then get a third of the benefit of the provision of a public good
that increases taxable income. Obviously, in this case an optimizing
monarch will provide public goods up to the point at which the marginal cost of the public good to the monarch is equal to one-third of
the increase in the national income that results from this provision.
Under the assumption that the monarch gets a specified percentage
of the national income in taxes, he will not spend a socially efficient
amount on public goods, but the benefits of law and order and of
minimal amounts of some other public goods are so extraordinary
that a less-than-Pareto-optimal supply is still of profound value. The
consumer surplus from a minimal level of government is so gigantic
that the provision of these minimal amounts can be of great significance in human history.[9]

VII

All that has been said so far shows the importance of the germ of truth in the argument of Banfield's quaint monarchist. Can the monarchist's insight and the foregoing argument be reconciled with the convictions most of us have in favor of democracy? When, if ever, do democracies benefit from a similarly encompassing incentive structure?

Though this paper will avoid any genuinely technical matters, we will need to be slightly less casual if we are properly to compare the incentives facing dictators and the leaders of democratic governments. Initially, we will need to develop a clear conception of the level of spending on public goods that an ideal and fully efficient government would have. Once this ideal is clear, it will be possible to understand how government by a self-interested optimizing autocrat, on the one hand, and government by a similarly self-interested democratic politician seeking reelection, on the other, would deviate from this ideal.

To get a model in which we can readily compare autocracies and democracies with an ideal government, we must define the society's income carefully and then go on to define the costs of the public goods that governments must provide. We must define the society's income to include nonmoney or "psychic" income and also properly distinguish between "gross" and "net" social income.

In general, official national income statistics do not capture changes in the quality of life or psychic income, but because these things depend partly on public expenditures, we need to include them. Obviously, socially desirable expenditures on public goods are worth more to the society than they cost; conversely, excessive or socially useless expenditures reduce the true income of the society. But the measures of national income defined in the national income statistics do not properly capture this. The national accounts treat all expenditures on final goods and services, whether by the government or the private sector, as contributing identically to national income, irrespective of whether government expenditures are at a socially efficient level or not. Thus conceptually we need to consider the increase in true (money + psychic) income that results from a given public expenditure, evaluated in terms of the consumers' willingness to pay for it when they honestly reveal their preferences.

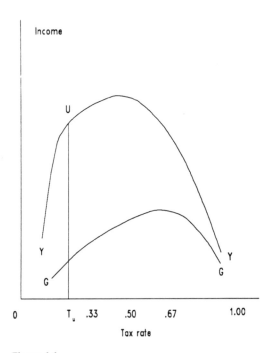

Figure 6.1

This increase in "true gross income" must be compared with the cost of the public expenditure that generated it. "True net income" is then obtained by *subtracting* public expenditure from true gross income, which is essentially income as defined in the national accounts plus or minus psychic income. We shall make the further simplifying assumption that there are no government surpluses or deficits, so tax revenue equals public expenditures. The true gross income for a society is then analogous to an individual's true pre-tax income, and the true net income for the society then is equivalent to true post-tax income for the individual. For the society as well as the individual, it is post-tax income that is relevant for welfare.

To make everything clear with simple pictures, let us look at a utopian situation with the aid of figure 6.1. Curve Y in this figure is true *gross* income as defined above. The percentage of national income taken in taxes is measured on the horizontal axis. Because I assume that tax collections are equal to expenditures on public goods, both income and expenditures on public goods are functions of the tax rate. When the level of public goods provision is inefficiently low (for example, in quasi-anarchy), devoting a larger percentage of national income to public goods necessarily increases gross income. To the right of the peak of the Y function, the damage to incentives from the high taxes needed to fund the public goods reduces income more than enough to offset any increase in productivity brought about by the additional public goods.

To look at changes in the level of *net* income or welfare, we must subtract the cost of public goods. This is not quite as simple as it seems, as the cost depends on how the tax burden is allocated among taxpayers. To make this allocation a precise one that will yield an unambiguous social optimum, I shall assume that there are Lindahl tax *shares* at *all* levels of taxes and public goods expenditures. That is, everyone shares the marginal (which here is, by assumption, also the average) tax burden in exactly the same proportion in which they share the benefits of public goods. Thus each individual's tax bill divided by total tax revenues equals his willingness-to-pay for the public good supply divided by the total willingness-to-pay of the society. With Lindahl tax shares, at lower-than-Pareto-optimal level of public expenditure there is *unanimous* support for more public expenditure, and at the higher-than-Pareto-optimal levels of public good provision, everyone wants less public spending. At every level of public good provision, however far from optimal it may be, all tax collections are by assumption efficiently directed to the provision of public goods.

We can now compare the welfare of citizens at each tax rate. The direct or cash cost of each level of public expenditure can be read off the G or "government" function in figure 6.1. The true gross or pre-tax income, Y, is shown at each weighted *average* tax rate for the society.[10] The vertical distance between the G function and the Y function gives the true net social income.

If the initial allocation of endowments is perfectly just, net welfare is necessarily maximized when Y exceeds tax collections by the largest amount. This is where tangents to the Y curve and the G function are parallel and where the marginal social benefit of public goods just equals their marginal cost. There is then a Pareto-efficient outcome at tax-spending level U, for utopia, in figure 6.1.

VIII

With the aid of the ideal conception just set out, we can examine the outcomes generated by autocratic and by democratic governments. Obviously, it would be easy to favor any type of government by assuming benevolent behavior of leaders of governments of that type whenever this led to better outcomes for the people at issue, and by assuming malicious behavior of the leaders of other kinds of governments. To be impartial, I will assume the same self-interested behavior at all times by all types of political leaders (and also by voters). Democratic political leaders will be assumed to care about nothing but maximizing their chances of election, and autocrats will similarly be assumed to exploit their domains entirely for their own purposes. Admittedly, I have, like many others, presented evidence elsewhere that unalloyed self-interest does not characterize most human beings.[11] Nonetheless, if a model is to be of any use, it must sacrifice descriptive accuracy to obtain manageable abstractions. The assumption of self-interest is much more realistic than any other assumption of comparable simplicity and impartiality. In the same spirit, I also abstract from "income effects" so that the willingness-to-pay for public goods does not change with changes in the distribution of income.

So, just as we used the rational self-interest of leaders of marauding bands to explain the establishment of peaceful order for large groups, we must in the same way ask what tax rate, and what disposition of tax revenues, will be most advantageous for the bandit-leader, once he has decided to be a king.

The rational self-interested autocrat will, of course, choose the tax rate that gives him the maximum attainable resources for his own purposes—for his palaces and other personal consumption, and most notably for the military power and war that will largely determine his status in relation to other autocrats and national leaders. As the Italian monarchist pointed out, a king will have the same incentive to care for his domain that a landlord has to fix the wiring in his property. But just as a landlord who owned all housing would have an incentive to charge monopoly rents, so the autocrat has an incentive to use his monopoly of violence in his domain to extract the maximum possible surplus for himself! Thus he will raise tax rates up to the point where any further increases would reduce tax collections.

It might seem that this would lead the autocrat to choose the highest point on the G function that is depicted in figure 6.1, but this is *not* correct. The autocrat will not (except in certain special cases) spend as much on public goods as the utopian government would have, and this entails that at any given tax rate social income and tax collections will be lower under autocracy than under an ideal government. For any given level of income of the society, every dollar the autocrat spends on public goods for the society is a dollar less that he can spend for his own purposes. It is in his interest to spend on public goods only so far as this expenditure increases the income of the society to such an extent that he gets his expenditures back in increased tax collections. Though an autocrat has an encompassing interest in his country, and this encompassing interest leads him to provide a peaceful order and other public goods of extraordinary value to his subjects, the very fact that his subjects inevitably get part of the society's income means that the autocrat will normally spend less on public goods than would a utopian government.

Suppose the revenue-maximizing tax rate for the dictator is 50 percent. Then the dictator will get 50 percent of the increase in social income that is generated by the provision of additional public goods. It follows that his interests are best served if he curtails his spending on public goods when the marginal dollar spent on public goods increases the society's income by two dollars, since at this point the last dollar spent on public goods will obviously bring him back just one extra dollar of tax revenue. If the revenue-maximizing tax rate for the monarch goes up, he will gain from providing more public goods.

In general, the rational autocrat will determine his profit-maximizing level of provision of public goods by calculating how "encompassing" his interest in the marginal social income is, and equating the marginal cost of public goods with the value of his share of the resulting increase in social income. It is expected that a fuller and more formal account of the determinants of the autocrat's level of provision, and an analysis of some interesting special cases, will be provided in a separate publication.[12]

In part because of the foregoing argument, we must go to figure 6.2 to find the optimal allocation for a self-interested autocrat. This figure not only presupposes a lower level of public good provision and corresponding reductions in the level of social income and tax receipts at each tax rate, but also examines the impact of using part of the proceeds of taxes for the autocrat's personal purposes on social income. In figure 6.1, *gross* income was higher to the right of the optimum *U* because there was more spending on public goods. This spending did

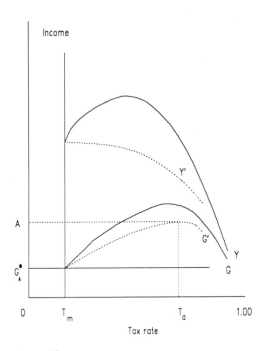

Figure 6.2

not increase gross income by as much as it increased expenditures on public goods, so the society's net income was reduced. But gross income and the amount of taxes that can be collected at any given tax rate were greater immediately to the right of T_u than at T_u. The tax receipts at the maximum of the tax receipts or G function in figure 6.1 could be attained only if all the money obtained from the tax receipts were devoted to the provision of public goods. When the autocrat uses much of the tax receipts for his own purposes, there will be a lower social income and a lower level of tax collections at each tax rate than would have occurred under ideal government.

Thus in figure 6.2 we depict a profit-maximizing expenditure on public goods by the autocrat, G_a^*, irrespective of the tax rate. If tax rates were not high enough to obtain G_a^*, there would be an inconsistency, so income is undefined to the left of T_m. The autocrat obviously chooses tax rates higher than T_m in order to obtain resources for his personal purposes. The excess burden of taxes tends to lower income, just as it did under ideal arrangements, but there is now no offsetting effect from a higher provision of public goods.

Thus the solid Y and G curves, analogous to those in figure 6.1, do not apply, and income decreases steadily as tax rates rise beyond the level needed to finance G_a^* of public good provision, as indicated by the dotted line Y'. This also reduces the level of tax receipts at any given tax rate,[13] so the optimum for the autocrat is found on the G' function. At the peak of this function, the difference between tax collections and expenditures on public goods is as great as it can be, and the autocrat has maximized the return from his domain. The surplus that the autocrat can use in whatever way best suits his ego is $0A$ minus $0G_a^*$.

Obviously, this leaves the autocrat's subjects with very much higher taxes than is in their interest, and these high taxes cost the subjects more than the amount they pay to the autocrat because they damage the incentive structure of the society and thus reduce income as well. As the peak of the G' function is approached from the left, a tiny increase in tax collections can be obtained only at the cost of a much larger drop in aggregate gross income, and the taxpayer's net income must fall by an even larger percentage than gross income. The autocrat nonetheless has an incentive to press all the way to the peak of the G' function. All taxes beyond those that would have been collected at tax rate T_m, moreover, are devoted to the ruler's wants rather than those of his subjects. Of course, the autocrat will not push tax rates above T_a, because this will reduce his tax collections.

The idea that it is irrational to raise tax rates beyond the level that maximizes tax collections is an old one. Joseph Schumpeter pointed this out in his article on "The Crisis of the Tax State," written in highly taxed Austria-Hungary not long before its defeat in World War I; there is even the germ of this idea in the fourteenth century in Ibn Kaldun's *Muqaddimah*.[14] Schumpeter's and Ibn Kaldun's important insight has been grossly misapplied and advertised as the "Laffer curve" in the United States in recent times, but this misapplication does not call the argument here into question.

The foregoing analysis should make it clear that, while the peaceful order a rational autocrat provides is vastly superior to violent anarchy, the rational autocrat's services are very expensive indeed. The rational autocrat uses his monopoly of power to take a huge part of the total gain from the social order for his own purposes. The distribution of income under autocracy gives much of the total taxable output to the autocrat, and the taxes or other exactions that he must impose to exploit his monopoly of the government introduce colossal inefficiency as well.

IX

With an ideal allocation and a self-interested autocrat's optimum as benchmarks, we can now explore how well democratic systems would work in relation to each. The democratic systems to be considered here are so simple that they have no close counterpart in reality. They nonetheless illustrate an advantage that relatively effective democratic systems have over autocracies and also reveal ways in which they systematically diverge from the utopian ideal depicted earlier. One model also illuminates a pathological problem in many democracies.

One prominent and simple possibility is to model the situation with a median-voter model in which it is assumed that all voters have single-peaked preferences. If at all sizes of the government everyone always pays a Lindahl *share* of the tax burden, the median voter who determines the outcome will also pay a Lindahl share, and we are back at the ideal allocation U in figure 6.1. If, realistically, we assume that there are significant departures from a Lindahl tax structure, then the outcome will depend on the tax share of the median voter.

To be specific, suppose the only tax is an income tax. The level of public expenditures would then be that sought by the voter of median income. If the median voter paid more than his Lindahl tax share, the level of provision of public goods would be somewhat too low; if he paid less than his Lindahl tax share, it would be somewhat too high. Since it is highly improbable that the median voter's tax rate is exactly his Lindahl share, the democratic outcome will almost never be Pareto-optimal. On the other hand, there is normally a positive income elasticity of demand for most public goods and usually also higher taxes for those with higher incomes, so there is no reason to believe that median-voter outcomes diverge dramatically from optimal allocations.

They certainly would tend to be vastly better than the autocratic outcome. Since the median voter certainly places a positive valuation on private goods, he would never vote for a tax rate at the maximum of the G function. If the allocation is anywhere close to this maximum, a reduction in tax rates generates a large increase in post-tax income at the cost of a tiny reduction in the provision of public goods. Accordingly, the median voter, even if his actual tax share were surprisingly far below his Lindahl share, would tend to vote for such a tax reduction, so tax rates would normally be much lower in a median-voter democracy than in an autocracy. The median voter, moreover, would have an incentive to vote only for those public expenditures that were of some benefit to him, so a median-voter democracy would not generate huge expenditures for the personal consumption of the government's leader akin to those at the autocratic optimum. In short, whatever plausible assumptions one chooses for a self-interested median-voter model of democracy, the outcomes appear to be vastly better for the citizenry than those that result from the self-interested autocrat.

One of the well-known problems of median-voter models with single-peaked preferences is that they do not capture the most serious distributional conflicts, which can bring on endless Arrovian cycles. The redistributional struggles and the policies to which they give rise will in general also mean that there are additional deadweight losses from the taxes and other policies that grow out of the distributional struggle. What, if anything, may be said about how a democracy will work when a governing party or president can for electoral advantage change the tax and subsidy structure, and thus redistribute income to "buy" the votes of a prospective majority?

X

To analyze this democratic difficulty most simply, I assume that proportional representation is excluded and there is instead a winner-take-all voting rule, such as applies to the presidencies in France and the United States and to seats in the House of Commons in Britain. With a winner-take-all voting rule, there is almost no purpose in having a small party, because no power can be attained without a majority. Similarly, it cannot be rational for a presidential candidate to seek less than a majority of the electorate. Thus, under a winner-take-all voting rule there will be a tendency toward two-party or two-candidate elections. I assume that no distributional coalitions or special interest groups play any role, so the outcomes depend entirely on the policies of the two parties or candidates, each of which maximizes the likelihood of victory. Because presidents or party leaders are by assumption self-interested, they have no inhibitions about using the tax and subsidy system to buy the support of a majority.

Here an important constraint on vote-buying redistribution arises from the "encompassing" character of the constituency each party must have in a two-party or two-candidate system. Because each party or president must get a majority to win anything, each must strive to please a constituency that will obtain a large fraction of the total income of the society—the fraction F for a party in a two-party system will not be far from one-half. If the income in the society rises or falls, the income of its constituents will on average rise or fall by FdY.

This encompassing interest gives the party or president an important stake in the well-being of the society. Incumbent parties and presidents want to run for reelection in circumstances in which they can credibly tell the voters, "you never had it so good," so they have a strong incentive to achieve good outcomes for the citizenry. Everyday observation confirms that presidents and leaders of encompassing political parties do indeed strive to be able to claim that there is "peace and prosperity" when they run for reelection. However, even a party or candidate with an encompassing constituency may still provide the best outcome of all for a given majority of the electorate by having some redistribution from the minority toward this majority. This can be true even though the deadweight loss from such a redistribution entails making national income lower than it would be otherwise.

The extent to which redistributive vote buying is expedient is limited by the difficulty of targeting the redistribution as well as by the encompassing interest of any majority coalition. The difficulties of targeting arise because the regions, occupations, income levels, or other identifiable attributes of voters that are used to determine whether they get a subsidy are not in general a perfect guide to what party they can be induced to support. A policy to subsidize persons in given categories will probably aid some individuals who prefer the alternative party. A subsidy may even induce the movement of voters who prefer the alternative party to the regions, occupations, or other categories that are subsidized. Thus much of the redistribution intended for the prospective majority will be "wasted" on those who support the other party. If the incumbent party attempts to tax those in the minority to subsidize the prospective majority, it will in practice tax some of those in the prospective majority and subsidize some of those in the minority. In general, only a proportion, P, of the redistribution targeted toward a prospective majority will be a net redistribution to it. An examination of plausible examples indicates that P could often easily be as low as .5.[15]

With the conceptual framework developed here, we can see both the social losses from democratic redistributions and the constraints on such redistributions when there are encompassing coalitions. Simply for convenience, let us suppose we start at the point in figure 6.2 depicting the optimum level of provision of public goods for the autocrat. The encompassing political leader with the strategy of using vote-buying redistribution to help obtain a majority will increase taxes and try to target the proceeds to his prospective majority. This redistribution, like the redistribution of the autocrat toward himself, will not increase gross income as the provision of more public goods would have; the taxes and subsidies will bring about deadweight losses. Thus gross as well as net income will decline to the right of T_m as they did as a result of the policy of the optimizing autocrat.

Nonetheless, the democracy with encompassing interests works incomparably better for the citizenry, even with uninhibited vote buying, than an optimizing autocrat. Suppose that the majority coalition earns exactly half of the national income and the difficulties of targeting dictate that P is also one-half. When the deadweight losses from redistributive vote buying become as large as the amount of the subsidy, the majority will gain from stopping the redistribution toward itself. Given the targeting difficulties, the net redistribution to the majority is only half of the subsidy, but the majority bears half of the reduction in national income that results from the *total* subsidy. Even if there were somehow costless and perfect targeting of subsidies, the redistribution would cease when the national income fell by double the amount of the subsidy.

To put the point generally, when the excess burden of the subsidy at the margin reaches P/F, it no longer pays the beneficiaries of the redistribution to carry it any further. At this point their share of the social loss from the redistribution just equals the net redistribution to them, and the upper bound on politically rational redistribution has been reached. Thus, when there are encompassing political parties or offices that determine democratic outcomes, the electoral gains from redistribution are limited, and these limits are more confining the greater the difficulty of targeting redistribution to a prospective majority.

Those who have not studied deadweight losses in the presence of *narrow* distributional coalitions may think that the foregoing constraints on vote-buying redistribution are not confining. A limit on redistribution that becomes effective only when the deadweight loss becomes (say) as large as the redistribution may not seem to be a binding constraint to those who have been brought up to believe that "all Harberger triangles are small." In fact, even in the richest democracies, narrow distributional coalitions often lead to deadweight losses that are substantial multiples of the amount redistributed to the members of the coalition, and in many underdeveloped nations the social losses from poor public policies account for most of the gap in per capita income between these countries and the developed world.[16]

To see the importance of the constraint on the losses from vote-buying redistribution with encompassing parties, consider the size of the excess burden that occurs when there is redistribution with tiny political parties (or with narrow special interest groups). Suppose that a political party or a special interest group represents a constituency that earns 5 percent of the national income. If there were no difficulties in targeting redistribution, it would pay this narrow interest to continue seeking redistributions to itself until the deadweight losses become twenty times as large as the redistribution. Thus democratic societies suffer colossal losses when their public policies become collections of measures won by special interest groups, whether the special interests take the form of lobbies or small political parties.

Though a democracy without *any* encompassing interest does suffer some losses that an autocrat with his encompassing interest would avoid, even a democracy of this kind has an important advantage for its citizens over an autocracy. Consider the situation at the autocrat's optimum at the peak of the G' function in figure 6.2. The autocrat has an incentive to choose this high tax rate and to keep all of the proceeds for himself (beyond the level T_m spent on public goods) because his gain comes exclusively from tax collections and other exactions: the post-tax income of his subjects has no direct impact on his welfare or choice of tax rate.

In a democracy with competitive political parties, even a political party that represented only 5 percent of the society would have *some* direct concern with the amount of net earned social income, because its members would get a little of this income. They would not, in other words, be quite at the peak of their G' function.[17] The vote-buying redistributions of a democracy with narrow parties would also differ from the autocrat's exactions in that they would be returned to the citizenry, or more precisely to various subsets of it. As governing coalitions changed over time, different subsets of the citizenry would gain from the changing redistributions. Thus for many citizens the distributional gains and losses would in the long run come close to balancing off, so that the only big losses would be the excess burdens. These are serious losses, but there are also large losses of efficiency in an autocracy from the "redistribution" to the autocrat, and the citizenry does not get any of this back.

XI

It is time to sum up and to call attention to the many important factors left out of the argument. We know from Schelling's argument in *Arms and Influence* that it is often rational for individuals to threaten or to employ violence. Because violence generates great losses without producing anything of value, there are phenomenal gains when anarchy is replaced by a peaceful order. Very small groups, such as the hunter-gatherer bands in environments that have not discovered settled agriculture, normally realize these gains through agreement and voluntary collective action. But the large populations that emerge after the development of crop production cannot, because of the logic of collective action, obtain law and order or other collective goods through voluntary cooperation.

Luckily, when populations are sizable, the invisible hand guides roving bandits to settle down and provide law and order and other public goods because this gives them more receipts in the form of tax revenues than they can obtain by roving banditry. The conqueror of a well-defined territory has an encompassing interest in that domain given by the share of any increase in the territorial income that he collects in taxes. This encompassing interest gives him an incentive to maintain law and order and to encourage creativity and production in his domain. Much of the economic progress and the development of civilization that has occurred in post-tribal times is explained by this incentive.

But the same rational self-interest that makes a roving bandit into an established monarch also makes him maximize his tax revenue and devote much of it to his purely personal purposes. This leads to a huge waste of resources and a considerable impairment of incentives due to high taxes.

In a democracy with encompassing and coherent political parties or with encompassing elective offices such as the presidencies in the United States and France, the invisible hand gives the highest political leaders an incentive to take account of the interests of the electorate. This shows up notably in the obvious desire of incumbent national leaders to be able to run for reelection on a record of peace and prosperity. Because a prospective majority may sometimes be made better off by a policy that includes some redistribution to them, democratic political leaders also have an incentive to generate some deadweight losses. But with encompassing parties or offices, the incentive for such redistribution is very limited. The incentives facing the self-interested leaders of encompassing political parties in a competitive democracy are accordingly more nearly consistent with those of the citizens than are the incentives of an autocrat.

The simple paradigm just described obviously leaves out many extraordinarily important factors, such as the role of the "rational ignorance" of the typical citizen in a democracy, the importance of distributional coalitions,[18] and so on. Some of the factors that have been left out often make democracies work badly, even when they have encompassing offices or parties. It would be a pity if the foregoing argument generates complacency (or even great optimism) about modern democracies.

XII

At the same time, our simple paradigm leaves out many factors that make autocracies work worse than the argument here would lead one to expect, and it also ignores many neglected advantages of democratic institutions. When an autocratic government is insecure, or for any other reason has a short time horizon, it no longer has an incentive to encourage the long-run investment that will increase the output of the domain in the long run—if the autocrat's time horizon is much shorter than the life of a capital good, he will gain more from expropriating that capital good than from protecting property rights in it. Thus insecure autocrats have often seized accumulations of property and imposed capital levies so high that they reduced tax collections in the long run. Of course, the short time horizons of elected politicians also cause severe problems.

The subset of democracies that have been viable in the long run are, however, almost the only governments that have been able regularly to arrange for a continuing orderly succession of leaders. When the autocrat dies or is deposed, there are no institutions that can be relied upon to select or install a new dictator peacefully. If institutions like the police and the judiciary derived their power from sources other than the former dictator, then the society would not really have been an autocracy: it would have been pluralistic and, if not democratic, at least an "institutionalized oligarchy," which I define as a semidemocracy. When a real dictator dies or is deposed, all institutions lose their authority, and there is no reliable means by which the society can ensure that it will get a new leader in an orderly way. Thus virtually the only societies in the world today in which there can be much confidence about what the government will be like a decade or two into the future are democracies. Thus to a great degree it is only in these societies that there is a predictable environment for long-run investment in capital goods, in research and development, and in enduring works of art.

The autocrat also has the problem that he cannot easily and straightforwardly make credible commitments. If he runs the society, there is no one who can force him to keep his commitments. Thus he is in a position roughly like that of minors in the United States, who cannot get credit cards because the law will not force them to repay their debts. The autocrat who looks forward to a long reign will obtain the greatest tax collections in the long run if his subjects believe that there will be no unscheduled new taxes or confiscations of wealth, for this will give them the greatest incentive to accumulate capital and to produce. The autocrat can promise that he will not impose any future taxes or confiscations that would make current investments unprofitable, but given his incentive to make that promise even if he intends to break it, the promise may not be credible.

This problem is far less serious in a pluralistic democracy. The independent judiciary systems of such societies make property rights much more predictable, and the pluralistic dispersion of power means that there are many powerful interests that have a stake in opposing any violations of property rights or failures to enforce contracts. The people who would have to pay any confiscatory taxes also have a right to vote, and that makes future tax rates and policies more predictable than they would be otherwise. All this makes an economy work better.

Thus it is probably not an accident that the richest countries in the world are mainly democracies. The undeniable correlation between democracy and high income is sometimes alleged to be due to a taste for democracy in high-income societies: democracy is a luxury. Though the demand for democracy may well rise with income, the causal sequence implied by the foregoing argument does not fit the facts. Though there are of course examples of dictatorships with very successful economies, relatively pluralistic and democratic countries generated the industrial revolution and were the first to copy it. After World War II, economic development and technological advance spread mainly from democracies to other countries, rather than the reverse. West Germany, Japan, and Italy grew with miraculous rapidity after their conversion to democracy, as did most of the democracies of continental Europe. The totalitarian societies of Eastern Europe grew rapidly for a time, but were unable to sustain this growth or even to ensure their viability.[19]

Some dictatorships have grown for a time at very rapid rates (I have calculated the *variance* of growth rates among dictatorships in recent decades and found it higher than that among democracies). But no society with a continuing absolute monarchy[20] or any other kind of dictatorship has ever reached a high level of development. Even areas with episodic dictatorships,[21] such as most of Latin America, have not been able to reach high levels of development. There is not much debate about how democracies fare in cultural and scientific competition, but they are sometimes thought to be at a disadvantage in war or military competition. David Lake has, however, carefully gathered all of the historical evidence on wars between democracies and dictatorships and discovered that democracies have been almost twice as likely to win their wars as have dictatorships.[22] It is not clear whether this is because of greater capabilities in fighting wars or to fewer mistakes in starting unsuccessful wars, but the result is favorable to democracy under either assumption.

So I conclude that the quaint Italian monarchist had a valid point, which helped us explain how the hidden hand leads to the emergence of government and thus helps to account for a large proportion of the history of civilization. But if the monarchist had carried the logic of his argument further, he would also have discovered a powerful case for democratic governments with encompassing institutions.

Notes

1. *The Moral Basis of a Backward Society* (Glencoe, IL: The Free Press/Research Center in Economic Development and Cultural Change, University of Chicago, 1958), p. 26. Charmingly, the monarchist who is quoted joined the Communist party a few weeks after making the statement, and then a few weeks later became a monarchist again.

2. *Arms and Influence* (New Haven, CT: Yale University Press, 1966), p. v.

3. See my *Logic of Collective Action* (Cambridge, MA: Harvard University Press, 1965).

4. Ibid.

5. Ibid.

6. James E. Sheridan, *Chinese Warlord: The Career of Feng Yu-hsiang* (Stanford: Stanford University Press, 1966), pp. 19 and 51–119. Feng is alleged to have been a better administrator of his domains than many other warlords. He was also exceptional among the warlords in being a Christian, and this may have added to his reputation among Western observers in China.

7. There is an earlier and, in some ways, analogous account of a king's incentive to improve property rights in Douglass North's valuable historical discussions, especially in his *Structure and Change in Economic History* (New York: W. W. Norton, 1981) and his book with Robert Thomas on *The Rise of the Western World* (Cambridge: Cambridge University Press, 1973).

8. Yale University Press, 1982.

9. Douglass North has previously emphasized the magnitude of the consumer's surplus from the provision of basic government.

10. Each person's tax rate must have a weight given by the percentage of the total revenue his Lindahl tax share would yield.

11. "The Role of Morals and Incentives in Societies," presented at a celebration of the 200th anniversary of Georgetown University.

12. This prospective publication grows out of the work of my colleague Martin McGuire and is being done jointly with him.

13. Another assumption is that the mix and level of public goods for the society are not altered by the fact that the autocrat takes a substantial share of social output through high taxation for his own purposes. This in turn requires the earlier assumption that there are no income effects. It also requires that all public expenditures affect taxable and nontaxable income impartially, so the autocrat does not have an incentive to emphasize those that raise taxable income.

14. Schumpeter's essay is reprinted, among other places, in *Joseph A. Schumpeter: the Economies and Sociology of Capitalism*, edited by Richard Swedberg (Princeton, N.J.: Princeton University Press, 1991), pp. 99–140. For Ibn

Khaldun's insight on this point see *The Muqaddimah, An Introduction to History*, translated from the Arabic by Franz Rosenthal (Princeton, N.J.: Princeton University Press, 1967), pp. 230–231.

15. Suppose that the incumbent party increases taxes on everyone to subsidize a majority, but that to make sure that it reaches the targeted majority it must make transfers to three-fourths of the electorate. One-third of the subsidy is then "wasted," and the prospective majority must bear its share, F, of the wasted subsidy (as well as of the deadweight loss on all of the subsidy). If three-fourths of the electorate is then subsidized and the prospective majority bears half of the cost of the misdirected third of the subsidy, its members' net gain is only half, or four-sixths minus one-sixth, of the subsidy. Thus their net gain from the subsidy is equal to half of the amount redistributed.

16. This is shown in my paper, "Why are international differences in per capita incomes so large and persistent?" (typescript, University of Maryland, 1990).

17. Though the excess burden of a given tax rate would be the same for a redistributive democracy and an autocracy, the excess burden of a given level of subsidies from democratic redistribution would not necessarily be the same as the same amount of autocratic spending. The subsidies from democratic redistribution might have a larger adverse effect on the incentives to work, or the autocratic spending might be more likely to be on socially costly wars, etc. Thus the G' function in figure 6.2 need not be the same for an autocracy and a redistributive democracy.

18. *The Rise and Decline of Nations.*

19. Given the nature of totalitarian societies, it is not straightforwardly possible to isolate what proportion of the social surplus has been used to serve the objectives of the conquerors or rulers of these societies and what proportion has been used to serve the interests of their subjects. The exceptionally high rates of forced saving, the high proportion of the GDP devoted to military expenditures, and the low standards of living in the Soviet-type societies indicate that an extraordinarily high proportion of output has been devoted to the purposes of the rulers, but the Soviet societies would have had some investment and military spending and some economic problems even under democratic governments, so the exact allocation of the social output between the rulers and the subjects can only be estimated. In the case of Hitler's Germany, ultimately about half of the GDP was used in the effort to augment and protect Hitler's domain.

20. It is unfortunately not possible directly to test the theory offered here by comparing the proportions of the national income used by governments in absolute monarchies and in democracies. Because absolute monarchies have usually existed only in historic and pre-industrial societies, one cannot meaningfully compare the proportions of the national income that the monarchs took in taxes with the proportions of the national income used by democratic governments in developed societies. This is partly because so

many of the activities of modern governments in the democracies are to transfer income or provide services to the citizenry (or to subsets of it). Because in ; the long run the electorate loses only the deadweight losses from this redistribution, its costs can not appropriately be compared with the autocrat's taxation for his personal purposes. In addition, in pre-industrial societies the total per capita output is not usually far above the subsistence level, so a conqueror can extract only a tiny proportion of total output, at least over the long run. Finally, the lack of the technological and cultural requirements for efficient large-scale administration also greatly limits the amount of surplus that a bandit-conqueror can feasibly extract (on the administrative difficulties, see my "Diseconomies of Scale and Development," in *The Cato Journal*, vol. 7, no. 1, Spring/Summer, 1987, pp. 77–97).

21. In those modern environments where democracies are familiar and often feasible alternatives, dictatorships frequently have to strive to be popular with the population as a whole or at least with large segments of it. It is therefore difficult empirically to distinguish modern popularity-dependent dictatorships from democracies; in some cases their actions are very similar. Thus the theory here makes no unambiguous predictions about the proportion of the GDP used by governments in such dictatorships and in democracies. It does, however, predict that future policies are more predictable in the stable democracies and that this is favorable to their growth.

22. David A. Lake, "Why Democracies Win Wars" (mimeo, University of California at Los Angeles).

II

Commitment and the Strategy of Conflict: A Few Players

7

Making Strategies Credible

Avinash Dixit and Barry Nalebuff

Thomas Schelling's way of framing strategic issues brings a new dimension to politics, business, and everyday life. If everything seems more complicated, it's more interesting too.

In this essay, we look at one small part of Schelling's universe—how to make strategies credible. This question allows us to bring together his contributions to bargaining, international conflict, and even the battle for self-control.[1] First, we describe the problem.

In most situations, mere verbal promises should not be trusted. As Sam Goldwyn put it, "A verbal contract isn't worth the paper it's written on."[2] An incident in *The Maltese Falcon* by Dashiell Hammett (filmed by Goldwyn's competitor Warner Brothers, with Humphrey Bogart as Sam Spade and Sydney Greenstreet as Gutman) illustrates this point. Gutman gives Sam Spade an envelope containing ten thousand dollars.

Spade looked up smiling. He said mildly: "We were talking about more money than this." "Yes sir, we were," Gutman agreed, "but, we were talking then. This is actual money, genuine coin of the realm. With a dollar of this, you can buy more than with ten dollars of talk."[3]

This lesson can be traced all the way back to Thomas Hobbes: "The bonds of words are too weak to bridle men's avarice."[4] Women's too, as King Lear discovered.

If a threat or promise is purely oral, why should you live up to it if it turns out not to be in your interest to do so? But if others believe you are not committed, they will look ahead and predict that you have no incentive to follow through, and your threat or promise will not have the desired effect.[5]

Strategic moves such as threats and promises attempt to change someone else's expectations about your response to his action. They will fail if he believes that you will not carry them out. Without any effect on others' expectations, there will be no effect on their actions.

Establishing credibility in the strategic sense means that you are expected to keep your promises and to make good on your threats. Commitments are unlikely to be taken at face value. Your commitment may be tested. Credibility must be earned.

Credibility requires finding a way to prevent going back. If there is no tomorrow, today's commitment cannot be reversed. The fact that deathbed testimony can never be altered leads the courts to give it tremendous weight. More commonly, there is a tomorrow (and a day after) so that we must explore the problem of how to maintain commitment over the long haul. "Feast today, for tomorrow we fast" is the excuse for putting on today what can be taken off tomorrow.

The Eightfold Path to Credibility

Making strategic moves credible is not easy. But it is not impossible, either. We now offer eight devices for achieving credible commitments. Like the Buddhist prescription for Nirvana, we call this the "eightfold path" to credibility. Depending on the circumstances, one or more of these tactics may prove effective. Behind this system are three underlying principles.

The first principle is to change the payoffs of the game. The idea is to make it in your interest to follow through on your commitment: turn a threat into a warning, a promise into an assurance. This can be done in a variety of ways.

1. Establish and use a reputation.

2. Write contracts.

Both these tactics make it more costly to break the commitment than to keep it.

A second avenue is to change the game to limit your ability to back out of a commitment. In this category, we consider three possibilities. The most radical is simply to deny yourself any opportunity to back down, either by cutting yourself off from the situation or by destroying any avenues of retreat. There is even the possibility of removing yourself from the decision-making position and leaving the outcome to chance.

3. Cut off communication.

4. Burn bridges behind you.

5. Leave the outcome to chance.

These two principles can be combined: both the possible actions and their outcomes can be changed. If a large commitment is broken down into many smaller ones, then the gain from breaking a little one may be more than offset by the loss of the remaining contract. Thus we have

6. Move in small steps.

A third route is to use others to help you maintain commitment. A team may achieve credibility more easily than an individual. Or you may simply hire others to act in your behalf.

7. Develop credibility through teamwork.

8. Employ mandated negotiating agents.

Reputation

If you try a strategic move in a game and then back off, you may lose your reputation for credibility. In a once-in-a-lifetime situation, reputation may be unimportant and therefore of little commitment value. But typically, you play several games with different rivals at the same time, or the same rivals at different times. Then you have an incentive to establish a reputation, and this serves as a commitment that makes your strategic moves credible.

During the Berlin crisis in 1961, John F. Kennedy explained the importance of the U.S. reputation:

If we do not meet our commitments to Berlin, where will we later stand? If we are not true to our word there, all that we have achieved in collective security, which relies on these words, will mean nothing.[6]

Another example is Israel's standing policy not to negotiate with terrorists. This is a threat intended to deter terrorists from taking hostages to barter for ransom or release of prisoners. If the no-negotiation threat is credible, terrorists will come to recognize the futility of their actions. In the meantime, Israel's resolve will be tested. Each time the threat must be carried out, Israel suffers; a refusal to compromise may sacrifice Israeli hostages' lives. Each confrontation with terrorists puts Israel's reputation and credibility on the line. Giving in means more than just meeting the current demands; it makes future terrorism more attractive.[7]

The effect of reputation is a two-edged sword for commitment. Sometimes destroying your reputation can create the possibility for a commitment. Destroying your reputation commits you *not* to take actions in the future that you can predict will not be in your best interests.

The question of whether to negotiate with hijackers helps illustrate the point. Before any particular hijacking has occurred, the government might decide to deter hijackings by threatening never to negotiate. However, the hijackers predict that after they commandeer the jet, the government will find it impossible to enforce a no-negotiation posture. How can a government deny itself the ability to negotiate with hijackers?

One answer is to destroy the credibility of its promises. Imagine that after reaching a negotiated settlement, the government breaks its commitment and attacks the hijackers. This destroys any reputation the government has for trustworthy treatment of hijackers. It loses the ability to make a credible promise, and irreversibly denies itself the temptation to respond to a hijacker's threat. This destruction of the credibility of a promise makes credible the threat never to negotiate.

Congress has a similar problem of maintaining consistency over time when it comes to tax amnesty programs. Such programs allow those who owe back taxes to pay up without penalty. This appears to be a costless way of raising more revenue. All those who have had second thoughts about cheating on their taxes give the government money. In fact, if it could be credibly established that there would never be another amnesty, then Congress could raise additional tax revenues at no cost. But, if amnesty was such a good idea once, why not try it again in a few years? Nothing prevents Congress from offering an amnesty on a regular basis. Then a problem arises. Cheating becomes more attractive because there will be the possibility of getting amnesty in the future.

Congress must find a way to prevent itself from ever repeating the amnesty program. In a *Wall Street Journal* article, Robert Barro and Alan Stockman propose that the government offer a tax amnesty, then renege on its promise and prosecute those who turn themselves in.[8] This will raise even more revenue than a simple amnesty. And after the government cheats on its amnesty, who would believe the government were it to try again? By destroying its credibility, the government can make a credible commitment not to offer an amnesty again; cheating will not be encouraged.

You will probably think this is an absurd idea, and with good reason. First, it will not work against strategically aware taxpayers. They will expect the government to renege on its promise, so they will not participate in the amnesty at all. More importantly, catching tax cheaters is not the only game in town. While double-crossing tax cheaters may be good in this game, it will cause greater harm to the government's reputation in others.

One of the most impressive examples of how to build a reputation belongs to the Mayflower Furniture Company. In a large billboard located along the Massachusetts Turnpike, they proudly advertise that they have gone 147 years without a sale. (Are they still waiting for their first customer?) This unconditional commitment to everyday low prices brings in a steady stream of customers. A sale might temporarily raise profits, but it would be another 147 years before they could repeat such a clever advertisement. Next year, we expect the sign will read 148 years. The reputation becomes self-perpetuating as it becomes more valuable.[9]

In all these instances, the player cultivates a reputation with the direct and conscious aim of creating credibility for his future unconditional commitments, threats, and promises. However, reputation can also arise for nonstrategic reasons and yet be just as powerful in achieving credibility. The feeling of *pride* in not breaking one's word is an example. Thomas Hobbes suggested that the weak bonds of words can be strengthened in two ways: a fear of the consequence of breaking one's word; or a glory, or pride, in not breaking it. Such pride is often instilled in people's value system through education or general social conditioning. It may even have the implicit social aim of improving the credibility of our manifold daily relationships. Yet we are not told to take pride in being honorable *because* it will bring us strategic advantage by making our threats and promises credible; we are told that honor is a good thing in itself.

Someone who has a reputation for being crazy can make successful threats that would be incredible coming from a saner and cooler person. In this way, apparent *irrationality* can become good strategic rationality. One can even cultivate such a reputation. A seeming madman, therefore, may be a superior strategist, because his threats are more readily believed.[10] Could Colonel Ghadafi and Ayatollah Khomeini have understood this principle better than the cool, rational leaders of Western nations trying to deal with them? We do not know, but we are willing to bet that your child who is too irrational to be deterred by your threats of punishment is a better instinctive game player than you are.

Contracts

A straightforward way to make your commitment credible is to agree to a punishment if you fail to follow through. If your kitchen remodeler gets a large payment up front, he is tempted to slow down the work. But a contract that specifies payment linked to the progress of the work and penalty clauses for delay can make it in his interest to stick to the schedule. The contract is the commitment device.

Actually, it's not quite that simple. Imagine that a dieting man offers to pay $500 to anyone who catches him eating fattening food. Every time the man thinks of a dessert, he knows that it just isn't worth $500. Before dismissing this example as incredible, just such a contract was offered by a Mr. Nick Russo—except the amount was $25,000. According to the *Wall Street Journal*:

> So, fed up with various weight-loss programs, Mr. Russo decided to take his problem to the public. In addition to going on a 1,000-calorie-a-day diet, he is offering a bounty—$25,000 to the charity of one's choosing—to anyone who spots him eating in a restaurant. He has peppered local eateries . . . with "wanted" pictures of himself.[11]

But this contract has a fatal flaw: there is no mechanism to prevent renegotiation. With visions of eclairs dancing in his head, Mr. Russo should argue that under the present contractual agreement, no one will ever get the $25,000 penalty because he will never violate the contract. Hence, the contract is worthless. Renegotiation would be in their mutual interest. For example, Mr. Russo might offer to buy a round of drinks in exchange for being released from the contract. The restaurant diners prefer a drink to nothing and let him out of the contract.[12]

For the contracting approach to be successful, the party that enforces the action or collects the penalty must have some independent incentive to do so.

In the dieting problem, members of Mr. Russo's family might also want him to be skinnier and thus would not be tempted by a mere free drink.

In business dealings, the contracting approach is more likely to succeed. A broken contract typically produces damages, so that the injured party is not willing to give up on the contract for naught. For example, a producer might demand a penalty from a supplier who fails to deliver. The producer is not indifferent about whether the supplier delivers or not. He would rather get his supply than receive the penalty sum. Renegotiating the contract is no longer a mutually attractive option.

Think of what happens now if the supplier tries the dieter's argument. The supplier attempts to renegotiate on the grounds that the penalty is so large that the contract will always be honored and the producer will never receive the penalty. This is just what the producer wants and hence he is not interested in renegotiation. The contract works because the producer is not solely interested in the penalty; he cares about the actions promised in the contract.

It is possible to write contracts with neutral parties as enforcers. A neutral party is someone who does not have any personal interest in whether the contract is upheld. To make enforcement credible, the neutral party must be made to care about whether or not the commitment is kept by creating a reputation effect. In some instances, the contract holder might lose his job if he allows the contract to be rewritten. Schelling (1989) provides a remarkable example of how these ideas have been implemented. In Denver, one rehabilitation center treats wealthy cocaine addicts by having them write a self-incriminating letter that will be made public if they fail random urine analysis. After placing themselves voluntarily in this position, many people will try to buy their way out of the contract. But the person who holds the contract will lose his job if the contract is rewritten; the center will lose its reputation if it fails to fire employees who allow contracts to be rewritten.

The moral is that contracts alone cannot overcome the credibility problem. Success requires some additional credibility tool, such as employing parties with independent interests in enforcement or a reputation at stake. In fact, if the reputation effect is strong enough, it may be unnecessary to formalize a contract. This is the sense of a person's word being his bond.[13]

Cutting off Communication

Cutting off communication succeeds as a credible commitment device because it can make an action truly irreversible. An extreme form of this tactic arises in the terms of a last will and testament. Once the party has died, renegotiation is virtually impossible. (For example, it took an act of the British parliament to change Cecil Rhodes's will in order to allow for female Rhodes Scholars.) In general, where there is a will, there is a way to make your strategy credible.

For example, most universities set a price for endowing a chair. The going rate is about $1.5 million. These prices are not carved in stone (nor covered with ivy). Universities have been known to bend their rules in order to accept the terms and the money of deceased donors who fail to meet the current prices.

One need not die trying to make commitments credible. Irreversibility stands watch at every mailbox. Who has not mailed a letter and then wished to retrieve it? And it works the other way. Who has not received a letter he wishes he hadn't? But you can't send it back and pretend you've never read it once you've opened the letter.

Before the practice became widespread, a successful commitment device was to mail one's bill payments in unstamped letters with no return address. Mailing a letter with no return address is an irreversible commitment. The post office used to deliver such letters, and the receiver could accept delivery by paying the postage due. A utility or phone company knew that such a letter was likely to contain a check and preferred to pay the postage due rather than wait another billing cycle before receiving payment (or another unstamped letter with no return address).

The solution to the companies' problem came when the post office changed its policy. Letters without postage are no longer delivered to the addressee; they are returned to the sender if there is a return address and not delivered if there is no return address. Now the company can commit itself not to receive a letter with postage due.

But what if you put the company's address as both the mailing address and the return address? Now the post office has someone to return the letter to. (Remember, you didn't hear this idea here first.) And if it begins to spread, rest assured that the post office rules will be changed so that letters without a stamp are not even returned to the sender.

Of course, this strategy is not without drawbacks; Schelling (1960, p. 39) is quick to remind us of the difficulties in cutting off communication as a device to maintain commitment. If you are incommunicado, it may be difficult if not impossible to make sure that others have complied with your wishes. You must hire others to ensure that the contract is being honored. For example, wills are carried out by trustees, not the deceased. A parental rule against smoking may be exempt from debate while the parents are away, but unenforceable too.

Burning Bridges behind You

Armies often achieve commitment by denying themselves an opportunity to retreat. This strategy goes back at least to 1066, when William the Conqueror's invading army burned its own ships, thus making an unconditional commitment to fight rather than retreat. Cortés followed the same strategy in his conquest of Mexico. Upon his arrival in Cempoalla, Mexico, he gave orders that led to all but one of his ships being burned or disabled. Although his soldiers were vastly outnumbered, they had no choice but to fight and win. "Had [Cortés] failed, it might well seem an act of madness. . . . Yet it was the fruit of deliberate calculation. . . . There was no alternative in his mind but to succeed or perish."[14]

Destroying the ships gave Cortés two advantages. First, his own soldiers were united, each knowing that they would *all* fight until the end because desertion (or even retreat) was an impossibility. Second, and more important, is the effect this commitment had on the opposition. They knew that Cortés must either succeed or perish, while they had the option of retreat into their homeland. They chose to retreat rather than fight such a determined opponent. For this type of commitment to have the proposed effects, it must be understood by the soldiers (yours and the enemy's), not just by the armchair strategists. Thus it is especially interesting that "the destruction of the fleet [was] accomplished not only with the knowledge, but the approbation of the army, though at the suggestion of Cortés."[15]

This idea of burning one's own ships demonstrates the evolution of strategic thinking over time. The Trojans seemed to get it all backward when the Greeks sailed to Troy to rescue Helen.[16] The Greeks tried to conquer the city, while the Trojans tried to burn the Greek ships. But if the Trojans had succeeded in burning the Greek fleet, they would simply have made the Greeks all the more determined opponents. In fact, the Trojans failed to burn the Greek fleet and saw the Greeks sail home in retreat. Of course the Greeks left behind a gift horse, which in retrospect the Trojans were a bit too quick to accept.[17]

In modern times, this strategy applies to attacks on land as well as by sea. For many years, Edwin Land's Polaroid corporation purposefully refused to diversify out of the instant photography business. With all its chips in instant photography, it was committed to fight against any intruder in the market.

On April 20, 1976, after twenty-eight years of a Polaroid monopoly on the instant photography market, Eastman Kodak entered the fray: it announced a new instant film and camera. Polaroid responded aggressively, suing Kodak for patent infringement. Edwin Land, founder and chairman, was prepared to defend his turf:

This is our very soul we are involved with. This is our whole life. For them its just another field. . . . We will stay in our lot and protect that lot.[18]

Mark Twain (1980, p. 73) explained this philosophy in *Pudd'nhead Wilson*:

Behold, the fool saith, "Put not all thine eggs in one basket" . . . but the wise man saith, "Put all your eggs in one basket and WATCH THAT BASKET."

After years of litigation, Polaroid won a complete victory. Kodak was forced to withdraw its film from the market.[19] Although Polaroid restored its dominance over the instant photography market, it lost ground to competition from portable video recorders and minilabs that developed and printed conventional film in one hour. Lacking bridges, Polaroid began to feel trapped on a sinking island. With a change in philosophy, the company has begun to branch out into video film and even conventional film.

One need not literally burn bridges, nor ships that bridge oceans. One can burn bridges figuratively by taking a political position that will antagonize certain voters. When Walter Mondale said in accepting the 1984 Democratic presidential nomination that he *would* raise taxes if elected, he was making such a commitment. Voters who believed in supply-side economics were irretrievably lost, and this made Mondale's position more credible to those who favored a tax increase in order to reduce the deficit. Unfortunately (for Mondale), the group of voters antagonized by this move turned out to be far too large.

Finally, building rather than burning bridges can also serve as a credible source of commitment. In the December 1989 reforms in Eastern Europe, building bridges meant knocking down walls. Responding to massive protests and emigration, East Germany's Prime Minister Egon Krenz wanted to promise reform but didn't have a specific package. The population was skeptical. Why should they believe that the vague promise of reform would be genuine and far-reaching? Even if Krenz was truly in favor of reform, he might fall out of power. Dismantling parts of the Berlin Wall helped the East German government make a credible commitment to reform without having to detail all the specifics. By (re)opening a bridge to the West, the government forced itself to reform or risk an exodus. Since it would be possible to leave in the future, the promise of reform was both credible and worth waiting for. Reunification was to be less than a year away.

Leaving the Outcome beyond Your Control

The doomsday device in the movie *Dr. Strangelove* consisted of large buried nuclear bombs whose explosion would emit enough radioactivity to exterminate all life on earth. The device would be detonated automatically in the event of an attack on the Soviet Union. When President Milton Muffley of the United States asked if such an automatic trigger was possible, Dr. Strangelove answered, "It is not merely possible; it is *essential*."

The device is such a good deterrent because it makes aggression tantamount to suicide.[20] Faced with an American attack, Soviet premier Dimitri Kissov might refrain from retaliating and risking mutually assured destruction. As long as the Soviet premier has the freedom not to respond, the Americans might risk an attack. But with the doomsday device in place, the Soviet response is automatic and the deterrent threat is credible.

However, this strategic advantage does not come without a cost. There might be a small accident or unauthorized attack, after which the Soviets would not want to carry out their dire threat, but have no choice as execution is out of their control. This is exactly what happened in *Dr. Strangelove*.

To reduce the consequences of errors, you want a threat that is no stronger than is necessary to deter the rival. What do you do if the action is indivisible, as a nuclear explosion surely is? You can make the threat milder by creating a risk, but not a certainty, that the dreadful event will occur. This is Thomas Schelling's idea of *brinkmanship*.[21] As he explained in *The Strategy of Conflict*,

Brinkmanship is . . . the deliberate creation of a recognizable risk, a risk that one does not completely control. It is the tactic of deliberately letting the situation get somewhat out of hand, just because its being out of hand may be intolerable to the other party and force his accommodation. It means harassing and intimidating an adversary by exposing him to a shared risk, or deterring him by showing that if he makes a contrary move he may disturb us so that we slip over the brink whether we want to or not, carrying him with us.

Brinkmanship scales down the size of the threat by making it a probability rather than a certainty, and then makes this diminished threat credible by leaving the outcome to chance. Schelling (1966, p. 70) uses a scene from the film *High Wind in Jamaica* to show how this works.

The pirate captain Chavez wants his captive to tell where the money is hidden, and puts his knife to the man's throat to make him talk. After a moment or two, during which the man keeps his mouth shut, the mate laughs. "If you cut his throat he can't tell you. He knows it. And he knows you know it." Chavez puts his knife away and tries something else.

Chavez might have kept the knife and tried brinkmanship, if only he had seen *The Maltese Falcon*. There Spade has hidden the valuable bird, and Gutman is trying to find out where it is.

Spade smiled at the Levantine and answered him evenly: "You want the bird. I've got it. . . . If you kill me how are you going to get the bird? If I know that you can't afford to kill me till you have it, how are you going to scare me into giving it to you?"

In response, Gutman explains how he intends to make his threat credible.

"I see what you mean." Gutman chuckled. "That is an attitude, sir, that calls for the most delicate judgement on both sides, because as you know, sir, men are likely to forget in the heat of the action where their best interest lies and let their emotions carry them away."[22]

Gutman concedes that he can't threaten Spade with certain death. Instead, he can expose Spade to a risk, a probability that things might get out of control in the heat of the moment.[23] Accidents do occur, and death is irreversible. Gutman cannot commit to killing Spade for sure if Spade refuses to talk. But he can threaten to put Spade in a position where Gutman can not guarantee that he will be able to prevent Spade from getting killed. This ability to expose someone to a probability of punishment can be enough to make the threat effective if the punishment is bad enough.

The greater the risk of Spade getting killed in this way, the more effective is the threat. But at the same time, the risk becomes less tolerable to Gutman, and therefore the threat becomes less credible. Gutman's brinkmanship will work if, and only if, there is an intermediate range of probabilities where the risk is large enough to compel Spade to reveal the bird's location, and yet small enough to be acceptable to Gutman. Such a range exists only if Spade values his own life more than Gutman values the bird in the sense that the probability of death that will frighten Spade into talking is smaller than the risk of losing his information that gives Gutman pause. Brinkmanship is not just the creation of risk, but a careful control of the degree of that risk.

The ability to get off the brink is a final aspect of control that is essential for effective brinkmanship. The threatened party must be able to reduce the risk sufficiently, often all the way to zero, by agreeing to the brinkman's terms. For example, Spade must have the assurance that Gutman's temper will cool down sufficiently quickly once he knows the secret. Otherwise you are damned if you do and damned if you don't, and there is no incentive to comply.

The conduct of America's trade policy illustrates brinkmanship without the control mechanism. The United States tries to compel the Japanese and the Koreans to open their markets to American exports (and also to export less to the United States) by pointing out the risk of more serious protectionist actions by Congress. "If we can't reach a moderate agreement, Congress will enact restrictions that will be a lot worse for you." The so-called voluntary export restraints on automobiles agreed to by Japan in 1981 were the result of just such a process. The problem with the regular use of such tactics in trade negotiations is that they can create risk, but cannot control it within the requisite range. When other issues are occupying the legislators' attention, the risk of protectionist action in Congress is too low to be an effective threat. On the other hand, when Congress is exercised about trade deficits, the risk is either too high to be acceptable to our own administration, or simply unresponsive to a modest foreign restraint and therefore an ineffective threat. In other words, the American system of checks and balances can create risk, but cannot control it effectively.

These ideas find their primary application in the use of nuclear brinkmanship as a deterrent. Now that the cold war is over and the arms race is winding down, we can examine nuclear brinkmanship in a cool analytical way that was hard to achieve earlier. Many argue that there is a paradox in nuclear weapons because they pose too big a threat ever to use. If their use cannot be rational, then the threat cannot be rational either. This is just the Gutman-Spade exchange writ large. Without the threat value, nuclear weapons are impotent in deterring minor conflicts.

This is why the Europeans feared that NATO's nuclear umbrella might prove a poor shield against the rain of superior Soviet conventional forces. Even if the United States was resolved to defend Europe, the argument went, the threat of nuclear response was not credible against small Soviet transgressions. The Soviets could exploit this using "salami tactics," a slice at a time. Imagine that there were riots in West Berlin and some fires. East German fire brigades come to help. Would the U.S. president press the nuclear button? Of course not. East German police arrive in support. The button? No. They stay, and a few days later are replaced by East German troops. At each point, the incremental aggression is too small to merit a drastic response. NATO keeps on redrawing the line of its tolerance. Eventually, the Soviets could be at Trafalgar Square, and NATO headquarters in exile would be wondering just when they had missed their chance.[24]

This conclusion was mistaken. The threat of a U.S. nuclear response to conventional Soviet aggression in Europe was one of brinkmanship. There are two ways for getting around the problem of redrawing the line. Brinkmanship uses both. First, you arrange to take the control for punishment out of your hands so as to deny yourself the opportunity to redraw the line. Second, you transform the precipice into a slippery slope. With each step further down the slope there is the risk of losing control and falling into the abyss. In this way, an opponent who tries to avoid your threat through salami tactics finds himself constantly exposed to a small chance of disaster. Each slice he takes, no matter how small, *may* be the proverbial last straw. *The essential ingredient in making this type of threat credible is that neither you nor your rival knows just where the breaking point lies.* A small risk of disaster can have the same threat value as the certainty of a smaller punishment.[25] The United States has used the nuclear threat by creating a risk that the missiles will fly even though at that time the government will be trying as hard as it can to prevent the attack. The United States' threat would be carried out only in spite of itself. The threat of nuclear weaponry is that it will be used inadvertently. Nuclear deterrence becomes credible when there exists the possibility for any conventional conflict to escalate out of control. The threat is not a certainty but rather a probability of mutual destruction.

With any exercise of brinkmanship, there is always the danger of falling off the brink. While strategists look back at the Cuban missile crisis as a successful use of brinkmanship, our evaluation would be very different if the risk of a superpower war had turned into a reality.[26] The survivors would have cursed Kennedy for recklessly and unnecessarily flaming a crisis into a conflagration. Yet in an exercise of brinkmanship, the risk of falling off the brink will sometimes turn into a reality. The massacre of the Chinese students in June 1989 is a sad example. The students occupying Beijing's Tiananmen Square were on a collision course with the hard-liners in their government. One side would have to lose; either the hard-liners would cede power to more reform-minded leaders or the students would compromise on their demands. During the confrontation, there was a continual risk that the hard-liners would overreact and use force to squelch the democracy movement. When two sides are playing a game of brinkmanship and neither side is backing down, there is a chance that the situation will get out of control, with tragic consequences.

In the aftermath of Tiananmen Square, government leaders became more aware of the dangers in brinkmanship—for both sides. Faced with similar democracy protests in East Germany and Czechoslovakia, the communist leaders decided to give in to popular demands. In Romania, the government tried to hold firm against a reform movement, using violent repression to maintain power. The violence escalated almost to the level of a civil war, and in the end President Nicolae Ceausescu was executed for crimes against his people.

Brinkmanship involves a fundamental trade-off. There is a value in being able to make a credible threat. But there is a cost in leaving one's fate to chance. In the case of nuclear deterrence, this requires accepting some risk of mutual destruction. Much of the debate about nuclear deterrence centers on this risk. Is there anything that can be done to lower the probability of nuclear war without losing the value of deterrence?

The answer is yes, but only to a limited extent. The exercise of brinkmanship has a Modigliani-Miller-like neutrality; to achieve deterrence, the probability of a bad outcome must remain above some constant (see Nalebuff 1987). An analogy might prove helpful. Suppose we try to make dueling safer by reducing the accuracy of the pistols. The likely outcome is that the adversaries will come closer to one another before firing. Suppose that the adversaries are equally good shots, killing the other person earns the reward of 1, and being killed incurs the penalty of -1. Then the optimal strategy is for the two to keep on approaching each other, and fire the moment the probability of hitting reaches 1/2. The probability of a fatal hit is the same (3/4) irrespective of the accuracy of the pistols. A change in the rules need not affect the outcome; all the players can adjust their strategies to offset it. This conclusion does not mean we must be resigned to the risk of nuclear war. To reduce the risks, the problem must be attacked at a more fundamental level. The payoffs have to be changed. Were French and German aristocrats to have used less accurate dueling pistols, that would not have helped them to live longer. Rather, they would have to have changed the honor code that initiated a duel at the drop of a glove. As the United States and the Soviet Union begin to share the same objectives, that changes the game, not just the rules.

Moving in Steps

Although two parties may not trust each other when the stakes are large, if the problem of commitment can be reduced to a small-enough scale, then the issue of credibility will resolve itself. The threat or promise is broken up into many pieces, and each one is solved separately (see Schelling 1960, p. 45).

Honor among thieves is restored if they have to trust each other only a little bit at a time. Consider the difference between making a single $1 million payment to another person for a kilogram of cocaine and engaging in 1,000 sequential transactions with this other party, with each transaction limited to $1,000 worth of cocaine. While it might be worthwhile to double-cross your "partner" for $1 million, the gain of $1,000 is too small, since it brings a premature end to a profitable ongoing relationship.

Whenever a large degree of commitment is infeasible, one should make do with a small amount and reuse it frequently. Homeowners and contractors are mutually suspicious. The homeowner is afraid of paying up front and finding incomplete or shoddy work. The contractors are afraid that after they have completed the job, the homeowner may refuse to pay. So at the end of each day (or each week), contractors are paid on the basis of their progress. At most each side risks losing one day's (or one week's) work.

As with brinkmanship, moving in small steps reduces the size of the threat or promise and correspondingly the scale of commitment. There is just one feature to watch out for. Those who understand strategic thinking will reason forward and look backward, and they will worry about the last step. If you expect to be cheated on the last round, you should break off the relationship one round earlier. But then the penultimate round will become the final round, and so you will not have escaped the problem. To avoid the unraveling of trust, there should be no clear final step. As long as there remains a chance of continued business, it will never be worthwhile to cheat. So when a shady character tells you this will be his last deal before retiring, be especially cautious.

A second feature of reducing the size of commitment is that you can compare how you do with the likely performance of those who follow in your footsteps. If they are likely to do better, then there is an advantage in waiting, or at least moving in small steps. To put this in context, we look at the antitrust case of the *United States v. IBM*. One of the many issues involved IBM's policy of leasing rather than selling its mainframe computers.

The government argued that IBM's emphasis on short-term leases constituted an entry barrier resulting in monopoly profits. IBM defended the practice as being in consumers' interest. It argued that a short-term lease insulates customers from the risk of obsolescence, provides flexibility when needs change, commits IBM to maintain its leased equipment (since it is responsible for the operation of the leased computers), and provides financing from the company with the deepest pockets (see Fisher et al. 1983).

Many find these arguments a convincing defense. Yet there is an altogether different strategic advantage to leasing. Leasing allows IBM to credibly maintain high prices.

Even a company without an outside competitor must worry about competing with its future self. When a new computer is introduced, IBM can sell the first models at very high prices to customers impatiently awaiting the technological advance. Once the computers are available in large numbers, there is the temptation to lower the price and attract more customers. The main cost of producing the computer has already been incurred in the development stage. Each additional sale is gravy.

But if customers expect that IBM is about to lower its price, they will wait to make their purchase. When the majority of customers are waiting, IBM has an incentive to speed up its price reductions and capture the customers sooner. For *durable* goods, in effect, a monopolist competes with its future self in a way that makes the market competitive (see Coase 1972).

Leasing serves as a commitment device that enables IBM to keep prices high. The leasing contracts make it much more costly for IBM to lower its price. When its machines are on short-term leases, any price reduction must be passed along to *all* customers, not just the ones who haven't yet bought. The loss in revenue from the existing customer base may outweigh the increase in new leases. In contrast, when the existing customer base owns its computers, this trade-off does not arise; the customers who already bought the computer at a high price are not eligible for refunds.

Thus leasing is an example of moving in small steps. The steps are the length of the lease. The shorter the lease, the smaller the step. Customers don't expect IBM to keep its price high when the steps are too big; they will wait for a price reduction and get the same machine a little later a lower price. But if IBM leases its computers only on short, renewable contracts, then it can credibly maintain high prices, customers have no reason to wait, and IBM earns higher profits.

College professors and authors encounter the same problem in the market for academic textbooks. If commitment were possible, publishers could make more money by bringing out new editions of a textbook on a five-year cycle, rather than the more common three-year cycle. Greater longevity would increase the text's value on the used-book market and consequently the student's initial willingness to pay when a new edition appears. The problem is that once the used books are out there, the publisher has a strong incentive to undercut this competition by bringing out a new edition. Because everyone expects this to happen, students get a lower price for their used books and thus are less willing to pay for the new editions. The solution for the publisher is the same as for IBM: rent books rather than sell them.

Teamwork

Often others can help us achieve credible commitment. Although people may be weak on their own, they can build resolve by forming a group. The successful use of peer pressure to achieve commitment has been made famous by Alcoholics Anonymous (and diet centers too). The AA approach changes the payoffs from breaking your word. It sets up a social institution in which pride and self-respect are lost when commitments are broken.

Sometimes teamwork goes far beyond social pressure and employs strong-arm tactics to force us to keep true to our promises. Consider the problem for the front line of an advancing army. If everyone else charges forward, one soldier who hangs back ever so slightly will increase his chance of survival without significantly lowering the probability that the attack will be successful. If every soldier thought the same way, however, the attack would become a retreat.

Of course it doesn't happen that way. A soldier is conditioned through honor to his country, loyalty to fellow soldiers, and belief in the million-dollar wound—an injury that is serious enough to send him home, out of action, but not so serious that he won't fully recover.[27] Those soldiers who lack the will and the courage to follow orders can be motivated by penalties for desertion. If the punishment for desertion is certain and ignominious death, the alternative of advancing forward becomes much more attractive. But soldiers are not interested in killing their fellow countrymen, even deserters. How can soldiers who have difficulty committing to attack the enemy make a credible commitment to killing their countrymen for desertion?

In ancient Rome, Schelling writes, falling behind in an attack was a capital offense. As the army advanced in a line, any soldier who saw the one next to him falling behind was ordered to kill the deserter immediately. To make this order credible, failing to kill a deserter was also a capital offense. Thus even though a soldier would rather get on with the battle than go back after a deserter, failing to do so could cost him his own life.[28]

The tactics of the Roman army live on today in the honor code required of students at West Point. Exams are not monitored, and cheating is an offense that leads to expulsion. But because students are not inclined to "rat" on their classmates, failure to report observed cheating is also a violation of the honor code. This violation also leads to expulsion. When the honor code is violated, students report crimes because they do not want to become guilty accomplices by their silence. Similarly, criminal law provides penalties for those who fail to report a crime as an accessory after the fact.

Mandated Negotiating Agents

If a worker says he cannot accept any wage increase less than 5 percent, why should the employer believe that he will not subsequently back down and accept 4 percent? Money on the table induces people to try negotiating one more time.

The worker's situation can be improved if he has someone else negotiate for him.[29] When the union leader is the negotiator, his position may be less flexible. He may be forced to keep his promise, or lose support from his electorate. The union leader may secure a restrictive mandate from his members, or put his prestige on the line by declaring his inflexible position in public. In effect, the labor leader becomes a mandated negotiating agent. His authority to act as a negotiator is based on his position. In some cases he simply does not have the authority to compromise; the workers, not the leader, must ratify the contract. In other cases, compromise by the leader would result in his removal.

In practice we are concerned with the means as well as the ends of achieving commitment. If the labor leader *voluntarily* commits his prestige to a certain position, should you (do you) treat his loss of face as you would if it were externally imposed? Someone who tries to stop a train by tying himself to the railroad tracks may get less sympathy than someone else who has been tied there against his will.

A second type of mandated negotiating agent is a machine. Very few people haggle with vending machines over the price; even fewer do so successfully.[30]

Conclusion

In describing the eightfold way to successful commitment, we have tried to bring together different elements and applications of strategic thinking. Sadly, there is no simple recipe for making strategies credible. The specifics of each situation are likely to differ in some significant aspects, and any general prescriptions for action could be misleading. In each situation, you will have to pull together principles of good strategy with other considerations. Where their dictates conflict with each other, you must evaluate the relative strengths of the different arguments.

We do not promise to solve every question you might have. The science of game theory is far from being complete, and in some ways strategic thinking remains an art. In that art, there is no greater influence than the vision provided by Thomas Schelling.

Notes

1. Schelling (1984, p. 63) calls this last topic "Strategic Egonomics," the strategy of consciously coping with one's own behavior.

2. *Bartlett's* (1968, p. 967).

3. Hammett 1983, p. 15.

4. Hobbes 1973, p. 71.

5. A *threat* is a response rule that punishes others who fail to cooperate with you—see Schelling 1960, pp. 35–36. A *promise* is an offer to reward someone who cooperates with you—see Schelling 1960, p. 43. The feature common to threats and promises is that the response rule commits you to an action that you would not take in its absence. If the rule merely says you will do what is best at the time, there might as well be no rule. There is no *change* in others' expectations about your future actions and hence no influence of the rule. Still, there is an informational role for stating what will happen without a rule; these statements are called *warnings* and *assurances*. These distinctions are introduced in chapter 5 of Schelling 1960.

6. John F. Kennedy speaking on July 25, 1961. The quote is taken from Ikle 1964, p. 67.

7. Even the Israelis have lost some of their reputation for toughness. Their willingness to swap 3,000 Arab prisoners for 3 of their air force pilots suggests that exceptions will sometimes be made.

8. *Wall Street Journal*, August 7, 1986.

9. Sadly, we must report that the Mayflower Furniture Company recently had its first sale, a going-out-of-business sale.

10. Schelling (1960, ch. 2) describes the enhanced credibility of a threat made by someone with bloodshot eyes.

11. *Wall Street Journal*, January 2, 1990, p. B1.

12. Even so, Mr. Russo might find it difficult to renegotiate with a large number of people simultaneously. If one person fails to agree, the renegotiation is held up. The idea of contracting with a large number of people in order to mitigate the renegotiation problem is suggested in Schelling 1960, p. 25.

13. On the other hand, among college professors there is a saying, "A handshake is good enough between businessmen. But when your university's dean promises you something, get it in writing."

14. Prescott 1896, ch. 8.

15. Prescott 1896.

16. Although the Trojans may have gotten it backward, the Greeks were ahead of the game. Schelling cites the Greek general Xenophon as an early example of this type of strategic thinking. Although Xenophon did not literally burn his bridges behind him, he did write about the advantages of fighting with one's back against an impassable ravine; see Schelling 1966, pp. 43–45 and Schelling 1984, pp. 195–212.

17. This interpretation and further mathematical analysis of strategic commitment may be found in Bulow et al. 1985.

18. This description and quote come from Porter 1983.

19. Not only did Kodak lose its share of the instant film market, it also lost all profits from the prior sales of Kodak instant cameras. Kodak provided rebates to all its customers who were stuck with its obsolete cameras.

20. Apparently, Khrushchev attempted to use this strategy, threatening that the Soviet rockets would fly *automatically* in the event of armed conflict in Berlin; see Schelling 1966, p. 39.

21. Schelling more or less invented this concept, and certainly pioneered its analysis. This section owes more than we can say to his books, *The Strategy of Conflict* (chs. 7, 8) and *Arms and Influence* (ch. 3). Many people erroneously say "brinkmanship"—which suggests the art of robbing an armored truck.

22. Hammett 1983, p. 169.

23. This can also be viewed as the strategic rationality of being irrational.

24. Such a hypothetical scenario was painted in an episode of the British television comedy series "Yes, Prime Minister."

25. Just how does one go about generating a threat that involves a risk? For example, suppose that during the Cuban missile crisis, one in six is the right risk of war for Kennedy to threaten. Then he might tell Khrushchev that

unless the missiles were out of Cuba by Monday, he would roll a die and if six came up, he would order the U.S. missiles to be launched. Quite apart from the horror this picture conjures up, it just won't work. If Khrushchev refuses to comply, and Kennedy rolls the die and six comes up, the actual decision is still in Kennedy's hands. He still has the powerful urge to give Khrushchev just one more roll of the die ("let's make it a two out three") before Armageddon. Khrushchev knows this, and knows that Kennedy knows that, too. The credibility of the threat collapses just as surely as if the elaborate mechanism of rolling the die had never been mentioned. An essential insight is that when a sharp precipice is replaced by a slippery slope, even Kennedy does not know where safety lies. It is as if he is playing nuclear Russian roulette instead of rolling a die. One number leads to disaster but he does not know which one that is. If the number comes up, he cannot change his mind and roll again.

26. During the Cuban missile crisis, Kennedy estimated the odds at between one out of three and even; see Allison 1971.

27. For a fascinating account of incentives used to motivate soldiers, see Keegan 1976.

28. The motive for punishing deserters is made even stronger if the deserter is given clemency for killing those in line next to him who fail to punish him. Thus if a soldier fails to kill a deserter, there are now two people who can punish: his neighbor and the deserter, who could save his own life by punishing those who failed to punish him.

29. The advantages of delegating authority when bargaining are described in Schelling 1960, p. 27.

30. According to the U.S. Defense Department, over a five-year period, seven servicemen or dependents were killed and thirty-nine injured by soft-drink machines that toppled over while being rocked in an attempt to dislodge beverages or change (*International Herald Tribune*, June 15, 1988).

References

Allison, Graham. 1971. *Essence of Decision: Explaining the Cuban Missile Crisis*, Boston: Little Brown & Co.

Bartlett's Familiar Quotations. 1968. Boston: Little, Brown & Co.

Bulow, Jeremy, John Geanakoplos, and Paul Klemperer. 1985. "Multi-market Oligopoly: Strategic Substitutes and Complements," *Journal of Political Economy*, 93: 488–511.

Coase, Ronald. 1972. "Durability and Monopoly," *Journal of Law and Economics*, 15, April.

Fisher, Franklin M., John McGowan, and Joen Greenwood. 1983. *Folded, Spindled, and Mutilated*, Cambridge, MA: MIT Press.

Hammett, Dashiell. 1983. *The Maltese Falcon*, San Francisco: Pan Books, Ario Press.

Hobbes, Thomas. 1973. *Leviathan*, London: J. M. Dent & Sons.

Ikle, Fred. 1964. *How Nations Negotiate*, New York: Harper and Row.

Keegan, John. 1976. *The Face of Battle*, New York: Viking Press.

Nalebuff, Barry. 1987. "Brinkmanship and Nuclear Deterrence: The Neutrality of Escalation," *Conflict Management and Peace Science*, 9, Spring: 19–30.

Porter, Michael. 1983. *Cases in Competitive Strategy*, New York: Free Press.

Prescott, William. 1896. *The History of the Conquest of Mexico*, vol. 1, London: Gibbings and Co.

Schelling, Thomas. 1960. *The Strategy of Conflict*, Cambridge, MA: Harvard University Press.

Schelling, Thomas. 1966. *Arms and Influence*, New Haven, CT: Yale University Press.

Schelling, Thomas. 1984. *Choice and Consequence*, Cambridge, MA: Harvard University Press.

Schelling, Thomas. 1989. "Strategy and Self-Command," *Negotiation Journal*, vol. 5, no. 4, October: 343–347.

Twain, Mark. 1980. *Pudd'nhead Wilson's Calendar*, New York: W. W. Norton.

8   Trusting Persons, Trusting Institutions

Russell Hardin

In *The Brothers Karamazov*, Dmitry Karamazov tells the story of a lieutenant colonel who managed substantial sums on behalf of the army. Immediately after each periodic audit of his books, he took the available funds to the merchant Trifonov, who soon returned them with interest and a gift. In effect, both the lieutenant colonel and Trifonov benefited from funds that would otherwise have lain idle, producing no benefit for anyone. Because it was highly irregular, theirs was a secret exchange that depended wholly on personal trust not backed by the law of contracts. When the day came that the lieutenant colonel was to be abruptly replaced in his command, he asked Trifonov to return the last sum, 4,500 rubles, entrusted to him.

Trifonov replied, "I've never received any money from you, and couldn't possibly have received any" (Dostoyevsky 1982/1880, p. 129).[1]

Dmitry Karamazov says that the lieutenant colonel implicitly trusted Trifonov. After his sad day of reckoning, the lieutenant colonel would presumably have said that Trifonov was not trustworthy. Unfortunately, Trifonov was trustworthy just so long as there was some longer-run incentive for him to be reliable in their mutually beneficial relationship. The moment there ceased to be any expectation of further gains from his relationship with the lieutenant colonel, Trifonov had no incentive to be trustworthy and, not surprisingly, he ceased to be. The lieutenant colonel might have thought Trifonov to be a man of honor who was, in that sense, trustworthy. If so, then, he clearly misjudged his man.

Had his dealings with Trifonov been reputable, the lieutenant colonel could have been protected by a contract that gave both parties

---

the right to be sued. "Who wants to be sued?" Thomas Schelling asks. Well, he notes in answer to his own question, "The right to be sued is the power to make a promise: to borrow money, to enter a contract, to do business with someone who might be damaged. If suit does arise, the 'right' seems a liability in retrospect; beforehand it was a prerequisite to doing business" (Schelling 1960, p. 43). The odd right to be sued is the "power to accept a commitment." It enables one to establish a strong commitment to fulfilling one's half of a bargain. Trifonov had no right to be sued by the lieutenant colonel, who, indeed, could not even publicly accuse him. And therefore Trifonov could be assumed to have only a commitment to gain as much as he could from his dealings with the officer. That is all that the lieutenant colonel should have trusted Trifonov to do.

Writings on trust often take the view that it involves something beyond merely reasonable expectations based in self-interest. Many philosophers suppose we should distinguish our trust of another individual from our expectations about that individual's behavior in particular respects (Baier 1986; Hertzberg 1988). Many writers also suppose that trust is an inherently normative notion (Elster 1979, p. 146). We can make some sense of such claims by supposing that they are really misplaced claims about trustworthiness rather than about trust. You might be trustworthy in the very strong sense that you would reciprocate even when it was against your interest to do so, as Trifonov might have returned the final 4,500 rubles.

Even then, my trust of you must be grounded in expectations that are particular to you, not merely in generalized expectations. If I always trust everyone, then I do not meaningfully trust anyone. Trust is therefore in part inherently a rational or intentional commitment or judgment. My expectations about your behavior may be grounded in my belief in your morality or fairness or, most commonly, self-interest. With no prior knowledge of you, I may initially treat you as though I trust you, but our relationship can eventually be one of trust only if there are expectations that ground the trust. As Karamazov's lieutenant colonel learned, inductively grounded expectations cannot be reliable for new contexts.

If the vague sense that trust requires more than rational expectations—expectations grounded in the plausible motivations of the trusted—is correct, then we are at a very early stage in the development of any theory to account for trust or even to characterize it. If the residual self-interest notion is largely correct, however, we already have the elements of a full-blown theory of trust that merely wants careful articulation and application. I will give an account of trust as essentially rational expectations about the—mostly—self-interested behavior of the trusted. The effort to construct such an account forces attention to varieties of interaction in which trust might arise and, hence, to differences in the plausible explanations of trust. The sense that trust requires more than reliance on the self-interest of the trusted may depend largely on particular kinds of interaction that, while interesting and even important, are not those of greatest interest in social theory.

I will present an account of trust as encapsulated interest, an account in which the truster's expectations of the trusted's behavior depend on rational assessments of the trusted's motivations. I will then argue that certain alternative, strongly-argued individual-level accounts of trust are implausible. Then I will turn to generalizations to trusting large numbers or institutions.

Trust as Encapsulated Interest

If Karamazov's lieutenant colonel had—anachronistically—read recent game theory, he might have concluded that it was irrational to cooperate with Trifonov in the first place. Their interaction was de facto a finitely iterated prisoner's dilemma. The usual argument against cooperating in such a game begins with the premise that one should treat the final play of a finite series of plays of the game as a one-shot game, in which one should defect. But if one should defect on the final play, then the penultimate play is de facto a final play in the sense that it can have no effect on anything thereafter, and so one should defect on the penultimate play as well. By tedious induction backward, one should defect already on the first play in the series.

If the backward induction argument is compelling, it is hard to see how rational individuals could ever enter into normal relationships of trust and exchange. All such relationships would have to be grounded in something extrarational, perhaps in normative commitments to be more decent than is rational. That there is apparently a great deal of trust in our lives then suggests that we are not rational. I think, on the contrary, that trust is eminently rational and that the backward induction argument is flawed. In brief, the flaw is this. Suppose I know that you are eminently rational and that you believe the backward induction argument. I also know that we could gain substantially from entering a series of exchanges that must terminate, perhaps unhappily, at some distant future point. I can now wreck your backward induction by simply cooperating at our first encounter. You may now suppose I am irrational, or you may reconsider your induction. Either way, you may now decide it is in your interest to reciprocate my cooperation, so that we both benefit far beyond what we would have got from continuous mutual defection. (I think you must reconsider your induction because, if I can get you to cooperate by acting cooperatively, you could do as well with others. That is to say, you must agree that it would be rational for *you* to cooperate initially rather than to defect.)[2]

Moreover, and more to the point here, if you think cooperation in finitely iterated prisoner's dilemma interactions is irrational, you must wonder at your own tendency initially to trust those whom you do not yet know well. All our relationships with people are of ill-defined but necessarily finite duration. The backward induction argument recommends initial distrust and, further, continued distrust. This is surely a recommendation for slow death by abnegation. Whatever the apparent force of the backward induction argument for rarefied game theorists, it appears that actual people in going societies regularly take the risk of initially cooperating to upset that argument. Only for that reason do we have going societies.

Various social scientific accounts of trust take for granted that trust is rational in the sense of being based on empirically grounded expectations of another person's (or an institution's) behavior (Barber 1983; Luhmann 1980). In effect, we do a reasonable job of reading tendencies and trends, such as those exhibited by a stock market or a large crowd of people such as doctors or politicians. Those who see trust as normative or otherwise extrarational argue that it is more richly a two-part relation than this view implies. Trust involves intentional or motivational moves by the trusted as well as by the truster. A rational analysis of trust of another intentional being, as opposed to trust of a force of nature (our trust in the sun's rising tomorrow), must attend to the rationality of both intentional parties. In this sense, sociological expectation accounts are only half-rational and they therefore fail to address the apparent concern of many moral philosophers. They have a liability not unlike that of the similarly half-rational Cournot theory of market behavior. A Cournot actor assumes regularity of behavior on the part of others in the market, but fails to take account of second-order effects of others' responses to his or her own actions.

A fully rational analysis of trust would not depend solely on the rational expectations of the truster, but also on the commitments, not merely the regularity, of the trusted. How can one secure commitments from someone whose love or benevolence does not guarantee good will toward oneself? The most common way is to structure incentives to match the desired commitment. You can more confidently trust me if you know that my own interest will induce me to live up to your expectations. Your trust then encapsulates my interest; it is a two-part intentional relation. On this view, as Schelling notes, "Trust is often achieved simply by the continuity of the relation between parties and the recognition by each that what he might gain by cheating in a given instance is outweighed by the value of the tradition of trust that makes possible a long sequence of future agreement" (Schelling 1960, pp. 134–135).

Several types of behavior often explained as moral can be clearly understood as self-interested. Promise keeping, honesty, and fidelity to others often make sense without any presupposition of a distinctively moral commitment beyond interest. Consider promise keeping, which has been the subject of hundreds of articles and books in moral theory during this century.[3] Hume says, without seeming to think the statement requires much defense, that the first obligation to keep a promise is interest (Hume 1978/1739–40, p. 523). The claim is obviously true for promises between close associates who have an ongoing relationship that they want to maintain. If I promise to return your book, I'll be encouraged to do so by frequent contact with you and frequent desire to make other exchanges with you. If I generally fail to keep such promises, I can probably expect not to enjoy as many exchanges and favors. Promising relationships typically are those in which exchanges are reciprocated over time. Because exchanges are resolutions of prisoner's dilemma problems (Hardin 1982a), promising relationships have the incentive structure of iterated plays of the prisoner' dilemma.

It is sometimes supposed, on the contrary, that promising is typically used to regulate relations with strangers.[4] Unless my worldly experience is extraordinary, this view is prima facie false. Promises to genuine strangers are rare, not least perhaps because they would not be trusted.[5] Schelling canvasses peculiar devices for securing compliance with promises in such difficult contexts as those between strangers (Schelling 1989). Establishing trust in such contexts requires strong measures, such as subjecting oneself to risk of real, often unrelated, harm if one fails to comply with one's promise. When we have to trust strangers in important matters, we commonly prefer to bind them through contracts under law.

The force that generally backs promises is the loss of credibility that follows from breaking one's promises.[6] Without credibility, one loses the possibility of making promises. This sounds suspiciously similar to Schelling's right to be sued. Why should anyone want the power to make promises? All I really want in my own interest is the power to receive them. And there's the rub, because promises are generally reciprocal. The real penalty here, as in Schelling's case if there were no right to be sued, is not that others will no longer rely on me, but that they won't let me rely on them (D. Locke 1986, p. 574). As is trust, promising is typically a two-part intentional relation.

Trust and promises are morally kin, just as much of the vocabulary of the two is cognate in its etymology. As with promising, future expectations, generally based in ongoing experience, contribute much of the force that binds in a trusting relationship. Trifonov and the lieutenant colonel could trust one another while future expectations of their relationship were motivating. Reputational effects, which can often put dishonest merchants out of business, were of no use to the lieutenant colonel because he himself could not afford to go public.

As this example illustrates, trust does not merely apply to another person but to another person under certain conditions. The particularity of many claims of trust can be explained by the particularity of interests at stake. I once had an acquaintance of whom many people said, with genuine force, that he was a person you could trust. Alas, that depended on who "you" were. Many people did not trust him at all because they thought him deceitful and manipulative. The latter group included people whose interests often conflicted with his and whose future value to him he had seemingly written off. He could be richly and deeply trusted by those who shared enough of his interests, not at all by those who did not. He was almost mythical in his capacity to put people into two distinct classes. Most of us are not mythical, but we can still make distinctions. Without a legally binding contract I might readily trust you to return the $10 I lend you for lunch, but quail at the thought of trusting you with $10,000—let alone 4,500 rubles that are not mine anyway.[7] In *Anna Karenina*, Count Vronsky's code of social rules was probably well understood by all concerned, who therefore had differential grounds for trust and distrust. As Tolstoy puts it, "The code categorically determined that though the card-sharper must be paid, the tailor need not be; that one may not lie to a man, but might to a woman; that one must not deceive anyone, except a husband; that one must not forgive an insult but may insult others, and so on" (Tolstoy 1949/1875–77, book I, p. 347). Karenin therefore could trust Vronsky with a gambling debt—but not with his wife.

Many of the things that one could trust Vronsky to do are different from the kind of sequential exchanges that can be modeled by the iterated prisoner's dilemma. Someone's trust in him would be a two-part intentional relation, because it would depend on Vronsky's intentional and arguably rational commitments. (They are simply rational if Vronsky adheres to the code just in case it fits his interests to do so. In choosing among debts to pay, he pays his fellow noble gambler, who could harm him socially or otherwise, rather than his tailor, who can only hassle him and refuse him further service.) Similarly, I can trust you to do what is in my interest in certain contexts because your doing so will fulfill some interest of your own. You need not necessarily give me something in return for something I give you. But the strategic relationship may be essentially the same as that for direct exchange. When I trust a political official who may be held at least somewhat accountable for failing to fulfill my interests, we are related in our intentions, though we may never meet.

Let us push the encapsulated interest view to the extreme. In Shizuko Go's *Requiem*, a painfully beautiful novel about the destruction of a vast web of social relationships through wartime deaths in the last months of World War II in Japan, the heroine Setsuko recalls "the familiar precept of perfect hospitality: 'We meet but once'" (Go 1985, p. 107).[8] There is strategic subtlety in this bit of popular wisdom. If I know we meet but once, my hospitality is not my half of a two-part relationship, not an initial move in a potential trust or exchange relationship. It does not encapsulate your interest in reciprocity over the long run. It is purely a gift or an expression of my hospitable character.

In Setsuko's case, the hospitable older woman whom she meets but once has a son whom Setsuko wishes to visit. Because the woman loves her son and wishes him well, interest should incline her to be nice to Setsuko on her singular visit. At the same time, independently of her interest, she may also be normatively motivated to kindness.

One could construct arguments for the rationality of developing strong normative commitments: for example, following a norm saves on decision costs in many contexts. But in many cases the behavior may simply be normative outright. Setsuko's older woman has been taught to be kind in certain circumstances of hospitality, and she might behave that way more or less independently of broad incentives to vary her degree of kindness. She has simply made a virtue of hospitality. She might also have made a virtue of trusting people. In both cases, she would presumably conclude that particular people whom she has tried and found repeatedly wanting are not worthy of hospitality or trust. Still, her initial stance is one of virtue rather than of calculated self-interest.

There are other possibilities. You might extend hospitality or trust in order to demonstrate to me that you have faith in my morality or character, to give me an opportunity to live up to your hopes even though I may have no incentive to reciprocate your action.[9] Or you may not wish to be the kind of person who acts toward another with distrust that is not based on solid evidence. Such motivations are apt to lead to disappointment in many contexts, but they might be statistically justified in certain milieus. In particular, they might be justified in contexts in which there are rich possibilities of further interactions. In such contexts, however, interest is likely to conspire with your hopes in getting me to reciprocate.

Trust as Ungrounded Faith or Belief

A common dictionary definition of trust reflects the sense that it is somehow more than mere expectations.[10] As *Webster's New World Dictionary* (1980, p. 1201, under "rely") puts it, "to *trust* is to have complete faith or assurance that one will not be let down by another [to *trust* in God]."[11] Abraham evidently had such complete faith in God as to be willing to sacrifice his beloved son merely on God's order. But apart from such trust in God, which may amount to a blanket acceptance that whatever God causes to happen must be for the best, it is hard to imagine anyone reasonably asserting "complete" faith in anyone.

Consider the infant who is not yet able to trust or to distrust, who depends on the actions of parents and others, and who merely accepts those actions. From this early relation "there gradually evolve attitudes which may be called trustful" (Hertzberg 1988, p. 316). Or, if that early relation is very bad or capricious, the child may develop an utter incapacity to trust. Because there is no question of choice in the matter, it is not sensible to say that the infant trusts its parents. Indeed, it may not be sensible to say that Abraham trusts God, given his beliefs. He might have failed to follow God's orders because of weakness of will or he might have revised his view of the goodness of God and the rightness of following his orders. But if Abraham could not revise his beliefs, then there was no question of choice for him any more than if his son had been taken from him by disease.

Given the way in which trust seemingly develops from infancy, one might suppose that trust "is not based on grounds" (Hertzberg 1988, p. 318). The older woman whose kindness impressed Setsuko seems to have been normatively motivated. If so, then her kindness to Setsuko was not necessarily based on grounds. But then it would be odd to say of the particular people to whom she was gracious that she trusted them to reciprocate. Her graciousness was almost entirely an expression of herself, without objective correlates, not specifically directed at particular people. If trust is selectively directed at only certain other people, but not based on grounds, then it must be capricious—unrelated to its objects and not a consistent expression of character. Such trust seems neither sensible nor meritorious.

The philosopher Annette Baier writes, "What is the difference between trusting others and merely relying on them? It seems to be reliance on their good will toward one, as distinct from their dependable habits, or only on their dependably exhibited fear, anger, or other motives compatible with ill will toward one, or on motives not directed on one at all" (Baier 1986, p. 234). Is there really a difference here? I rely on *you*, not just on anyone, because the experience that justifies reliance is my experience of you, not of everyone. Moreover, I can see you having good will toward me because it is generally in your interest to do so and against your interest to have ill will toward me. Perhaps you are an official in some organization or you have an ongoing relationship with me, either directly or indirectly through others. You benefit from that role or that relationship and you will want to maintain it through appropriate good will toward me. Your good will is probably quite restricted—there are many things you could not be expected to do on my behalf. My trust in you will probably also be restricted.

In some cases, you may have good reason to believe that someone loves you or has strong altruistic motivations toward you or people like you. Your trust still turns on a rational reading of that person's intentions. Trust does not depend on any particular reason for the trusted's intentions, merely on credible reasons. In fact, many of our trusting relationships, especially those of early life, are grounded in the love or altruism of others. That may be one reason why we associate moral qualities with trust.

On Baier's account, trust is an extension of the infant's relation to its parent, especially its mother. Yet, she notes, a "constraint on an account of trust which postulates infant trust as its essential seed is that it not make essential to trusting the use of concepts or abilities which a child cannot be reasonably believed to possess" (Baier 1986, p. 244). If this is so, then the encapsulated interest view of trust is inherently wrong because assessments of trustworthiness could only be based on instinctive, behavioral learning. They could not require straightforward rational accounting such as we indulge regularly when, for example, we revise a prior supposition and decide someone is, after all, not trustworthy. On the infant view, trust is a primitive and somewhat ineffable condition in which we sometimes find ourselves. Such trust cannot very well apply to people whom we know almost entirely through intellectual apprehension; yet people say they trust public figures, merely on the basis of what they have read about them. There surely is some element of the primitive and ineffable in many of our commitments, perhaps especially in the forms they can take. In particular, our capacity for trust must build in part on evolved instincts. But our trust itself is not necessarily as primitive as the "innate readiness of infants to initially impute goodwill to the powerful persons on whom they depend" (Baier 1986, p. 242). That readiness may be a necessary or at least important foundation on which the capacity for trust may be built.

Consider an adult instance of Baier's kind of trust. In Wagner's opera *Lohengrin*, Lohengrin is an utterly incredible, godlike figure who demands of Elsa that she trust him without doubt or query or all is lost. Elsa is a true Wagnerian heroine, prepared to submit to and adore her hero as her lord. She wants not only to trust him, but to marry him, so beautiful a person does he seem to be. By refusing to tell her why she should trust him, Lohengrin puts her in the relation of an infant to her all-powerful parent with no choice but to accept or perish. Elsa's fundamental problem is that she has no good way to explain Lohengrin's existence and powers. He has come from nowhere, no one has ever heard of him. The nearest theory available to

Elsa for understanding him is sorcery. That theory would make Lohengrin evil, not good. Given her understanding of the world, it would be stupid of her to trust him merely on his demand. In the end, it is hard for us mortals to avoid thinking of him as inhumane and partly evil in his supreme goodness. The view of trust that Lohengrin imposes is repulsive.

An account of the life of the infant and its necessary dependency might seem cogent as an account of how we come psychologically to be able to trust or to know. But that is not an account of what trust is or of how it works. It is not only preadult, it is prehuman. It is plausibly the way an infant bird works, turning a wide-open mouth to the sky with an instinct behaviorally equivalent to trust that good things will fall into it. Such instinctual considerations are arguably a compelling part of an account of knowledge, including knowledge that backs up trust, knowledge of the reliability of any particular other and of others in general. That kind of knowledge is inherently inductive, and one might suppose it wise to be skeptical of inductive knowledge until the run is fairly long. But our normal proclivities may be to make an optimistic assessment of a short but so-far positive inductive run. If we live in a culture in which that optimism typically is justified by longer-run experience, we have rich relationships from trusting others. Still, the act of trusting, though it may more nearly befall us than be chosen by us, is one that depends on objective data and is subject to correction if the data recommend.

The most significant sense in which trust may go beyond justified expectations is that many of us—more, no doubt, in some societies than in others—face a new case with optimism, with tentative trust. But we are not wildly irrational in our optimism, and we will withdraw our tentative trust if it proves to have been unwarranted. This is a minimally rational constraint on trust: One will not continue to trust another who repeatedly fails the trust. Moreover, we may be more optimistic toward new cases in richly structured than in anomic contexts. An account of the life of the infant child and its inherent dependency suggests the plausibility of evolutionary selection for openness that enables us later to be tentatively trusting.

Howard Margolis notes the social nature of most knowledge, a thesis that is well developed by Wittgenstein. "By and large the easiest and even the most reliable reason for believing X is to be aware that everyone else believes X" (Margolis 1987, p. 135). Trust in the knowledge of others may well have been a trait favored by natural selection in earlier times. And it must be reinforced for us by the way in which we are educated to understand our world. As children we had little alternative to following advice that could not be grounded in anything other than authority, and we were often rewarded by success when we followed it. For these and other reasons, as Margolis (1987, p. 45) notes, cognition is "intrinsically 'a-logical.'" We build our cognitions from patterns and from society, and in many cases we could no more justify them than we could prove basic laws of physics.

Trust as Inherently Moral

Trust is clearly a two-part relationship, although there is disagreement on what the parts are. On the encapsulated interest account, if I trust you, I have certain expectations about your behavior under various contingencies. Presumably those expectations are grounded in your behavior or apparent commitments. This notion can be augmented in at least two ways. First, my trust may be something about my character well beyond mere expectations of your contingent behavior. This appears to be Baier's view (Baier 1986). Second, some discussions of trust treat it, explicitly or implicitly, as an essentially normative concept. If you do not live up to my trust, I may conclude that you have violated my expectations in a way that merits moral censure, as though you were obligated by my trust or by whatever gave rise to it.

In many of our relationships, trust is perhaps a bit like altruism. I trust you more than can be enforced by withdrawing from future interactions with you, a weak sanction. My trust is virtually a gift. Or, better, it is a gamble. You may live up to my trust, and we may then go on to have a strong and mutually rewarding relationship. But you may also turn out to be a Trifonov who will turn on me when the moment for gain is ripe. One might go further, as Jon Elster does, to say that "Altruism, trust and solidarity are genuine phenomena that cannot be dissolved into ultra-subtle forms of self-interest" (Elster 1979, p. 146). This clearly makes sense for altruism because I can genuinely have your interests at heart independently of any causal connection back to my own interests. Most of us are probably altruistic to some extent, even if not to a very great extent. But it is not clear what is analogous about trust in Elster's view.[12] Many writers and perhaps most people in ordinary life seem, with Elster, to have some vague sense of a distinctively moral character to trust. But, in contrast to the case of altruism, it does not make sense to cut trust free of mooring in expectations and, hence, at least potentially, in interests. We cannot cut it free because our expectations will be grounded in factual assessments of the motivations of anyone we might trust, among the most important of which must be interests.

Of course, ascriptions of trust may be normatively loaded in some ways, just as expectations and other interpersonal terms may be. For trust to have normative bite, however, it must entail some degree of obligation. That is, it must depend on something specifically relational as, for example, a contract does. The trusted must do something that morally motivates the claim of obligation. I trust you because we have some kind of relationship or because, at least, you typically have some kind of relationship toward those in a relevant class. For example, I trust you because we have been through a lot together, or because you are a police officer and I am a citizen. Our ongoing relationship or our role relationship may generate mutually reinforcing expectations that each of us sees as obligating to some extent and that each of us may have reason to think the other sees as obligating.

"When someone's trust has been misplaced," the philosopher Lars Hertzberg writes, "it is always, I want to say, a misunderstanding to regard that as a shortcoming on *his* part. The responsibility rests with the person who failed the trust." He goes on to say that, "unlike reliance, the grammar of trust involves a perspective of justice: trust can only concern that which one person can rightfully demand of another" (Hertzberg 1988, p. 319; Hertzberg's emphasis).[13] On this view, I can only "trust" someone to do what that person already has a moral obligation to do. This is a definitional move that, if accepted, makes unnecessary Hertzberg's several pages of argument while raising many ancillary questions. On whose moral theory do I ground your obligation, one might wonder, yours or my own? Hertzberg's redefinition also makes "trust" a nearly otiose category.

Perhaps we could rescue the sense that trust is inherently moral by reserving the term "trustworthiness" for those whose reciprocity is motivated by character or morality rather than by interest. One might then suppose it plausible to speak of *trust* only in cases of trustworthiness and to speak of *reliance* when reciprocity is grounded in interest. Unfortunately, this restriction would imply that we generally cannot be sure whether we trust or merely rely because the data on another's character, morals, and interests are likely to be confounded. Among close associates, indeed, the bulk of the data are likely to be the same. But it would be absurd for the lieutenant colonel to say he only thought he trusted Trifonov, that he now realized he had not trusted him at all. He *had* trusted him, and therefore he had been swindled by him.

When our trust proves to be misplaced, we are likely to say, "But I trusted her." Indeed, we are likely to say this in many contexts in which we could not truthfully say, "But she gave me a commitment." Our trust depends on actions of the other but it is commonly not authorized by those actions, as it might be in the case of a contract or promise. In its common understanding, therefore, trust is not essentially normative, it does not imply an obligation on the part of the trusted, who may not even be aware of the trust placed in her. Hertzberg seemingly moralizes the notion of trust by simply defining it as coupled with assumed obligations. His concept of trust may still be a two-part relation, but it is a very one-sided relation with all of the burden on the trusted.

Unless one makes something like the definitional move that rules out the application of trust to any cases but those of moral obligation, it does not seem likely that trust can be moralized. It is an attitude that can be grounded in moral obligations, as public officials may be regarded as morally obligated to behave in certain ways toward their constituents. But it need not be. And it can be grounded in expectations about the moral commitments of others. But, again, it need not be.

In this respect trust is clearly different from promising and many other moralized notions. We may say that someone who makes a promise is obligated by it. This is merely a conventional, not a logical claim. There is a long tradition of claiming that to break a promise is to be logically self-contradictory.[14] To make a promise is to proclaim an obligation; to break it is to prove that proclamation false. In more recent writings, the logical entailment of an obligation to keep a promise is tricked up out of the meaning of the ordinary words 'I promise,' which are taken to entail fulfillment. If we reject such an analysis, we may still suppose that competent people who make promises thereby assume some obligation, which, however, may fall short of actually requiring them to keep all their promises. But with trust we cannot even formulate an analogue of either the conventional or the logical account of an obligation. It is I who promise and who thereby assume an obligation. But if it is I who trust, it is the trusted who would have to be burdened with an obligation.

The Social Grounding of Trust

Those who use the term "trust" readily apply it to institutions and institutional actors, such as banks, nations, and political leaders. Many plausible psychological and normative accounts of individual behavior may be hard to generalize to apply to institutional behavior. A theory of trust that does not generalize to institutions is of limited interest in political theory and international relations. As observers of politics we often speak in analogies that may be fallacies of composition. For example, we may try to explain peaceful Anglo-American relations by saying England and the United States trust each other.

If our notion of trust comes from understandings of individual behavior and character, the term may be entirely out of place in application to a nation, group, or institution. There may be ways to interpret the notion to apply it to such actors, but it is not likely to be prima facie applicable without interpretation. It is now a commonplace understanding that interest does not readily generalize from individual to group or national levels. It should not surprise us to find that trust, which is commonly at issue just because interests are at stake, does not readily generalize either. Nevertheless, the encapsulated interest conception of trust can be generalized to fit institutions.

Advocates of moralized conceptions of trust at the individual-level argue that trust is inherently a two-part relation, that it is not merely rational expectations about the behavior of others. Sociological accounts of trust, such as that of Bernard Barber (1983), seem, however, to account for trust as simple expectation grounded in large-number regularities. Barber's interest in trust grows in large part out of his more general concern with the role of professionalism in our lives. We cannot know enough to judge the competence of the professionals who serve us; therefore, we must essentially trust them to some extent. Niklas Luhmann (1980) focuses on our need to trust (that is, to have stable expectations about) large institutional aspects of life, such as the stability of our currency or the reliability of our political leaders during crises that could lead to foolish war.

On these accounts, large-number stability in the behavior of relevant others or other types can be a reason for expecting more of the same behavior. Large-number regularities can play a stronger role: They can affect one's incentive to act as others do. My expectations of your behavior may turn in large part on my expectations of behavior of people like yourself in our society. For example, consider marital fidelity. I might suppose that the best norm for marriage is to be utterly faithful until death do us part. If all followed that norm, I might firmly believe, ours would be a better world. Suppose the woman I wish to marry believes the same. We therefore publicly vow to be faithful forever. Should we believe each other? Perhaps. But only in the sense that we really are committed *at this moment*. Whether we will still be committed in a few years may depend very much on the laws and norms of our society.

In Verdi's *La Traviata*, Germont wishes to discourage the former courtesan Violetta from continuing her life with his son, Alfredo. Violetta says that, alas, she can love no one but Alfredo. Changing his tack, Germont points out that "men are often fickle." Violetta involuntarily says, "Oh God," and Germont, given the opening, demolishes her hope. He sings:

> One day, when time has dispelled
> the charms of love,
> tedium will set in quickly.
> What happens then? Think—
> The deepest feelings
> can bring you no balm,
> *since heaven has not blessed*
> *this union.* (Verdi 1946/1853, Act 2, Scene 1, p. 9)

The blessing of heaven was, of course, to be secured from earthly institutions that would then protect Violetta's claims on Alfredo by, at the very least, making it illegal for him to marry anyone else. Like Schelling's contractor, Violetta understood that restricting one's freedom might be necessary to securing desirable ends. Of course, as with Schelling's contractor, her greater concern was to restrict someone else's freedom to secure desirable ends.

Recall also Vronsky's code of ethics. Given the prevalence of this code among his class, Vronsky was virtually incapable of convincing anyone he would behave otherwise toward anyone's beautiful wife than he behaved toward Karenin's Anna. In this respect, trust, like expectations and knowledge, is in part inherently a social construction. Even if they were trustworthy, Vronsky and Alfredo would have no way to convince others.

If divorce is impossible and infidelity is severely sanctioned, we who wish to swear fidelity until death may find it quite easy to trust one another. If infidelity and opportunities for it are rampant, however, we may be unable to trust one another with anything short of an act of faith. In many contexts your capacity to make a commitment about how you will behave depends on the normal expectations of behavior. You cannot easily establish a commitment to a much more demanding standard of behavior. Genuinely normative commitments may depend on or interact with incentive structures.

Society offers two general categories of controls to individuals who can benefit from constraining themselves. There are the elaborate, large-scale controls of the law in a relatively extensive society. And there are the particular, small-scale controls of ongoing relationships of family, friends, and what we might crudely call geographical associates—those with whom we will almost inescapably be thrown into further dealings. Between these two categories there are institutionalized religious controls that blend elements of both. Where social controls fail we are left with our own personal devices of internal motivations.

One of the best and most useful of internal motivations is interest, which leads us to and through much of the best that life has to offer. To suppress interest, so that it does not lead us in ways we might consider wrong, is to put ourselves at war with ourselves. In waging that war we are supported by social controls based in our own longer-term interest. A strong network of laws and conventions is needed to make any kind of behavior reliable if it is likely to conflict with powerful considerations of interest. Neither the law nor conventions worked to secure faithfulness from Vronsky and Alfredo. And few of their peers would expect faithfulness from them.

Trusting Institutions

On the encapsulated interest account, trust and cooperation are related problems. They are not always the same problem. Cooperation may generally require conditions that make for trust, but not all trusting relationships are sensibly grounded in ongoing cooperation. Some trusting relationships depend on love or altruism from the trusted, and some involve only a loose concatenation of interests, nothing like direct exchange or pursuit of common goals. The latter may be especially typical of political life, where it may be vital to establish something analogous to trust for institutions, so that citizens may prosper and institutions and nations may cooperate.

Some, including the usually very sensible Hume (1978/1739–40, p. 537), have supposed that government requires public-spirited people to make it work well. In practice most political institutions are staffed by individuals whose motives are heavily if not entirely self-interested. To gain our trust, they will have to work in our interest. Hence, the general problem is to make it the interest of various officials to work in our interest. We do this in part by making some officials directly answerable to citizens and in part by making other officials answerable to these. Both these controls are likely to be very loose, but the latter sounds especially weak. What we need to complete the picture is a theory of how the general interest can be served by a government of millions of bureaucrats who are fundamentally self-interested, who are motivated not by unusual public spirit, but only by income and career.

In crude outline, the most plausible theory is one that takes James Madison's analysis down to the level of individual officials. In defense of the U.S. Constitution, he writes, "In framing a government which is to be administered by men over men, the great difficulty lies in this: you must first enable the government to control the governed; and in the next place oblige it to control itself." He recommends, "Ambition must be made to counter ambition" (Madison 1961/1788, p. 322). How? If I violate the norms determined by our bureaucratic mission, you and others are likely to find it in your interest to oppose me (Hardin 1988a, pp. 526–527). Sometimes the enticements to malfeasance are so great that they infect almost everyone in a relevant agency, as we often hear of police units that succumb to bribery or even direct involvement in such profitable crimes as illegal drug trade. But commonly, even in such extreme cases, someone will have a strong career interest in bringing them to account. Strong moral commitment beyond interest may help and may be common, but it may also lead officials into taking the law into their own hands, and it cannot be reliable.

Often we expect institutions to be more stable than individuals. Many institutional promises and threats are more reliable than their individual equivalents. Consider some examples. The nuclear deterrent threat is credible because it does not depend on a particular individual's commitment to act in the relevant moment. As has widely been discussed, the individual might choose, once deterrence had failed, to act as a humanitarian rather than as an avenger or an automaton programmed to retaliate. The reliability of retaliation approaches certainty if it is institutionalized in the form of many actors prepared to act in related but not entirely centrally controlled ways.[15] Similarly, many of us might trust our fortunes to a bank more readily than to most individuals, perhaps including close friends and relatives with whom we expect our relationships to last our lifetimes.

Aristotle argued that the best of all governments would be a good monarchy and the worst would be a bad monarchy, or tyranny. The differences between a good and a bad democracy would be less great. To reduce variance, we might choose democracy as the preferred form of government in general. There may be little or no empirical study of Aristotle's factual claims, but they sound sensible. Government by the many may induce a kind of regression toward the mean and hence much greater predictability.

Seldom in history has anyone gone so far toward establishing institutional trust as has Soviet President Mikhail Gorbachev, head of a system that has exhibited extraordinary variance. He has made some previously possible Soviet threats virtually impossible by putting institutional barriers in their way. For example, in inviting the reformation of the East European regimes and the dismantling of the iron curtain, he has greatly reduced the possibility of a sudden Soviet conventional attack on West Europe. By withdrawing troops and certain materiel he has made it virtually impossible to launch a secret attack without first visibly warning of attack during the necessary restoration of troops and equipment to the European theater. The obstacles he has created consist of institutional structures that can impede individual audacity.

Such institutional arrangements are appealing partly because they stabilize our expectations. Institutional behavior regresses toward the mean to average out the variance of individual behavior. Our expectations may not be grounded in any theory or explanation of why they are justified, but simply in experience. For example, political trust of many kinds may be easier in the Soviet Union now than it was a generation ago, although many of the older generation may still be reticent in trusting others with their opinions. And it must be harder in China now than it was shortly before the June 1989 massacre in Tiananmen Square.

One might suppose that trustworthy (that is, reliable) institutions are reliable because the right people are in the right places in them. But banks and many other institutions do not very rigorously select people for their roles, and it seems unlikely that reliability emerges from simple goodwill on the part of individuals in those roles. Most of us are somewhat like bank tellers: we are secured in our normal honesty by institutional arrangements that make significant dishonesty risky, even difficult. Much of what looks like honesty is essentially self-interest at work.

Institutional arrangements may secure our expectations, and hence our trust, with the devices of self-interest, just as our own individual arrangements do. I become trustworthy by establishing a reputation and by setting myself up for real losses if I betray a trust. Those who fail to learn such lessons are seen as capricious and adolescent. Public officials and institutions also must live by the reputations they establish.

John Dunn has argued that the failure of political philosophers to consider trust is a source of weakness in their theories (Dunn 1988; also see Dunn 1984). He evidently understands trust to be a form of encapsulated interest—he often speaks of "rational trust." He is concerned to restore Locke's view that society turns power over to its governors, "whom the Society hath set over it self, with this express or tacit Trust, That it shall be imployed for their good, and the preservation of their Property" (Locke 1988/1690, p. 381). The relationship of citizens to government is one of trust, not one of contract,[16] and it is the possibility of this relationship and its working that are to be explained. No matter how one comes down on the textual warrant in Locke for this view, it offers an insightful and compelling reconstruction of the otherwise incoherent move to justify government from a supposed grounding in contract or consent.

To bring trust into political theory requires a micro-level account of how government works at the macro level. This will largely be an account of rational expectations of what government and its agents are likely to do. But the expectations will be rational not because they extrapolate from current and past actions, as might be adequate for a sociological account of credible expectations. Merely institutionalizing government and the implementation of policies should lead to greater stability of expectations, and hence to greater trust in this sociological sense. To reach Dunn's concern, the expectations must also be rational in the sense of depending on the rational commitments of officials. Rationally grounded trust in officials therefore requires that the officials be responsive to popular needs and desires. To have incentive to be responsive, they must be somehow accountable, most plausibly, perhaps, through competitive elections.

Many aspects of individual trust of political institutions deserve much more extended discussion. Institutions, for example, play a role in underwriting even interpersonal trust. As Hume says of contracts, if they "had only their own proper obligation, without the separate sanction of government, they wou'd have but little efficacy in [all large and civiliz'd] societies. This separates the boundaries of our public and private duties, and shews that the latter are more dependant on the former, than the former on the latter" (Hume 1978/1739–40, p. 546). Hobbes may exaggerate the extent to which powerful institutional sanctions are required for grounding trust and promises, but he is not radically mistaken.

Concluding Remarks

Many social and moral norms are primarily manifestations of encapsulated interest, as trust is. Because this is so, we can count on others enough even to take an unduly optimistic view of them. We can afford to be trusting in general until our trust proves to be badly misplaced. If, in contrast, we had come to be distrusting in general, the result would surely be far worse than what we have. Presumably, it would look much more akin to much of international relations, as in the Cold War between East and West, in which distrust often seemed to be the baseline and trust to be, until recently, an unreachable goal.

Would it make sense for an individual to go through life without initial trust toward new acquaintances? One might be always distrusting until reputational or other evidence recommended trust in a particular case, and no doubt some people are initially distrustful to such a degree. For many people, such a stance would be too tedious and would cost more in lost opportunities than it would save in avoided harms. To act according to the backward induction argument would not generally be in their interest.

Perhaps our willingness to open by tentatively trusting others, even if only in small ways, underlies a commonplace claim that even the market and other more or less purely exchange relations depend on a general level of trust. Some economists consider this general level of trust a public good that is nevertheless voluntarily provided by individuals through their piecemeal actions (Arrow 1972; Hirsch 1978, pp. 78–79). There may be less extrarationality here than seemingly meets the eye. If our expectations are stabilized at a high enough level of cooperativeness, we may finally be able to treat much of the behavior we expect to encounter as a relatively benign force of nature, just as microeconomic theorists of the market essentially do.

Under typical circumstances in large markets, I can have very stable expectations of fairly good results from my entering ordinary exchanges. My trust in "the market" may be like my trust in the sun's rising tomorrow. I will correct specific details of my trust when any dealer out there violates it. But otherwise I will treat each dealer as benign, at least in the sense of not malignant. If I share Adam Smith's view that most dealers are likely to share my interests (because they must serve my interests to serve their own), I may even think of them as positively benign. The public good of generalized trust, then, may not require a moral foundation. It may be little more than an encapsulation of the self-interest of all or most of us.

Notes

I wish to thank Richard Zeckhauser for causing this paper to be written, for using its topic to cajole me into meeting deadline promises, and for lively discussions and commentaries on the topic and earlier drafts of the paper. I also wish to thank participants in his seminar on the papers of this book at Harvard and participants in the informal Tuesday evening seminar on contemporary moral and social theory at the University of Chicago for their cogent comments on an earlier draft. In particular, Avon Leong, Jay Patel, and Alan Wertheimer wrote valuable, extensive commentaries. Finally, I thank Richard Arneson, Howard Margolis, Jonathan Riley, and Duncan Snidal for their comments. All of these people raised far more questions than I have answered.

1. Trifonov's misappropriated rubles thereafter thread their complex way through Dostoyevsky's entire novel, wrecking lives while motivating the plot.

2. For more extensive discussion, see Hardin 1982b, ch. 9. The conclusion of the backward induction argument has become a virtual dogma despite the fact that many, perhaps most, discussants think it perverse. Its appeal as a dogma may simply be that it is cute and perversely contrary to common sense.

3. For more extensive discussion of promising in its strategic variety, see Hardin 1988b, pp. 41–44, 59–65.

4. Baier says that exchange of promises typically requires "one to rely on strangers over a period of time" (Baier 1986, p. 246).

5. The social psychologist David Good apparently shares my experience. He says, "Rarely is it the case that exchanges requiring trust are ahistorical single cases" (Good 1988, p. 33).

6. As Baier herself recognizes in her "Promises, Promises, Promises" (Baier 1985).

7. This is a large part of Baier's concern in Baier 1986 (see p. 236 and passim thereafter).

8. That precept is striking in the most ordinary circumstances, but it seems almost dreadful in the context of Setsuko's recollection of it. It was, she notes, "literally true of everything that happened now."

9. As suggested by Alan Wertheimer. Or you may act according to Gregory Kavka's Copper Rule of doing unto others what they do unto you, even when it is not strictly in your interest (Kavka 1986, pp. 347–348). Hence you may be trustworthy toward me because I am trustworthy toward you.

10. Hertzberg (1988) wishes to show a difference in the "grammars" of reliance and trust. He draws on discussions of trust by Wittgenstein. Unfortunately, he is misled in some cases by the English translation he uses, because the words Wittgenstein uses in German are as nearly equivalent to *reliance* as to *trust*, in Hertzberg's senses. Wittgenstein's words translated as *trust* by Denis Paul and G. E. M. Anscombe include *gläubig hinnehmen* and *sich auf etwas verlassen* (Wittgenstein 1972, §§159 and 509).

11. Locke supposed that atheists could not consistently be trusted because they would not fear ultimate retribution from God. On his account, then, trust is essentially a matter of rational expectations grounded in the rationality of the trusted.

12. Elster's concern is with altruism, and he does not spell out the analogous nature of trust implied in his brief aside.

13. Talk of the grammar of trust is risky. We might also look to its etymology, where among other things we find that it has an explicable common root with "tryst."

14. Such an argument already appears in Wollaston 1738, pp. 8–20 (cited in Dunn 1984).

15. The success of a deterrent strategy may not require anything near certainty of retaliation, because even a small risk is too much to invite.

16. Dunn's view constitutes a major revision of Lockean thought. (See further, Laslett 1988, pp. 114–117.)

References

Arrow, Kenneth J. 1972. "Gifts and Exchanges," *Philosophy and Public Affairs*, 1: 343–362.

Baier, Annette. 1986. "Trust and Antitrust," *Ethics*, 96: 231–260.

Baier, Annette. 1985. "Promises, Promises, Promises," in Baier, *Postures of the Mind: Essays on Mind and Morals*, London: Methuen, 1985.

Barber, Bernard. 1983. *The Logic and Limits of Trust*, New Brunswick, NJ: Rutgers University Press.

Dostoyevsky, Fyodor. 1982/1880. *The Brothers Karamazov*, trans. by David Magarshacks, London: Penguin.

Dunn, John. 1988. "Trust and Political Agency," in Gambetta 1988, pp. 73–93.

Dunn, John. 1984. "The Concept of 'Trust' in the Politics of John Locke," in *Philosophy in History*, Richard Rorty, J. B. Schneewind, and Quentin Skinner, eds., pp. 279–301, Cambridge: Cambridge University Press.

Elster, Jon. 1979. *Ulysses and the Sirens*, Cambridge: Cambridge University Press.

Gambetta, Diego, ed. 1988. *Trust: Making and Breaking Cooperative Relations*, Oxford: Blackwell.

Go, Shizuko. 1985. *Requiem*, Tokyo: Kodansha.

Good, David. 1988. "Individuals, Interpersonal Relations, and Trust," in Gambetta 1988, pp. 31–48.

Hardin, Russell. 1988a. "Constitutional Political Economy: Agreement on Rules," *British Journal of Political Science*, 18: 513–530.

Hardin, Russell. 1988b. *Morality within the Limits of Reason*, Chicago: University of Chicago Press.

Hardin, Russell. 1982a. "Exchange Theory on Strategic Bases," *Social Science Information*, 2: 251–272.

Hardin, Russell. 1982b. *Collective Action*, Baltimore: Johns Hopkins University Press for Resources for the Future.

Hertzberg, Lars. 1988. "On the Attitude of Trust," *Inquiry*, 31: 307–322.

Hirsch, Fred. 1978. *Social Limits to Growth*, Cambridge, MA: Harvard University Press.

Hume, David. 1978/1739–40. *A Treatise of Human Nature*, L. A. Selby-Bigge and P. H. Nidditch, eds., Oxford: Oxford University Press.

Kavka, Gregory. 1986. *Hobbesian Moral and Political Theory*, Princeton, NJ: Princeton University Press.

Laslett, Peter. 1988. "Introduction," in J. Locke (1988/1690), pp. 3–126.

Locke, Don. 1986. "Review of Baier (1985)," *Philosophical Quarterly*, 36: 571–574.

Locke, John. 1988/1690. *Two Treatises of Government*, student edition, Peter Laslett, ed., Cambridge: Cambridge University Press.

Luhmann, Niklas. 1980. *Trust and Power*, New York: Wiley.

Madison, James. 1961/1788. *Federalist*, no. 51, in *The Federalist Papers*, Clinton Rossiter, ed., pp. 320–325, New York: New American Library.

Margolis, Howard. 1987. *Patterns, Thinking, and Cognition*, Chicago: University of Chicago Press.

Schelling, Thomas C. 1989. "Promises," *Negotiation Journal*, 5: 113–118.

Schelling, Thomas C. 1960. *The Strategy of Conflict*, Cambridge, MA: Harvard University Press.

Tolstoy, Leo. 1949/1875–77. *Anna Karenina*, Oxford, trans. by Louise and Aylmer Maude, Oxford: Oxford University Press.

Verdi, Giuseppe. 1946/1853. *La Traviata*, New York: G. Schirmer, libretto by Francesco Maria Piave. (Quotations in my translation.)

Webster's New World Dictionary. 1980. New York: Simon and Schuster, second college edition.

Wittgenstein, Ludwig. 1972. *On Certainty*, trans. by Denis Paul and G. E. M. Anscombe, New York: Harper.

Wollaston, William. 1738. *Religion of Nature Delineated*, London, sixth edition (cited in Dunn 1984).

9   Gifts and Bribes

Robert Klitgaard

The chapters in this volume are a tribute to a man who knows that tributes may have strategic uses. What seems to be a gift may really be a bribe; what looks like praise may be insincere and self-serving. When he retired as president of the Ford Foundation, McGeorge Bundy summarized his experience as "never a bad meal, never an unkind word." Some time after he retired as president of the United States, Dwight Eisenhower was asked how his golf game was doing. "I'm playing much better," he said, "but I'm not winning as often."

Tom Schelling understands all this. So writing a tribute to him is an intimidating task. You know he will be reading every sentence strategically.

Do I exaggerate? In 1988 I dedicated a book to Tom, whose letter of thanks quickly proceeded to analysis.

I have been giving a little thought to strategic issues in dedication, even to some of the ethics.

The reader of a dedication, I think, perceives some combination of admiration, indebtedness, and personal subordination. Pupils dedicate to masters, not masters to pupils, but pupils may respectfully dedicate to their former masters even when they have been exalted beyond the master. So the personal subordination can be historical rather than contemporary. The reader probably assumes that the indebtedness expressed in the dedication goes beyond the book; people who helped with a book get thanked in the preface; the dedication implies a relation that is broader, deeper, longer, or more personal.

Dedicating is also a little like name-dropping. But the common kind of name-dropping is surreptitious; the owner of the dropped name doesn't know who dropped it in company and whether it was legitimate or fraudulent. The dedication, in contrast, is visible to the person so honored, and he or she can even guess something about the nature of the public into which the name has been dropped. It is therefore much more disciplined. And it is much more likely than surreptitious name-dropping to be reciprocal, or even overbalanced . . .

I dedicated one book, my latest one. It was to Willi Fellner, who had been the best teacher I ever had and the most devoted, who advised me to go to Harvard to complete my graduate work rather than return to Berkeley, where he personally wanted me. We were then colleagues at Yale for five years. He was about the finest gentleman I ever knew. When I dedicated the book he had just died. My feelings were ambivalent. I wished that he could know that I had dedicated my book to him but I realized that, had he not died just as I was putting the front matter in final shape, it would probably not have occurred to me to dedicate the book to him. Anyway, his widow was pleased. But I mention this in order to confess that I got pleasure out of the envy that I thought people would feel toward me for having been close enough to Willi Fellner to take the liberty of dedicating my book to his memory.

Tom went on for a page or two more, and of course his letter made me happy. But there was something unsettling about it as well. What a mind, this Schelling fellow: dedication as name-dropping, as a ploy! As always, he yanks your perspective to a new vantage point. And once you look at things his way, you can't stop. Before you know it you are reanalyzing other sorts of academic tributes strategically.

Take book-jacket blurbs. Can the blurber always tell the whole truth about a colleague's work: "This is a so-so book," or "It's almost worth the $21.95 purchase price"? No. Faced with a request to praise the less-than-thrilling work of someone you know, your challenge is to provide something flattering but not false. "Timely" and "relevant" are good choices, as they can pertain to the topic if not the book. "Important" is a little stronger but still can be linked to the subject and not necessarily to the author's contribution.

One of Tom's blurbs demonstrates the technique. "This is a careful book on a delicate and important subject and is distinguished by its lucidity, its candor, and its integrity." "Careful" and "important subject" are safe. The brilliant choice is "distinguished." As an adjective, it is favorable indeed. But as a verb it can refer to horrid birthmarks as well as intellectual landmarks. Strictly speaking, Tom's use of the verb is noncommittal, but it retains the adjective's aura, thereby solving masterfully a classic blurb-provider's problem.

Acknowledgments can have strategic dimensions. Purporting to be humble and deferential, they can be sneakily self-enhancing. When an author thanks others for their excellent books and articles, he may incidentally imply that his own work has emerged from the best brains of the generation and now occupies the summit of current knowledge.

Thanking readers can have a similar function. Despite the author's obligatory "errors remain my own," acknowledging others' help may be an attempt to implicate them in one's views, to vest the paper in the authority of those cited.[1]

Acknowledgments may degenerate into simple name-dropping. A well-known sociologist damages his cause with this first sentence of a preface: "The idea for this book came to me during a walk with Erik Erikson one morning in a New England graveyard."

Credibility in acknowledging is enhanced by subtlety, irony, self-deprecation. Alexander Nehamas (1985, p. ix) thanks kind and patient friends for reading earlier drafts, many of whom

often proved me wrong. But I suppose that even in a book about Nietzsche I can be Socratic enough to believe that they thereby made the book, and myself, better than we otherwise would have been.

Susan Glimcher, who was the first to read the completed manuscript, not only also proved me wrong but, in addition, persuaded me that, every now and then, I might conceivably be right. This is a different benefit, but it is equally crucial. I don't know what I would have done without it.

Stanley Cavell has three wonderful pages of thanks in *Must We Mean What We Say?* (1976, p. xiii). Halfway through them, he inserts this short, winning paragraph: "First books tend to over-ambitiousness, and nowhere more than in the bulk of debts they imagine themselves able to answer for."

Tom's acknowledgments are usually scant but elegant. Take *Arms and Influence* (1966, p. viii):

I have had so much help in writing this book that I am tempted to break the rules and let others share the blame as well as any credit. Forceful critics have had a good deal of impact on its shape and style. Two of them, Bernard Brodie and James E. King, Jr., out of great dissatisfaction with the manuscript and even greater affection for its author, took extraordinary pains with every chapter and I must not only thank them here but record that they remain unsatisfied. Others who unhesitatingly told me where I was wrong, or my language unclear, or my book badly structured, or who added ideas or lent me examples were [list].

Footnotes, too, can be self-serving. Citations can attempt to bully readers into agreeing with dubious propositions. And they can purport to enhance the importance of one's topic by citing the luminaries who have struggled with it previously—implying also, perhaps, that the greats didn't provide what the lucky reader is about to partake.[2]

Book reviewers, too, face strategic problems of credibility and hurt feelings. Reviews also offer a chance to drop names and to associate with or dissociate oneself from an author, a topic, an approach. The genre permits negative judgments, even antitributes. My favorite opening line is, "There are many strange and wonderful words that could be used to describe this book, but the best, I think, is 'bad.'"

Tom Schelling couches his criticisms more kindly. Of a book on foreign aid: "On some points, the writer may disagree with the authors only because he is free to depart from the framework they set for themselves, or because, a first approximation having been made by Brown and Opie, a second approximation can now be offered" (1955, p. 608). In the preface to the original edition of *The Strategy of Conflict*, he writes: "And I owe a special word of appreciation to R. Duncan Luce and Howard Raiffa, whose *Games and Decisions* has been of immeasurable help; if I have often focused critical remarks on the book, it is only because the inevitable lot of a definitive survey is to serve as a definitive target" (1960, p. vi).

The title of Tom's classic critique (1963) of Kenneth Boulding's *Conflict and Defense* conveys his main point: "War without Pain and Other Models." Tom's comment on the presentations at a conference on nonviolent resistance is adroit (1967, p. 302). "One has to admit that it could work," his paper begins, thereby undercutting the propensity to avoid useful work on nonviolent resistance by indulging in definitional debates or accusations of blue-skying. Instead, Tom encourages the analysis of tactics, favorable and adverse conditions, and track records.

So, sensitized by Schellingesque considerations, one worries that even a festschrift may have strategic dimensions. A tribute may, while purporting to elevate another, be transmogrified by self-esteem. "This distinguished person was my friend, I his confidant and intellectual peer. I am equipped to tell you what was especially fine about his work." Naipaul (1988, p. 295) notes that this attitude can even contaminate obituaries.

A number of people who wrote about Alan after his death wrote with that part of their personalities that had almost been created by Alan's flattery. Their obituaries were curiously self-regarding; as much as to Alan . . . these people paid tribute to themselves for having known and befriended Alan, for having spotted his talent and sensibility, having been singled out by him for his confidences, his confessions of sadness.

A festschrift calls for praise, but the academic scruple calls for honesty, and because no one is perfect this implies criticism; some of the tensions of blurbing and reviewing reemerge. Moreover, a festschrift contribution is both a tribute and a performance: it acknowledges a valued other in part by demonstrating one's own valuable, other-like capabilities. How one writes—the quality of the rhetoric and the apparent investment made in it—affects the credibility of one's kind words.

How to proceed? Despite the dangers, I think the occasion calls for more than an impersonal, academic article. One of the nicest compliments to the tributee is that he has generated distinctive personal links, not just professional and intellectual ones. It is the personal voice that makes this sort of essay a gift.

Policy Analysis à la Schelling

A tribute to Tom Schelling could cover any of the many problems and disciplines over which he has ranged. I want to emphasize the way he approaches problems, what Tom can teach us about doing policy analysis.

Though a theorist, he is fascinated by real examples and finds them indispensable for developing theory. "In my own thinking." Tom writes in the preface to *The Strategy of Conflict* (1960, p. vi), "they have never been separate. Motivation for the purer theory came almost exclusively from preoccupation with (and fascination with) 'applied' problems; and the clarification of theoretical ideas was absolutely dependent on an identification of live examples."[3]

This passion has led him to topics ranging from foreign aid and international economics to diplomacy, war, and terrorism, from crime to altruism, from collective action to the nature of the self. In the long, discussion-paper version of his "Hockey Helmets" essay (1972), an index shows readers where to locate the many examples he uses along the way because, Tom notes, they are what many readers most want to find.

Tom unpacks concepts, rebuts simplistic solutions, expands the range of alternatives. "I am drawing a distinction, not a conclusion," he writes, prototypically, in an article on organizations. In this piece he distinguishes exercising from defining responsibility, standards that impose costs from those that do not, costs arising from an act from those prompted by the fear of that act, wanting to do the right thing from figuring out what the right thing is, discouraging what is wrong from doing what is right, and the firms of economic abstraction from businesses as "small societies comprising many people with different interests, opportunities, information, motivations, and group interests." Regarding an organization, he says, "It may be important to know who's in charge, and it may be as difficult as it is important" (1974, pp. 82, 80, 83).

Policy analysis à la Schelling means analysis that *enriches*. Through a combination of simplifying theory and elegant example, he forces us to realize that there are not one or two but a multiplicity of, say, military strengths, public goods, types of discrimination, nonviolent behaviors, actions that affect others, ways to value a human life. "My conjectures," he says of his analysis of various kinds of organized crime, "may at least help to alert investigators to what they should be looking for; unless one raises the right questions, no amount of hearings and inquiries and investigations will turn up the pertinent answers" (1971, p. 649). Not for him normal science's quantitative demonstration that a qualitative point from simplifying theory cannot be rejected at the usual level of significance.

And not for him the policy recommendation of what might be called "normal policy analysis." Tom is after enriching principles, and "principles rarely lead straight to policies; policies depend on values and purposes, predictions and estimates, and must usually reflect the relative weight of conflicting principles" (1966, p. vii).

In a little-known essay, Tom reviews "the non-accomplishments of policy analysis" in fields from defense to energy to health to education. Policy analysis as customarily practiced has made so little difference because the usual paradigm is wrong.

If policy analysis is the science of rational choice among alternatives, it is dependent on another more imaginative activity—the invention of alternatives worth considering. . .

The point I would make is that policy analysis may be doomed to inconsequentiality as long as it is thought of within the paradigm of rational choice. . .

[P]olicy analysis may be most effective when it is viewed within a paradigm of conflict, rather than of rational choice. . . . Analysing the *interests* and the *participants* may be as important as analysing the issue. Selecting the alternatives to be compared, and selecting the emphasis to be placed on the criteria for evaluation may be what matters, and the creative use of darkness may be as much needed as the judicious use of light. (1985, pp. 27–28)

What is the paradigm of policy analysis that Schelling rejects? The analyst is given the objectives, alternative actions, and perhaps constraints. The analyst then assesses the likely effects of the various actions. He or she calculates which alternative maximizes the objectives, and from this a prescription for action is derived.

This rejected paradigm conceives of the analytical problem as the leap from givens to prescriptions, from the "if" to the "then." This conception borrows from economics. Under idealized assumptions, economic science is able to derive powerful statements about optimal courses of action. Seduced, the analyst may accept a lot of unrealistic restrictions on the "if" for the thrill of an unassailable "then." But as Tom points out, in real policymaking the intellectual problem is often a different one: how to discover, how to be more creative about, the objectives, the alternatives, and the constraints. In other words, how to understand, expand, and enrich the "if."

The rejected paradigm says that the policymaker's problem is deciding among many given courses of action. Schelling's version turns this radically around. The problem is understanding, indeed generating, the objectives and the range of alternatives. Once policymakers have done that, they usually do well at making decisions. They are already pretty good at the "then" part; they may need help on the "if."

On this view, policy analysis provides not so much a set of answers that politicians should adopt and bureaucrats implement, but a set of tools and examples for enriching the appreciation of alternatives and their consequences.

This conception of policy analysis has another implication that has to do with the lamentable reluctance of politicians to adopt and bureaucrats to implement the excellent advice of policy analysts. "Economic policy professionals are . . . well accustomed to frustration" notes Arnold C. Harberger (1984, p. 428). "Proposals aimed at improving policy must run a veritable gauntlet of hazards . . . on their way to implementation. Most proposals do not survive, and those that do may emerge so mutilated or distorted that they no longer serve their intended purposes."

Gerald M. Meier (1984, pp. 223, 229, 230) asks,

But how to gain acceptance of more appropriate policies? This remains the most underdeveloped part of the development economist's subject. . . . To become more persuasive, the development economist needs to become a student of public policy, and to determine why particular policies are adopted and not others. . . . . Development economics is on the edge of politics and the edge of management. To be more effective in policymaking, it must venture more into each territory.

Under the standard paradigm, it is at first baffling why one's optimal advice is not pursued—until one notes that, unlike oneself, policymakers and bureaucrats have selfish agendas. Aha.

But to the policy analyst clued in by Tom Schelling, the resistance of politicians and functionaries may mean more. Politicians' resistance may be a sign that the analyst does not understand the operative "objective functions." Bureaucrats' resistance may indicate that the analyst has more to learn about the alternatives and the constraints. In most real policy problems, the objectives, alternatives, and constraints are not "given."

So, when confronted with the apparently stupid or self-serving reluctance of the real world to heed our advice, we should listen carefully and learn. The words and actions of the politicians and the bureaucrats may provide invaluable clues for appreciating what the objectives and alternatives really are and might be. And, after listening. our task as analysts is to use theoretical tools and practical examples to expand and enrich *their* thinking about objectives, alternatives, and consequences. At least part of the failure of standard policy analysis to make a difference stems from the way many analysts conceive of "answers" in public policy.

Tom Schelling's style is as distinct as his enriching objective. His papers are essays in the first person, packed with care and taste and touches of humor.

Sometimes promises are enforced by a deity from which broken promises cannot be hidden. "Certain offenses which human law could not punish nor man detect were placed under divine sanction," according to Kitto. "Perjury is an offense which it may be impossible to prove; therefore it is one which is particularly abhorrent to the gods." This is a shrewd coupling of economics with deterrence: if divine intervention is scarce, economize it by exploiting the comparative advantage of the gods. If their intelligence system is better than that of the jurists, give them jurisdiction over the crimes that are hardest to detect. The broken promises that are hardest to detect may, like perjury, fall under their jurisdiction. But be careful not to go partners with anyone who does not share your gods. (1989, p. 118)

Stylistically as well as substantively, Tom recasts the predominant paradigm of policy analysis. He is an enricher of the "if," a catalyst for one's own creativity. In what he writes and how, he is aware of the importance of intangibles like perceptions, inclinations, and will—in the policymaker and in the reader as well.[4]

What Can Be Done about Corrupt Tributes?

This volume is a tribute to Tom Schelling in the sense of "something given, done, or said, as a gift, testimonial, etc., to show gratitude, respect, honor, or praise." Tom is a lot to be thankful for.

I would now like to turn to another sort of tribute, "any forced payment or contribution, as through bribery."[5] We have already seen that praise can be used corruptly, that a tribute in the first sense can become a tribute in the second. But now we turn to corruption with no praise attached: a payoff to a public official.

Avoiding the Practical Problem

Like many of the topics Tom has studied, corruption is a sensitive subject. In the developing countries, because of what Gunnar Myrdal (1989, pp. 406–407) called "diplomacy in research," scholars have tended to avoid the topic altogether. "The taboo on research on corruption is, indeed, one of the most flagrant examples of this general bias . . . [which] is basically to be explained in terms of a certain condescension on the part of Westerners." Some social scientists aver that bribes cannot be distinguished from transactions, that to try to do so is to import Western or one's own normative assumptions. A bribe, a fee for service, a gift—analytically, it is said, they are the same. So we should not talk too much about corruption or, if we do, not be too critical of it.

But as many poor countries have slid into deeper economic trouble, the sheer fact that corruption is so widespread and so devastating to economy and society has become impossible to avoid. People within the developing countries have led the outcry. Increasingly and around the globe, a central issue in popular uprisings and election campaigns is corruption and what to do about it.

Policy analysis has lagged. True, scholarly work shows how rent seeking and "directly unproductive profit-seeking activities" can be harmful by distorting incentives (Rose-Ackerman 1978, Srinivasan 1985, Inman 1987, and Meier, forthcoming). Recent research on influence activities in organizations reveals other sources of distortion

(Milgrom and Roberts 1988, Milgrom 1988). And new empirical work does show—no surprise to people living in poor countries—that corruption in fact does harm (Gould 1980, Gould and Amaro-Reyes 1983, Noonan 1984, Márquez et al. 1984, Cariño 1986, Klitgaard 1988, and United Nations 1990).

But little is said about how to reduce corruption. Typical is a study carried out under the auspices of the World Bank's Management and Development Series in 1983. The authors expend all their energies to support this simple conclusion: "Corruption has a deleterious, often devastating, effect on administrative performance and economic and political development (Gould and Amaro-Reyes 1983, abstract, p. 34). None of the monograph's eighty-six footnotes refers to strategies for fighting corruption. After showing corruption to be a bad thing, the authors note, as though in an afterthought, that "governments may increasingly wish to consider possible measures to counteract this scourge," and then they simply list, without examples or supporting arguments, four vague, general, and therefore unhelpful "possible measures."[6]

Why this lack of practical work on corruption? Many citizens of developing countries shy away from the subject because they are simply exhausted by it; many have adopted a fatalistic attitude. A recent article from Guatemala illustrates an alarmingly widespread view. The author begins, "When in a society the shameless triumph, when the abuser is admired: when principles end and only opportunism prevails; when the insolent rule and the people tolerate it, when everything becomes corrupt but the majority is quiet because their slice is waiting . . . " After a series of such laments, the author concludes, "When so many 'whens' unite, perhaps it is time to hide oneself; time to suspend the battle, time to stop being a Quixote; it is time to review our activities, reevaluate those around us, and return to ourselves" (Altolaguirre, 1990).

The reluctance of scholars to address corruption from a practical perspective sometimes has a different source: they do not want to accuse people of being corrupt. The frustrated citizen asks rhetorically, "What can be done if the people on top do not care?" The scholar may also ask, "If I look at corruption, don't I accuse a people of being morally derelict?"—and this in the academic culture is forbidden.

Both these questions have force. But I think it is useful to recall some words from Tom Schelling's essay "Command and Control" (1974, pp. 83–84):

An organization, business or other, is a system of information, rules for decision, and incentives; its performance is different from the individual performances of the people in it. An organization can be negligent without any individual's being negligent. To expect an organization to reflect the qualities of the individuals who work for it or to impute to the individuals the qualities one sees in the organization is to commit what logicians call the 'fallacy of composition.' Fallacy isn't error, of course, but it can be treacherous.

The subject of Tom's essay is the social responsibility of business, but his insight applies to corruption as well. The fallacy of composition lurks here, too. It is too often assumed that organizations or entire governments are corrupt simply because people are immoral; and, it is concluded, nothing can be done to curb corruption except generations of moral education.

But let us pursue Tom's idea. Is it possible that organizations can alter their "systems of information, rules for decision, and incentives" to reduce corruption? How?

Types

Corruption is the misuse of office for private ends. It can involve the misuse of policy instruments—tariffs and credit, irrigation systems and housing policies, the enforcement of laws and rules regarding public safety, the observance of contracts, and the repayment of loans—or simple procedures. Its extent ranges from rare to widespread; in some developing countries, corruption has become systemic.

On occasion a corrupt act may be socially harmless, even helpful. For example, it may allow the circumvention of a stupid rule, or it may effect a kind of politically stabilizing redistribution. Under some circumstances, "speed money" can be efficient.[7] But as careful studies repeatedly show, corruption is usually pernicious. When corrupt behavior is widespread, it deforms economic growth, undermines political legitimacy, and demoralizes both public officials and ordinary citizens.

Corruption can involve promises, threats, or both; can be initiated by the public servant or the interested client; can entail acts of omission or commission; can involve illicit or licit services; can be inside or outside the public organization. The borders of corruption are hard to define and depend on local laws and customs.[8] The first task of

Table 9.1
Types of corruption encountered within the Philippines Bureau of Internal Revenue (1975)

	External corruption
Lagay	Speed money and payments for supposedly free paperwork. Extensive, small sums. Taxpayer paying bribe gains, but overall taxpayers lose.
Extortion	Assessors threaten taxpayers with higher rates, preying on their ignorance or their unwillingness to subject their cases to costly litigation. Fairly extensive, and political dynamite. Taxpayers lose.
Arreglo	Assessors and taxpayers collude to reduce tax liabilities. Widespread, large sums. Taxpayer paying bribe gains, but noncorrupt taxpayers lose and government loses millions in revenues.
	Internal corruption
Embezzlement	Employees make off with funds collected. Widespread, especially in provinces. Government loses millions in revenues.
Fraud	Overprinting of tax stamps and labels. Not very widespread, not very costly.
Personnel scams	Choice positions within the BIR allocated for bribes. Systematized, widespread in provinces. Contributes to BIR's culture of corruption.
Delaying remittances	Tax collectors take the float on funds received. Fairly extensive, small losses.
Corruption of internal investigations	BIR's Internal Security Division rendered ineffective, exacerbating all the Bureau's problems of corruption.

policy analysis, Tom Schelling has taught us, is to disaggregate the concept at hand and look at concrete examples.

Consider the problems faced by Justice Efren Plana when he took over the Philippines' Bureau of Internal Revenue (BIR) in 1975. Positions within the bureau were being bought and sold. One job that paid $10,000 a year was going for $75,000 because of its lucrative opportunities for corruption. Plana also found embezzlement, fraud, counterfeiting, extortion of taxpayers, *lagay* or money to speed up paperwork, *arreglos* or side payments to reduce tax liabilities, and corrupt internal investigation and enforcement. Table 9.1 presents a summary.

Confronted with this botanical garden of illicit activities in an environment as corrupt as the Philippines, many people would have

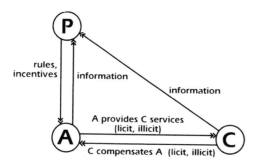

Figure 9.1
A principal-agent-client model

concluded that nothing could be done. Plana, however, launched what proved to be a successful campaign to reduce corruption. How he did so is instructive.

The Usefulness of Economic Metaphors

Plana asked why so much corruption existed inside the BIR. Some have ascribed corruption to cultures (be they dictatorial, personalistic, or gift-giving)[9] or racial groups ("mulatto states" are more prone to corruption, according to Samuel Huntington, as are certain Orientals, according to Max Weber).[10] Still others have pointed out that corruption is prevalent when social norms are in flux or break down, or during a boom or a bust. Corruption has been blamed on too much capitalism and competition as well as on too little; on colonialism and on the withdrawal of the colonial powers; on traditional regimes and on the breakdown of traditions.

Plana proceeded at a different level. He looked at the motives and opportunities facing agents within the BIR. We can appreciate this approach, I think, by using economic metaphors to analyze corruption. First, imagine a *public agent* trading off her benefits from undertaking a corrupt act against the costs to her of doing so. (A similar analysis can be made of the person—or *client*—offering the bribe.) Second, imagine a *principal* like Justice Plana—for the moment assumed to be noncorrupt—facing another trade-off: between the social benefits of reducing the agent's corrupt activity and the social costs of taking various steps to obtain that reduction. The combination of these two metaphors is a *principal-agent-client model* (see figure 9.1).

The public official is an agent pledged to act on behalf of the principal to produce public services. But the agent can use her position to reap private benefits in transactions with the client. These transactions may create public bads. The agent engages in them depending on their costs and benefits to her (as in Wilson and Herrnstein 1985, pp. 41–62 and 531–535). The principal's problem is to induce the agent to create the optimal amounts of public goods and bads.

Much recent economic theory concerns itself with the principal-agent problem and its extensions, including the problems of implementing a "unified governance structure," which includes incentives, information systems, decision rules, hierarchical structures, and the control of "influence activities." Useful references include Williamson 1985, Hart and Holmstrom 1987, Milgrom and Roberts 1989, and Holmstrom and Tirole 1989. The complexity of the problem of a real principal like Plana soon outstrips available models, but one can usefully continue with economic metaphors. For heuristic purposes, I have found it useful to put the principal's tools for controlling corruption into five categories:

1. Selecting the agents (and training them).

2. Altering the incentives facing agents and clients (for both efforts and results).

3. Collecting and processing information on the agents' and clients' efforts and results.

4. Restructuring the agent-client relationship (for example, reducing monopoly powers, clarifying rules and procedures to limit agents' discretion, changing decision rules, and indeed, redefining the mission of the organization).

5. Raising the moral costs of corruption (for example, with ethical codes and changes in the organizational culture).

Production functions connect each of these anticorruption tools with changes in the levels and location of various types of corruption. The principal needs to know: how big a reduction in corruption is he likely to get for how extensive (and expensive) a policy change (a factual question about the production functions), and how much this reduction is worth compared with the direct and indirect costs of the reforms themselves (an evaluative question, which also of course has factual elements).

The evaluative question is complicated and outstrips our current ability to model and estimate. The benefits of reducing corruption should be assessed in terms of efficient allocation (static), better incentives (dynamic), political legitimacy, distributional equity, and other dimensions. The costs of anticorruption measures will be gauged in terms of money, but also in terms of politics, organizational red tape, and organizational culture. Moreover, the principal cares not only about corruption but also about the primary business of his agents and agency (for example, collecting taxes, convicting criminals, or distributing pharmaceuticals). The principal is also involved with other agents in other "games." These may interact with his efforts to reduce corruption, and he has to be attentive to these externalities.

Metaphorically, the policy-analytic problem plays out this way. First, the principal analyzes his organization. He examines the agents' behavior (and the corrupt public clients') and assesses where and how much corruption occurs. Experience as well as theory indicates that an organization is most vulnerable to corruption at points where agents enjoy greater monopoly power over clients, have greater discretion over the provision of a licit or illicit service, and take actions that are more difficult to monitor. Reducing monopoly power is a key element in the literature on rent seeking. A stylized equation holds: corruption = monopoly + discretion − accountability.

Second, the principal evaluates the various costs (and possible benefits) that different kinds of corrupt activities entail, and to whom.

Third, he assesses the various policies through which he can affect the calculations of potentially corrupt officials and citizens. He imagines enacting these policies and asks, "As I turn the dial and spend more resources on them, how do various kinds of corruption respond and how much does turning the dial cost?" To allocate his resources efficiently, he must choose the appropriate types of corruption to attack and the appropriate types and levels and sequences of anticorruption policies to employ. An anticorruption campaign should not be pushed so far that its costs outweigh the benefits in reduced corruption. Reducing corruption is only one of the ends he seeks, and it is a costly one.

Using these metaphors has proved useful with policymakers in developing countries. Table 9.2 is a heuristic framework designed to help policymakers think more creatively about ways to control corruption. Notice how it uses economic intuitions without a mathematical model.

Table 9.2
Controlling corruption: A heuristic framework for policymakers

A. Select agents.

1. Screen out the dishonest (past records, tests, predictors of honesty).
2. Exploit outside "guarantees" of honesty (networks for finding dependable agents and making sure they stay that way).

B. Set agents' rewards and penalties.

1. Change rewards.
a. Raise salaries to reduce the need for corrupt income.
b. Reward specific actions and agents that reduce corruption.
c. Use contingent contracts to reward agents on the basis of eventual success (e.g., forfeitable nonvested pensions, performance bonds).
d. Link nonmonetary rewards to performance (training, transfers, perks, travel, publicity, praise).

2. Penalize corrupt behavior.
a. Raise the severity of formal penalties.
b. Increase the principal's authority to punish.
c. Calibrate penalties in terms of deterrent effects and breaking the culture of corruption.
d. Use nonformal penalties (training, transfers, perks, travel, publicity, loss of professional standing, blackballing).

C. Obtain information about efforts and results.

1. Improve auditing and management information systems.
a. Gather evidence about possible corruption (red flags, statistical analysis, random samples of work, inspections).
b. Carry out "vulnerability assessments."

2. Strengthen information agents.
a. Beef up specialized staff (auditors, computer specialists, investigators, surveillance, internal security).
b. Create a climate where agents will report improper activities (e.g., whistle-blowers).
c. Create new units (ombudsmen, special investigatory committees, anti-corruption agencies, inquiry commissions).

3. Collect information from third parties (media, banks).

4. Collect information from clients and the public (including professional associations).

5. Change the burden of proof, so that the potentially corrupt have to demonstrate their innocence (e.g., public servants with great wealth).

D. Restructure the principal-agent-client relationship to leaven monopoly power, circumscribe discretion, and enhance accountability.

1. Induce competition in the provision of the good or service (privatize, public-private competition, competition among public agents).

2. Limit agents' discretion.
a. Define objectives, rules, and procedures more clearly and publicize them.
b. Have agents work in teams and subject them to hierarchical review.

c. Divide large decisions into separable tasks.

d. Limit agents' influence (change decision rules, change decision makers, alter incentives).

3. Rotate agents functionally and geographically.

4. Change the organization's mission, product, or technology to render them less susceptible to corruption.

5. Organize client groups to render them less susceptible to some forms of corruption, to promote information flows, and to create an anticorruption lobby.

E. Raise the "moral costs" of corruption.

1. Use training, educational programs, and personal example.

2. Promulgate a code of ethics (for civil service, profession, agency).

3. Change the corporate culture.

Justice Plana made moves in each of the areas described in the framework, as table 9.3 summarizes. (The other successful cases of reducing corruption I have studied can also be usefully assimilated in this framework.) As Plana described it to me, his strategy had three parts. First, establish a new performance evaluation system with the help of BIR employees and link incentives to it. Then collect various sources of information about corrupt activities. Third, fry some big fish, meaning the rapid punishment of high-level violators. This later step signaled to the BIR and the public that the rules of the game had changed.

Within three years, Plana had knocked out the internal market for jobs and extortion, greatly reduced *arreglos* and internal corruption, and reduced *lagay*. Tax revenues were up, and even those opposed to Ferdinand Marcos lauded Plana's sensational success (for more details, see Klitgaard 1988).

Information

In fighting corruption, Justice Plana emphasized information and incentives; this recalls Tom Schelling's reminder that "an organization, business or other, is a system of information, rules for decision, and incentives." As Susan Rose-Ackerman writes (1986, p. 131),

All public bureaucracies must resolve two fundamental problems. First, they must specify individual tasks in a way that is consistent with each official's information-processing capabilities, and, second, they must motivate officials to carry out their duties conscientiously. It is pointless for low-level officials to

Table 9.3
What Justice Plana did: Applying the framework for policymakers

A. Select agents.

1. Investigated past records to weed out the dishonest. Used professional criteria for recruitment and appointment. Created new rules against nepotism.

2. Exploited external "guarantees" of honesty by using military and civilian intelligence personnel as information agents.

B. Set agents' rewards and penalties.

1. Rewards: Installed a new performance evaluation system, which proded incentives for more efficient, less corrupt tax collection. Cleaned up the personnel transfer system. Used prizes, travel, perks, praise as incentives.

2. Penalties: Dismissed and prosecuted high-level violators. Raised the pain of dismissal by publicizing the names and stories of offenders.

C. Obtain information about efforts and results.

1. Implemented a red-flag system for identifying possibly corrupt agents. Installed another system to spotlight possible tax evaders.

2. Strengthened the role of information agents (Internal Security Division, Fiscal Control Division). Appointed a special staff of senior "heroes" and young, outside CPAs to investigate suspicious cases and some randomly selected cases.

3. Used third parties to obtain credible information (Commission on Audit monitored tax remittances; intelligence agents inspected financial records of BIR officials; undercover operations).

4. Did not use clients or public, but did involve the media heavily.

5. Did not change the burden of proof.

D. Restructure the principal-agent-client relationship to leaven monopoly power, circumscribe discretion, and enhance accountability.

1. Used performance monitoring and targets for tax collection to stimulate competition among agents.

2. Limited agents' discretion: centralized handling of large cases; more controls over remittances, stamps, etc.; greater use of banks to collect funds; some changes in tax laws; greater supervision.

3. Rotated field agents geographically.

4. Did not redefine the organization's mission, product, or technology.

5. Did not organize taxpayers or civic groups.

E. Raise the "moral costs" of corruption.

1. Held "reorientation seminars" and set pristine personal example.

2. Promulgated values of public service.

3. Changed corporate culture: toastmaster's club, glee club, athletics, morning masses at the BIR, participatory management in creating new performance evaluation system.

know what they ought to do if they are not motivated to do it and equally futile to design a sophisticated motivational system that is ineffective because bureaucrats lack crucial information.

Information about corruption is hard to obtain. Bribery is rarely proved; accusations of bribery may be abundant and motivated by considerations other than the truth. Legal activity in this area may be a misleading indicator. Unlike many other policy issues, the information sought will probably not involve survey data, economic indicators, and the like. More ingenious, indirect means must be devised.

For example, in Plana's case and in the successful anticorruption efforts I have studied, policymakers used such information-gathering devices as:

• Finding "heroes" within the organization—people known to be clean—and having them examine a sample of cases, decisions, or offices for evidence of corruption (and more generally of inefficiency).

• Convening inquiry commissions, as proved so successful in 1989 in Zimbabwe.

• Using undercover agents.

• Devising new, often indirect measures of corrupt behavior (for example, the wealth or spending habits of top officials; the prevalence of illegal activities that would be abetted by official corruption).

• Involving the public through devices ranging from hotlines to citizens' committees to random samples of clients.

In addition, "participatory diagnosis" proves surprisingly useful: that is, involving officials within corrupt institutions in the analysis of corrupt activities. In my experience, as long as one is not looking for particular individuals who are corrupt, it is surprising how much information about corruption can be obtained from officials within a supposedly corrupt organization. They are able and willing to identify places vulnerable to corruption, even to design workable changes.

Information systems are important in the fight against corruption. Improving them involves several steps: reconsidering objectives; developing measures of success; and assessing tasks, efforts, and outcomes.

Specifying objectives comes first, then come performance measures. Experience shows that the participation of employees is crucial in both: for a review of the linkages between participation and incentive systems, see Levine and Tyson 1990. Without employees' involvement, one is likely to get the wrong answers and—even if somehow the right answers are obtained—employees are likely to resist the changes proposed.

Task definition is also crucial. In the words of James Q. Wilson (1989, pp. 173–174),

People matter, but organization matters also, and tasks matter most of all.
The principal challenge facing public managers is to understand the importance of carefully defining the core tasks of the organization and to find both pecuniary and nonpecuniary incentives that will induce operators to perform those tasks as defined.

Measuring performance is not easy, especially in the public sector. But even when performance is hard to calibrate, groups of professionals may be able to provide useful information. Sometimes, a kind of peer review procedure can be used to rank performance.

The organization's clients can provide information about corruption, if they have channels for reporting their impressions—such as telephone hotlines, suggestion boxes, client surveys, the press, ombudsmen, client oversight groups, radio call-ins, and political organizations. Involving the public is also important for political reasons: anticorruption campaigns fail without public support (Etzioni 1982).

Incentives

When performance measures become more available, incentives should be linked to them. This is hardly a new idea. Adam Smith observed, "Public services are never better performed than when their reward comes only in consequence of their being performed, and is proportioned to the diligence employed in performing them" (1976, p. 678).

Incentives are crucial in a campaign against corruption. As Justice Plana explained to me, this was his first priority.

We needed a system to reward efficiency. Before, inefficient people could get promotions through gifts. So, I installed a new system for evaluating performance. I got the people involved in designing the system, those who did the actual tax assessment and collection and some supervising examiners. [Incentives were] based upon the amount of assessments an examiner had made, how many of his assessments were upheld, the amounts actually collected—all depending on the extent and type of the examiner's jurisdiction.
In no time, the examiners were asking for more assignments and were more conscious of their work.

After the agency's employees have been involved in defining objectives, performance measures, and so forth, then one can begin to attack corruption: creating information systems to detect it, enhancing incentives to discover and prosecute it, and stiffening the penalties for those who partake in it.

Reforming incentives faces many obstacles; for a recent review within the private sector, see Mitchell, Lewin, and Lawler 1990. In the public sector, difficulties of measurement, civil service rules, budget problems, and politics add further complexities. Yet recent years have seen examples of incentive reforms that enhance productivity and discourage corruption (Klitgaard 1989). Here are some ideas.

One might *experiment* with bonuses contingent on meeting agreed-upon performance targets. "If the customs bureau generates at least 20 percent more revenue in the next six months, then 10 percent of this additional amount will be go to customs officials as a bonus and 90 percent will go to the treasury. If the target is not met, no bonus." An experiment along these lines succeeded in Bolivia in 1986. In contrast, national commissions that intend to reform incentives for all agencies all at once may never get off the ground.

Team-based or even organization-wide incentives may be more feasible than individual incentives. For example, an emerging lesson from efforts in the United States to reform incentives for teachers is that competition within the same school threatens the egalitarian culture of most public schools. More effective are incentives that reward, if variably, everyone in a given school (Darling-Hammond and Berry 1988, pp. 51–68). Similar issues arise in the modern corporation.[11]

Incentives include money but also more. Because of salary erosion and compression over the last decade in most Third World countries, financial incentives should now be emphasized. But incentives also include training, travel, special assignments, transfers, awards, favorable recognition, and praise. And apart from fines and sackings, penalties can include negative publicity, peer pressure, restrictions, transfers, the loss of discretion or autonomy, and the loss of professional status. Plana publicized the names of BIR offenders, creating thereby the punishment of shame and simultaneously communicating to the public that things had changed.

Information itself turns out to function as a reward. When an information system enables employees to evaluate their own attainments as well as those of the people working around them, it provides a powerful incentive (Israel 1987, ch. 5).

Tactically, one may wish to begin a reform of public sector incentives with the easiest cases. Revenue-raising agencies are prime candidates for two reasons: results are relatively easy to measure; and because they increase revenues, incentive schemes and anticorruption efforts can be self-financing. It is advisable to begin with simple incentive systems based on short-run outcomes instead of complicated, multiple-objective evaluations over a long time period.

The choice of penalties (and of those to be penalized) should be made with an eye on cracking what might be called the culture of corruption. When corruption is systematic, cynicism and alienation spread widely. Experience with successful anticorruption campaigns suggests that a severe penalty to a "big fish" is one way to begin to subvert that culture. The big fish must be a clearly important case, one that has or can be given public prominence, and one that cannot be interpreted as a political vendetta. For this last reason, it is best that the first big fish should come from the political party in power.

Policy Analysis

The foregoing has been only a schematic treatment of the complex problem of corruption. It has tried to illustrate briefly the usefulness of policy analysis in the sense I have attributed to Tom Schelling. One tries to unpack the concept, even an emotively loaded one; one disaggregates the types of corruption. One approaches a sensitive subject by highlighting not the moral failures of individuals but the structural failures of information and incentives. One uses a simplifying theory to obtain, not an optimizing model under restrictive assumptions, but a framework that stimulates the creativity of policymakers and managers in their varied and unique circumstances.

Tributes Differ

We have seen that a tribute in the sense of praise may sometimes be corrupt and a tribute in the sense of bribery may sometimes be efficient; many social scientists would like to leave matters there. I would like to conclude by separating the two. This volume's tribute to Tom Schelling is a gift, only metaphorically the repayment of our intellectual debt; its motivation, content, and significance is as different from a transaction as love is from paying a telephone bill.

Many anthropologists have followed Marcel Mauss's teaching that tributes such as gifts and praise are "in theory voluntary, disinterested and spontaneous, but are in fact obligatory and interested. The form usually taken is that of the gift generously offered, but the accompanying behaviour is formal pretence and social deception, while the transaction itself is based on obligation and economic self-interest" (1967, p. 1). "It is the law of the gift," wrote H. Newell Wardle (1931, p. 658),

that it may not be summarily refused without giving offense, and a counter gift must be tendered in due season. The Maori of New Zealand class with theft failure to offer the return gift. Neglect to offer or refusal to take a gift is a declaration of war among Dyak tribes of Borneo. The Northwest Coast tribes acknowledge the potlatch to be "fighting with favors" in place of "war by deeds."

He went on to supply many other examples and concluded by noting, "Striving for prestige and the feeling of the need of reciprocity are not absent in gift giving in modern societies."

Wardle's analysis appeared in an old edition of the *Encyclopedia of the Social Sciences*. The newest edition contains no entry under "gifts." Instead, the subject is treated under "exchange and display," and I think this is a telling shift. As members of the class of reciprocities or transactions, are gifts and bribes alike in their essentials? Do these two senses of "tribute" collapse into one?

Those who lean toward answering yes have been predominant in analyses of corruption and indeed in the social sciences. A series of functionalist "explanations"—really, loaded descriptions—have been given of bribery and related acts. Bribes are akin to market prices, say some; to log-rolling, say others; to the cutting of red tape, say still others. Good points, all; but too often they have been taken as conclusions instead of the starting points for further analysis. To note a theoretical similarity and then shrug one's shoulders is the last thing that should be appreciated by an admirer of Thomas C. Schelling.[12]

Look at some differences. A bribe has a purpose: to move the recipient to serve the briber's interests. The more impersonal the medium, the better. The bribe must be delivered secretly; the recipient is usually ruined if the bribe becomes known. The bribe is exchanged for a service, and this equivalence means that the size of the bribe is important. It is intended to create an obligation. A bribe is an act of self-interest.

A gift differs from a bribe along all these dimensions. A gift is a token of affection. Its context is a personal relationship, and its intent is to convey a personal feeling. A gift is the more suitable the more it expresses the recipient's interests and the giver's tastes. Secrecy is not essential, though a gift may be a secret; in general, the recipient is glad to acknowledge the giver. The size of the gift is unimportant. What matters is how the donor expresses identification with the recipient, for this identification is what a gift declares. The gift is wholly the recipient's and in the limit creates no obligation.

In the ideal case, a gift conveys love. John T. Noonan, Jr., writes (1984, p. 695),

> The donee's thanks are but the ghost of a reciprocal bond. That the gift should operate coercively is indeed repugnant and painful to the donor, destructive of the liberality that is intended. Freely given, the gift leaves the donee free. When the love the gift conveys is total, donor and donee are one, so the donor has no one to whom to respond. Every gift tries to approximate this ideal case. A present of any amount is a gift when it conveys love.

Noonan could have been describing the purpose of the tribute we offer in this volume to our colleague and mentor Tom Schelling. We owe much to Tom but only in a highly metaphorical fashion. When we say we are indebted to his work and his example, we mean we are thankful for the gifts he has given to all of us. We present these essays to Tom not ás a payback but as an act of love.

Notes

1. Thanks to Richard Zeckhauser and his seminar of helpful critics for productively pummeling an earlier draft of this essay. Nancy Jackson's editing improved the presentation, though perhaps not as much as she hoped. Emmett Keeler, Elizabeth Rolph, and John Rolph provided encouragement and useful suggestions, and an emotional outburst by Gus Haggstrom ("You're all over the *map* in this thing!") induced a slight tightening of the essay's borders. I have been unable to take all their advice into account, and the usual caveat protecting these courteous people from further responsibility is, of course, in order.

2. Among the luminaries who have worried about the topic of this chapter—the differences between gifts and bribes—are St. Augustine, Gregory VII, Martin Luther, Lord Clive, Marcel Mauss, Peter Blau, and John T. Noonan, Jr.

3. An earlier classic on the strategy of conflict contained a similar sentiment: "Just as some plants bear fruit only if they don't shoot up too high, so in the

practical arts the leaves and flowers of theory must be pruned and the plant kept close to its proper soil—experience" (Clausewitz 1976, p. 61).

4. A military example of this theme: "[W]e are necessarily dealing with the enemy's intentions—his expectations, his incentives, and the guesses that he makes about our intentions and our expectations and our incentives. . . . This is why so many of the estimates we need for dealing with these problems relate to intangibles. The problem involves intangibles. In particular, it involves the great intangible of what the enemy thinks we think he is going to do" (Schelling 1964, p. 216).

5. These definitions (and others related to taxes and levies) appear in *Webster's New World Dictionary* (1979).

6. Another example is Dey 1989, p. 510: "Understanding the microeconomic basis of corruption is the aim of this paper, not suggesting ways of fighting it. Yet a few remarks about the general lines of attack seem to be in order"; followed by a paragraph of schematic advice.

7. Illicitness itself causes inefficiencies here, as Rose-Ackerman (1978, ch. 5) demonstrated. When speed money is legal and customers in a queue are allowed to determine the size of the bribe (or better, payment) offered, then such payments can be an efficient way of auctioning places in line (Lui 1985).

8. For an interesting differentiation of forms of corruption—or "the politics of the gut"—in Africa, see Bayart 1989, pp. 87–138.

9. For example, Karnow (1989) ascribes corruption in the Philippines to the *compradazgo* system, a ritual network of relatives and adopted relatives that commands the loyalty of Filipinos more than any formal institution, and the cultural trait of *utang na loob*, "the debt of gratitude."

10. Weber was reluctant to attribute causation but was "inclined to think the importance of biological heredity was very great" (1958, p. 31).

11. Kanter (1989, ch. 9) emphasizes the importance of performance-based pay. She says the five key trade-offs in incentive systems are individual vs. group contributions, whole agency vs. units, discretion of management vs. automatic or target-based, relative to base pay vs. relative to the value of the contributions to the agency, and a single system vs. multiple systems.

12. Camerer (1988) provides a game-theoretical analysis of gifts as signals and symbols. Noonan brilliantly presents and then rebuts the reductionist view that no useful distinctions can be drawn among bribes and other reciprocities (1984, pp. 687–690 695–699).

References

Altolaguirre, Marta. 1990. "Cuando Sucede. . ," *La Prensa* (Guatemala City), 22 February, my translation.

Bayart, Jean-François. 1988. *L'État en Afrique: La Politique du Ventre*, Paris: Fayard.

Camerer, Colin. 1988. "Gifts as Economic Signals and Social Symbols." *American Journal of Sociology*, 94, supplement.

Cariño, Ledivina V., ed. 1986. *Bureaucratic Corruption in Asia: Causes, Consequences, and Controls*, Quezon City, The Philippines: JMC Press.

Cavell, Stanley. 1976. *Must We Mean What We Say?* Cambridge: Cambridge University Press.

Clausewitz, Carl von. 1976. *On War*, ed. and trans. Michael Howard and Peter Parfet, Princeton, NJ: Princeton University Press.

Darling-Hammond, Linda, and Barnett Berry. 1988. *The Evolution of Teacher Policy*, Santa Monica, CA: The RAND Corporation.

Dey, Harendra Kanti. 1989. "The Genesis and Spread of Economic Corruption: A Microtheoretic Interpretation," *World Development*, 17, no. 4, April.

Etzioni, Amitai. 1982. "The Fight Against Fraud and Abuse," *Journal of Policy Analysis and Management*, 2, Fall.

Gould, David J. 1980. *Bureauctratic Corruption and Underdevelopment in the Third World: The Case of Zaire*, New York: Pergamon Press.

Gould, David J., and José A. Amaro-Reyes. 1983. "The Effects of Corruption on Administrative Performance: Illustrations from Developing Countries," Staff Working Paper No. 580, Management and Development Series. Washington, D.C.: The World Bank.

Harberger, Arnold C. 1984. "Economic Policy and Economic Growth," in *World Economic Growth*, Harberger, ed., San Francisco: ICS Press and International Center for Economic Growth.

Hart, Oliver, and Bengt Holmstrom. 1987. "The Theory of Contracts," in *Advances in Economic Theory—Fifth World Congress*, Truman Bewley, ed., Cambridge: Cambridge University Press.

Holmstrom, Bengt, and Jean Tirole. 1989. "The Theory of the Firm," in *Handbook of Industrial Organization*, R. Schmalensee and R. Willig, eds., Amsterdam: North-Holland.

Huntington, Samuel. 1968. *Political Order in Changing Societies*, New Haven, CT: Yale University Press.

Inman, Robert P. 1987. "Markets, Government, and the 'New' Political Economy," in *Handbook of Public Economics*, vol. 2, Alan J. Auerbach and Martin Feldstein, eds., Amsterdam: North-Holland.

Israel, Arturo. 1987. *Institutional Development: Incentives to Performance*, Baltimore: Johns Hopkins University Press.

Kanter, Rosabeth Moss. 1989. *When Giants Learn to Dance: Mastering the Challenge of Strategy, Management, and Careers in the 1990s*, New York: Simon and Schuster.

Karnow, Stanley. 1989. *In Our Image: America's Empire in the Philippines*, New York: Random House.

Klitgaard, Robert. 1988. *Controlling Corruption*, Berkeley and Los Angeles: University of California Press.

Klitgaard, Robert. 1989. "Incentive Myopia," *World Development*, 17, no. 4, April.

Levine, David I., and Laura D'Andrea Tyson. 1990. "Participation, Productivity, and the Firm's Environment," in *Paying for Productivity: A Look at the Evidence*, Alan S. Blinder, ed., Washington, D.C.: The Brookings Institution.

Lui, Francis T. 1985. "An Equilibrium Queuing Model of Bribery," *Journal of Political Economy*, 93, no. 4, August.

Márquez, Marcela, Carmen Antony, José Antonio Pérez, and Aida S. de Palacios. 1984. *La Corrupción Administrativa en Panamá*, Panama City: Instituto de Criminología, Universidad de Panamá.

Mauss, Marcel. 1967 (1925). *The Gift: Forms and Functions of Exchange in Archaic Societies*, trans. Ian Cunnison, New York and London: W.W. Norton.

Meier, Gerald M. 1984. *Emerging from Poverty: The Economics That Really Matters*, New York: Oxford University Press.

Meier, Gerald M., ed. 1991. *Politics and Policy Making in Developing Countries: Perspectives on the New Political Economy*, San Francisco: ICS Press and International Center for Economic Growth.

Milgrom, Paul. 1988. "Efficient Contracts, Influence Activities, and Efficient Organizational Design," *Journal of Political Economy*, 96 no. 1.

Milgrom, Paul, and John Roberts. 1988. "An Economic Approach to Influence Activities in Organizations," *American Journal of Sociology*, 94, supplement.

Milgrom, Paul, and John Roberts. 1989. "Economic Theories of the Firm: Past, Present, and Future," *Canadian Journal of Economics*, XXI, 3, August: 444–458.

Mitchell, Daniel J. B., David Lewin, and Edward E. Lawler III. 1990. "Alternative Pay Systems, Firm Performance, and Productivity," in *Paying for Productivity: A Look at the Evidence*, Alan S. Blinder, ed., Washington, D.C.: The Brookings Institution.

Myrdal, Gunnar. 1989 (1968). "Corruption as a Hindrance to Modernization in South Asia," in *Political Corruption: A Handbook*, Arnold J. Heidenheimer, Michael Johnson, and Victor T. LeVine, eds., New Brunswick, NJ: Transaction Publishers.

Naipaul, V. S. 1988. *The Enigma of Arrival*, New York: Vintage.

Nehamas, Alexander. 1985. *Nietzsche: Life as Literature*, Cambridge, MA: Harvard University Press.

Noonan, John T., Jr. 1984. *Bribes*, New York: Macmillan.

Rose-Ackerman, Susan. 1978. *Corruption: A Study in Political Economy*, New York: Academic Press.

Rose-Ackerman, Susan. 1986. "Reforming Public Bureaucracy through Economic Incentives?" *Journal of Law, Economics, and Organization*, 2, no. 1, Spring.

Schelling, Thomas C. 1955. "American Foreign Assistance," *World Politics*, VII, no. 4, July.

Schelling, Thomas C. 1960. *The Strategy of Conflict*, Cambridge, MA: Harvard University Press.

Schelling, Thomas C. 1963. "War without Pain and Other Models," *World Politics*, 15, no. 3, April: 464–487.

Schelling, Thomas C. 1964. "Assumptions about Enemy Behavior." In *Analysis for Military Decisions*, E. S. Quade, ed., Santa Monica: The RAND Corporation.

Schelling, Thomas C. 1966. *Arms and Influence*, New Haven, CT: Yale University Press.

Schelling, Thomas C. 1967. "Some Questions on Civilian Defence," in *The Strategy of Civilian Defence: Non-violent Resistance to Aggression*, Adam Roberts, ed., London: Faber and Faber.

Schelling, Thomas C. 1971. "What Is the Business of Organized Crime?" *The American Scholar*, 40, 4, Autumn

Schelling, Thomas C. 1972. "Hockey Helmets, Concealed Weapons and Daylight Saving: A Study of Binary Choices with Externalities," Discussion Paper No. 9, Cambridge, MA: Kennedy School of Government.

Schelling, Thomas C. 1974. "Command and Control," in *Social Responsibility and the Business Predicament*, James W. McKie, ed., Washington, D.C.: The Brookings Institution.

Schelling, Thomas C. 1985. "Policy Analysis as a Science of Choice," in *Public Policy and Policy Analysis in India*, R. S. Ganapathy et al., eds., New Delhi: Sage.

Schelling. Thomas C. 1989. "Promises," *Negotiation Journal*, 5, no. 2, April.

Smith, Adam. 1976 (1776). *An Inquiry into the Nature and Causes of the Wealth of Nations*, Oxford: Oxford University Press.

Srinavasan, T. N. 1985. "Neoclassical Political Economy, the State and Economic Development," *Asian Development Review*, 3, no. 2.

United Nations. 1990. *Corruption in Government*, TCD/SEM. 90/2. INT-89-R56, New York: United Nations Department of Technical Co-operation for Development.

Wardle, Newell. 1931. "Gifts," *Encyclopedia of the Social Sciences*, vol. VI. New York: Macmillan.

Weber, Max. 1958 (1904–1905). *The Protestant Ethic and the Spirit of Capitalism*, trans. Talcott Parsons, New York: Charles Scribner's Sons.

Webster's New World Dictionary of the American Language. 1979. Second college ed., Cleveland: William Collins.

Williamson, Oliver. 1985. *The Economic Institutions of Capitalism*, New York: Free Press.

Wilson, James Q. 1989. *Bureaucracy: What Government Agencies Do and Why They Do It*, New York: Basic Books.

Wilson, James Q., and Richard J. Herrnstein. 1985. *Crime and Human Nature*, New York: Simon and Schuster.

10

The Strategic Use of Contracts with Third Parties

Jerry R. Green

One of the most important ideas in modern game theory was first stated systematically in chapter 2 of Thomas Schelling's *The Strategy of Conflict*. Schelling points out that a player may benefit by agreeing to diminish his own payoffs in some circumstances, because this commitment changes his own incentives and hence can influence the equilibria of the game he is playing.[1] Unilateral action to diminish one's own payoffs is not often credible. To make such a commitment credible, a player can sign a contract promising a third party part of the payoff he would otherwise keep for himself. Because the third party will enforce his rights under the contract, the payoff modification has been made credible to other participants in the game or bargaining situation.

This stratagem is of considerable practical importance. When firms have market power, it is well recognized that the ability to commit to a business strategy may be of great competitive advantage.[2] Unfortunately, the most effective threats are often the least credible. Establishing a reputation is one way to bind oneself to such actions.[3] Another way to sustain aggressive strategies is to hire an agent (or a manager of the firm) whose job it is to execute these business plans. By thus separating ownership and control of the firm and by tying the manager's compensation offer to the firm's profits, one might make otherwise incredible threats. Another way to commit to strategically advantageous actions is to become heavily indebted. Because limited profits will be of no value if they cannot cover the indebtedness, the firm will try extreme measures in an attempt to make enough profits that there is something left for the owners. This should convince the competition that the firm will compete aggressively, and in light of this they may back off. In this case the outside "third party" is not a single individual but rather the collectivity of all creditors of the firm.[4]

Finally, in administrative and political contexts, the credible commitment is commonly effected by making a binding promise to one group that it will be treated exactly like another. It is then possible to avoid acquiescing to either group's demands by arguing that, "if I do it for you I will have to do it for them." In this case each group plays the role of the "third party" vis-à-vis the other.

The idea behind using contracts or irrevocable promises to gain an advantage rests on a two-phase conceptualization of the economic interaction. In the first phase, contracts are used to modify the payoffs of a game or a bargaining situation. They may also modify the control relationships by reassigning the rights to make or reject an agreement with the other side. In the second phase, the modified game is played, or the altered bargaining situation resolved.

Schelling recognizes that contracts made in the initial phase are not automatically credible. Arrangements with the partner must be observable and irrevocable if they are to be incorporated into the other player's understanding of the game and hence to influence the equilibria. Schelling writes,

When one wishes to persuade someone that he would not pay him more than $16000 for a house that is really worth $20000 to him, what can he do to take advantage of the usually superior credibility of the truth over a false assertion? Answer: make it true. . . . [T]he buyer could make an irrevocable and enforceable bet with some third party, duly recorded and certified, according to which he would pay for the house no more than $16000 or forfeit $5000.[5]

But how is the contract made irrevocable? If secret or private renegotiation is possible, the contract will have no credibility.[6] To prevent renegotiation, one must either invoke a reputational argument or make communication between the principal and his partner impossible.[7] Finally, an effective contract requires that the partner not be able subsequently to contract with the opponent in a way that would undo the incentives originally created. As Schelling notes,

In the example of the self-inflicted penalty through the bet, it remains possible for the seller to seek out the third party and offer a modest sum in consideration of the latter's releasing the buyer from the bet, threatening to sell the house for $16000 if the release is not forthcoming.[8]

Assuming that the contract can be made observable, irrevocable, and immune to modification by further bilateral contracting between the partner and either the principal or his opponent, how should the resulting economic interaction be modeled? Who are the active players and what communication channels are open? If the principal can remove himself from the situation entirely, a two-person game is now to be played between the partner and the opponent.[9] If, as in Schelling's house purchase example, it is the partner who can be cut off from any remaining interaction, the principal's payoffs have been modified by virtue of his contract, and it is he who still bargains with the seller, the partner playing no active role. Alternatively, the contract can require the assent of both the principal and the partner before an agreement with the opponent can be consummated.

The effect of the bet—as of most such contractual commitments—is to shift the locus and personnel of the negotiation in the hope that the third party will be less available for negotiation. . . . If all interested parties can be brought into the negotiation the range of indeterminacy remains as it was. . .[10]

When the principal has the power to reach an agreement with the opponent without the partner's consent, we will say that the latter is a "silent partner." (Alternatively, the principal could be a silent partner if he gave an agent irrevocable power to negotiate against the opponent without his further intervention.) If the contract requires that both the principal and the partner agree before any resolution is final, we will call them "cosignatories." Control of negotiations with the opponent is as much a part of the contract design as is the compensation to be paid to the partner when the outcome of the negotiations is known. We ask whether an observable irrevocable contract between a principal and his partner could be beneficial when the parties know that the final result will be obtained through an interaction among all of them. And if a contract is beneficial, should it be one in which one of the two contractually bound agents is the silent partner of the other, or should they be cosignatories?

We will reassess Schelling's statement, asking whether the existence of the contract affects the "range of indeterminacy." That is, is the solution of the resulting three-person bargaining problem the same, as far as the principal and his opponent are concerned, as the solution to their original two-person problem?[11]

Although Schelling's ideas were well known and well appreciated, it is only very recently that the strategic advantages of contracting with third parties have been examined in economic applications. For example, a firm can issue securities that effectively modify the return to the original equity holders much as if a Schelling-like "bet" had been made with an outsider. Here the third party is not any single player but rather is the debt market as a collective entity.[12] Other potential third parties are the firm's employees, especially if a union exists, or even the firm's customers, if a long-term contract can be signed with them. In this line of research the firm's original equity holders continue to be the strategic players in the product market interaction with actual and potential competitors.[13]

The other way of credibly altering product market behavior is to hire managers who are independent of the owners and who are compensated according to contractually determined performance measures.[14] Now the third party is the active player in the second-stage product market game, and it is assumed that the original equity holders can withdraw credibly from further negotiations.[15]

Recent more abstract game-theoretic analyses, closer in spirit to this chapter,[16] ask whether and to what extent the original equilibria of the game between two principals can be altered when the principals are represented by agents whose payoffs are contractually determined.

These papers implicitly follow Schelling in assuming that the principals can isolate themselves from the actual playing of the game—that is, the principals become the silent partners. With contracts in place, the game is played by the partner and the opponent. Here, however, I shall assume that the principals remain active participants. Their incentives may have been modified by the contractual arrangements they have made with their respective representatives, but all players are active in the second-phase game. The crucial decision, it turns out, is not which of the partners shall deal with the opponent, but rather whether agreement shall require the assent of both partners or just one of them.

Is this presumption of active principal behavior realistic? Consider some real-world agency relationships: lawyers under contract to negotiate between potential litigants, for example, or investment bankers retained by a raider and a target firm in a potential takeover, or the realtors acting for the buyer and the seller in a typical sale of a house. There is nothing to prevent one of the litigants from contacting the other and proposing a settlement without going through the attorneys. A target firm could issue a public statement about some defensive actions it might take, effectively communicating with the raider without the investment banker's approval. The buyer could negotiate specific terms directly with the seller of the house. Whether or not these contacts are advantageous, they do seem possible.

In these situations the actual negotiation is more complex than can be modeled by a two-person game involving only the two representatives. Indeed the legal, ethical, and professional prohibitions regarding direct communication between a principal and the agent of the other party, or between the two principals once agents have been retained, testify that these activities are not irrelevant and severe sanctions are required to prevent their occurrence.[17]

These examples teach us a mixed lesson. Genuine isolated bilateral play between the representatives is rarely the right model of interaction, but neither is totally unrestricted three- (or four-) player bargaining. I shall nevertheless explore the latter possibility because previous research has concentrated on the former, and it is useful to establish another benchmark. I hope to discover whether Schelling's conclusions about the effectiveness of agency necessarily hinge on the conditions that renegotiation is impossible and only two of the three players can participate in the second phase of the interaction.

If the principal is able, for example, to cut himself off from all further communication, then the underlying situation is really not a symmetric bargaining model at all. In Schelling's example, if the buyer can offer the third party the incentive contract to buy the house and then become incommunicado, why can he not make a take-it-or-leave-it offer to the opponent, cutting off communication in just the same way? If he can cut himself off from the partner but not from the opponent, could not the opponent become an unwanted intermediary, carrying verifiable enforceable messages between the partner and the principal?

The next section of the paper establishes the basic model, describes the nature of contracts, and discusses four solutions that can be used to resolve the range of indeterminacy and thus to determine the outcome. It will be shown that, in the most plausible models of the second phase of the negotiation process and for the most commonly observed compensation arrangements, a contract that involves a silent partner can potentially shift the outcome in favor of the principal, whereas one in which the principal and his partner are cosignatories cannot be beneficial. The following section shows that a contract requiring cosignatories can benefit the principal only if its results are not monotonically related to the underlying outcome of a bargaining game. A brief summary concludes.

Contracts and Trilaterial Bargaining: Cosignatories and Silent Partners

In this section we pursue Schelling's idea that one of the two bargainers can enter into an observable and irrevocable contract with a third party. We assume that the opposing player cannot offer this agent a contract, nor can he offer to buy him out of the contract he has made with the first player or compensate him for not enforcing all of its provisions. If any of these actions were possible, then, as Schelling shows, the arrangement could not be beneficial to the principal.

For concreteness, we suppose that the principal and the opponent have the opportunity to divide $1. If they fail to agree on how the dollar is to be divided, they each get zero. In this bargaining situation there is a "range of indeterminacy," the set of all allocations of the dollar in two parts t and $1 - t$, which represents the possible outcomes of the agreement that are at least as good for each of the players as what he would achieve by refusing to agree at all.

A contract between the principal and his partner will transform this two-player situation into a three-player bargaining problem. The principal can agree to divide his share of the underlying bargain t with the partner, giving the partner $x(t)$ and retaining $t - x(t)$ for himself. Thus if the contract specifies that the partner's share shall be $x(t)$ when the principal's share of the underlying bargain is t, the range of indeterminacy of the two-person problem has been translated into a "range of indeterminacy" for the three players given by all payoffs of the form $(t - x(t), 1 - t, x(t))$, for the principal, opponent, and partner, respectively. (Throughout this chapter we will maintain this ordering and will alternatively refer to the participants as players 1, 2, and 3, respectively. This is most often the form followed when we give a geometrical description of contracts and alternative possible payoffs; see below.)

Competitive Partners and Up-Front Contracting Fees

We assume that the principal has access to a number of potential partners before the contracting. Competition among these agents will result in a contract that gives the partner exactly his opportunity cost but no more than that. Any payment that the third party foresees himself getting as a result of the contract can be extracted from him in advance by requiring him to bid against other potential partners for the right to enter the agreement with the principal. In this way the principal's total payoff is one minus the opponent's payoff in the resulting bargain. Thus the best contract will be the one that minimizes the opponent's payoff, irrespective of how it allocates the remainder between the principal and his partner.

Whether a contract is acceptable to the partner, and whether it is better for the principal than the original bilateral bargaining problem, depends on how the "ranges of indeterminacy" created by these contracts will be narrowed down to a unique definitive outcome. The resolution of bargaining indeterminacy is a far more straightforward task in the original two-person game than it is in the post-contract three-person environment. With only two players, and with no reason to believe that one has more bargaining ability than the other, splitting the range in half is the obvious choice. This is the solution that would occur to any outside arbitrator, it has the virtue of simplicity, and it is selected by all formal theories of bargaining. In the three-person case there is no natural midpoint to select. A more elaborate approach to the bargaining problem is required in multilateral cases. We will examine several alternative theories of bargaining, each of which corresponds to a social norm.[18] The players are assumed to understand this norm and to use it to predict the allocation resulting from the contract.[19] Which of these theories is most appropriate depends on whether a silent partner has delegated signature authority or whether both partners must assent in renegotiation, and on whether certain types of extracontractual transfers are observable. These issues will be explored further below, after the solution concepts have been explained.

Before analyzing optimal contracts, one should ask whether a contract will be offered at all. The principal has the option of remaining in the two-person case, which is likely to provide a fifty-fifty split between the opponents, as discussed above. A contract will be beneficial to the principal only if the opponent can be held to a share of less than one-half. As we explore alternative methods of resolving the range of indeterminacy in the presence of a contract, and analyze the effects of different contracts between the principal and his partner, we will focus on whether the final result will give the opponent strictly less than one-half. Only in that case will the contract be executed.

Geometric Description of Three-Person Bargaining Problems

To develop some intuition, let us describe the problem geometrically, as shown in figure 10.1. Figure 10.1a shows how any allocation of a dollar into three parts corresponds to a point in the equilateral triangle. The vertices represent the extremes at which one of the three players receives the whole dollar. A point such as c in the interior shows a division in which the share of player i is the length of the line drawn perpendicular to the side opposite player i's vertex. In any equilateral triangle, the sum of these lengths is the same regardless of the point from which we take these perpendiculars. Thus we can use this two-dimensional figure to display all the possible partitions of a fixed amount into three parts.

Figure 1b shows a contract $x(t)$ between the principal and his partner in which the partner has paid a lump-sum fee of f. Each point on the curve results from the payment of the fee f and the contractually specified transfer $x(t)$ following the underlying division of the dollar into parts t and $1 - t$ for the principal and the opponent. If an agreement is reached, the sum of the payoffs is $1. For example, if $t = 0$ is the underlying agreement, the resulting payoffs are at point a, because the opponent gets $1, the principal gets the fee f minus the contractually agreed amount $x(0)$ that he gives to his partner, leaving $f - x(0)$ as his share of the total. The partner gets $x(0) - f$, and the opponent gets $1.

If the players fail to reach an agreement, the payoffs will be $(f, 0, -f)$ respectively. The lump-sum fee shifts the original divisions of the dollar, shown as a solid triangle, in favor of the principal and against the partner. In the dotted triangle, which has been shifted to the left by the amount f, we show how the division of the dollar is determined relative to the threat point inclusive of the payment of the lump-sum fee. The relevant region in which an agreement can lie is shown as B. These are all the possible payoff allocations in which no player gets less than he could have achieved in the disagreement outcome, and the terms of the contract have been followed. Note that the option to default to the disagreement outcome may eliminate some ranges of t as possible underlying agreements. (As shown, the agreement to set $t = 0$, which would result in point a, is eliminated for this reason.) We do allow the players to agree on a randomization over possible values of t. That is why the shaded region, consisting of all convex combinations of points along the $x(t)$ locus meeting the

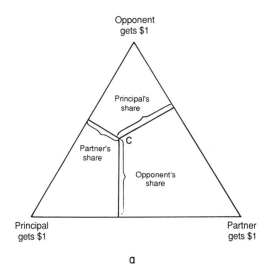

Opponent
gets $1

Principal's
share

Partner's
share

C

Opponent's
share

Principal
gets $1

Partner
gets $1

a

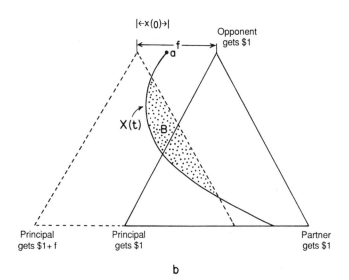

|←x(0)→|

Opponent
gets $1

←—— f ——→

•a

X(t)

B

Principal
gets $1+ f

Principal
gets $1

Partner
gets $1

b

Figure 10.1

criterion of no default to disagreement, is included in the bargaining region.

The magnitude of the fixed fee does not affect the subsequent bargaining outcome. If the principal and his partner negotiate a fixed fee for signing the contract, it is a form of sunk cost, or a bygone. It will have shifted payoffs in the game and the location of the disagreement point by exactly the same amount. Therefore we neglect the fixed fee when discussing solutions to the bargaining game. We will solve the bargaining problem and examine the payoff of the opponent. If and only if this falls short of one-half, the principal's results—the fixed fee combined with the bargaining outcome—will be better than he could have achieved without a contract.

Alternative Solutions to Three-Person Bargaining Problems with Cosignatories and Silent Partners

A simple example of a contract will help us examine four solution concepts, two each for the cases of cosignatories and silent partners. In the context of this example we will see the differences among these solutions and the way they incorporate the rights of the partner to participate in the agreement, to enforce the contract, and to observe the activities of the principal and the opponent. We conclude that one of the two solutions discussed in each case is to be preferred and base the analysis in the next section on these two.

First consider the simple "sharing contract" in which the principal promises the partner a fixed share α of any portion of the allocation he receives. If the principal and the opponent achieve shares t and $1 - t$ respectively, the partner receives αt and the principal retains $(1 - \alpha)t$. The underlying allocations for this problem are shown in figure 10.2a. The fixed fee f is determined endogenously, in such a way that the total payment received by the partner, net of any fee he has paid, is zero. This is because there are a large number of potential third parties ready to enter into contracts with this principal if there are positive rewards to be had and willing to compete with each other for the right to do so. As described above, we can neglect the fixed fee in our analysis of whether the opponent's share falls short of one-half. Thus we consider the contract as shown in figure 10.2b, which is the same as in figure 10.2a but without the transfer from the principal to the partner in the amount f.

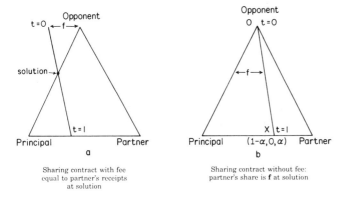

Figure 10.2

Consider first the case in which the partner is a cosignatory. Unless all three players agree, the disagreement outcome results; groups of two players are powerless. Therefore the description of the set of underlying allocations contains all the information relevant to this problem and determines the final allocation. Once t is determined, the contract is enforced and results in the final allocation $((1 - \alpha)t,$ $(1 - t), \alpha t)$.

If, on the other hand, the third party is a silent partner, the principal and the opponent can threaten to impose an agreement that they reach without consulting or compensating him. They have the right to do so because the principal has not given the partner the right to veto the agreement. This case requires a more detailed analysis of the situation, with an explicit examination of the power of coalitions comprising a subset of the players. A description of the feasible set of underlying agreements is not a complete picture of the bargaining environment.

For the example of a sharing contract, this analysis is particularly simple. Only the coalition consisting of the principal and the opponent has the power to reach and enforce an underlying agreement. Neither of the two-person coalitions involving the partner has any power at all. Therefore to model contracting with a silent partner, we need to look at the set of allocations that are obtainable by the three players together and the set that can be reached by the principal and the opponent as a pair.

Let us now return to the case of a cosignatory in which the bargaining region is the sole determinant of the outcome. The selection of a unique outcome from a set of possibilities is the classical bargaining problem. Analysts of bargaining and negotiation, observing actual outcomes and defining desirable guiding principles, have sought to identify the allocations that will or should result. The rule by which an outcome is generated from the underlying possibilities is called a bargaining solution. The most well-known bargaining solutions are those discovered and analyzed by Nash, Shapley, and Harsanyi. We will explore these, and one other solution, to see what they predict about the benefits of strategic contracting with a third party. Specifically, we will see what they predict about which point on the segment OX in figure 10.2b will result.

The Nash bargaining solution[20] would select the underlying allocation in which $t = 2/3$, resulting in the payoffs $(2(1 - \alpha)/3, 1/3, 2\alpha/3)$. This outcome results because the Nash solution is invariant to the scale in which any player's payoffs are measured.[21] Thus the zero-sum situation shown in figure 10.2b is the same as the non-zero-sum situation in which the principal and the partner gain a unit of utility *each* for every unit given up by the opponent.[22] Symmetry across individuals therefore requires that the two individuals who benefit from higher values of t get twice the weight in determining the outcome as the one individual who loses as t rises. Under the Nash solution the principal stands to gain from a contract such as the one proposed. The mere presence of the partner as a passive player is enough to shift the solution to the opponent's disadvantage.

An alternative to the Nash solution is the iterated Steiner solution defined in Green 1983. This solution is based on the idea that in a zero-sum situation the trade-off between the players should be determined by the maximization of a linear weighting of the individuals' utilities.[23] Because we have no theory of which weights to use for the three players,[24] we should admit any possible weighting scheme and then ensure the anonymity and fairness of the procedure by randomizing the assignment of weights to players. This procedure selects a subset of the set of possible allocations but does not, in general, result in a unique solution. It narrows down the possibilities. If we accept the premise that the ultimate solution should be the same whether the problem is as originally given or whether the narrowed-down set of allocations were the specified set from which a selection is to be made, we are led naturally to the idea of repeating the process (randomizing weights and maximizing weighted utilities), using at each step the allocations that survived the prior stage. When this has been repeated over and over again, it has been shown that a unique outcome emerges. We call this outcome the *iterated Steiner solution*.[25]

In the example at hand, for any weights w_1, w_2, w_3 not all equal, the maximal allocation is at $t = 0$ if $w_1 + w_3 < w_2$ and at $t = 1$ if this inequality is reversed. Thus, randomizing the roles of the players we get a randomized outcome of $t = 0$ with probability 1/3 and $t = 1$ with probability 2/3 if the second-largest weight is high relative to the smallest, and the randomized outcome with the probabilities reversed if the second-largest weight is close to the lowest. (The exact conditions will depend on α, but this is not important for our argument.) Thus taking one step of this process limits the result to the middle third of the segment OX in figure 10.2b. By iteration we clearly converge to the midpoint, where the opponent's payoff is exactly one-half. Thus, unlike the Nash solution, the iterated Steiner solution predicts that there is no advantage for this particular fixed-share contract between the principal and his partner. We will show that this property holds for an important class of contracts, but that for a more general set of contracts there is an advantage.

In the case of silent partners the bargaining outcome depends on the abilities of smaller coalitions to achieve results independent of the coalition of the whole. In the present example the only two-player coalition that has any power at all is that of the principal and the opponent. Their attainable set is shown in figure 10.3.

How might the possibilities for this two-player coalition affect the outcome of the three-player bargain? One possibility is that the principal and the opponent see that they can guarantee for themselves the maximum total payoff of 1 without cooperating with the partner. To achieve this they must agree to set $t = 0$. Then the principal does not have to share with the partner at all. Were they to agree to anything else, the three-person coalition would be strictly more advantageous than their two-person coalition; consequently the partner could rightfully claim a share of the surplus his cooperation in the three-person coalition helped to generate. Thus the principal and the opponent could agree to pretend that they have settled on $t = 0$ and argue that therefore the partner should get nothing. But they could then effect a secret transfer from the opponent to the principal, compensating him for colluding in this fictitious and unfair division. If such a secret transfer is possible, they can credibly claim that they do not need the partner's cooperation in order to achieve for the two of them the full

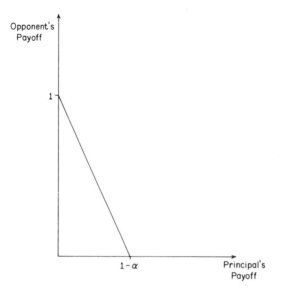

Figure 10.3

payoff that the three-person coalition could reach. By symmetry the principal and the opponent share the total of one equally. This solution concept coincides with the Shapley value.[26] Under this solution the opponent gets one-half, and thus the principal would gain nothing by offering a contract to a partner.

The notion of surreptitious transfers can be criticized on two grounds. First, our analysis of the contracting problem depends on the fact that the contract is observable. It seems contrary to the spirit of this analysis that the transfer could be kept a secret, thus undermining the contract. Second, even if a secret transfer were feasible, there is no reason to expect that it would take place after the agreement between the principal and the opponent has openly been reached. Having obtained all the gains from trade in full view of the partner and any enforcement powers that the partner has brought to monitor the contractual arrangements, the opponent has no reason to give anything to the principal under the table. And the principal has no legal claim to enforce against him because the promise of such a transfer was clandestine. For this reason we reject the analysis based on the Shapley value and must look for another solution concept for the games (with nontransferable utility) that result from contracting with a silent partner.

What threat by the coalition of the principal and the opponent is possible when they must honestly stick with the agreed-upon division? One possibility is that the two players would choose the allocation at which they receive the same payoff, in this case $1 - \alpha/2 - \alpha$ each. This leaves a surplus of $\alpha/(2 - \alpha)$ that can be obtained by the coalition of the whole. It is natural that the partner have a claim on this equal to that of the other players. Thus the overall solution is $((3 - 2\alpha)/3(2 - \alpha), (3 - 2\alpha)/3(2 - \alpha), \alpha/3(2 - \alpha))$. The other notable bargaining solution that can be applied to nontransferable utility games in characteristic function form is the Harsanyi value.[27] Because the opponent's share is less than one-half for all values of α, sharing contracts are advantageous to the principal.

Whether the egalitarian allocation between the principal and the opponent will be used as their threat against the partner is not obvious. It does have considerable normative appeal. However, there is a clear trade-off between efficiency and equity, a trade-off that might very well lead to a credible choice of threat that gives the opponent somewhat more than the principal.[28] Indeed, if there is even a relatively minor departure toward efficiency in the present example, the opponent will get more than one-half, in which case the contract will have been disadvantageous to the principal. Thus, unless one can be sure that equal division will be used as the threat, the efficacy of sharing contracts is an empirical matter.

To summarize, we have presented four solutions, two for the case of cosignatories and two for the case of silent partners. When the third party is a cosignatory, we looked at the Nash solution and at the iterated Steiner solution. The former, although seeming to lead to the conclusion that contracts are beneficial, gives excessive power to the partner because of the assumption that the solution is invariant to linear transformations of the payoffs.[29] This solution is more likely to be appropriate when payoffs are in utility units than when the payoffs are directly comparable, as in the zero-sum problem we have presented. The iterated Steiner solution leads to the conclusion that contracts with cosignatories cannot help the principal do any better than he could by bargaining with the opponent in the absence of a contract.

In the case of silent partners we looked at the Shapley λ-transfer value and the Harsanyi value. We reject the former as a model of this situation because it implicitly allows for secret side payments, which are not credible, even if they were feasible. The latter solution seems quite appropriate if the resolution of the threat is likely to be determined on egalitarian grounds as between the threatening parties. Under that assumption the contract with a silent partner will be unambiguously beneficial. In more general circumstances in which the threat embodies a compromise between equity and efficiency, and no secret side payments can be made, the efficacy of the contract is possible but not by any means certain.

More General Contracts

In this section we will look at contracts more general than the simple sharing contract of the last section to see what the iterated Steiner solution and the Harsanyi value (and its generalizations) imply about the potency of contracts with cosignatories and silent partners. We will see that the effectiveness of contracts with cosignatories depends essentially on whether the interests of the principal and his partner are always coincident, as in the fixed-share contract of the last section, or whether their interests are in some cases opposed, as in the contract discussed by Schelling as described in the introduction. The former type of contract will be called *monotonic* because both the principal and the partner have payoffs that are strictly increasing with (hence monotonic in) t. The latter type is called *nonmonotonic*. In figure 10.4 we show the payoffs for the principal and the partner in a general monotonic contract and in the particular nonmonotonic contract of chapter 2 of *The Strategy of Conflict*.

In any monotonic contract with cosignatories the principal gets exactly one-half when we resolve the indeterminacy by using the iterated Steiner solution. This can be seen by referring to figure 10.5. The original monotonic contract is shown by the shaded region. After one application of the maximization of a linear function of the payoffs, the set of allocations shrinks to the region indicated between points X and Y. The exact shape of this region depends on the contract. However, the interval XY is always precisely the middle third of the segment OZ, and the boundary of the region between X and Y is monotonic in the sense that as one moves along either side of it (from X to Y), both the principal's and the partner's payoffs increase. Thus this set has all of the characteristics of a bargaining region generated by a monotonic contract to allocate the division of \$1 subject to the constraint that the principal and the opponent both receive at least one-third. Clearly, successive iterations of this problem will converge

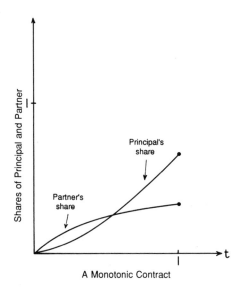

A Monotonic Contract

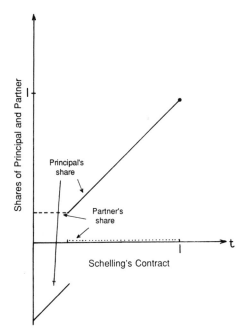

Schelling's Contract

Figure 10.4

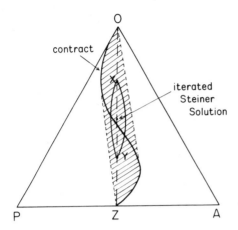

Figure 10.5

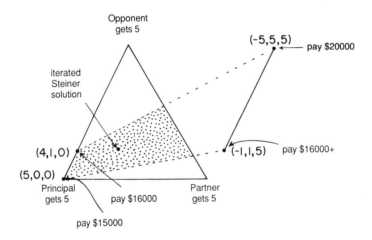

Payoffs are shares of $5000 surplus (in thousands).
Shaded area is the bargaining region for Schelling's contract.

Figure 10.6

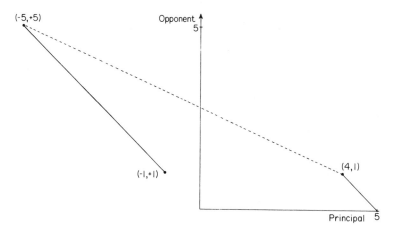

Feasible utilities (with randomization) for Principal and Opponent
when Agent is a Silent Partner in Schelling's house-sale contract.

Figure 10.7

upon the midpoint of OZ, at which point the opponent receives exactly one-half.[30]

Nonmonotonic contracts with cosignatories may benefit the principal. For example, consider the contract suggested in chapter 2 of *The Strategy of Conflict*, as described in the introduction. This contract is nonmonotonic, because the partner's payoff falls from $5,000 to zero as the price paid by the principal drops below $16,000. The allocations generated by this contract are shown in figure 10.6. Assuming that all agreements must give players a payoff at least as great as they would achieve at the disagreement point, the bargaining region is the set of outcomes spanned by the underlying agreements that give all players at least a non-negative share of the $5,000 surplus that can be generated by the trade. This region is shown as the shaded area in figure 10.5. It can be shown that the iterated Steiner solution as applied to this bargaining region is approximately (2,670, 950, 1,480). Note that the opponent can be held to a value far below his $2,500 share of the $5,000 surplus available.[31]

Now let us consider the case of contracts with a cosignatory and the associated resolution of the range of indeterminacy associated with the Harsanyi value. Figure 10.7 shows the utility possibility set available to the principal and the opponent under the contract that Schelling suggests. Here the egalitarian solution would select $t = 2/3$, and the Harsanyi value for the opponent would be $2,222. If the threat of this coalition is not egalitarian but rather reflects a balance between the egalitarian allocation and a more efficient one, the opponent's payoff is further reduced. This is an essential difference between monotonic contracts (such as the fixed-share contract of the last section) and nonmonotonic contracts (such as the Schelling contract of *The Strategy of Conflict*). As usual, Schelling's insights were correct: there is substantial power to be gained by making an observable and irrevocable nonmonotonic contract with either a cosignatory or a silent partner.

Conclusions

Schelling asked whether the outcome of a bargaining problem can be favorably influenced by contracting with a third party in an observable and irrevocable manner. Reexamining this question, we find that if the contract is monotonic, in that the contracting parties' interests are always aligned, then a beneficial result is possible only if the partner is silent, unable to veto the agreement between the principal and the opponent. If the third party is made a cosignatory, the contract will not be beneficial. Even in the monotonic case with a silent partner, favorable results are not assured. They depend on the nature of the threats that the principal and the opponent are able to make. To the extent that credible threats will embody efficiency considerations rather than equity, these contracts will likewise be impotent.

Matters are quite different if nonmonotonic contracts, such as the contract discussed by Schelling in *The Strategy of Conflict*, are possible. Then either cosignatories or silent partners can be used to influence the results of the bargaining problem in favor of the principal.

Notes

1. Indeed Schelling shows this to be the case for payoff modifications that are, in every case, decreases, and hence easily credible when there is a form of free disposal of utility. This theme has recently been explored by Ben-Porath and Dekel (1988).

2. These commitments may affect the payoff of the competitors as well as the payoff of the firm in question, as for example in the case of preemptory, strategic building of excess capacity to deter entry; see Spence 1977. In this chapter we will be concerned with strategies that alter one's own payoffs but do not directly affect the payoffs of competitors or opponents.

3. Reputational effects are also a theme that can be traced to Schelling; indeed they are featured in *The Strategy of Conflict* as well. Much recent research has been devoted to how threats based on reputation might become sustainable in dynamic contexts, in the presence of imperfections of information or when mutually damaging deterrent strategies exist.

4. These two examples and the relevant related literature are discussed further, later in this section.

5. Schelling 1960, p. 24.

6. See Katz 1987 or Dewatripont 1988.

7. With an explicit extensive form model of the contracting process, such as that in Hart and Moore 1988, there is a last moment at which legally binding commitments can be made; making a commitment at that time is a way of ensuring that it cannot be modified. We shall not follow this route.

8. Schelling 1960, p. 25.

9. This is the situation assumed in most of the recent purely theoretical literature; see Katz 1987 and Fershtman, Judd, and Kalai 1989. Some of the applied literature presumes that the agent takes over the principal's possible moves in the game, while other contributions assume that the principal continues to act on his own behalf. See the further discussion below.

10. Schelling 1960, p. 25.

11. The one asymmetry between the principal and his opponent is that the former has a first-mover advantage in contracting with an agent. If the opponent could react by taking an agent of his own in response, a four-person bargaining problem, instead of a three-person problem, would result. Does the principal gain from his first-mover advantage in this case? This problem is discussed in Green 1989.

12. The effect of such financial market strategies on product market behavior has been studied by Brander and Lewis (1986) and Maxsimovic (1986).

13. Contracts with employees are studied in Dewatripont 1987, 1988 and contracts with customers are examined in Aghion and Bolton 1987. These papers are primarily concerned with the issue of credible commitments between the equity holders and the third party. Therefore their main focus is on making the contract secure against renegotiation.

14. See Williamson 1964, 1985.

15. This situation has been studied by Sklivas (1987) and Fershtman and Judd (1987a). Complications arise when there is incomplete information about firm characteristics that are relevant both to the third party and to the product market rivals. Signaling and contractual precommitment become intertwined. See Poitevin 1989a, 1989b, 1989c and Gertner, Gibbons, and Scharfstein 1988.

16. See Katz 1987, Fershtman and Judd 1987b, and Fershtman, Judd, and Kalai 1989.

17. It would be interesting to study the creation and policing of the institutions through which such forbidden communication is monitored. This process probably involves the reputation of the agents, who are the long-run players, and the competitive environment in which they operate.

18. Each of these theories of bargaining, or solutions, can be based on a set of axioms that uniquely determine the nature of the solution. Space limitations preclude any more than the briefest discussion and comparison of the axioms here.

19. The saliency of certain norms, such as "split the difference," may be useful in that negotiation costs are reduced. Although our analysis ignores negotiation and bargaining costs, we note that one important justification for assuming all players understand that a particular norm will apply is that they know which norms are efficient in avoiding such costs.

20. See Nash 1950.

21. This is because utilities are determined only up to linear transformation and because the Nash solution is based, among other axioms, on the hypothesis that the solution should be independent of this representation.

22. Take the utility weights to be $1/(1 - \alpha)$ and $1/\alpha$ for the principal and the agent.

23. A central axiom of that theory is called linearity, or additivity. This axiom and its consequences for bargaining problems without transferable utility have been explored by Maschler and Perles (1981), among others.

24. The obvious choice, equal weights, would not yield a determinate answer. Because the problem is one of pure division, all divisions would result in the same value of the objective function being maximized.

25. This nomenclature is due to the Steiner point, a related concept in the geometry of convex sets. The Steiner point is that point obtained when the weights are random and uniformly distributed over the set of all possible weighting schemes. Because the uniform distribution of weights does not have a firm normative foundation, we consider all possible symmetric weighting methods. Without a specific distribution of weights, iteration is needed to overcome the non-uniqueness problem.

26. See Shapley 1969. He called this solution the λ-transfer value because there may not have been a way to transfer utility freely among the players and he was looking for the scaling of utilities (the λ's) such that transfers would not be necessary at the solution point.

27. See Harsanyi 1959.

28. There is a fair amount of experimental evidence on problems very similar to the two-person situation faced by the principal and the opponent. When α

is high, reasonable players will depart from equal division in favor of the player who has the more to gain.

29. Invariance to the units of measurement means, for example, that the solution does not change if one player keeps whatever share of the dollar he attains but another can exchange his share at a highly favorable rate, say $10 for every penny.

30. See Green 1989.

31. The author has created a computer program that calculates the iterated Steiner solution. This program, and several enlightening examples calculated using it, are available from the author upon request.

References

Aghion, P., and P. Bolton. 1987. "Contracts as a Barrier to Entry," *American Economic Review*, 77: 388–401.

Ben-Porath, E., and E. Dekel. 1988. "Coordination and the Potential for Self-Sacrifice," Stanford GSB research paper, no. 984.

Brander, J. A., and T. R. Lewis. 1986. "Oligopoly and Financial Structure: The Limited Liability Effect," *American Economic Review*, 76: 956–970.

Dewatripont, M. 1987. "Entry Deterrence under Trade Unions," *European Economic Review*, 31: 149–156.

Dewatripont, M. 1988. "Commitment through Renegotiation-proof Contracts with Third Parties," *Review of Economic Studies*, 60: 377–390.

Fershtman, C., and K. Judd. 1987a. "Equilibrium Incentives in Oligopoly," *American Economic Review*, 77: 927–940.

Fershtman, C., and K. Judd. 1987b. "Strategic Incentive Manipulation in Rivalrous Agency," Hoover Institution Working Paper in Economics, E-87-11.

Fershtman, C., K. Judd, and E. Kalai. 1989. "Observable Contracts: Strategic Delegation and Cooperation," Tel Aviv University working paper, no. 8–89.

Gertner, R., R. Gibbons, and David Scharfstein. 1988. "Simultaneous Signalling to the Capital and Product Markets," *RAND Journal of Economics*, 19: 173–190.

Green, J. 1983. "A Theory of Bargaining with Monetary Transfers," Harvard University discussion paper, no. 966.

Green, J. 1989. "Commitments with Third Parties," Harvard University, mimeo.

Harsanyi, J. C. 1959. "A Bargaining Model for the Cooperative N-Person Game," in *Contributions to the Theory of Games, IV*, pp. 325–356, Princeton, N.J.: Princeton University Press.

Hart, O., and J. Moore. 1988. "Incomplete Contracts and Renegotiation," *Econometrica*, 56: 755–786.

Katz, M. 1987. "Game-Playing Agents: Contracts as Precommitments," Princeton University discussion paper.

Maschler, M., and M. Perles. 1981. "The Super-Additive Solution for the Nash Bargaining Game," *International Journal of Game Theory*, 10: 163–193.

Maxsimovic, V. 1986. *Capital Structure in Stochastic Oligopoly*, Ph.D. dissertation, Harvard University.

Nash, J. F. 1950. "The Bargaining Problem," *Econometrica*, 28: 155–162.

Poitevin, M. 1989a. "Moral Hazard and the Financing of Entrepreneurial Firms," Université de Montréal, working paper 8914.

Poitevin, M. 1989b. "Financial Signalling and the 'Deep Pocket' Argument," *RAND Journal of Economics*, 20: 26–40.

Poitevin, M. 1990. "Strategic Financial Signalling," *International Journal of Industrial Organization*, vol. 8, no. 4, December: 499–518.

Schelling, T. C. 1960. *The Strategy of Conflict*, Cambridge, MA: Harvard University Press.

Shapley, L. S. 1969. "Utility Comparison and the Theory of Games," in *La Decision: Aggregation et Dynamique des Ordres de Preference*, pp. 251–263, Paris: Editions du CNRS.

Sklivas, S. 1987. "The Strategic Choice of Managerial Incentives," *RAND Journal of Economics*, 18: 452–460.

Spence, A. M. 1977. "Entry, Capacity, Investment and Oligopolistic Pricing," *The Bell Journal of Economics*, 8: 534–544.

Williamson, O. E. 1964. *The Economics of Discretionary Behavior, Managerial Objectives in the Theory of the Firm*, Englewood Cliffs, NJ: Prentice-Hall.

Williamson, O. E. 1985. *The Economic Institutions of Capitalism*, New York: Free Press.

11

Thomas Schelling and the
Analysis of Strategic
Behavior

Vincent P. Crawford

It is difficult to recall how the world looked before we first saw it with
the aid of Thomas Schelling's vision. The challenge is particularly
great for one who read *The Strategy of Conflict* before developing his
own view of economics. Reading and rereading Schelling's work over
the years has taught my subconscious mind the trick of presenting his
ideas to my conscious mind without citation, leaving it to rediscover
the original source weeks, months, or even years later. Memory
rarely does justice to the original, and there is much to be gained by
keeping Schelling's influence at the conscious level. This essay
is an attempt to ease that task by identifying the distinctive features
of his view of strategic behavior—his "theory of interdependent
decision"—and tracing its effects on game theory and the analysis of
strategic interactions in economics.[1]
   Schelling has perhaps the strongest game-theoretic orientation of
any applied economist, and he surely has the strongest interest in
applications of those who have made important contributions to
game theory. His preference for questions of strategy, no doubt partly aesthetic, seems to stem primarily from a deep-seated belief that
some form of strategic interdependence underlies many important
questions in economics, and most of those that are not yet well
understood. His predilection for strategic questions is apparent even
in his essays on individual decision making. In his most recent book,
Choice and Consequence,[2] he argues that many familiar phenomena—
from Christmas clubs to addiction to the delegation of certain kinds of
medical treatment decisions—are best understood by viewing the individual as a collection of different selves with different preferences
at different times: Not even Robinson Crusoe can ignore strategic
interactions!

Most economists are now convinced, many through Schelling's influence, that the effects of strategic interdependence are neither negligible nor inherently intractable. But Schelling remains conspicuous, among those who have done important work in game theory, in taking as much pleasure in its applications as in the theory itself. As he wrote in the preface to the first edition of *The Strategy of Conflict*,

The essays are a mixture of "pure" and "applied" research. To some extent the two can be separated, . . . [but] in my own thinking they have never been separate. Motivation for the purer theory came almost exclusively from preoccupation with (and fascination with) "applied" problems; and the clarification of theoretical ideas was absolutely dependent on an identification of live examples. For reasons inherent either in the subject or in the author, the interaction of the two levels of theory has been continuous and intense.

His sensitivity to the interdependence of theory and applications led directly to Schelling's greatest contribution, his leading role in showing how von Neumann and Morgenstern's [1953 (originally published in 1944)] theory of games could help to explain economic behavior. Schelling pioneered the delicate art of translating the subtleties of real economic interactions—as opposed to parlor games and toy market examples—into the language of game theory, enormously expanding the possibilities for fruitful applications. His analyses of the resulting models introduced now-central concepts like common knowledge and perfectness, and clarified the roles of the timing of decisions and information flows. To deal with the combined elements of coordination and conflict often encountered in applications, he alloyed Nash's notion of strategic rationality with essential admixtures of common sense and knowledge derived from experience, forging a stronger tool for explaining strategic behavior. His work transformed game theory and economics.

Schelling's view of strategic behavior stands out most clearly in his analyses of bargaining and coordination in *The Strategy of Conflict*, *Arms and Influence*, and *Micromotives and Macrobehavior*. The next section sets the stage for a discussion of Schelling's analyses by describing the theory of games as he found it. The following section discusses Schelling's theory of interdependent decision against the background of the traditional approach to bargaining and coordination. There is also a brief conclusion.

Traditional Game Theory

Most research in game theory and its applications follows the lead of von Neumann and Morgenstern (1953) in seeking to deduce from the structure of the game the implications of the hypothesis that individuals' decisions are "rational" in some agreed-upon sense.[3] For want of a better term, I call such theories *traditional*. Although traditional game theory is formally normative, it is most often used to describe or predict behavior under the assumption that individuals are rational. The resulting view of strategic behavior is an extreme one, but it still characterizes almost all pure research in game theory, and it continues to dominate applications.

A traditional game-theoretic analysis begins with a complete description of the strategic environment, which could be any situation in which individuals are affected by each other's decisions. This description must include, in particular, any opportunities for individuals to communicate and any commonly observed variables they might use to correlate their decisions. The *game* that describes the strategic environment is defined by listing the interacting individuals, traditionally called *players*, and specifying the decisions they must make and the information they have when making them, how their decisions jointly determine the outcome, and their preferences over outcomes. A player's decisions are summarized by his *strategy*—a complete contingent plan for playing the game, specifying a feasible decision at each point at which he might need to make one, as a function of what he knows at that point. A player's feasible strategies are thus jointly determined by his information and his feasible decisions, and specifying a strategy choice for each player uniquely determines an outcome in the game.

In games (unlike individual decision problems) players sometimes find it advantageous to randomize their strategy choices. Such randomized choices are called *mixed* strategies, in order to distinguish them from unrandomized choices, which are called *pure* strategies. Players' uncertainty about their ultimate pure-strategy choices, or about how their strategies determine the outcome, is easily handled by thinking of outcomes and strategies as probability distributions. Players' preferences are extended to probability distributions by assigning numerical *payoffs* to the possible deterministic outcomes in such a way that players choose as if to maximize the mathematical expectations of their payoffs.

The standard formalizations of the idea of rationality in games build on Nash's (1951) notion of an equilibrium point. A *Nash equilibrium* (often shortened to *equilibrium*) is a combination of strategies, one for each player, such that each player's strategy maximizes his expected payoff, given the others' strategies. A Nash equilibrium is a kind of rational-expectations equilibrium. Because players' strategies are complete contingent plans, they must be thought of as chosen *simultaneously*—not necessarily at precisely the same time, but without knowledge of each other's choices—at the start of the game. Players' strategy choices therefore depend on their predictions of each other's choices. If all players predict the same combination of strategies, then the predicted strategies are consistent with payoff maximization if and only if they are in equilibrium.

These concepts can be illustrated in a simple model of bargaining by ultimatum. There are two players, I and II, and two feasible contracts, X and Y. Player I proposes one of these contracts to Player II, who must either accept or reject it. If he accepts, the proposed contract determines the outcome; if he rejects, the outcome is a third alternative, Z. Player I prefers Y to X to Z, and Player II prefers X to Y to Z; and each player's preferences are represented by assigning the payoffs 2, 1, and 0 to these outcomes, with higher payoffs assigned to better outcomes.

I consider two versions of this game, distinguished by whether Player II can observe which contract Player I has proposed before deciding whether to accept. In each case, players are assumed to know the structure of the game, including what each player knows. Common sense suggests that, in either case, Player II will accept whichever contract Player I proposes, and Player I will therefore propose the contract he himself prefers.

It is instructive to see how these conclusions emerge from an equilibrium analysis. Player I has two pure strategies, "X" and "Y" (for propose X and propose Y) in each case. If Player II cannot observe Player I's proposal, he also has only two pure strategies, "A" and "R" (for Accept and Reject). The game can then be represented by the payoff matrix

II

	A	R
X	2 1	0 0
Y	1 2	0 0

I (label on left side, between rows X and Y)

in which Player I chooses between rows and Player II chooses between columns, and Player I's and Player II's payoffs are in the lower left and upper right corners of the cells of the matrix, respectively. It is clear from the matrix that Player II's strategy A *dominates* his strategy R, in that it yields him a payoff as high, or higher, for any strategy Player I chooses. Payoff maximization therefore requires that Player II choose strategy A, hence that Player I choose strategy Y. Thus, the strategy combination (Y;A), already identified as the commonsense outcome, is the only equilibrium in this version of the game.

In the second version of the game, Player II can observe Player I's proposal before deciding whether to accept. The game is then *dynamic*, in that players' decisions are no longer simultaneous. Nevertheless, defining players' strategies as complete contingent plans again makes it possible to describe their decisions as simultaneous strategy choices.[4] Player I has the same two pure strategies as before, X and Y; but Player II now has four pure strategies, "A,A", "A,R", "R,A", and "R,R" (for Accept X or Y, Accept X but Reject Y, etc.), because he now has enough information to make his decision depend on which contract Player I proposes. This version can be represented by the expanded payoff matrix

II

	A,A	A,R	R,A	R,R
X	2 1	2 1	0 0	0 0
Y	1 2	0 0	1 2	0 0

I (label on left side, between rows X and Y)

The commonsense outcome, now represented by the strategy combination (Y;A,A), remains an equilibrium. But there are two other equilibria, ($Y;R,A$) and ($X;A,R$), one with X the outcome instead of Y. In each of these equilibria, Player II plans, contrary to common sense, to reject one of Player I's possible proposals. But Player I's expectation that Player II would reject that proposal deters him from making it, so that Player II's planned rejection does not reduce his payoff and is thus not inconsistent with equilibrium.

A simple refinement of Nash's notion of equilibrium makes the theory's predictions accord better with common sense. Because the rationale for playing equilibrium strategies does not depend on the starting point of the analysis, players' strategy choices should meet the same standard of rationality throughout the game. An equilibrium analysis should therefore require equilibrium play not only in the game taken as a whole, but also starting from any situation that might arise during play. An equilibrium whose strategies remain in equilibrium starting from any such situation is called a *perfect* equilibrium. The commonsense outcome is the unique perfect equilibrium in each version of the game. Because the first version is static, its equilibrium is perfect by definition. Perfectness in the second version requires that Player II choose rationally following each of Player I's possible proposals. Player II must therefore play A,A in any perfect equilibrium, and equilibrium in the entire game then requires that Player I play Y.

Nash's notion of equilibrium had its roots in von Neumann's (1928) analysis of zero-sum two-person games, as extended by von Neumann and Morgenstern (1953). A zero-sum game is one in which players' payoffs sum to zero for all strategy combinations, so that players' interests are strictly opposed in the sense that what one player gains, the other necessarily loses. When there are only two players, this perfect opposition of interests makes mutually beneficial coalitions impossible. This reduces the strategic aspects of the game to a conflict over distribution, and considerably simplifies the analysis.

Although people without formal training in game theory often seem to think intuitively in zero-sum terms, situations of pure conflict are very rare. As Schelling noted in *The Strategy of Conflict*, there are important elements of common interests even in parlor games (which are played in part for pleasure, not just to win) and in war. However, von Neumann and Morgenstern's theory of zero-sum two-person games yielded important insights, and was widely perceived as more convincing than their generalization to non-zero-sum games. As a result, it exerted strong and lasting influences on how game theorists analyze more general games and on how economists view game theory.

Von Neumann and Morgenstern began by considering the strategies that give players the highest payoff guarantees, independent of their opponents' strategy choices (such strategies exist, under very weak assumptions). Although such strategies are plainly too conservative in non-zero-sum games, von Neumann and Morgenstern showed that they are in what is now called Nash equilibrium in any zero-sum two-person game in which mixed strategies are allowed, thereby establishing the existence of equilibrium for such games. They also showed that, as long as the players in a zero-sum two-person game follow the prescriptions of their theory, it does not matter whether, or how, they coordinate their strategy choices; whether a player observes his opponent's strategy before choosing his own; or whether players can discuss the game or make binding agreements before they play it.

Although zero-sum two-person games are very special, these strong implications gave considerable promise that a more general theory would capture something of the richness of strategic interactions in economic environments. Seeking the greatest possible generality, von Neumann and Morgenstern extended their theory to non-zero-sum n-person games by continuing to summarize players' strategic possibilities by the highest payoffs that each possible coalition of players can guarantee its members, independent of the strategies chosen by players outside the coalition, and suppressing all other details of the structure of the game. They then proposed a characterization of the outcomes that might emerge, given these guarantees, when players are rational and have complete freedom to communicate and form coalitions. Their characterization laid the foundation for modern cooperative game theory. Although it is a true generalization of their theory of zero-sum two-person games (in which single players are the only possible coalitions, and players' payoff guarantees are all that matter), its prescriptions are much less specific and far less compelling.

Nash (1951) generalized von Neumann and Morgenstern's theory of zero-sum two-person games in a different way, retaining its structural detail and, recognizing the limited relevance of payoff guarantees in non-zero-sum games, focusing instead on the more precise idea of rational expectations implicit in von Neumann and Morgenstern's analysis. His proof of the existence of equilibrium in a wide class of non-zero-sum n-person games laid the foundation for the modern theory of noncooperative games and paved the way for many fruitful economic applications. Although cooperative game theory has also been successfully applied in economics, most economists, Schelling included, have found the noncooperative approach more useful.

The great strengths of traditional noncooperative game theory as a positive theory of strategic behavior are its generality and flexibility, and the modeling discipline of deriving behavioral assumptions from a compelling notion of rationality. Many superficially plausible explanations prove to be consistent with rationality only in implausibly contrived models. The idea of rationality is therefore often of considerable help in distinguishing good explanations from bad ones, even when behavior is not expected to be completely rational. One might imagine another behavioral hypothesis providing the same kind of discipline, but none yet suggested is as simple, as powerful, or as compelling as the idea of rationality.

With these strengths come certain weaknesses. Perhaps the most important of these is the fact that the rationale for Nash equilibrium analysis depends on the assumption that all players expect the same strategy combination to be chosen. As we shall see, this assumption is far from innocuous in bargaining and coordination games.

Ironically, in addition to requiring that players have the same expectations even when rationality yields ambiguous prescriptions, the traditional approach also makes it difficult or impossible to model players' attempts to bring their expectations into line (or to respond sensibly to the likelihood that their expectations are different). Players who believe that their expectations are likely to differ might respond by choosing strategies that are "robust" to such differences; by trying to change the rules of the game; by talking about how to play it; or by trying to learn from their past experience with analogous games. However, a traditional analysis of these responses would have to be carried out in an expanded, all-inclusive game that takes these possibilities into account. An equilibrium analysis of such a game normally inherits any ambiguity in the analysis of the original game.

This and other weaknesses convinced many economists that noncooperative game theory had little or nothing to say about the strategic interactions they found most interesting. Fortunately for us, Schelling was unwilling to conclude that the strategic issues raised by the applications that fascinated him were intractable, or to push the applications into the background and develop the theory of games as a branch of mathematics. Instead he confronted the weaknesses of the traditional approach, retaining what he found convincing and useful, and replacing the rest with something better suited to the task.

Schelling's Theory of Interdependent Decision

The cornerstones of Schelling's theory of interdependent decision are his analyses of the "applied" bargaining and coordination problems that began his fascination with questions of strategy. A brief review of traditional game-theoretic approaches to these problems is necessary for a full appreciation of Schelling's contributions. For simplicity, I assume that players bear uncertainty (if at all) only about each other's strategy choices.

The first clear demonstration of noncooperative game theory's potential to elucidate bargaining and coordination problems was Nash's (1953) analysis of the bargaining problem faced by two players who can meet before playing a game and make a binding agreement about how to play it. Nash's 1953 analysis built on his 1950 cooperative analysis of bargaining, in which he sought to express the payoffs that fully informed players could rationally "anticipate" as a function of the data of the bargaining problem. There, he showed that one such function, now called the Nash bargaining solution, is uniquely characterized by plausible axioms that extend the commonly accepted principle of equally sharing the gains from an agreement to a wide class of bargaining problems. Nash's innovation in his 1953 paper was to construct an explicit noncooperative model of the bargaining process and to use his notion of equilibrium to characterize its players' rational responses to its possibilities. In that model, players make simultaneous, once-and-for-all demands, expressed in utility terms. If their demands are feasible, taken together, bargaining ends with a binding agreement that yields them the utilities they demanded; otherwise the process ends in disagreement. Any pair of demands that leads to an outcome that is at least as good as disagreement for each player and is *efficient*, in the sense that there is no feasible alternative that both players would prefer, is in equilibrium in this demand game. A player who reduced his demand, starting from such a pair, would lower his payoff with no compensating benefit; and a player who increased his demand would cause a disagreement, again lowering his payoff.

Although Nash allowed players' demands to vary continuously, his analysis can be illustrated in a discrete version of his demand game. Suppose that two players, I and II, have four dollars to share, that dollars are indivisible, and that to get any money they must agree on how to share all four dollars. Denoting players' possible demands by their dollar amounts, setting players' payoffs equal to the number of dollars they receive, and iteratively eliminating each player's dominated strategies, $0 and then $4, yields the payoff matrix

		II	
	$1	$2	$3
$1	0 / 0	0 / 0	3 / 1
I **$2**	0 / 0	2 / 2	0 / 0
$3	1 / 3	0 / 0	0 / 0

It is clear that each efficient outcome that both players prefer to disagreement corresponds to an equilibrium, and that each pure-strategy equilibrium leads to an efficient outcome.

Nash's noncooperative analysis of bargaining is important because it explains, within the theory, why bargaining is a problem, and thereby provides a framework in which the effectiveness of bargaining strategies can be evaluated. The view of bargaining it suggests can be described more precisely as follows. Although there are normally many efficient agreements that are better than disagreement for both bargainers, all of them are consistent with the idea of rationality that underlies Nash's notion of equilibrium, which is therefore no help in choosing among them. Thus, bargaining is likely to generate a great deal of uncertainty about how players will respond to its multiplicity of equilibria, even when there is no other uncertainty in the bargaining environment. Unless the bargainers find a way to resolve this uncertainty, they may not realize any of the gains from reaching an agreement: At the heart of the bargaining problem lies a coordination problem.

Nash (1953) suggested two complementary resolutions of this coordination problem. In one, he suggested that the normative force of his 1950 bargaining solution might focus players' expectations on the associated equilibrium in the demand game. In the other, he outlined a mathematical "smoothing" argument that leads to the same conclusion.

Two other suggested resolutions of the bargaining problem deserve mention. The first of these is a general theory of equilibrium selection in games with multiple equilibria, developed over the past two decades by Harsanyi and Selten and described in detail in their 1988 book. This theory follows the traditional pattern of Nash's resolutions in that it always selects a particular equilibrium in a way that is determined entirely by the structure of the game. Unlike other traditional equilibrium refinements, however, it rests on a model of the process by which players form their expectations that allows their strategies to respond in sensible ways to the difficulty of coordination. Interestingly, it also prescribes the Nash bargaining solution in games like the discrete version of his demand game just described. Harsanyi and Selten's arguments for this conclusion are both more sophisticated and more plausible than Nash's, but they are also dauntingly complex. (This criticism has more than the usual force here, since the theory purports to describe players' thought processes directly.) Harsanyi and Selten's theory of equilibrium selection also applies to a wide variety of coordination problems whose structures are different from the demand game's. It is, in fact, still the only comprehensive attempt to resolve such problems within traditional noncooperative game theory.

Rubinstein (1982) suggested yet another resolution, which has recently been very influential. He replaced Nash's demand game with a dynamic model of the bargaining process, in which players take turns proposing agreements to each other. A player can accept his partner's latest proposal at any stage, in which case it becomes a binding agreement, taking effect immediately. But if he rejects a proposal, he must wait until the next stage (an exogenous interval of time) before making a counterproposal. This process continues indefinitely until a proposal is accepted, but the players prefer to reach a given agreement sooner rather than later. Rubinstein showed that this model has a unique perfect equilibrium, in which the player who has the right to make the first proposal chooses it so as to extract all of his partner's surplus from accepting it, taking into account that his partner's alternative is to make a counterproposal, chosen in the same way, but one stage later. In equilibrium, this first proposal is always accepted. Thus, the players always reach an efficient agreement, and the rules of bargaining in Rubinstein's model completely eliminate the coordination problem. How players share the surplus is completely determined by their time preferences, and it is generally advantageous to make the first proposal. But when players discount the future at the same rate, this advantage disappears as they discount the future less and less (or as the time between offers approaches zero), and the perfect equilibrium outcome then approaches the Nash bargaining solution.

Schelling, like Nash, took it for granted that coordination is the essence of the bargaining problem. He rejected any suggestion that bargaining outcomes are completely determined by the rules that govern the bargaining process, independent of all other factors; or that bargaining somehow ceases to be a problem if bargainers are well informed about the bargaining environment. In his words (*The Strategy of Conflict*, p. 70),

> Most bargaining situations ultimately involve some range of possible outcomes within which each party would rather make a concession than fail to reach agreement at all. In such a situation any potential outcome is one from which at least one of the parties, and probably both, would have been willing to retreat for the sake of agreement, and very often the other party knows it. Any potential outcome is therefore one that either party could have improved by insisting; yet he may have no basis for insisting, since the other knows or suspects that he would rather concede than do without agreement. Each party's strategy is guided mainly by what he expects the other to accept or insist on; yet each knows that the other is guided by reciprocal thoughts. The final outcome must be a point from which neither expects the other to retreat; yet the main ingredient of this expectation is what one thinks the other expects the first to expect, and so on. Somehow, out of this fluid and indeterminate situation that seemingly provides no logical reason for anybody to expect anything except what he expects to be expected to expect, a decision is reached. These infinitely reflexive expectations must somehow converge on a single point, at which each expects the other not to expect to be expected to retreat.

The overall view of bargaining that follows from this argument is similar to Nash's, and very different from Rubinstein's. Yet Schelling, like Rubinstein, emphasized the dynamic aspects of bargaining, and would have been the first to acknowledge that Nash's demand game is too stylized to provide an adequate basis for a complete analysis.

Nash's (1953, p. 129) defense of his specification provides little help in reconciling Schelling's view of bargaining with this emphasis on dynamics:

Of course, one cannot represent all possible bargaining devices as moves in the non-cooperative game. The negotiation process must be formalized and restricted, but in such a way that each participant is still able to utilize all the essential strengths of his position.

In appendix B of *The Strategy of Conflict* (see also Harsanyi and Selten 1988, pp. 23–26), however, Schelling outlined a dynamic model with the detail his analysis required, but a structure consistent with his view of bargaining as primarily a coordination problem.

In Schelling's model, there are no artificial restrictions on players' strategies: the only rules are a fixed deadline and the stipulation that any agreement reached by the deadline will be enforced. The cost of delaying agreement is negligible until the deadline is reached. The absence of restrictions on strategies makes them complex dynamic decision rules, difficult even to describe. Nevertheless, Schelling was able to show that the bargaining game has a perfect equilibrium corresponding to each of the efficient equilibria in Nash's demand game. More generally, even if there is no deadline, players' strategies can be thought of as chosen simultaneously; and in any equilibrium in which they reach an agreement, each player's strategy must be such that the lowest utility his partner can make him accept and the lowest utility he can make his partner accept determine an efficient outcome. These lowest utilities function just like the demands in Nash's demand game, and the resulting agreements correspond precisely to those reached in its efficient equilibria.[5]

Curiously, this argument applies not only to *tacit* bargaining, in which bargainers can communicate only by taking actions that directly affect their payoffs, as in Nash's demand game, but also to *explicit* bargaining, in which they can also communicate by sending nonbinding "cheap talk" messages with no direct payoff implications.[6] This is surprising, because when players' preferences are identical, coordination problems are easily resolved (in practice, if not in theory) by discussing them in advance; explicit coordination is then very different from tacit coordination. But when players' preferences about how to coordinate are opposed, as they are in bargaining problems, cheap talk cannot *by itself* coordinate their expectations. Well-informed bargainers have nothing to communicate except what shares of the surplus they expect to receive, and whatever a bargainer expects, it is to his advantage to convince his partner that he expects more rather than less. It follows that both explicit and tacit bargaining have much in common with tacit coordination. It does *not* follow that it does not matter whether bargaining is tacit or explicit. This point is important, because it clearly matters a great deal in practice; why else prohibit conspiracies in restraint of trade? In Schelling's view, the effect of cheap talk is determined by how it interacts with other factors that affect the coordination process.

Schelling's analysis rests on a deep understanding of the logic of equilibrium analysis and of what it can and cannot be expected to accomplish, only recently reflected in the formal literature. Define a *rational* player, as in individual decision theory, as one who maximizes his expected payoff, given some set of expectations about the uncertainty he faces that are not inconsistent with anything he knows. As Schelling noted in the passage quoted above, for rational bargainers to reach a given agreement, they must both expect to reach that agreement. Expectations that led one bargainer to insist on receiving more than his partner expected him to get could not be realized by any feasible agreement. Expectations that led one bargainer to insist on receiving less than the other expected him to get would lead bargainers to continue bargaining, time permitting, and well-informed bargainers would avoid strategies that leave room for an agreement, but not enough time to reach an efficient one.

The fact that the traditional rationale for equilibrium analysis depends on the assumption that players' expectations are the same was well understood before *The Strategy of Conflict*. In the quoted passage, Schelling took this logic an important step further by considering the requirements for consistency between rational bargainers' expectations and their expectations about each other's expectations, and so on. He observed that any difference between bargainers' expectations, at any level, could lead to a difference between the agreements they expected, and thereby prevent or delay agreement. Thus, for bargainers to expect to reach a given agreement, they must both expect that they both expect to reach it, and so on ad infinitum. In the terminology later introduced by Lewis (1969) and Aumann (1976), for an agreement to be reached in equilibrium, it must be supported by expectations that are *common knowledge*, in the sense that bargainers know each other's expectations, know that they know them, and so on ad infinitum.[7]

The stringency of this requirement makes traditional resolutions of bargaining and coordination problems, in which players' expectations are based entirely on deductions from an equilibrium-selection principle, very fragile. The Nash bargaining solution, for instance, responds to the symmetries of the discrete demand game described above by prescribing the strategy combination ($2,$2). Thus, if it is common knowledge that players are rational, and that they subscribe to the Nash solution, it is common knowledge that each expects his partner to demand $2. This makes it rational for each player to demand $2, so that players' expectations are realized and their strategy choices are in equilibrium.

If, however, both players subscribe to the Nash solution and know that they both subscribe to it, but (contrary to common knowledge) Player I does not know that Player II knows that Player I subscribes to it, then it is not inconsistent with common knowledge of rationality for Player I to believe that Player II (believing that Player I has a different bargaining solution in mind) expects Player I to demand $3. If Player I believes this, he will expect Player II to demand $1, and will therefore demand $3. Similarly, it is not inconsistent with rationality for Player II (who knows that Player I subscribes to the Nash solution and knows that Player I knows that Player II does) to expect Player I to demand $2. If Player II expects this, he will demand $2. Thus, even though both players are rational, both subscribe to the Nash solution, and both know that they both are rational and subscribe to the Nash solution, their strategy choices need not be in equilibrium, and need not conform to the Nash solution.

The same difference between players' expectations, with the same result, could arise if it were common knowledge that they both subscribe to the Nash solution, but not that they are rational, or if either failure of common knowledge occurred at an even lower level in the hierarchy of expectations. In this game, common knowledge of rationality without common knowledge of a coordinating principle (or vice versa) places no restrictions whatsoever on players' behavior. In more general games, common knowledge of rationality may yield some restrictions, but it provides little help in resolving coordination problems.

Schelling acknowledged that bargainers' expectations can sometimes be coordinated from the start by a simple symmetry principle based on the structure of the game, like the one that underlies the Nash solution. But to attract bargainers' joint attention strongly enough to induce the required common knowledge by itself, even approximately, a principle must stand out extremely clearly. Bargainers who are not game theorists are unlikely even to notice the mathematical invariances that make the Nash solution salient to game theorists, except in environments in which those invariances reduce to symmetries as clear-cut as the fifty-fifty split in "divide the dollar" (the well-known special case of Nash's 1953 demand game in which two players must agree on how to share a dollar between them, with their payoffs equal to the money amounts they receive). In most real environments, the clues that are most helpful in coordinating bargainers' expectations are usually provided by principles of a different sort. Even a bargainer whose notion of rationality is highly refined must predict which principle his partner is likely to focus on, unless he is confident that his partner's notion of rationality is equally refined (and that his partner is confident of this, and so on). To the extent that these principles cannot be deduced from a refined notion of rationality, their influence makes the theory inherently empirical, even for normative purposes.

Typically, no one principle stands out very clearly, and bargainers initially expect, or at least hope for, more than is collectively feasible. Coordination therefore takes time. This point has profound implications for the analysis of bargaining, and of coordination in general. The time required for coordination is also time in which players can employ a wide variety of tactics to influence the outcome; these tactics interact with coordinating principles in complex ways. Also, although there is no obstacle in principle to an equilibrium analysis of the entire coordination process, the final outcome of the process is likely to be affected by the difficulty of coordination, hence unlikely to be adequately modeled *within* an equilibrium that is selected by applying traditional equilibrium refinements that do not take that difficulty into account. Equilibrium analysis is then far more likely to be useful in characterizing the outcome of the coordination process than in describing players' initial expectations.[8]

Schelling called the outcomes identified by the coordinating principles most likely to attract players' joint attention *focal points*. His analysis of focal points has become part of the folklore of economics. To learn more about them, he made a detailed study of anecdotal empirical evidence (mostly from international relations) and became a pioneer in experimental economics, drawing on the analogy between bargaining and tacit coordination to design a series of elegant and illuminating experiments.[9] He found that focal points are most often derived from the structure of the game, from how it is described or the social context in which it is played, or from the history of play in analogous games. He also identified a number of empirical regularities in the underlying principles, which are plainly essential in understanding real bargaining and coordination. Although the idea of a focal point is easy to explain or illustrate by example, it has proven tantalizingly difficult to formalize.[10] Its importance is acknowledged, however, even by those who are made most uncomfortable by the lack of a formal theory.

The power of focal points to determine bargaining outcomes and the subtleties of bargainers' strategic uses of this power are illustrated in the experiments reviewed in Roth (1987), which were carried out in environments with structures very close to Schelling's model of bargaining. The agreements Roth and his collaborators observed were heavily influenced by focal equal-sharing principles. Their subjects appeared to share a common "relevance" ranking of these principles, and usually agreed to share the surplus according to the most relevant principle they could implement, given the information publicly available plus whatever private information they found it advantageous to reveal, on the understanding that it would be used to determine the outcome in this way. These results are particularly informative because they were obtained in environments that placed no artificial restrictions on subjects' bargaining strategies. In related experiments, subjects' agreements were heavily influenced by historical precedents based on their prior experience with analogous games. In each case, the results provide striking confirmation of Schelling's view of bargaining as a coordination problem, and of the importance of focal points in resolving it.

Schelling's analyses of bargaining tactics have been even more influential. His main innovation in this area is the realism of his specifications of the rules that govern players' interactions, in particular his sensitivity to their opportunities to change the rules. (His discussions of the means by which agreements are enforced, in particular, have important implications for the theory of incentives.) Schelling's analyses of tactics are informed by a sophisticated understanding of notions such as perfectness and the use of actions with direct payoff implications to signal private information (as in Spence's 1974 celebrated analysis of market signaling), which were integrated into the formal literature much later.

The best known of the tactics Schelling discussed is the commitment. A *commitment* is any action by which a player restricts his future options (usually by making an irrevocable decision or by lowering his payoffs for certain actions). Paradoxically, the "weakness" caused by such a restriction can be advantageous in a non-zero-sum game. Suppose, for instance, that in the discrete demand game discussed above, Player II can commit himself to a demand and communicate his commitment to Player I before Player I chooses his demand. If he commits himself to demand $3, Player I's best choice is to demand $1. When Player II's commitment opportunity is included in the specification of the game, this is, in fact, the unique perfect equilibrium outcome. It is not difficult to show that both the irrevocability of Player II's commitment and his ability to communicate it to Player I before he chooses his demand are essential for the commitment to work.

Schelling also showed that familiar tactics like the threat and the promise can be given precise meanings in his framework, as commitments to contingent decision rules. If, for instance, Player I can commit himself, before Player II's opportunity to commit in the game just described, to demand $3 unless Player II demands $2, then Player II's best choice is to commit himself to demand $2; when players' commitment opportunities are included in the specification of the game, this is the only perfect equilibrium outcome. Player I's contingent commitment makes his threat to demand $3 credible, neutralizing Player II's commitment advantage. Without Player I's commitment, Player II would commit to demanding $3 as before, and Player I would have no recourse but to demand $1.

In practice, the uncertainty bargainers face and the complexity of their commitment possibilities makes the use of these tactics far less cut-and-dried than in my examples. Coming to grips with these complicating factors led Schelling to a deeper understanding of bargaining impasses, which is arguably his most important contribution to the theory of bargaining. In *The Strategy of Conflict*, he outlined a model in which it may be rational for bargainers to attempt commitment to incompatible positions, even though they know that this entails an inefficient risk of disagreement. In his words (p. 39):

In threat situations, as in ordinary bargaining, commitments are not altogether clear; each party cannot exactly estimate the costs and values to the other side of the two related actions involved in the threat; the process of commitment may be a progressive one, the commitments acquiring their firmness by a sequence of actions. Communication is often neither entirely impossible nor entirely reliable; while certain evidence of one's commitment can be communicated directly, other information must travel by newspaper or hearsay, or be demonstrated by actions. In these cases the unhappy possibility of both acts occurring, as a result of simultaneous commitment, is increased. Furthermore, the recognition of this possibility of simultaneous commitment becomes itself a deterrent to the taking of commitments.

Although the conclusion Schelling reached here may now seem almost commonplace, when he wrote (and for long afterward) it was widely believed that rationality implies that bargainers will reach an efficient agreement. With few exceptions, game theorists and economists who studied bargaining did not seriously question this belief and instead spent their time deducing the implications of efficiency and theorizing about which efficient agreement would emerge. Schelling's analysis of commitment was a bold, much-needed step toward bringing the theory of bargaining into line with reality.[11]

Another important tactic is the manipulation of risk—Schelling's term for the deliberate creation, by delay or other means, of a situation in which both bargainers are at risk as long as they do not reach agreement. A bargainer may thereby outlast his partner, capturing most or all of the remaining surplus. Schelling's crucial insight is that the manipulation of risk can allow a bargainer to make a threat credible even if the outcome being risked is too terrible to contemplate with certainty. Schelling's analysis of this tactic foreshadowed the recent work on noncooperative models of bargaining with asymmetric information,[12] and anticipated the large literature on "war of attrition" models, first formally analyzed by the biologist Maynard Smith (1974) and now extensively applied in biology and economics.

The capstone of Schelling's theory of interdependent decision is his analysis, in chapter 7 of *Micromotives and Macrobehavior* (originally published as Schelling 1973), of the dynamics of strategy choices in games played repeatedly in populations. This analysis helps to fill the gaps in traditional analyses of bargaining and coordination due to their lack of a convincing account of behavior when players' expectations are not coordinated from the start. There is no obstacle in principle to a traditional analysis of the coordination process, in which players choose dynamic decision rules that are in perfect equilibrium in the entire repeated game. However, this kind of analysis rarely describes real coordination processes adequately, and would in any case compound the multiple equilibrium problem rather than help to resolve it. Schelling therefore assumed, instead, that players focus on their decisions in the game that is repeated, adjusting them over time in sensible—but not strictly "rational"—ways.

To learn more about the implications of this hypothesis, Schelling made a number of simplifying assumptions, which define a model that is ideally suited to the study of historical coordination processes. From now on, "game" refers to the game that is repeated, and "strategy" refers to players' decisions in that game. In Schelling's model, all players in the population are identical, and players' strategies are identified, so that it is meaningful to say that different players choose the same strategy, or that a player chooses the same strategy in different stages. Players choose only pure strategies, of which each player has only two. Each player's payoff is completely determined by his own strategy and the population frequencies of the other players' strategies, so that it makes no difference "who did what" among the other players.[13] Finally, the population is sufficiently large that excluding a single player's strategy has a negligible effect on the population frequencies.

Almost any sensible assumption about how players adjust their strategies implies that strategies with higher current expected payoffs are chosen more often in the immediate future. It is natural to hope that the implied dynamics of the population strategy frequencies converge over time to some limit. Such a limit must normally be a *stationary* point, at which the population frequencies have no tendency to change. If the dynamics converge, no matter where they start, to a given stationary point, that point is said to be *globally stable*. Because global stability is usually too much to hope for in coordination games, Schelling focused instead on stationary points that are *locally stable*, in the standard sense that the dynamics converge to the stationary point after any sufficiently small departure from it.

It is a remarkable instance of simultaneous discovery that Schelling's model of games played in populations and the notion of local stability he employed are virtually identical to the model of the dynamics of strategy frequencies in animal populations proposed by the biologists Maynard Smith and Price (1973) and Maynard Smith (1974) and their notion of "evolutionary stability."[14] (This coincidence may be partly explained by the fact that, like Schelling, evolutionary game theorists emphasize coordination rather than conflict and believe that learning and adaptation are important determinants of strategic behavior.)

Schelling's techniques for analyzing games played repeatedly in populations could be used to study the emergence of focal points based on historical precedent in bargaining. Their power is better illustrated, however, by using them to study the emergence of conventions to solve a different kind of coordination problem. As a by-product, the analysis sheds some light on the effect of group size on coordination and cooperation, which has long been a puzzle in traditional game theory.

Suppose that there are a number of identical players, who choose simultaneously between two effort levels, 1 and 2. The minimum of their effort-level choices determines total output, which they share equally. Each player's effort cost increases as his effort level rises; but effort is sufficiently productive that if all players choose the same effort level, the resulting output shares more than repay their costs. Thus, players have identical preferences about how to coordinate, with each player's payoff maximized when all players choose effort level 2. But if anyone shirks, the balance of the other players' efforts is wasted.

This game has a long history in economics and political theory. It is similar in structure to some recently proposed models of Keynesian effective demand failures (as in the papers surveyed in Cooper and John 1988). It can also be viewed as a formalization of the stag hunt example Rousseau used in his discussion of the origins of the social contract (see for instance Lewis 1969, p. 7). In the stag hunt, each member of a group of hunters must independently decide whether to hunt a stag with the others or to hunt rabbits by himself. Effort level 2 corresponds to hunting a stag, which depends for success on the cooperation of every hunter in the group. Effort level 1 corresponds to hunting rabbits, which yields a lower return than a successful stag hunt but requires no cooperation, and therefore involves no risk of coordination failure.

Suppose, for definiteness, that output *per capita* is twice the minimum effort level and each player's unit cost of effort is one. Then, for any number of players, the game can be represented by the following payoff table, whose entries give each player's share of total output, net of his effort cost, as a function of his effort level and the minimum effort level:

minimum effort level

		2	1
player's effort level	2	2	0
	1	1	1

It is easy to verify that this game has two pure-strategy Nash equilibria, one in which all players choose effort level 2 and one in which all choose effort level 1; all players prefer the former equilibrium to the latter. Because the efficient outcome in which all players choose effort level 2 is an equilibrium, there are no incentive problems as they are normally characterized in economics. Moreover, the argument in favor of playing this equilibrium does not depend on game-theoretic subtleties; it is the obviously "correct" coordinating principle.[15]

To realize the effficient outcome, however, players must overcome a more subtle kind of incentive problem. A rational player who chooses effort level 2 must do so because he believes that the correctness of the coordinating principle that dictates this choice is sufficiently obvious that it is more likely than not that *all* of the other players with whom he is playing the game will believe that its correctness is sufficiently obvious to all. Although the argument for this principle does not depend on the number playing the game, it is easy to show by informal experiment that most people consider this a good bet when they are playing with only one other player, but not when they are playing with many other players. (Note that these beliefs are self-confirming!) This observation is strongly confirmed in controlled experiments involving repeated play of a version of this game with seven effort levels, reported in Van Huyck, Battalio, and Beil (1990) (see also the discussion and further references in Crawford 1991). In those experiments, populations of fourteen to sixteen subjects simultaneously playing the game rapidly converged to the lowest effort level and stayed there, but subjects playing the game in pairs randomly selected from the same populations persistently chose much higher effort levels.

The striking difference in behavior between large and small groups can be better understood by using Schelling's techniques to compare the dynamics of the population strategy frequencies when players are paired at random to play a two-person version of the stag hunt game with the dynamics when the same players play an *n*-person version of

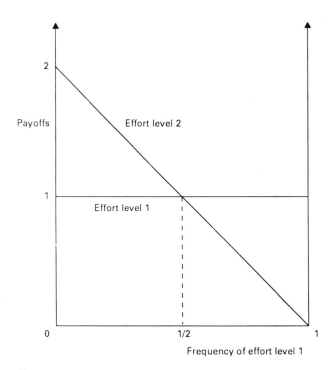

Figure 11.1
Stag hunt with random pairing

the game simultaneously. In each case, a player's expected payoff is completely determined by his own effort level and the population frequencies. In the random pairing model, a player's expected payoff is a frequency-weighted average of his effort level's payoffs when his partner chooses effort levels 1 and 2, and therefore a linear function of the population frequencies. In the simultaneous-play model, a player's expected payoff depends nonlinearly on the population frequencies, as illustrated below.

When players have only two pure strategies, a simple graphical stability analysis is possible. Figures 11.1 and 11.2 graph the expected payoffs of effort levels 1 and 2, for a representative player in the random-pairing and simultaneous-play models, respectively, against the population frequency of effort level 1.

It is clear from figure 11.1 that there are three stationary points of the population dynamics in the random-pairing model, with population frequencies 0, 1/2 (the frequency that equalizes the expected

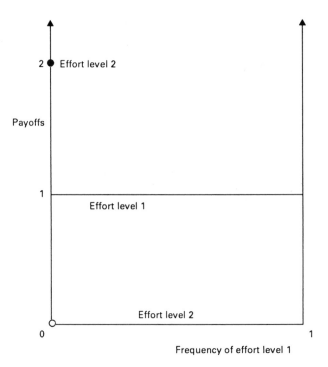

Figure 11.2
Stag hunt with simultaneous play

payoffs of the two effort levels), and 1. Each of these points corresponds to a Nash equilibrium in the two-person version of the stag hunt game. The stationary points with frequencies 0 and 1 are locally stable, and the stationary point with frequency 1/2 is unstable.[16] The outcome to which the dynamics converge is determined by the population's initial strategy frequencies, which are in turn determined by players' initial effort-level choices. If, as experiments with the two-person stag hunt game suggest, most players initially choose effort level 2, the population converges to the efficient equilibrium. (This experience will, if anything, make players even more likely to make the analogous initial choice the next time they encounter this kind of situation.) It is clearly also possible, however, for the population to get stuck forever at the inefficient equilibrium.

In figure 11.2, the expected payoff of effort level 1 is constant as before, but there is now a sharp drop in the expected payoff of effort level 2, which falls from 2 to 0 as the population frequency of effort level 1 rises above 0. This discontinuity reflects the fact that, when all members of the population play the stag hunt game simultaneously, each player's payoff can be drastically altered by a single other player's choice, no matter how large the population.[17] There are two stationary points in this version of the game, with population frequencies 0 and 1. Each corresponds to a Nash equilibrium in the n-person version of the stag hunt game. The equilibrium in which all players choose effort level 1 is locally stable; but the equilibrium in which all choose effort level 2 is unstable, because if even one player switches to effort level 1, it then has the higher payoff. Thus, unless all players initially choose effort level 2, which experiments suggest is highly unlikely, the population will converge to the inefficient equilibrium in which all players choose effort level 1. (This experience will make players more likely to make the analogous initial choice the next time they encounter this kind of situation.) This convergence to the inefficient equilibrium occurs despite the existence of an efficient equilibrium that meets the most stringent traditional game-theoretic standards of rationality. Plainly, something like Schelling's analysis of games played repeatedly in populations is necessary to explain the coordination failures commonly observed in this kind of game.

Conclusion

In this chapter, I have tried to illustrate Thomas Schelling's contributions to the analysis of strategic behavior by discussing the work on bargaining and coordination that forms the analytical core of his theory of interdependent decision. This approach does not do justice to the advances in economic theory Schelling's work in game theory made possible. Many of these advances stem from his contributions to the art of modeling economic, political, and social interactions. He did more than anyone else to reveal their common structure and to make it clear that bargaining and coordination are pervasive phenomena rather than special cases. Equally significant are the tools he developed to analyze these problems. These are important in many other contexts and are used every day (consciously or not) by everyone who thinks seriously about strategic interactions.

I have also left much unsaid about Schelling's leading role in policy analysis. He is, of course, a world-renowned expert on the problems of nuclear deterrence and many other questions in international relations. He is less well known, but no less a leader, for his work in fields as disparate as addiction (which he views, illuminatingly, as a struggle between man and himself) and segregation. His most recent fascination is with policies to combat the greenhouse effect, focusing on strategies by which independent, sovereign nations might overcome the special difficulties of this vital bargaining problem.

I hope that, despite these omissions, my discussion conveys something of the power and originality of Thomas Schelling's mind, his seriousness and intellectual honesty, and the inspiration his efforts to make game theory applicable can provide.

Notes

1. I owe thanks to J. Luis Guasch, John McMillan, Joel Sobel, Maxwell Stinchcombe, and Richard Zeckhauser for many helpful suggestions, to Yong-Gwan Kim for research assistance, and to the National Science Foundation for financial support.

2. Titles not otherwise identified refer to Schelling's books, cited in the references. I have made no attempt to provide comprehensive references to the work of other authors.

3. Game theorists invariably agree that the notion of rationality in games should be consistent with the traditional expected-utility characterization of rationality in individual decisions, and they often agree on what it means to play particular games rationally. However, there is still no accepted general definition of rationality in games.

4. Although what players plan to do in contingencies that do not arise, given their strategies, may seem irrelevant, it is impossible for them to evaluate the rationality of their strategy choices without predicting the consequences of alternative choices.

5. This argument makes clear that Rubinstein's 1982 resolution of the bargaining problem is sensitive to his model's restrictions on players' strategies and his assumption that delay is the only potential source of inefficiency. In most applications, bargainers are free to choose the timing of their offers and counteroffers; and the cost of delay is often far less important than the risk of disagreement due to coordination failure. (This risk is not adequately modeled by the common practice of viewing discounting as reflecting a chance that the bargaining process will be exogenously terminated after any given stage.) Coordination then remains the essence of bargaining, even if bargainers approach agreement by a sequence of alternating offers. The dynamic give-and-take of real bargaining is surely, at least in part, a robust response to this coordination problem.

6. In economic models, it is often possible for messages with no direct payoff implications to convey information in equilibrium. In equilibrium, a message means, in effect, "I like what you do when I say this better than anything

I could get you to do by saying something else"; information is transmitted by the message-sender's implied choice among the message-receiver's possible responses to messages. Crawford 1990 reviews the theory strategic communication through cheap talk and discusses the theoretical and experimental literature on explicit bargaining.

7. For simplicity, I have assumed (following Schelling) that bargainers have point expectations. Schelling's discussions of the importance of common knowledge for the rationality of playing equilibrium strategies, originally published in 1956 and 1957, are apparently the earliest in the literature. See Brandenburger and Dekel 1989 for an overview of the recent formal literature on this question.

8. See Lucas 1986 for an eloquent defense of this view in a somewhat different context.

9. Schelling's experiments captured his colleagues' imaginations to an unusual degree; see for example Tobin's comments, quoted in Zeckhauser 1989, p. 158.

10. See, however, the complementary analyses of coordination in games played repeatedly in Schelling 1973, discussed below, and Crawford and Haller 1990.

11. Of course, Schelling's view of bargaining as a coordination problem makes it possible to explain impasses as coordination failures even without considering bargainers' incentives to attempt commitment. But such explanations are unlikely to change the minds of those convinced that rationality implies efficiency when the model also has efficient equilibria. Schelling's analysis of commitment suggests models in which rationality *requires* bargainers to risk an impasse; see for example Crawford 1982.

12. This work is surveyed, with an eye to its use in empirical analyses of strike data, by Kennan and Wilson 1989.

13. In Schelling 1971, reprinted in abbreviated form as chapter 4 of *Micromotives and Macrobehavior*, Schelling considered the alternative possibility that players interact locally, with each player's payoff determined by his own strategy and the strategies chosen by his near neighbors.

14. In the biological models, it is assumed that the game determines individuals' expected reproduction rates and players inherit their parents' strategies. See Crawford 1991 for a summary of evolutionary stability theory and further references. Maynard Smith and Price allowed players to have more than two pure strategies, but considered only the case in which they are paired at random to play a two-person game. Schelling allowed players to interact in much more general ways, as discussed below.

15. However, with the exception of Harsanyi and Selten's 1988 theory of equilibrium selection, this argument is not reflected in traditional equilibrium refinements.

16. The stationary point with frequency 1/2 corresponds to a mixed-strategy equilibrium, here realized by a mixture of pure strategies with the appropriate population frequencies. It is a coincidence that the stationary points that correspond to pure-strategy equilibria are locally stable and the one that corresponds to a mixed-strategy equilibrium is unstable. It is easy to find examples with stable mixed-strategy equilibria, or with unstable pure-strategy equilibria.

17. This discontinuity is not pathological in any of the traditional senses of the word. The curves in figure 11.2 are only approximations of the discrete point sets associated with the possible strategy frequencies in a finite population playing pure strategies. Effort level 2's point set could be filled in continuously (though steeply) if desired.

References

Aumann, Robert. 1976. "Agreeing to Disagree," *Annals of Statistics*, 4: 1236–1239.

Brandenburger, Adam, and Eddie Dekel. 1989. "The Role of Common Knowledge Assumptions in Game Theory," in *The Economics of Missing Markets, Information, and Games*, Frank Hahn, ed., New York: Oxford University Press.

Cooper, Russell, and Andrew John. 1988. "Coordinating Coordination Failures in Keynesian Models," *Quarterly Journal of Economics*, 103: 441–463.

Crawford, Vincent P. 1982. "A Theory of Disagreement in Bargaining," *Econometrica*, 50, 607–637; reprinted in Ken Binmore and Partha Dasgupta, eds., *The Economics of Bargaining*, New York: Basil Blackwell, 1987.

Crawford, Vincent P. 1990. "Explicit Communication and Bargaining Outcomes," *American Economic Review Papers and Proceedings*, 80: 213–219.

Crawford, Vincent P. 1991. "An 'Evolutionary' Interpretation of Van Huyck, Battalio, and Beil's Experimental Results on Coordination," *Games and Economic Behavior*, 3: 25–59.

Crawford, Vincent P., and Hans Haller. 1990. "Learning How to Cooperate: Optimal Play in Repeated Coordination Games," *Econometrica*, 58: 571–595.

Harsanyi, John, and Reinhard Selten. 1988. *A General Theory of Equilibrium Selection in Games*, Cambridge, MA: MIT Press.

Kennan, John, and Robert Wilson. 1989. "Strategic Bargaining Models and Interpretation of Strike Data," *Journal of Applied Econometrics*, 4: S87–S130.

Lewis, David K. 1969. *Convention: A Philosophical Study*, Cambridge, MA: Harvard University Press.

Lucas, Robert E. 1986. "Adaptive Behavior and Economic Theory," *Journal of Business*, 59: S401–S426; reprinted in Robin Hogarth and Melvin Reder, eds.,

Rational Choice: The Contrast Between Economics and Psychology, Chicago: University of Chicago Press, 1987.

Maynard Smith, John. 1974. "The Theory of Games and the Evolution of Animal Conflicts," *Journal of Theoretical Biology*, 47: 209–221.

Maynard Smith, John, and G. R. Price. 1973. "The Logic of Animal Conflict," *Nature, London*, 246: 15–18.

Nash, John. 1950. "The Bargaining Problem," *Econometrica*, 18: 155–162.

Nash, John. 1951. "Non-cooperative Games," *Annals of Mathematics*, 54: 286–295.

Nash, John. 1953. "Two-Person Cooperative Games," *Econometrica*, 21: 128–140.

Roth, Alvin. 1987. "Bargaining Phenomena and Bargaining Theory," in *Laboratory Experimentation in Economics: Six Points of View*, Alvin Roth, ed., New York: Cambridge University Press.

Rubinstein, Ariel. 1982. "Perfect Equilibrium in a Bargaining Model," *Econometrica*, 50: 207–211; reprinted in Ken Binmore and Partha Dasgupta, eds., *The Economics of Bargaining*, New York: Basil Blackwell, 1987.

Schelling, Thomas. 1960. *The Strategy of Conflict*, Cambridge, MA: Harvard University Press; second edition 1980.

Schelling, Thomas. 1966. *Arms and Influence*, New Haven, CT: Yale University Press.

Schelling, Thomas. 1971. "Dynamic Models of Segregation," *Journal of Mathematical Sociology*, 1: 143–186.

Schelling, Thomas. 1973. "Hockey Helmets, Concealed Weapons, and Daylight Saving: A Study of Binary Choices with Externalities," *Journal of Conflict Resolution*, 17: 381–428.

Schelling, Thomas. 1978. *Micromotives and Macrobehavior*, New York: W. W. Norton.

Schelling, Thomas. 1984. *Choice and Consequence*, Cambridge, MA: Harvard University Press.

Spence, Michael. 1974. *Market Signaling: Information Transfer in Hiring and Related Screening Processes*, Cambridge, MA: Harvard University Press.

Van Huyck, John B., Raymond C. Battalio, and Richard O. Beil. 1990. "Tacit Coordination Games, Strategic Uncertainty, and Coordination Failure," *American Economic Review*, 80: 234–248.

Von Neumann, John. 1928. "Zur Theorie der Gesellschaftsspiele," *Mathematische Annalen*, 100: 295–320; translated by Sonya Bargmann in A. W. Tucker and R. D. Luce, eds., *Contributions to the Theory of Games, Volume IV*, Annals of Mathematics Study No. 40, Princeton, NJ: Princeton University Press, 1959.

Von Neumann, John, and Oskar Morgenstern. 1953. *Theory of Games and Economic Behavior*, New York: John Wiley and Sons; first edition 1944, second edition 1947.

Zeckhauser, Richard. 1989. "Reflections on Thomas Schelling," *Journal of Economic Perspectives*, 3: 153–164.

III

Choice and Consequence:
Just Oneself

12

Endowment and Contrast in Judgments of Well-Being

Amos Tversky and
Dale Griffin

In a recent educational television program, an amnesic patient was asked about his childhood and high-school experiences. Verbally fluent, he was able to converse about daily events, but could not remember any details about his past. Finally, the interviewer asked him how happy he was. The patient pondered this question for a few seconds before answering, "I don't know."

As Tom Schelling observed, "We consume past events that we can bring up from memory" (1984, p. 344). Thus, the memory of the past is an essential element of present well-being. As our opening anecdote suggests, the present alone may not provide enough information to define happiness without reference to the past. Yet memories have a complex effect on our current sense of well-being. They represent a direct source of happiness or unhappiness, and they also affect the criteria by which current events are evaluated. In other words, a salient hedonic event (positive or negative) influences later evaluations of well-being in two ways: through an *endowment* effect and a *contrast* effect. The endowment effect of an event represents its direct contribution to one's happiness or satisfaction. Good news and positive experiences enrich our lives and make us happier; bad news and hard times diminish our well-being. Events also exercise an indirect contrast effect on the evaluation of subsequent events. A positive experience makes us happy, but it also renders similar experiences less exciting. A negative experience makes us unhappy, but it also helps us appreciate subsequent experiences that are less bad. The hedonic impact of an event, we suggest, reflects a balance of its endowment[1] and contrast effects. This chapter explores some descriptive and prescriptive implications of this notion.

A few examples illustrate the point. Consider a professor from a small midwestern town who attends a conference in New York and enjoys having dinner at an outstanding French restaurant. This memorable event contributes to her endowment—she is happier for having had that experience—but it also gives rise to a contrast effect. A later meal in the local French restaurant becomes somewhat less satisfying by comparison with the great meal she had in New York. Similarly, exposure to great theater is enriching, but makes it harder to enjoy the local repertory company. The same principle applies to accomplishments. A successful first novel contributes a great deal to the author's endowment and self-esteem, but it also reduces the satisfaction derived from future novels if they are less successful.

The effects of endowment and contrast also apply to negative events. Some people, dominated by a negative endowment, become depressed and unable to enjoy life in the aftermath of a bad experience; others are elated by the contrast between the present and the bleak past. People may vary in the degree to which their reactions are dominated by endowment or by contrast. Note that the endowment-contrast dimension of individual differences is distinct from the more familiar dimension of optimism-pessimism. Optimism-pessimism normally refers to positive or negative expectations regarding the future, whereas the endowment-contrast dimension refers to the manner in which the evaluation of the present is determined by the comparison with the past. Both endowment and contrast, of course, depend on memory. With no memory, there can be no endowment and no contrast, just immediate pleasures and pains.

There is little novelty in suggesting that well-being depends both on the nature of the experience that is being evaluated and on the standard of evaluation. Furthermore, many authors have observed that satisfaction is directly related to the quality of the experience, or its endowment, and inversely related to the evaluation standard, which serves as a contrast. Perhaps less obvious is the observation that the same (past) event makes a dual contribution to well-being—a direct contribution as endowment and an inverse contribution as contrast. Although these effects have been discussed in the well-being literature (under various names), we know of no explicit attempt to integrate them.

The distinction between endowment and contrast does not depend on the character of the event itself; any hedonic experience could affect our well-being through the endowment it generates and through the contrast to which it gives rise. The endowment depends primarily on the quality and the intensity of the event, whereas the contrast depends primarily on its similarity or relevance to subsequent events. A great meal at a French restaurant in New York will probably not reduce your ability to enjoy a Chinese meal back home; similarly, while a great theater performance may spoil your taste for the local repertory company, you will probably continue to take pleasure in concerts or even high-school plays.

Because the contrast effect depends on similarity or perceived relevance, it is susceptible to framing and other cognitive manipulations. The same sequence of events can produce varying degrees of satisfaction depending on whether an early event is viewed as similar or relevant to the evaluation of later events. Thus, happiness should be maximized by treating positive experiences as endowments and negative experiences as contrasts. To achieve this goal, one should find ways to treat the positive experiences of the past as different from the present (to avoid a sense of letdown). By the same token, one should compare present conditions to worse situations in the past (to enjoy the benefits of a positive contrast). This prescription raises some intriguing questions that lie beyond the scope of this chapter. Are people who emphasize the endowment of positive events and the contrast of negative events generally happier than those who do not? And how much freedom do people have in the framing of hedonic events?

Here we report some preliminary explorations based on experimental manipulations of endowment and contrast. In the next section we vary the quality and the relevance of past events and investigate their effects on judgments of well-being. We propose a simple method for assessing the relative contributions of endowment and contrast in these studies, and we apply this analysis to some experiments of Schwarz, Strack, and their colleagues (see Schwarz and Strack 1990), and to the study of expectation effects. In the last section of the chapter, we discuss the use of choice and of judgment for the assessment of well-being, illustrate the discrepancy between the two procedures, and relate it to the relative contribution of endowment and contrast.

Studies of Endowment and Contrast

The following two experiments employ the same design to study the effect of a past event on present judgments of happiness. In the first study, we use fictitious scripts to investigate the role of endowment and contrast in judgments regarding the well-being of another person. In the second study, subjects rated their own satisfaction following an actual experience.

In our first study, subjects were given a "story"—a description of two events, allegedly taken from an interview with a student—and were asked to rate the happiness of that student. In each case, the earlier event was either positive or negative, and the later event was neutral. Four types of events were used in the study: a date, a term paper, a party, and a movie. The two events presented to the subject could be of the same type (e.g., two term papers or two parties) or of different types (e.g., a date followed by a party, or vice versa). This arrangement gives rise to a 2 × 2 (between-subjects) design in which a neutral event is preceded by either a positive or a negative event that could be of the same type or of a different type.

Because the second event is always neutral, we can focus on the endowment and the contrast effects produced by the first event. For events of different types, we expect an endowment effect, with little or no contrast. Judged happiness, therefore, should be relatively high when the first event is positive and relatively low when the first event is negative. For events of the same type, however, both contrast and endowment effects are expected. As a consequence, a related positive event should produce less happiness than an unrelated positive event, whereas a related negative event should produce less unhappiness than an unrelated negative event. For example, an excellent paper followed by an average paper should produce less satisfaction than an excellent paper followed by an average party because the original paper makes a subsequent paper (but not a subsequent party) somewhat disappointing by contrast. On the other hand, a bad paper followed by an average paper should produce less dissatisfaction than a bad paper followed by an average party.

Sixty-four students participated in our first experiment, which was administered in a class setting in four groups of approximately sixteen students each. All subjects received the following instructions:

On the next few pages you will find several descriptions of life events experienced by high-school students. These are everyday sorts of events that you or your friends have probably experienced some time in your high-school career.

Your task will be to read these stories carefully and try to understand how the person felt during these episodes. Each individual narrator will present two vignettes from his or her own high-school experience. The vignettes were all gathered during the narrator's junior year in high school. After each pair of stories, you will be asked to rate the feelings of the narrator.

Each story-teller was asked to recount two experiences. First, they were asked to describe an experience from the week before, and then they were asked to describe something that had happened that very day. These narratives were given orally, so the grammar and prose are not perfect.

Each story is very short, so please take your time and try to imagine what the scene looked like and felt like to the narrator. Especially try to imagine how the narrator was feeling as he or she recounted the story.

The events refer to four domains: a date with a young woman, performance in a course, the planning of a party, and the reaction to an Australian movie. Three events were constructed for each domain: positive, neutral, and negative. Recall that for each story (i.e., a pair of events), the present event was always neutral and it was preceded by either a positive or a negative event that was either related or unrelated. Each respondent evaluated four stories, one in each quality/ relation condition (i.e., positive/related, positive/unrelated, negative/ related, and negative/unrelated). The following story describes a negative event involving class performance followed by a related neutral event; an unrelated neutral event is also given for comparison.

Tim's Story

(Past, Negative)

What happened last week? Last week, let's see. I had a bad day. A really, really bad day. In the morning, I had a quiz in French. I was so tired and I just couldn't keep my mind on the problems. And then with about 10 minutes to go in the period, I sort of woke up and realized that I was in bad trouble. I had sort of puttered on the first page of a three-page quiz and there was no way I was going to finish. I almost broke out in a cold sweat; the quiz wasn't very important or anything, but it was like a dream where I was racing against time and my heart was pounding and there was no way I was going to get finished. So I felt bad about that all morning, not to mention embarrassed at blowing the quiz, and then in the afternoon I got a test back in Chemistry. I had almost failed it; it was a pretty hard test and everything, but it just made me want to give up. I was just stunned, not to mention tired. Good grades in Chemistry are important to me because I want to take sciences in college. So I skipped track practice that day and just went home. I didn't want to deal with anything else bad that could happen to me.

(Present, Related)

What happened today? I had three classes this morning, but since one of them is Civics, it wasn't too bad. In Civics, we discussed political issues that have been in the news. That was o.k., mostly a break from taking notes in other

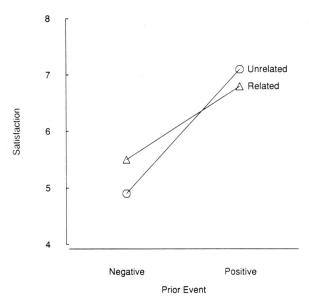

Figure 12.1
The effect of prior events

classes. First period I had Geometry, and we had a substitute teacher so we just did our homework in class. Before lunch I had French, which I am taking instead of Spanish this year. We practiced our conversations, which we have to present next week. That's pretty much it, I think.

Story 2 (Present, Unrelated)

What happened today? Well, I had another lunch with Susan. We had a pretty good time. We talked most of the time, about classes and some people we both know. Mostly we talked about the English class, though, and the way that exams were given. We argued some about whether the professor was fair, but we both agreed that the exams were aimed more at trivial detail than were the lectures. We ate pretty slowly, but both made it to our one o'clock classes. It was hard to get a feeling for what was going on, but I think she liked me well enough.

The dependent variable was a rating of happiness on a scale ranging from 1 (very unhappy) to 10 (very happy). Subjects were asked "On the day that Tim answered these questions: How happy do you think he was with his life overall?" Because there were no significant differences between the responses to the different types of events, the results were pooled. Figure 12.1 displays the average rating of happiness in each of the four conditions, averaged across subjects and stories. The results confirmed our predictions. There was a significant interaction between the quality of the past event (positive or negative) and its relation (related, unrelated) to the present event, $F(1,60) = 6.71$, $p < .02$. As expected, we observed a significant endowment effect: in both the related and unrelated conditions, judged satisfaction was higher for the positive than for the negative prior event. Furthermore, there was a significant contrast effect: for the positive prior event, satisfaction was higher in the unrelated ($M = 7.1$) than in the related condition ($M = 6.8$), whereas for the negative prior event, the pattern was reversed ($M = 4.9$ for the unrelated condition, and $M = 5.5$ for the related condition). For example, the memory of a good date last week diminished the satisfaction with a neutral date this week, but it enhanced the satisfaction with a neutral movie this week. The memory of a painful date, on the other hand, enhanced the satisfaction with a neutral date this week, while it diminished the satisfaction with a neutral movie this week.

To aid in the interpretation of experimental data, we find it useful to express judgments of satisfaction as an additive combination of endowment and contrast effects. We assume that the endowment effect E_{12} is given by the sum of the endowments of the first and second events, denoted E_1 and E_2 respectively, and that the contrast effect C_{12} is expressible as the signed hedonic discrepancy between the two events d_{12}, weighted by their degree of relatedness r_{12}. Thus, we obtain the form

Satisfaction = Endowment + Contrast

$$= E_{12} + C_{12}$$
$$= E_1 + E_2 + r_{12}d_{12}.$$

To apply this scheme to the results of our first study, let S denote the rating of satisfaction. For simplicity, we suppose that the grand mean has been subtracted from all observations, so S is expressed as a deviation score. Let S^+ and S^- be respectively the responses in a condition where the first event was positive or negative, and let S_r and S_u denote the responses in a condition where the two events were related or unrelated. Let E^+ and E^- denote the endowment associated with a positive or negative event, and let C^+ and C^- denote the contrast associated with a positive or negative event, respectively. Because the second event in this study was always neutral we can neglect its endowment, and set $E_2 = 0$. Naturally, the contrast associated with a prior positive event is negative, $C^+ < 0$, and the contrast associated with a prior negative event is positive, $C^- > 0$. We also assume that, for unrelated events, $r_{12} = 0$, hence the contrast term vanishes in that case. Judgments of satisfaction in the present design can be represented as:

	Negative	Positive
Unrelated	$S_u^- = E^-$	$S_u^+ = E^+$
Related	$S_r^- = E^- + C^-$	$S_r^+ = E^+ + C^+$

We use this model to estimate the effect of contrast and endowment. For the experimental results shown in figure 12.1, the total endowment effect is

$$E = E^+ - E^- = S_u^+ - S_u^- = 7.1 - 4.9 = 2.2.$$

As we assume the unrelated events involve no contrast, the overall endowment effect is simply the difference between mean satisfaction in the cells representing positive and negative unrelated events. The contrast associated with the positive first event is

$$C^+ = S_r^+ - S_u^+ = 6.8 - 7.1 = -.3.$$

Similarly, the contrast associated with the negative first event is

$$C^- = S_r^- - S_u - S_u^- = 5.5 - 4.9 = .6.$$

Thus, the total contrast effect in this experiment is $C^- - C^+ = .9$, which is considerably smaller than the endowment effect, as can be seen in figure 12.1.

In our second study, subjects rated their own satisfaction with actual experiences. Seventy-two subjects took part in a computer-controlled stock-market game played for real money. Subjects were given information about different stocks and were asked to construct a portfolio from these stocks. They were told that the computer would simulate the market and that their actual payoffs would depend on the performance of their portfolios. Each session included an initial game (with a payoff of $2 or $6) and a later game (with a payoff of $4) separated by a filler task involving no gains or losses. As in the first study, we manipulated two variables: (a) the payoff in the first game and (b) the similarity or relatedness of the first and the second games. In the related condition, subjects played essentially the same game with different stocks. In the unrelated condition, the games

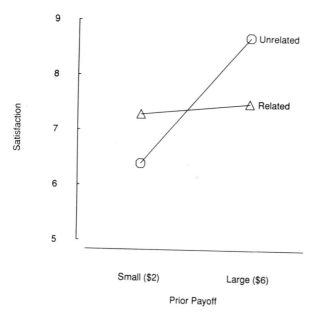

Figure 12.2
The effect of prior payoffs

involved different markets (stocks versus commodities) and used different procedures for portfolio construction. After subjects played both games, they were asked to rate their overall satisfaction with the experience, using a ten-point scale.

This design allows us to test the following hypotheses regarding judged satisfaction. First, the difference between the low ($2) and the high ($6) payoffs will be greater in the unrelated than in the related condition. This prediction follows from the assumption that for the unrelated games, the difference reflects a pure endowment effect. In the related games, however, the positive endowment will be reduced by a negative contrast, whereas the negative endowment will be reduced by a positive contrast. Second, the negative contrast effect following the high payoff (when $d_{12} > 0$) will be larger than the positive contrast effect following the low payoff (when $d_{12} < 0$), as suggested by the notion of loss aversion (Kahneman and Tversky 1984).

The pattern of results displayed in figure 12.2 supports the endowment-contrast analysis. In the unrelated condition, where there is pure endowment and no contrast, those who received the larger payoff in the first game were considerably more satisfied

($M = 8.7$) than those who received the smaller payoff in the first game ($M = 6.4$), $t(33) = 1.95$, $p < .05$, one-tailed. However, in the related condition, where contrast and endowment worked in the opposite directions, there was essentially no difference between the satisfaction of those who received the larger reward in the first game ($M = 7.5$) and those who received the smaller reward in the first game ($M = 7.3$).

The decomposition scheme introduced in the first study is also applicable to the results of the present study. Here too, E_2 is a constant, and hence can be ignored in the analysis. To simplify matters, we also assume that the difference between the satisfaction derived from the high prior payoff and the low prior payoff in the unrelated games yields an estimate of the total endowment effect:

$$E = S_u{}^+ - S_u{}^- = 8.7 - 6.4 = 2.3.$$

The positive contrast (the increase in satisfaction caused by a low expectation) was

$$C^- = S_r{}^- - S_u{}^- = 7.3 - 6.4 = .9,$$

and the negative contrast (the decrease in satisfaction caused by a large expectation) was

$$C^+ = S_r{}^+ - S_u{}^+ = 7.5 - 8.7 = -1.2.$$

Note that the overall endowment effect was about the same in the two experiments, but the overall contrast effect, $C = C^- - C^+ = 2.1$ was doubled in the present study. As implied by loss aversion, people's disappointment with a "loss" of $2 was greater than their satisfaction with a "gain" of $2.

Applications of the Endowment-Contrast Scheme

Our conceptual scheme for the integration of endowment and contrast effects, described above, can be applied to two studies conducted by Schwarz, Strack, and their colleagues (see Schwarz and Strack 1990). In one experiment, Strack, Schwarz, and Geschneidinger (1985) instructed subjects in one group to recall and write down a very negative event in their lives; subjects in another group were instructed to recall and write down a very positive event in their lives. Within each group, half of the subjects were asked to recall a recent

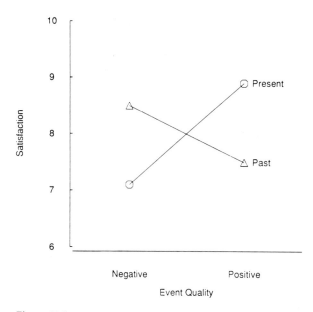

Figure 12.3
The effect of past vs. present events

event, and half were asked to recall a past event. Subjects were then asked to rate their well-being on a ten-point scale. This procedure yields a 2×2 (between-subjects) design in which the recalled event was either positive or negative, in the present or in the past. For the events in the present, the results were hardly surprising. Recalling a positive present event made people feel good, whereas thinking about a negative present event made people feel less happy. The results for past events were more surprising: ratings of well-being were higher for those who recalled a past negative event than for those who recalled a past positive event (see figure 12.3). We have replicated this result at Stanford.

The endowment-contrast scheme provides a natural account of these findings. For the events in the present, there is no room for contrast, hence we get a positive endowment effect for the positive event and a negative endowment effect for the negative event. The recall of past events, however, introduces a contrast with the present, which is positive for negative events and negative for positive ones. We assume here that the present is neutral. This contrast component offsets the relatively weak endowment component of past events, thereby producing the observed reversal.

Again, let S^+ and S^- refer to judged satisfaction when a positive or negative event, respectively, has been brought to mind. (As before, we first subtract the grand mean from each observation and operate on deviation scores). Let S_c and S_p refer to the judgments associated with a current and a past event, respectively. We can represent the average judgment in each cell as follows:

	Negative	Positive
Current	$S_c{}^- = E^-$	$S_c{}^+ = E^+$
Past	$S_p{}^- = E^- + C^-$	$S_p{}^+ = E^+ + C^+$

The total endowment effect is

$$E = E^+ - E^- = S_c{}^+ - S_c{}^- = 8.9 - 7.1 = 1.8.$$

The contrast associated with the positive first event is

$$C^+ = S_p{}^+ - S_c{}^+ = 7.5 - 8.9 = -1.4.$$

The contrast associated with the negative first event is

$$C^- = S_p{}^- - S_c{}^- = 8.5 - 7.1 = 1.4.$$

The total contrast effect in this experiment is $C = C^- - C^+ = 2.8$. In this study, therefore, the contrast effect is considerably greater than the endowment effect.

More generally, thinking about positive events in the past (e.g., a tour of the Greek islands, or a happy time at summer camp) calls attention to the less exciting present. This is the stuff of which nostalgia is made. On the other hand, recalling some bad times in the past (e.g., failing a test or being lonely) reminds us that the present, although imperfect, could be a great deal worse. While Strack et al. (1985) see mood as the carrier of endowment, we do not regard mood as a necessary condition for an endowment effect. We shall address this difference in emphasis at the conclusion of this section.

In another study, Schwarz, Strack, Kommer, and Wagner (1987) required subjects to spend an hour either in an extremely pleasant room (spacious, nicely furnished, and decorated with posters and flowers) or in an extremely unpleasant room (small, dirty, smelly, noisy, and overheated). After the session, subjects were asked to assess general satisfaction as well as satisfaction with regard to their current housing situation. The room influenced the rating of overall satisfaction; subjects who were placed in the pleasant room reported

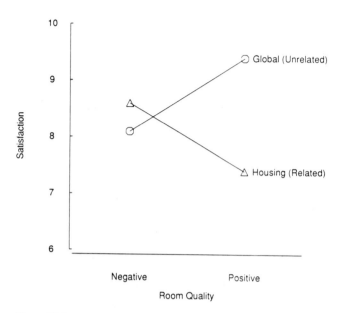

Figure 12.4
The effect of room quality

higher overall life satisfaction than those in the unpleasant room. However, subjects' rating of their normal living conditions exhibited the opposite pattern (see figure 12.4). Those placed in the unpleasant room reported higher satisfaction with their housing than those who had been in the pleasant room. This pattern is naturally interpreted as a contrast effect. One's own room appears less attractive when compared with the pleasant room than when compared with the unpleasant room. Because contrast depends on the relevance or the similarity of the standard to the target, the contrast effect of the experimental room was confined to the evaluation of housing, and did not extend to the rating of life satisfaction. A specific event, therefore, is likely to have a significant contrast effect in the domain to which it belongs, and little or no contrast effect in others.

Using the notation introduced earlier, let S^+ and S^- denote, respectively, judgments of satisfaction for the pleasant and unpleasant rooms, and let S_r and S_u denote, respectively, judgments of satisfaction for the related (housing) and unrelated (life satisfaction) domains. The analysis of these results is then identical to the analysis of the first study. In particular, the total endowment effect is

$E = S_u{}^+ - S_u{}^- = E^+ - E^- = 9.4 - 8.1 = 1.3.$

The contrast effect associated with the positive first event is

$C^+ = S_r{}^+ - S_u{}^+ = 7.4 - 9.4 = -2.0.$

The contrast effect associated with the negative first event is

$C^- = S_r{}^- - S_u{}^- = 8.6 - 8.1 = .5.$

As one might expect, the contrast effect produced by the room is considerably larger $(C = C^- - C^+ = 2.5)$ than its endowment effect.

Although different in focus, our analysis is generally compatible with that offered by Schwarz and Strack (1990). They assume the operation of contrast effects and focus on the role of emotion or mood in generating endowment. Our account assumes the existence of endowment effects, produced through either mood or other processes, and focuses on the factors that control the relative strength of endowment and contrast.

Expectations as Contrast and Endowment

Much psychological research on the assessment of well-being has focused on the role of expectations. It has been shown in many contexts that the same event can be perceived as more or less satisfying, depending on whether a positive or negative expectation has been induced (Feather 1966; Shrauger 1975). Whether a given test score is pleasing or disappointing will depend on whether the student was led to expect a low or a high score (Schul 1988). Expectation effects are generally interpreted as contrast. Indeed, people are commonly advised to lower their expectations in order to avoid disappointment. In line with our previous analysis, we propose that expectations produce endowment as well as contrast. We are relieved when a dreaded event does not happen, but the memory of anxiety and fear still haunts us long afterward. Imagine that you have been living two weeks with the possibility that your child has leukemia. Further tests now prove your worries unfounded. Despite your elation at this news, we suspect that you are worse off for the experience. In such circumstances, the endowment effect of a negative expectation has a strong impact on your well-being long after the specific worry has been relieved.

Much as unrealized fears can generate negative endowment, un-realized hopes can give rise to positive endowment. Consider the experience of someone who owns a lottery ticket. Because the probability of winning is very small, the failure to win does not cause much disappointment. However, the dream of becoming an over-night millionaire could produce enough pleasure to offset the mild disappointment of not winning the lottery. Indeed, it appears that many people enjoy playing the lottery even when they do not win. The contrast between prior expectations and the actual outcome is especially sensitive to the probability of winning. As the probability of winning increases, the costs of disappointment (contrast) seem to increase faster than the benefits of hope (endowment). Holding expected value constant, therefore, playing long odds should be more pleasurable than playing short odds. Losers on long odds had sweeter dreams than losers on short odds; and their disappointment was also less bitter. This analysis suggests another reason for the attractiveness of long shots, in addition to the overweighting of small probabilities (Kahneman and Tversky 1979).

The present conception of well-being is guided by the observation that people derive pleasure and pain not merely from the positive and the negative events they experience, but also from the memory of past events and the anticipation of future events (Elster 1985; Loewenstein 1987). Like the memories of past events, expectations of future events, we suggest, serve both as endowment and as contrast. Expectations not only control the evaluation of future events, they have a hedonic impact of their own—whether or not the event they refer to actually comes to pass. Our hedonic portfolio encompasses memories and expectations; successes and failures of the past, hopes and fears of the future. In the words of Tom Schelling, "We consume good news and bad news," (1984, p. 344).

The Assessment of Well-Being: Choice versus Judgment

The studies described here were concerned with judgments of satis-faction or happiness, which have served as a major source of data for students of well-being (Argyle 1987; Diener 1984). Another paradigm for the study of welfare focuses on choice rather than on judgment. In this paradigm, a person is said to be better off in State A than in State B if he or she chooses State A over State B. Indeed, the concept of utility has been used in economics and decision theory in two different senses: (a) experience value, the degree of pleasure or pain associated with the actual experience of an outcome, and (b) decision value, the contribution of an anticipated outcome to the overall attractiveness of an option (Kahneman and Tversky, 1984). Experience values are generally measured by judgmental methods (e.g., self-reports or judgments by observers), although physiological measures (e.g., blood pressure or heart rate) are occasionally used. Decision values are inferred from choices using an appropriate model such as expected utility theory or the theory of revealed preference. The distinction between experience and decision values is rarely made explicit because, with a few notable exceptions (e.g., March 1978; Schelling 1984; Sen 1982), it is commonly assumed that judgment and choice yield the same ordering. In many situations, however, experience values, as expressed in self-ratings, appear to diverge from decision values, as inferred from choice.

First, choice and judgment may yield different results because of moral considerations and problems of self-control. We commonly avoid certain pleasurable experiences because they are immoral, illegal, or fattening. On the other hand, there are times we cannot resist experiences that will ultimately make us unhappy, because of a lack of self-control. Choice, therefore, could conceal rather than reveal one's "true preferences." Second, a choice-judgment discrepancy is likely to arise if the decision maker's prediction of the consequences of a choice is inaccurate or biased. A common bias in the prediction of utility is a tendency to overweight one's present state or mood. Some perceptive consumers have learned to avoid doing their weekly grocery shopping either when they are very hungry (because they would buy too much) or after a very large meal (because they would not buy enough). A related source of error is the failure to anticipate our remarkable ability to adapt to new states. People tend to overestimate the long-term impact of both positive events, such as winning a lottery or receiving tenure, and negative events, such as injury or personal loss (Brickman, Coates, and Janoff-Bulman 1978). The ability to predict future well-being depends largely on the nature of the experience. People generally have a reasonable idea of what it is like to lose small sums of money or to have a bad cold, but they probably do not have a clear notion of what it means to go bankrupt or to lose a limb. For illuminating discussions of the role of adaptation and the problems of predicting one's own future satisfaction, see Kahneman and Snell 1990, and Kahneman and Varey 1990.

But even if the judgment, like the choice, precedes the experience of the consequence, the two tasks can give rise to different answers because they highlight different aspects of the problem. When people are asked to assess the hedonic value of some future states (e.g., new jobs) they try to imagine what it would feel like to experience those states. But when asked to choose among these states, they tend to search for reasons or arguments to justify their choice. Consequently, the two procedures could lead to different results. For example, Tversky, Sattath, and Slovic (1988) have shown that the most important attribute of a multidimensional decision problem is weighted more heavily in choice than in judgment, presumably because it provides a convenient rationale for choice. Recall the stock-market study, presented in the first section of this chapter. Given a choice, subjects would surely elect to participate in the negative contrast condition, where they earn $10, rather than in the positive contrast condition, where they earn $6. Yet subjects who had a lower total endowment ($6) and a positive contrast were just as satisfied as subjects who had a higher total endowment ($10) and a negative contrast. It appears that the choice depends primarily on the payoffs, whereas judgments of satisfaction are more sensitive to the contrast.

To explore the choice-judgment discrepancy, we presented the following information to some sixty-six undergraduate students.

Imagine that you have just completed a graduate degree in communications and you are considering one-year jobs at two different magazines.

(A) At Magazine A, you are offered a job paying $35,000. However, the other workers who have the same training and experience as you do are making $38,000.

(B) At Magazine B, you are offered a job paying $33,000. However, the other workers who have the same training and experience as you do are making $30,000.

Approximately half the subjects were asked "Which job would you choose to take?" while the other half were asked "At which job would you be happier?" The results confirmed our prediction that the comparison with others would loom larger in judgment, and that the salary would dominate the choice. Eighty-four percent of the subjects (27 out of 32) preferred the job with the higher absolute salary and lower relative position, while 62 percent (21 out of 34) of the subjects anticipated higher satisfaction in the job with the lower absolute salary and higher relative position ($\chi^2(1) = 14.70$, $p < .01$).

We further explored the relation between choice and judgment in the assessment of an actual experience using a within-subjects design. Thirty-eight undergraduate students participated in a study of "verbal creativity" involving two different tasks. One was described as a test of "cognitive production": the ability to come up with many words that fit a sentence. The other task was described as a test of "grammatical production": the ability to produce many words of a particular grammatical type. Subjects were told that their payoffs would depend on their performance in these tasks.

All subjects performed both tasks, each of which consisted of a practice trial followed by a payoff trial. In one task, subjects were told that their performance was below average on the practice trial and about average on the payoff trial. In the other task, subjects were told that they performed above average on the practice trial and about average on the payoff trial. Thus, the performance of each subject allegedly improved on one task and declined on the other task. The order and type of task were counterbalanced. The payoff in the declining condition ($3) was higher than the payoff in the improving condition ($1). Thus, one task paired a larger payoff with an unfavorable comparison. The other task paired a smaller payoff with a favorable comparison. After each task, subjects were asked to rate their satisfaction with their performance on a ten-point scale. Following the completion of both tasks, subjects were asked "If you could do just one task, which would you choose to do?"

As predicted, the payoffs loomed larger in choice than in judgment, or equivalently, the contrast was weighted more heavily in judgment than in choice. Of the twenty-eight subjects whose ratings were not identical on the two tasks, 75 percent chose the high-payoff task, whereas 54 percent expressed greater satisfaction with the low-payoff task. This reversal pattern is significant ($p < .05$ by a McNemar test of symmetry).

These studies show that judgments of satisfaction and choice can yield systematically different orderings. Furthermore, it appears that choice is determined primarily by the payoffs, which reflect the endowment effect, whereas the judgment is more sensitive to comparison or contrast. The salary or payoff one receives provides a more compelling reason for choice than the contrast between one's own salary and the salary of others. This contrast, however, is a very salient feature of the experience, as reflected in the judgment task. Note that the present use of *contrast* is consistent with, but considerably broader than, the concept invoked in the first part of this chapter. There the term refers to the indirect contribution of a past event to current well-being, whereas here it refers to the standard of reference by which the relevant outcomes are evaluated, which may be determined by prior experience or by other factors, such as the salary of colleagues.

The choice-judgment discrepancy raises an intriguing question: which is the correct or more appropriate measure of well-being? This question cannot be readily answered, and perhaps it cannot be answered at all, because we lack a gold standard for the measurement of happiness. We believe that both choice and judgment provide relevant data for the assessment of well-being, although neither one is entirely satisfactory. Since, as we argue below, the two methods seem to be biased in opposite directions, a compromise between them may have some merit.

Perhaps the most basic principle of welfare economics is Pareto optimality: an allocation of resources is acceptable if it improves everybody's lot. Viewed as a choice criterion, this principle is irresistible. It is hard to object to a policy that improves your lot just because it improves the lot of someone else even more. This is a pure endowment argument that neglects contrast altogether. Policies that ignore contrast effects can create widespread unhappiness, however. Consider, for example, a policy that doubles the salary of a few people in an organization and increases all other salaries by 5 percent. Even though all salaries rise, it is doubtful that this change will make most people happier. There is a great deal of evidence (e.g., Brickman 1975; Brickman and Campbell 1971; Crosby 1976) that people's reported satisfaction depends largely on their relative position, not only on their objective situation.

Both experimental and survey research on happiness have shown that judgments of well-being are highly sensitive to comparison or contrast and relatively insensitive to endowment effects. Perhaps the most dramatic illustration of this phenomenon concerns the effect of windfall gains and personal tragedies. Judged by their ratings, lottery winners are no happier than others, and quadriplegics are only slightly less happy than healthy people and no less happy than paraplegics (Brickman et al. 1978). Surveys indicate that wealthier people are slightly happier than people with less money, but substantial increases in everyone's income and standard of living do not raise the reported level of happiness (Easterlin 1974).

Do these data reflect rapid adaptation that negates the immediate impact of any endowment—as implied by the treadmill theory of happiness (Brickman and Campbell 1971)? Or do they reflect a normalization of the response scale that makes the ratings of ordinary people and paraplegics essentially incomparable? (As if the paraplegic answers the question: how do I feel relative to other paraplegics?) There is no simple answer to these questions. Obviously, everyone would choose to be healthy rather than paraplegic, and rich rather than poor. But it is not obvious how to demonstrate that the rich are actually happier than the poor if both groups report the same level of well-being. At the same time, it is clear that an adequate measure of well-being must distinguish between rich and poor, and between paraplegic and quadriplegic.

It seems that judgments of well-being are insufficiently sensitive to endowment, whereas choice is insufficiently sensitive to contrast. The exclusive reliance on either method can lead to unreasonable conclusions and unsound recommendations. Welfare policy derived from Pareto optimality could result in allocations that make most people less happy because it ignores the effect of social comparison. On the other hand, a preoccupation with judgment has led some psychologists to the view that "persons with a few ecstatic moments in their lives may be doomed to unhappiness" (Diener 1984, p. 568), hence, "if the best can come only rarely, it is better not to include it in the range of experiences at all" (Parducci 1968, p. 90). These conclusions are justified only if endowment effects are essentially ignored. A few glorious moments could sustain a lifetime of happy memories for those who can cherish the past without discounting the present.

Notes

This work was supported by a grant from the Alfred P. Sloan Foundation. It has benefited from discussions with Daniel Kahneman, Lee Ross, and Richard Zeckhauser. This is a slightly modified version of a paper that appears in *Subjective Well-being*, edited by F. Strack, M. Argyle, and N. Schwartz (1990).

1. Our use of this term to denote a component of hedonic experience should be distinguished from the endowment effect demonstrated by Thaler (1980), through which the acquisition of material goods influences subsequent choices.

References

Argyle, M. 1987. *The Psychology of Happiness*. London: Methuen.

Brickman, P. 1975. "Adaptation Level Determinants of Satisfaction with Equal and Unequal Outcome Distributions in Skill and Chance Situations," *Journal of Personality and Social Psychology*, 32: 191–198.

Brickman, P., and D. T. Campbell. 1971. "Hedonic Relativism and Planning the Good Society," in *Adaptation Level Theory: A Symposium*, pp. 287–302, M. H. Appley, ed., New York: Academic Press.

Brickman, P., Coates, D., and R. Janoff-Bulman. 1978. "Lottery Winners and Accident Victims: Is Happiness Relative?" *Journal of Personality and Social Psychology*, 36: 917–927.

Crosby, F. 1976. "A Model of Egoistical Relative Deprivation," *Psychological Review*, 83: 85–113

Diener, E. 1984. "Subjective Well-Being," *Psychological Bulletin*, 95(3): 542–575.

Easterlin, R. A. 1974. "Does Economic Growth Improve the Human Lot? Some Empirical Evidence," in *Nations and Households in Economic Growth*, pp. 89–125, P. A. David and M. W. Reder, eds., New York: Academic Press.

Elster, J. 1985. "Weakness of Will and the Free-Rider Problem," *Economics and Philosophy*, 1: 231–265.

Feather, N. T. 1966. "Effects of Prior Success and Failure on Expectations of Success and Failure," *Journal of Personality and Social Psychology*, 3: 287–298.

Kahneman, D., and J. Snell. 1990. "Predicting Utility," in *Insights in Decision Making*, R. Hogarth, ed., Chicago, IL: University of Chicago Press.

Kahneman, D., and A. Tversky. 1979. "Prospect Theory: An Analysis of Decision Under Risk," *Econometrica*, 47: 263–291.

Kahneman, D., and A. Tversky. 1984. "Choices, Values and Frames," *American Psychologist*, 39: 341–350.

Kahneman, D., and C. Varey. 1990. "Notes on the Psychology of Utility," in *Interpersonal Comparisons of Well-Being*, J. Roemer and J. Elster, eds., Chicago, IL: University of Chicago Press.

Loewenstein, G. 1987. "Anticipation and the Valuation of Delayed Consumption," *Economic Journal*, 97: 666–684.

March, J. G. 1978. "Bounded Rationality, Ambiguity, and the Engineering of Choice," *The Bell Journal of Economics*, 9(2): 587–608.

Parducci, A. 1968. "The Relativism of Absolute Judgments," *Scientific American*, 219: 84–90.

Schelling, T. C. 1984. *Choice and Consequence*, Cambridge, MA: Harvard University Press.

Schul, Y. 1988. *Expectations, Performance, and Satisfaction*, unpublished manuscript, The Hebrew University of Jerusalem.

Schwarz, N., and F. Strack. 1990. "Evaluating One's Life: A Judgment Model of Subjective Well-Being," in *Subjective Well-Being*, F. Strack, M. Argyle, and N. Schwartz, eds., Oxford: Pergamon Press.

Schwarz, N., F. Strack, D. Kommer, and D. Wagner. 1987. "Soccer, Rooms, and the Quality of Your Life: Mood Effects on Judgments of Satisfaction with Life in General and with Specific Domains," *European Journal of Social Psychology*, 17: 69–79.

Sen, A. 1982. *Choice, Welfare and Measurement*, Cambridge, MA: MIT Press.

Shrauger, J. S. 1975. "Responses to Evaluation as a Function of Initial Self-Perception," *Psychological Bulletin*, 82: 581–596.

Strack, F., M. Argyle, and N. Schwartz, eds. 1990. *Subjective Well-Being*, Oxford: Pergamon Press.

Strack, F., N. Schwarz, and E. Geschneidinger. 1985. "Happiness and Reminiscing: The Role of Time Perspective, Affect, and Mode of Thinking," *Journal of Personality and Social Psychology*, 49(6): 1460–1469.

Thaler, R. 1980. "Toward a Positive Theory of Consumer Choice," *Journal of Economic Behavior and Organization*, 1: 39–60.

Tversky, A., S. Sattath, and P. Slovic. 1988. "Contingent Weighting in Judgment and Choice," *Psychological Review*, 95(3): 371–384.

13

Preferences or Principles:
Alternative Guidelines for
Choice

Dražen Prelec and
R.J. Herrnstein

"Profound moral conviction was the basis of Mr. Gladstone's political influence," remarked Bertrand Russell, explaining: "Invariably he earnestly consulted his conscience, and invariably his conscience earnestly gave him the convenient answer." From the perspective of a rational agent, the humor in Russell's joke ought to be cryptic, but, of course, it is not, especially to those whose conscience is not as obliging and versatile. There is something odd about the suggestion that one's conscience reliably serves one's self-interest, but why? At the level of common sense, we all recognize that actions are shaped by such things as values, rules, vows, obligations, and principles, which are in part our own creation but which can also appear to us as an external constraint, over which we have little control. Can that idea be incorporated into an empirically sound, but theoretically consistent, theory of choice?

In this essay,[1] we would like to suggest the importance, for the social sciences generally, of having a theory of human nature and action within which the paradox inherent in Gladstone's decision-making style would find some natural explanation. We do not have such a theory in any rigorous sense of the term, and we do not think a fully satisfactory one is available, despite the efforts of philosophers and others who have thought long and hard about these matters. Hence the essay will have the more modest aim of showing the need for a *psychology of legal/moral reasoning and interpretation* that would describe how people use principles in decision making, as well as how principles are integrated with rational cost-benefit calculations.

Rational choice theory seems to be readily reconciled with the existence of explicit *moral* principles, at least for those cases in which individual compliance can be monitored by the community. It is well understood that a collection of individually maximizing agents may often fail to find a collective optimum when confronting prisoners' dilemmas or common grazing lands, if they are not guided by explicit rules. But what of *prudential* rules of self-management (Schelling 1985)? If we are rational individually, why do we need anything more to guide us? If we prefer to weigh less, be in better shape, or stop drinking, why do we not just do so? The fact that prudential rules exist indicates that the tendency to form, and follow, rules requires some explanation at the level of individual psychology.

Introspection suggests that moral and prudential principles tap a common psychological mechanism, although the object of concern is different. We may feel guilty or remorseful for having overslept or overspent or broken a diet, just as for violating a law or a duty or a social obligation. We may feel virtuously good for declining the chocolate cake or for contributing to charity. Violating a convention for which there is no corresponding internalized principle probably engenders only embarrassment, not guilt, and that only when our violation has been detected by others. Conforming to a convention lacking an internalized principle may confer no further benefit than the avoidance of embarrassment, and no warm glow of virtue.

The next section of the essay defines rules or principles and explores their possible function. We then discuss why rule-governed behavior resists assimilation to the rational cost-benefit model. This same issue is taken up again in the following section, but now with respect to so-called divided self models, which view the individual agent as a collection of noncooperating but individually rational subunits. The essay concludes with a short summary of the basic differences between rational and rule-governed action.

Systematic Biases in Cost-Benefit Calculation

By one definition, a principle does not *supplement* ordinary cost-benefit analysis, but rather *replaces* it (Etzioni 1988). In other words, by invoking a principle one does not add another consideration onto what Janis and Mann (1977) call the "decisional balance-sheet"; instead one discards the balance-sheet altogether, at least provisionally. There is nothing wrong with thinking about the costs and benefits of a marriage before the vow[2]; afterward, such calculations probably foreshadow the end of the marriage.

In our view, a behavioral policy in regard to some action or class of actions is a rule or principle[3] if, and only if, it overrides cost-benefit calculation with respect to that action. Within the normative economic theory, the approach is to fit rules and principles into the utilitarian calculus. Our claim, in contrast, is not that the standard approach is unworkable, but that the issue is clarified by proceeding as if there are two distinct ways of deciding on a course of action, only one of which involves the utilitarian calculus. The second method is used not merely because the calculations are often hard to do, as they certainly are. Even when the calculation is easy, as subsequent examples will show, we often invoke a guide to behavior that abjures doing the mental arithmetic of cost-benefit analysis.

Perhaps a clarification of the word *rule* might be useful. Within the tradition of "bounded rationality" theorizing in economics, decision-making rules have been viewed as a necessary response to the daunting complexity of the decision problems faced by both individuals and economic organizations. The tradition probably can be traced to Herbert Simon (1957), and shows its influence today in the work of Heiner (1983) and Nelson and Winter (1982), among many others. Simplifying somewhat, we could say that a rule, in this view, is a behavioral policy that produces satisfactory results in the long run, without burdening the decision maker with case-by-case cost-benefit calculations. This is what Etzioni refers to as "rules of thumb" (1988, chapter 10), and Nelson and Winter (1982) as "routines."

Our focus of attention is on the sort of personal rules that arise, not to routinize calculation, but to overcome weaknesses of our natural cost-benefit accounting system, weaknesses of which we are aware and for which the rule or principle serves as a partial antidote. For example, parents who are not themselves religious may try to inculcate religious belief in their children, because they feel that the principles of a religious life lead believers to make better choices than nonbelievers do. Some parents may inculcate belief because they think that *society* is better served by believers, but our point is that some parents may do so because they think their *children* are better served by being believers.[4]

Such rules need not be imposed by parents or other agents who have our interests in mind; they may also be "constructed" by ourselves as we see the need for them. We may observe, for example, that our alcohol drinking is creeping upward—our taste for alcohol is pushing us beyond what we perceive as an optimal level of consumption—and decide to adopt a one-drink-a-day policy, which may be an improvement without being quite optimal. We may realize the risks of drinking, but find ourselves at times unable to act sensibly in light of our realization. In the final section we discuss briefly this contrast between internally and externally imposed rules or principles, but until then, the distinction will be set aside.

Rules or principles cannot be a perfect antidote under all conditions, for if they were, then they would be equivalent to a perfect cost-benefit analysis, which is, by assumption, not possible. One might expect to find rules proliferating in exactly those choice domains where a natural utilitarianism produces results that we do not find satisfactory. Rules or principles presumably improve performance over the results of our faulty cost-benefit analyses, but not to virtual optimization.

At least three different forms of trouble afflict ordinary cost-benefit analysis. Each can be described as a biasing asymmetry or mismatch in the disposition of the costs relative to the benefits that flow from an action. The tacit assumption is that a decision maker must choose between taking or not taking a course of action. The consequences of not taking the action are, for simplicity's sake, assumed to be a fixed standard of reference against which we compare the results of combining the costs and benefits of the action. We omit here, as we do elsewhere in this essay, the complexities of strategic interactions, in which present choices affect the outcomes of future choices through their influence on other agents. What difficulties may we encounter in this calculation?

1. *Temporal mismatch*, in which the cost and benefit are separated by a substantial time interval.

2. *Saliency mismatch*, in which one element of the cost-benefit pair is vivid and easy to imagine, whereas the other is not.

3. *Scale mismatch*, in which one element of the cost-benefit pair is perceived to have impact only in an aggregate sense (that is, only if the same action is repeated many times, or on a larger scale).

We will refer to these mismatches as asymmetries of time, saliency, and scale, respectively. In all three cases, cost-benefit analysis fails because it assigns the wrong weights to one or the other, or both, of the elements of the pair, given the person's long-run valuations. The excessive discounting of future consequences is amply demonstrated by both casual observation and experimental research (Ainslie 1975), hence the asymmetries of time. As regards saliency, the importance of vividness has been demonstrated in the domain of probability judgments by Tversky and Kahneman (1981), and it seems likely that a comparable bias would afflict judgments about utility and value.

The third mismatch, asymmetries of scale, which could also be described as the "drop in the bucket" phenomenon, has been analyzed by Herrnstein and Prelec (in press) in the context of so-called *problems of distributed choice*. There are situations in which the economically significant variables are aggregates of many temporally distinct decisions, each of which, individually, has little impact (rates of cigarette consumption, frequency of exercise, or social interaction, etc.). But, to the extent that decision makers ignore these impacts, their choices may in the long run be predictably suboptimal.[5]

The first, and most critical psychological function of a rule, according to the line of thought being pursued here, is to *disengage* the cost-benefit calculus, because it is subject to distortion by one or another of the asymmetries. If this is true, then we should be able to trace specific rules to specific (possibly multiple) mismatches in the cost-benefit accounting. Here are some examples.

Rules Pertaining to Health and Personal Safety

Decisions that affect health are clear examples of distributed choice (or scale mismatch), because the cost of engaging in some unhealthy or risky action is negligible unless the action becomes a permanent pattern or lifestyle. Try, for example, to evaluate the cost or the benefit of

(i) one cigarette;

(ii) one slice of chocolate cake;

(iii) one car trip with a seat belt;

(iv) one visit to the health club;

(v) one more day at the beach, away from work.

In some of these examples, a temporal mismatch is also present (e.g., the health risks from smoking), but it is conceptually a distinct problem, and one that may not be of primary importance. Consider the seat-belt case. The cost, if it appears, is instantaneous; it is also vivid (the saliency mismatch does not apply). Furthermore, if you survive the trip, there are no insidious aftereffects—the balance sheet is cleared. Hence the problem is primarily one of scale.

Presumably, the cost-benefit problem in the seat-belt case could be tackled either "in the small" (i.e., for the one-shot decision) or "in the large" (i.e., whether one should buckle up always, or never). Neither format is convenient for a cost-benefit analysis, because of the mismatch in scale. In the large problem, the probability of harm that follows from a no-buckle-up policy can perhaps be appreciated, but how does one aggregate, across hundreds of trips in the car, the modest comfort increases garnered by not buckling up? In the small problem, the comfort can perhaps be appreciated, but the tiny probability of harm in one trip has little subjective meaning. The aggregate benefits of seat-belt use outweigh those of not using them, so, if we could correctly solve either the long or the short cost-benefit problem, we would use the belts.[6] Adopting a policy signifies that we are disinclined to solve the problem in terms of costs and benefits.

It could be argued that even though the stakes "in the small" are difficult to grasp, nothing prevents one, in principle, from solving the large cost-benefit problem and, as a result, deciding always to use seat belts. But although subjectively we may feel that we have decided "once and for all" to use seat belts, objectively we are not given the opportunity to make such a choice. The objective situation presents us only with choices "in the small," each covering precisely one trip; if it were possible to buy a car that would not start with seat belts unbuckled, then one could choose a policy. As it is, a person may *decide* on a policy, but that is no guarantee that he or she will indeed follow it, when confronted with the reality of one trip at a time.

For people who regularly use seat belts, it may seem odd to categorize this activity with such notoriously conflictual matters as too much chocolate cake or smoking cigarettes or chronic absenteeism from work. Regular seat-belt users may want to distinguish between policies adopted with little or no internal fuss, and those we continually struggle to maintain against the temptations of defection. But, on the other hand, not everyone uses seat belts regularly and effortlessly. To them, the seat-belt issue may naturally sort itself with chocolate cake or absenteeism. Such questions as the relative universality of a particular decision-making conflict or the intensity of the conflict are important and deserve consideration. But, here, we will have little more to say about them (the final section comments on the motivational force attached to principles), beyond observing that conflicts may be more or less common, and more or less intense, and still exemplify scale mismatches.

Rules That Build Up and Maintain Character, or "Personal Identity"

People derive satisfaction from their internal moral standing or, more generally, from the subjective correspondence between their self-image and some ideal. But maintaining such an image is usually a problem of distributed choice. A character trait, for example, is the product of many separate decisions, any given one of which could have been reversed without major impact. It is probably true that a person can consider himself honest, generous, brave, in spite of a few deceptions, or occasional acts of cheapness or cowardice. (However, is this a truth for a moralist to advertise?) For example, the choice between truth and falsehood, in the small, pits the often clear and instantaneous benefits of a lie against the minute blemish to one's self-image of truthfulness incurred from a single lie. The problem of distributed choice is that the outcome of this decision may tip toward steady lying even if one believes that "honesty is the best policy."

Rules for Spending or Saving Decisions

Ordinary overspending may often be primarily due to a temporal mismatch—the expensive magazine picked up at the check-out counter, which you bought impulsively and would not have bought had you been making the decision a few moments before you reached the end of the check-out line. But some forms of overspending are probably more a matter of saliency mismatches. In "home shopping clubs," for example, television viewers are shown products that can be ordered by phone. It is probably clear to anyone that money spent to purchase a product (for, say, $19.95) will not be available to spend on something else—there will be a loss, in other words, of $19.95 in general purchasing power. But where, specifically, will the sacrifice be felt? Most people do not know. This creates an initial bias for overspending—the benefit is concrete and visible, while the cost is an unspecified and abstract corollary. The bit of consumption that will be canceled by the purchase is not present to the mind, to make its case felt.[7]

The success of home shopping clubs cannot be attributed to the immediacy of reward (i.e., the time mismatch does not apply). Products purchased over the telephone may not arrive for weeks, possibly well after the charge has been debited against one's account, given the vagaries of billing and shipping. Nor could one argue that the decision to buy is driven by the immediate *expectation* of using the product, because the loss in expected purchasing power is also realized immediately.

Undersaving, in general, may reflect the simultaneous operation of all three mismatches. First, the benefits of savings are delayed; second, the benefits of savings may be imagined at the level of aggregate future income, which is not appreciably affected by single acts of current consumption; third, the benefits are less concrete, given the uncertainty surrounding one's future circumstances.

Prohibition against Crime and Self-Abuse

Pure examples of a temporal mismatch are hard to find; they would be cases in which the delayed consequence was clear and hinged on a single action. Some criminal acts probably fall in this category (Wilson and Herrnstein 1985), especially "crimes of passion" that are committed in full knowledge that punishment is probable. Other examples might include drug, alcohol, or sexual binges, in which the negative hangover phase is fully expected, but discounted.

When Opportunities and Information Have Negative Value

Our hypothesis is that rules or principles take over in situations where cost-benefit analysis systematically fails at the personal level. But can the use of rules itself be rationalized by a more complete inventory of individual preferences, one that would capture a taste for following principles? We think not. Without going into technical detail, and omitting the complexities that arise in strategic interactions between rational actors, the modern conception of the rational agent derives from three fundamental psychological assumptions:

Assumption (1) A person's preferences over a given set of outcomes of choices are independent of how the choices are constrained.

Assumption (2) All aspects of individual psychology bearing on choice can be resolved into matters of taste (preferences) or knowledge (information).

Assumption (3) A person chooses the most preferred outcome, given the information at his or her disposal.

From these three postulates flow two elementary theorems about how changes in opportunities, information, and preferences should affect the utility or welfare derived from a choice situation:

Theorem (1) Expanding opportunities can only increase personal welfare in the utility-maximizing sense.

Theorem (2) Having more information can only increase personal welfare, similarly defined.

It is important to recognize the utter generality of these deductions, at the purely individual level (i.e., in the absence of multiperson externalities). They are valid without regard to a person's tastes, or the extent to which he understands the choice situation; they constitute the empirical rock bottom of the rational model. Thus, it is significant that decisions involving principles will often produce violations of the two theorems.

Costly Opportunities

Suppose that you are given an opportunity to do something, which, upon consideration, you decline. If the rational model is correct, your welfare should be unchanged—you are exactly where you were before the declined offer. And indeed, insofar as *tastes* are concerned, the prediction holds: if you are about to order steak from a restaurant menu when the waiter informs you of a special unlisted dish, you can reject this new possibility without impairing your enjoyment of the steak.

But now suppose, instead, that you are an unemployed football player, invited to join one of the "replacement" teams during the 1987 football strike. If you reject the offer, the regret over lost income may make you suffer. But if you accept the offer, you may regret having violated a personal rule against strike-breaking and may wish the situation had never arisen.[8] The clearest challenge to rational choice theory is posed by the case in which the individual declines the offer, but feels worse off for having had the opportunity. Such phenomena are recorded in speech, when we say things like, "It is a tempting opportunity, and I'd like to take it, but I regret I cannot accept." While such expressions of regret are sometimes merely conventional, in many cases they are sincere. Yet, if the opportunity failed to pass a comprehensive cost-benefit analysis, why regret declining it?

If the job offer is perceived as a temptation, and not just something one either wants to accept or reject, then it can be neither refused nor accepted without cost. An option to do or not to do something becomes a temptation when it presents an opportunity to break a personal principle. For this reason, it is considered unkind, if not worse, to offer cigarettes to a recently converted nonsmoker, or cakes to someone on a diet, or drinks to an ex-alcoholic, or a sexual proposition to someone else's faithful spouse. Some social and legal institutions specifically shield people from temptations, such as minimum wage laws and prohibitions on the sale of sexual favors, blood, body parts, and so on. To be sure, society as a whole may have an interest in such prohibitions, but our point is that individuals may favor them as devices for controlling their own behavior as well. Below, we offer a psychological hypothesis about why temptations always impose costs; here we emphasize that, insofar as a temptation is just an expansion of a choice set, it cannot reduce individual welfare within classical cost-benefit theory. If it is not just an expansion of a choice set, the problem for the normative theory is to explain what it is.

Note, also, that the best solution, in the utility-maximizing sense, would be to be compelled to accept a temptation, so that you can enjoy whatever makes it a temptation to begin with, but be absolved from the responsibility, which is to say, from the costs of violating a principle. ("The devil made me do it.") On the other side of the coin of reduced utility with an expanded choice set is the paradox of increasing utility when the choice set is reduced. ("Get thee behind me, Satan.")

If constraints on choice can improve welfare, there will be incentives for manufacturing constraints even though none "really" exist. A reformed alcoholic, for example, may have a policy of not walking down streets with many bars on them, but he is not really prevented in any physical way from doing so (Schelling 1980, 1985). The constraint is a mental construction. In a similar vein, if a person can find an alternate principle that will permit a tempting action with no (or much reduced) cost, then he is in the best of all possible worlds: he may think he has really had his cake and eaten it too. When a reforming alcoholic accepts brandy after a dinner party, excusing himself by saying (and believing) that he did not want to offend his host, we may think he is kidding himself. This internal jockeying of choice sets makes no sense within rational choice theory, yet it is probably familiar to everyone.

Just as accepting or rejecting temptations has costs, costs may be incurred when someone is presented with an opportunity to *affirm* a principle. Consider two hypothetical situations:

Scenario 1: You buy an expensive bottle of wine that turns out to be mediocre; you drink it, making note not to buy it again.

Scenario 2: You order a comparable bottle in a restaurant (for the same price); after a great deal of thought, you decide not to send it back; however, your dinner has been spoiled.

The opportunity set in Scenario 2 is strictly larger, because it includes the option of returning the wine (not available in Scenario 1). How can this produce a lower "utility" level? By not sending the wine back, you have sacrificed a principle (something like "Get the fair value for purchases"), probably for pragmatic, cost-benefit reasons (e.g., avoiding a scene, embarrassment if the establishment refuses to take back the wine, personal acquaintance with the owner). The violation of principle exacts an additional cost, which is absent from Scenario 1.

When a rule is not followed, it must be because of cost-benefit reasons like these, because some other rule predominated, or because of physical restraint. It is our intuition that the subjective utility level will be *directly* related to how strong or compelling a reason there was for breaking the rule. If, for example, physical restraint was involved, rule breaking per se exacts little if any subjective cost. Or, to pick another example, homicide in self-defense is no crime at all, whereas homicide to avenge an uncollected debt is first-degree murder. The law mirrors our subjective sense of transgression. The subjective cost for breaking a rule rises with one's perceived margin for behaving otherwise. The perception of freedom of action is costly.

Costly Knowledge

A famous experiment of Stanley Milgram illustrates how information may hurt, in contradiction to the second theorem. In Milgram's experiment, many subjects discovered that they were willing to cause great apparent harm to another person, if pressed sufficiently hard by the experimenter, who represented himself as a scientist associated with Yale University.[9] For most subjects, participation in the experiment was a disagreeable experience, although they later felt it had taught them a useful lesson about themselves and other people (Milgram 1974). Although the cost was partly due to the stress of the actual experiment, the more significant source of suffering was presumably the knowledge that one had failed a test of an important principle.

Some subjects obediently delivered the entire series of ostensibly painful and harmful shocks; other subjects abruptly resigned from the experiment. Two principles were evidently vying for control—something like "Do no harm," versus "Respect legitimate authority"—and subjects were guided by one or the other. It is relevant, though perhaps regrettable, that the defiant subjects were more unhappy about their experience as subjects than the obedient ones, as if to say that, on the average, it costs more psychologically to violate the principle of respecting authority than of doing no harm. Subjects who behaved cruelly evidently felt less anguish than those who behaved admirably, but, in all cases, subjects suffered psychologically as they served in the study.

It is so easy to empathize with the discomfort of having participated in such an experiment that it takes some thought to see how puzzling it appears on strictly rational grounds. The procedure clearly provided fresh information about one's own behavioral dispositions, especially for those who complied with the instructions.[10] Although the information may be disturbing, it also provides an opportunity for the person to take morally corrective measures. A rational person may suffer as a result, but this is preferable, presumably, to remaining ignorant of one's profound susceptibility to authority. That is how many outsiders viewed Milgram's data, as a significant and welcome addition to our knowledge of human nature.

Curiously, it seems that the concerns over the ethical aspects of the study, of which there were many, derived from the fact that we all (i.e., the nonparticipants) benefited from its publication, at the expense of the actual participants (this issue is discussed in Herrnstein 1974). We are all now duly warned about following orders, etc., and, statistically, we know that there is a more than an even chance that we would have given the entire sequence of shocks. But no one will lose sleep over this—indeed, one could even conjecture that no nonparticipant would feel great anguish even if *all* of the experimental subjects complied. There is a vast difference between knowing that one might have broken a principle, and actually doing so.

Valuable Misinformation

If information can be costly, it should come as no surprise that misinformation can be valuable, as illustrated by a hypothetical problem posed in Kahneman, Knetch, and Thaler (1986). Imagine yourself lying on the beach on a hot day, thinking about how nice it would be to have a cold beer. A friend offers to get one, from a place nearby—which, in the two versions of the story, is described as either a "fancy resort" or a "run-down grocery store." Not knowing the price of the beer, the friend requests instructions about the maximum amount that she should pay.

Kahneman, Knetch, and Thaler report that the subjects' median reservation price was $1.50 for the grocery store, and $2.65 for the resort, the lower grocery-store price reflecting presumably a matter of principle (e.g., "Don't pay more than the customary price"). Suppose, now, that the friend goes to the grocery store and finds that the price is $1.75. What should she do? Purchase the beer, and explain, upon returning, that the grocery store was unfortunately closed, but that just down the road there was a fancy resort . . .

Multiple Selves and Ainslie's Theory of Rule Formation

It has been recognized for some time by a small but growing group of economic and behavioral theorists that in some situations, opportunities or information have negative value for the decision maker, even at the individual level. Aside from the work of Kahneman, Knetch, and Thaler (1986), which is concerned with the narrower issue of perceptions of fairness, these researchers have typically maintained the analytical techniques of the rational model, but viewed the person as being composed of several "subagents," each of which may have distinct preferences, as well as access to private information (Ainslie 1975, 1982, 1986; Elster 1986; Schelling 1980; Thaler and Shefrin 1981; Winston 1980).

Observed from the outside, a single person would exhibit the behavior of a collective of rational agents, which, as formal game theory indicates, will not always be consistent with the one-person axioms of rationality. There are many games (the prisoner's dilemma being only the most famous example) in which individually rational play produces poor results and in which the elimination of some strategies would improve everyone's payoffs. The promise of this approach is to understand perceived suboptimalities in individual choice, by game-theoretic analogy, as the result of harmful strategic interactions between individually rational subsections of the self.

These attempts, however, also fall short, for lack of a key analytical instrument—something that would provide an analytics of *legal reasoning*. To develop this argument, we turn first to the work of George Ainslie, which, although less formal, contains an account of how rules and principles emerge from a strategic struggle for mastery within a single individual.

Ainslie proposes a theory of extraordinarily simple underlying assumptions. Because of an inherent characteristic of time perception—documented experimentally (Ainslie 1975)—people are prone to a systematic ambivalence about actions that create an initial benefit (or cost) followed, after some delay, by a larger cost (or benefit). When the moment of choice is relatively far away, we intend to give proper weight to the later consequence; however, when the moment of choice arrives, the smaller but earlier consequence overshadows the later one, causing an "impulsive" reversal of the original preference.

This intertemporal inconsistency sets the stage for an internal struggle between the individual's long- and short-term interests. Since the short-term interest is most often the "executive" (i.e., the one that actually makes the choice), it is naturally positioned to sabotage the intentions and plans of the long-term interest, unless the latter can alter the structure of rewards and punishments that are effective at the moment of choice. Ainslie has proposed a number of devices by which the long-term interest can prevail, but the most interesting, for our purposes, is the stratagem of *private rules*, or *side bets*.

The key step in the private rule strategy is to convince the short-term interest that the current decision will constitute a binding precedent for a long series of future choices. A current decision to, say, indulge some temptation becomes a sign that the temptation will be indulged on all such occasions. A single bite of the forbidden dessert, for instance, destroys the expectation that the diet will be followed in the future. The short-term interest is thus kept in line, as it were, by the threat of a severe and *immediate* loss in expectations for future outcomes.

Linking this account with our previous discussion, we could say that a principle is a mechanism serving the long-term interest, for the purpose of correcting the three types of cost-benefit mismatches discussed earlier. It amplifies the scale of the decision; it transforms unclear consequences into vivid ones; and, by staking future expectations on present choices, it brings the future to bear on the present. But this argument now brings us to a central difficulty. Suppose that at the time of decision, the short-term interest is inclined to choose one way, but is reined in by the presence of some overarching rule. What is to prevent the short-term interest from interpreting the rule so that it does not apply to *this* particular case, which after all must differ in some respects from previous occasions when the rule was invoked, or, if that option is too farfetched, from invoking another, stronger principle that overrides the original one? At the moment of choice, the short-term interest is both the judge and the jury for any disputes over interpretation, which makes mysterious its presumed fidelity to the interpretations as they were originally laid down.

The Internal Marketplace of Principles

A missing element of the story, then, is some account of the psychological force by which a rule can fend off the challenge of immediate short-term interests. In addition, we need to understand the extent to which a rule can be stretched, or defeated by another dominating rule. These two issues are discussed in turn.

In Pavlovian, or classical, conditioning, the powers of one stimulus are, to some degree, imparted to another. In Pavlov's famous experiment on dogs, the power of dry meat powder to elicit salivation was transferred to a metronome or other arbitrary signal. The arbitrary signal is differentially associated or correlated with the natural (or previously conditioned arbitrary) stimulus.[11]

Much of the modern work on Pavlovian conditioning has dealt with the transference of motivational or emotion-eliciting powers across stimuli. For example, subjects will value an arbitrary signal that has been differentially associated with something they value to begin with. The ambiance of a room in which one has eaten numerous delicious meals acquires an aesthetic value in its own right. Collectors of books, documents, or old phonograph records treasure the feel, look, smell, and heft of their objects of interest, even though their fundamental value as collectibles depends on other attributes, such as rarity, age, and content.

Similarly, the arbitrary features of stimuli differentially associated with undesirable states of affairs become motivationally negative. The look and sound of a harsh teacher become disagreeable in their own right. We avoid his or her presence when we can. The disinfectant smell of hospitals has become a conditioned aversive stimulus for people who have endured fear, pain, or sorrow in that environment.

Society exploits our susceptibility to Pavlovian conditioning to inculcate social values. Social interactions are permeated with essentially arbitrary conventions of behavior and address, which arise in a history of conditioning that members of a community share. We are rewarded for politeness, punished for rudeness, and the differential association of those rewards and punishments with particular modes of behavior endow those modes of behavior with motivational power of their own. If we are successfully conditioned, we feel good about our good manners, bad about bad manners. That internalized increment or decrement may be sufficient to tip the scales toward politeness when the external circumstances might have evoked rudeness.

Conditioning attaches motivational power to arbitrary stimuli, and then, by some ill-understood process akin to reasoning or induction, that power may spread far from the particulars originally experienced, into a more or less logically coherent structure of stimuli and the perceived relations among them. Politeness becomes, not merely particular conditioned responses to particular stimuli, but a systematic approach to behavior in social settings. Having been conditioned aversively to avoid doing dangerous things like touching hot stoves or stepping off the curb into the street, we feel some of the attendant anxieties when we confront what we know or perceive to be new dangers. The value instilled in us by the external environment for good health habits may be elaborated internally into principles for staying fit.

On the face of it, the Pavlovian conditioning of values can be subsumed under standard economic analysis as a device for creating tastes. But, in fact, moral and prudential choices often involve deciding which of these articulated systems of internalized relations—or principles—applies in a given instance, then acting accordingly.

Our discussion of the selection among, or substitution of, alternate rules can be focused by means of the following example. Suppose that one particular Friday evening, a person chooses between going to an entertainment movie or a documentary film about famine in Africa (the proceeds of which will be donated to charity). It is the last showing for both movies. The person chooses the entertainment film, thus revealing his preference.

Now, to change the problem slightly, suppose that Friday after lunch, the person has the opportunity to take off early and see one of the two films (again, the last opportunity to see either one). He refuses the entertainment film, but might in fact go see the documentary. On narrow revealed preference grounds, this choice is irrational. Whatever the objective cost of taking the afternoon off, it is not affected by the movie that he sees: the benefits of either movie—hedonic, moral, or educational—are no doubt technically separable in preference from the benefits that are derived from several hours' work.

It is not hard to reconstruct the internal argument that leads to the preference reversal. The person may have a rule against taking off early—especially for play—no doubt acquired from a history of conditioning. The documentary, however, is a hard case: In a sense it might be "work," especially if the film is not *too* enjoyable. In addition, there is a secondary principle at stake, namely, contributing to charitable causes, analogously acquired. Such ambiguities form the raw material for a decision to leave work, but they need to be shaped into a principle that has sufficient power to sanction the original desire to leave.

It is doubtful that rational calculation can shed much light on this process. Careful decision analysis may help us decide whether in a particular instance it is better to go against principle (one would rationally assess the costs of sacrificing the principle—a hard but not impossible task), but it does not help in deciding whether the principle actually applies to the issue at hand.

Decision analysis, which codifies the model of rational behavior and extends it into areas where uncertainty reigns, operates by resolving each problem into either a matter of preference or a matter of information. Let us start with the most obvious question. Does the documentary constitute work or play? This does not seem to be a matter of information, in the sense of uncertainty about some objective "state of the world." For example, if you think that it is work, and another person thinks that it is play, then your disagreement is not of the type that can be resolved by a scientific debate. There is no critical *fact* that establishes the correct labeling.

There is a temptation then to shift the question into the domain of tastes, which so often serves as the catch-all category for any nonobjective matter. But the thought processes one would go through in trying to classify the film do not seem to correspond to an interrogation of subjective *preference*. Quite possibly, the person has a good idea of how much he would enjoy each film; his doubt has to do with whether to allow himself this violation of principle.

What we see in the example, then, is a rather complete (and characteristic) fusion of tastes and beliefs. Our theory suggests that, up to a point, the probability of going to the documentary film may increase as the price (i.e., donation) rises. If one believes that seeing the film is work, then it can be seen (and enjoyed); if one believes that it is entertainment, then the enjoyment will be corrupted by the knowledge that a personal rule has been violated.

We also see that the arena in which principles compete is somewhat autonomous. If we were trying to convince someone to go see the film, we would not appeal to preferences, but would rather try to present him with an alternative interpretation or principle. This is the method of seduction through rhetoric: to provide arguments that sanction one's inclinations.

Divided-self models capture something important in describing moral ambivalence as a struggle—a game—between different, temporally segregated aspects of the individual. The problem is that they do not have much to say about the rules by which this game is conducted—and that is because the psychological processes that make the game possible are not well captured by variations on preferences and information (the twin building blocks of rational modeling).

In this paper, we have tried to show that action by rules or principles entails a distinct mode of decision making, irrespective of whether the rules pertain to moral or prudential concerns, whether the decisions are profound or trivial. Table 13.1 lists the main contrasts between this legal/moral mode and the familiar procedures of decision analysis. Instead of evaluating trade-offs among the competing arguments of the utility function (such as risk versus expected return), the process revolves around a search for a unique principle that covers the decision at hand and that is not dominated by another more powerful principle.

This second mode of decision making has not yet benefited from the sustained economic and psychological research and attention that have been bestowed on the rational-agent model, perhaps because there is no normative theory to set the agenda. But if rules and prin-

Table 13.1

	Action by decision analysis	Action by rule or principle
Goal	Maximize a given criterion	Discovery of, and adherence to, appropriate criterion
Method	Logical/empirical	Legal
Internal structure	Compensatory dimensions or attributes	Hierarchy of principles
Main cognitive activity	Assessment of multiattribute value functions; prediction of uncertain events	Interpretation; judgments of grouping and similarity

ciples do in fact arise because of fundamental defects in individual decision making, then a model of rule-governed action will have no shortage of applications in economics and the other social sciences.

Notes

1. An earlier version, by Prelec alone, was presented at the session, "Socioeconomics: The Roles of Power and Values," at the annual meeting of the American Association for the Advancement of Science, San Francisco, January 14–19, 1989. The present version has had the benefit of many useful comments and suggestions from Thomas Schelling, Richard Zeckhauser, and other members of the seminar on public policy at the Kennedy School of Government. Jonathan Riley provided helpfully skeptical comments. We are much in their debt. Many of the ideas presented here were developed as resident fellows, in 1988–89, at the Russell Sage Foundation, to which we owe much thanks for supporting our work.

2. In the vow, we may foreswear calculating "sickness," "health," "richer," "poorer."

3. Richard Zeckhauser has pointed out (personal communication) that the term *principle* seems to refer to deeper guidelines for conduct, which require additional elaboration before they can be applied in a given instance. Rules, on the other hand, are relatively unambiguous directions for action. That distinction in usage will not be observed here, although it may prove to be useful in more detailed analyses.

4. We refer here to the benefits from choices made as a believer, which would have been different for a nonbeliever, not the benefits (e.g., respect, deference, etc.) that believers receive from other people by virtue of being believers.

5. For a further discussion of the theory and relevant experimental evidence, see Herrnstein and Prelec (in press), Herrnstein and Vaughan 1980, or Prelec 1982.

6. More likely, we would use the belts on some occasions and not on others, depending on how comfort and risk measure up. The very fact that we seize on using them always (or, for some people, never) suggests that a rule, rather than a cost-benefit calculation, is guiding behavior.

7. There is a parallel here with the so-called invisible lives problem in public project risk-management. It is notorious that life-saving funds are more easily appropriated if they will benefit a visible group than if they benefit an anonymous sample from the population. For example, expenditures for traffic safety are typically lower than the level that would be justified by a lives-saved analysis.

8. For completeness, we can round out the set of contingencies by mentioning that either acceptance or rejection could be accompanied, not by regret, but by satisfaction: acceptance providing the satisfaction of, for example, extra money, or rejection providing that of upholding solidarity with the strikers. However, there is no challenge to the standard choice theory when an additional option yields additional benefits.

9. Subjects were instructed to give what appeared to them to be a series of progressively more severe electric shocks (but which were not really shocks at all) to another "subject" (an actor, in fact), who was seated in another room, but whose screams and pleadings could be clearly heard, as punishments for "incorrect" responses in a learning experiment.

10. Milgram (1974) showed that virtually everyone thinks he would be defiant under experimental conditions that in fact elicit obedience from about two-thirds of the subjects.

11. Extensive research has refined Pavlov's rudimentary theory, according to which stimulus powers were transferred as a result of mere temporal contiguity and, in addition, the response being elicited was assumed to be unchanged in form. It is well known now that conditioned responses may differ systematically from unconditioned responses, and that mere contiguity is neither necessary nor sufficient to produce conditioning. An up-to-date account of this form of conditioning can be found in Mazur 1986. For present purposes, the modern refinements can be set aside.

References

Ainslie, George. 1975. "Specious Reward: A Behavioral Theory of Impulsiveness and Impulse Control," *Psychological Bulletin*, 82: 463–509.

Ainslie, George. 1982. "A Behavioral Economic Approach to the Defense Mechanisms: Freud's Energy Theory Revisited," *Social Science Information*, 21: 735–779.

Ainslie, George. 1986. "Beyond Microeconomics: Conflict among Interests in a Multiple Self as a Determinant of Value," in *The Multiple Self*, J. Elster, ed., Cambridge: Cambridge University Press.

Elster, Jon, ed. 1986. *The Multiple Self*, Cambridge: Cambridge University Press.

Etzioni, Amita. 1988. *The Moral Dimension: Toward a New Economics*, New York: The Free Press.

Heiner, Ronald A. 1983. "The Origin of Predictable Behavior," *American Economic Review*, 73: 560–595.

Herrnstein, Richard J. 1974. "Measuring Evil," *Commentary*, June: 82–88.

Herrnstein, Richard J., and Drazen Prelec. In press. "Melioration: A Theory of Distributed Choice," *Journal of Economic Perspectives*.

Herrnstein, Richard J., and William Vaughan, Jr. 1980. "Melioration and Behavioral Allocation," in *Limits to Action: The Allocation of Individual Behavior*, J. E. R. Staddon, ed., pp. 143–176, New York: Academic Press.

Janis, Irving, and Leon Mann. 1977. *Decision making: A Psychological Analysis of Conflict, Choice, and Commitment*, New York: The Free Press.

Kahneman, Daniel, Jack Knetch, and Richard Thaler. 1986. "Fairness as a Constraint on Profit Seeking: Entitlements in the Market," *American Economic Review*, 76: 728–741.

Mazur, James E. 1986. *Learning and Behavior*, Englewood Cliffs, NJ: Prentice-Hall.

Milgram, Stanley. 1974. *Obedience to Authority: An Experimental View*, New York: Harper & Row.

Nelson, Richard R., and Sidney G. Winter. 1982. *An Evolutionary Theory of Economic Change*, Cambridge, MA: Harvard University Press.

Prelec, Dražen. 1982. "Matching, Maximizing, and the Hyperbolic Reinforcement Feedback Function," *Psychological Review*, 89: 189–230.

Schelling, Thomas C. 1980. "The Intimate Contest for Self-Command," *The Public Interest*, no. 60, Summer: 94–118.

Schelling, Thomas C. 1985. "Enforcing Rules on Oneself," *Journal of Law, Economics, and Organization*, 1: 357–374.

Simon, Herbert A. 1957. *Models of Man: Social and Rational; Mathematical Essays on Rational Human Behavior*, New York: Wiley.

Thaler, Richard, and Hersh M. Shefrin. 1981. "An Economic Theory of Self-Control," *Journal of Political Economy*, 89: 392–410.

Tversky, Amos, and Daniel Kahneman. 1981. "The Framing of Decisions and the Psychology of Choice," *Science*, 211: 453–458.

Wilson, James Q., and Richard J. Herrnstein. 1985. *Crime and Human Nature*, New York: Simon and Schuster.

Winston, Gordon C. 1980. "Addiction and Backsliding," *Journal of Economic Behavior and Organization*, 1: 295–324.

14   Coping with Common Errors in Rational Decision Making

Howard Raiffa

Any *descriptive* account of how real people make choices would show that formal, reasoned analysis plays little part in the process. Yet *normative* analysis lays out elaborate rules for how superrational individuals should, in some sense, make decisions. Somewhere between those extremes lies the terrain in which I am primarily interested: the use of analytical methods to guide the deliberations of decision makers. I call that *"prescriptive* analysis."

This trichotomy (descriptive, normative, and prescriptive) is not standard (see Bell, Raiffa, and Tversky 1988). Prescriptive analysis is usually considered a subset of normative analysis, but it is something more. A prescriber who wants to give relevant, constructive advice to ordinary (not superrational) people must be sensitive to descriptive realities, and so my craft combines art with science.

In this chapter I would like to make some descriptive remarks about how prescriptive analysis is usually done and to point out some common shortcomings of such prescriptive analyses. Then I will offer some suggestions for coping with common errors in doing prescriptive analysis, primarily those that arise in using incomplete or inadequate decision trees.

Decision trees are made, not born, and it is a myth that there is a unique "right" tree for a given problem. In practice, decision trees, like real trees, grow, but for different reasons. Sometimes a very small tree—dubbed a "sapling" by Behn and Vaupel (1982)—could capture the simplest essence of the problem, but its analysis might not be compelling to the analyst or the client. As its shortcomings are examined, the tree is often embellished to highlight its inadequacies. And so it grows. But the more intricate the tree, the more inputs (often subjective ones) have to be assessed. Artful compromises must be made that balance realism, complexity, and transparency.

Decision analysis is often criticized for aiming no higher than trying to find the best of a *prespecified* set of alternative strategies. But nothing is prespecified in practice. Alternatives and options have to be created, and analysis and creativity should be mutually supportive. It's easier to generate creative options at a given node of a partially structured tree than to be creative with a blank piece of paper. Normatively, prescriptive analysis should help creativity; descriptively, it all too often inhibits creativity; prescriptively, analysts should consciously engage their clients in dialogues about improving their menu of choices. Better a choice between exciting alternatives than pedestrian ones.

It's not easy to construct a complicated decision tree, but some recent technological developments have helped. Computer aids make it easier both to draw complicated trees and to communicate results to clients. Once trees are drawn, computers make it easy to do sensitivity analysis. Influence diagrams (Shachter 1986, Howard and Matheson 1984) are now extensively used to help analysts interact with clients in structuring the dependencies in a problem, and useful computer programs can convert influence diagrams to decision trees. For complex problems it is easier for the analyst and client to interact using influence diagrams than decision trees. These new tools should be kept in mind as I recite some of the errors caused by incomplete trees.

Analysis at the Tips of the Tree: Life Goes On

Imagine that the analyst, along with his client, structures a problem in terms of a decision tree (see figure 14.1). To simplify the use of pronouns, I'll assume that it is *Mr.* Analyst and *Ms.* Decision Maker.) Not everything can be included on the tree—and that's one source of problems. The analyst must cut off the tree at some horizon. When assigning utilities for consequences at the tips of the tree, the analyst must keep in mind that life continues after the artificially imposed horizon. In comparing and evaluating any two terminal consequences, he must go beyond the tangible payoffs gained along the paths to C' and C''. If C' has better future possibilities and flexibility than C'', then most analysts would take that difference into account in assigning utility values to C' and C''.

In a large design project, for tractability reasons, one might at first ignore problems of implementation. Suppose that strategy Q is, in the

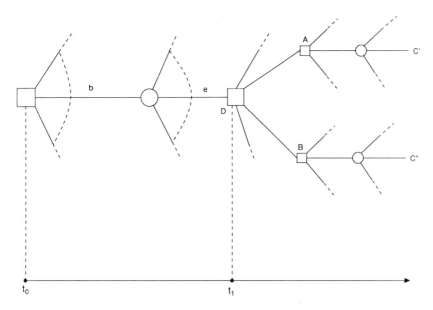

Figure 14.1
Schematic decision tree

abstract, better than strategy R, but harder to implement. Ideally, the analyst should formalize the implementation phase in the decision tree and work backward from the end—a normative suggestion for prescriptive analysis. A prescriptive suggestion might be to do a rough *qualitative* analysis of the implementation phase and to modify the *quantitative* evaluations of strategies subjectively, in a way that reflects these implementation considerations. These observations about what to do at the tips of the tree are a prelude for the next complication that is not ordinarily accommodated by analysts.

The literature is replete with arguments about whether formal analysis is better or worse than holistic intuitive analysis. There is a role for subjective intuitive analysis within a formal framework.

Analysis at Intermediate Nodes: Subjectively Incorporating Flexibility

Once the analyst has assigned utilities at the tips of the tree, in the usual rollback procedure he computes derived utility values for decision nodes A and B. He finds, let us say, that A has a higher utility value than B (see figure 14.1). But now assume that the tree is incomplete and that at node B there is more flexibility than at A—perhaps enough more so that the decision maker really would prefer to be at B than at A. One might say that the decision tree should be embellished to reflect this flexibility, but it may not be easy to do so. To patch up such blemishes in decision trees, a pragmatic analyst and decision maker might adjust the values at A and B to reflect this sense of flexibility, just as they would adjust a value at the tip of the tree. Of course, if you demand that this adjustment be made more formally, the analyst would be driven into structuring a more complete version of the decision tree. But that effort may not be worth making—and effort of analysis is also not included in the decision tree.

I recognize the danger inherent in such loose advice. What prevents an advocate of some position from overruling the implications of objective analysis? Moreover, the client may not have a responsible way to impute subjective values for such factors as flexibility. If these are issues, then my advice would be to do a bit more formal analysis—but not necessarily a complete job.

Embellishing a Tree in Real Time

In real time, decision trees sprout new branches. Suppose a tree is structured and analyzed (as in figure 14.1), and the decision maker, starting at time t_0, follows the optimum strategy by going down choice-branch b. Then chance, in real time, responds with outcome e: in real time, the decision maker is now perched at node D at time t_1. The bulk of the original tree has been stripped away by the passage of time, and the decision maker and her analyst should rethink the options at node D at time t_1. They usually do. New branches, more detail, more depth, at both decision and chance nodes, can be added beyond D. Certainly this would be wise. But if this is to be the practice, how should the analyst and client view the original tree at time t_0? They suspect at the outset that if they ever reach D in real time, they will embellish the tree at that point. If they suspect a far richer potential embellishment at one node than at another, should this difference not be reflected in the analysis of the original tree—at least intuitively?

Working backward with the original decision tree, suppose that the utility value at node D is 70 units. Imagine that the analyst and the decision maker are at time t_0 at the beginning of the tree, and the analyst reflects, "If at time t_1 my client ends up at node D, then I will suggest that we embellish the tree at D. It would be surprising to me if on such further reflection we ended up with an evaluation of 70. Without making this analysis, and from the perspective of time t_0, the value we will get at D at time t_1 has some subjective probability distribution, and for present action purposes, I'm interested in my client's certainty equivalent of this distribution. If in consultation with my client I think 70 is a reasonable certainty equivalent, I'll go along with the present analysis. If I think 70 underestimates the value at D because of flexibility, I'll doctor up that value."

Subjective Pruning

Consider another variation of the problem. Constructing a decision tree, the analyst and decision maker find there are definitely at least three (a,b,c) choices, perhaps a fourth (d) at the initial decision node. Assume they have examined choices a, b, and c, finding b the best so far. Say b's utility score is 80. Should the analyst painfully examine alternative d? Conceptually the problem can be depicted as in figure 14.2. If detailed analysis shows that the evaluation of d is less than or equal to 80, the conditional value of this information would be zero;

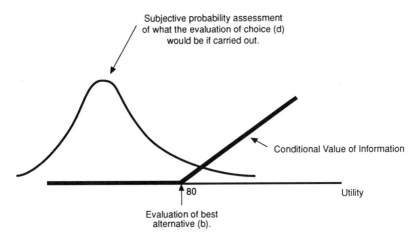

Figure 14.2
Conceptual analysis of the worth of analysis

above 80 the conditional value increases linearly. It's like an option with a strike price of 80. To determine formally whether to analyze choice d, the analyst would have to compare the *expected* value of the conditional information to be gained by analysis against the cost of such analysis. But it may be clear without any formal analysis that choice d should be pruned. If the problem isn't clear, then perhaps a full analysis should be made. Still there is the possibility of a partial, primitive, analysis. Very rarely in my experience as an analyst have I made formal calculations of the value of doing analysis. However, informal, subjective assessments of the expected value of information are done all the time.

Changing Values

Let's simplify and complexify at the same time. Suppose the decision tree involves only cash flows and the decision maker cares only about her final asset positions at the tips of the tree. But somewhere along the way an external event θ can happen that's quite independent of the decision maker's actions. Assume this event will not affect the final asset values at the tips of the tree, but might affect her attitudes toward risk. For example, a sickness in the family might require additional major expenses. In other words, her utility function for assets X might function as $u(X/\theta)$. Before θ is known, the analyst should work with the expected utility function

$U(X) = E_\theta u(X/\theta).$

In other words, to get the operational utility of X, which we call $U(X)$, the analyst should expect out (over θ) the conditional utilities for X given θ. In practice analysts rarely add that θ-branch to the tree. Nevertheless, they should be working with an intuitive assessment of the function $U(.)$, all things considered.

Changing Selves

The usual decision tree depicts a sequence of decision nodes that will be reached over a period of time. Suppose the analyst and decision maker both know that the decision maker's later values will, in all likelihood, be different from those she now professes. Let's label her divided selves DM-Now and DM-Later, where DM stands for decision maker. The issue is that the values of DM-Now may differ from those of DM-Later. But an analyst who is advising DM-Now might wish to consider DM-Later's actions not under control of DM-Now. After some preaching about the anomalies of divided selves, the analyst might wish to treat the decision node controlled by DM-Later as a chance node from the perspective of DM-Now. It's DM-Now's values that he should be analyzing—at least if his client agrees to that approach. Schelling (1988) and Elster (1979) have written fine essays about the problems of divided selves from descriptive and normative viewpoints. The decision analyst, from a *prescriptive* point of view, must decide not only who his client is, but must apply a bit of therapy.

In standard decision analysis, it's never advantageous to limit flexible action in the future if it can be preserved without a cost penalty. But in practice decision makers often deliberately limit their future choices. If the analysis, however, distinguishes between DM-Now and DM-Later, it makes perfectly good analytical sense for DM-Now to restrict the action domain of DM-Later.

Undervaluing Information

If the accumulation of information is costly and if the information will not change any subsequent action *on the decision tree*, then it should not be collected. That seems like sage advice, yet it may be oversimplified. In medicine, for example, information that is irrelevant for medical action purposes may have value for life purposes (e.g., information that reveals how long a patient will live). According to the clinical-medical, decision-tree formulation, such information should not be collected. But the tree is incomplete from the perspective of the patient who might want to use such information for personal, nonmedical reasons. This example seems like a special case, but often the expected value of information is undervalued because the decision tree is not complete.

Ignoring External Market Instruments

Once again, consider the case of a decision tree in which only monetary flows are of interest; no psychological features are important. We'll consider two cases of an incomplete tree.

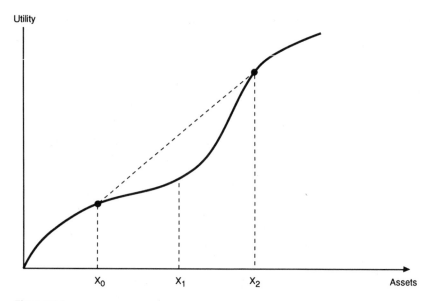

Figure 14.3
Concavifying a utility function with a dip

Concavifying Convex Dips in Utility Function

Suppose that the decision maker has a utility function with a convex portion—perhaps representing an aspiration level (see figure 14.3). The analyst assigns utilities to the tips of the tree, expects out, and works backward. But suppose in real time the real outcome results in asset value X_1, which falls in a valley in the decision maker's utility function. She could then seek a nearly fair lottery (there are lots of these around) that would end up with an asset value of X_0 and X_2. Hence for operative purposes, when other financial instruments are available, the utility value of X_1 should not be $U(X_1)$, but the operative utility function should result from the concavification of U. For example, if X_1 were in the middle of the $[X_0, X_2]$ range and if fair bets were available, then the decision maker's derived utility value for X_1 should be

$$U^*(X_1) = .5U(X_0) + .5U(X_2).$$

The message generalizes. If at the tip of the tree you would not rest content but take some corrective action, then the utility value at the tip should reflect that strategic option.

Another example: a lottery with a negative expected, incremental value may still be desirable even for a risk-averse individual. Why? Because if it is negatively correlated with other market instruments, it may be a desirable component of a diversified portfolio.

Price Dependencies among Financial Instruments

Modern finance theory often can get objective answers for the pricing of uncertain market instruments without resorting to subjective expected utility theory. Take the case of a market option in a given security with an exercise price at a given target date. The consequences of that option can be completely replicated by a dynamic strategy of buying and selling the security itself and of buying and selling relatively risk-free bills. Because the securities and bills are fully priced by the market, we can derive [as did Black and Scholes (1973)] the "correct" market value of the option. If the option were not so priced, the arbitrageurs would go to work and equilibrate the prices.

More generally, if several financial instruments are strongly dependent, in the sense that one instrument can be expressed as a dynamic, adaptive combination of the others, then there must be a mathematical relation among the valuations of these instruments. Otherwise, market pressures will adjust prices to mirror the mathematical constraints.

Consider the following extreme example. The decision maker is asked for her certainty equivalent of a lottery that pays off x_i, if event E_i occurs, for $i = 1, \ldots, m$. She, possibly with the help of her analyst, assigns probabilities to events and utilities to incremental monetary values, computes her expected utility, and gets her certainty equivalent, the price she would just be willing to sell the lottery. But now suppose in an extreme case that the lottery matches exactly what 1,000 shares of IBM stock will yield in the same time period. Her certainty equivalent for the lottery, given the availability of the market, should now roughly be the price of the 1,000 shares. She could, by going long or short on the stock, hedge her bet. Her lottery is identical to a tradeable commodity that has, as far as she is concerned, an objective price. Now let's generalize. Suppose that the lottery has a high correlation with a portfolio of stocks (or let's say the market portfolio) that can be objectively priced out. Surely this should be relevant for the decision maker's assessment. Analysts very often

ignore these market opportunities for hedging of risk and their implication for evaluation of risky options. In some sense, if the market
is ignored, the decision maker's tree is incomplete. Completing her
tree does not necessarily make the analysis more difficult, but sometimes *easier* and more objective.

The Corporate Manager as Decision Maker

A corporate manager who is solely concerned about the financial welfare of the stockholders does not need to know their utility functions
when making a corporate investment. The manager assumes that
each stockholder is risk-averse and is fully diversified among instruments. In other words, for the component of uncertainty in the investment that is probabilistically independent of the market, expected
monetary value is appropriate. This is because each shareholder
holds (or better yet, should hold) only a trivial portion of the equity of
the company and therefore of the contemplated investment. Essentially shareholders should, and by and large do, diversify away that
component of the corporate investment uncorrelated with market behavior. But there remains the component that is market related. Investors should also diversify this part of their portfolio, and when
they do so efficiently, the by-now classical result says that the expected values of the cash flow should be discounted by the "beta-
adjusted" rate.

The point of all this is that if the single investment under investigation is embedded into the financial environment, then the analysis
becomes surprisingly simpler. In this case, completeness does not introduce complex intractability but rather simpler tractability.

Ah, but *will* the manager, as contrasted to *should* the manager, be
solely concerned about the group of fully diversified stockholders? To
this end let's put ourselves in the role of the analyst working with a
corporate CEO who has to make an important investment decision.
What are Ms. Decision Maker's concerns? Empirically, this is an interesting question about descriptive decision making. But roughly,
she would be concerned about her obligations to herself (her financial
returns, including bonuses, salaries, stock options, her future administrative flexibility, her sense of doing what's right, etc.), her obligations to employees, to stockholders, to creditors, and to society. This
is a typical complex, multiple-attribute problem, with several kinds
of stakeholders affected by the decision.

Let's assume that the analysis will not be shared openly with the stakeholders, but revealed only to the CEO. A common error is to do an analysis that is too restrictive—for example, to consider only the collectivity of stockholders, or only the CEO's utility for the monetary consequences to herself. Even if the latter focus were erroneously adopted, it would be important not to consider this decision in isolation. The manager cannot diversify the way the investment stockholders can, but she can hedge and diversify within the firm in ways that would make sense for her, for employees, and perhaps for the board of directors. The particular investment must be embedded in the environment of the firm's other investments and possible hedging and diversification activities. The CEO, employees, and her board of directors may want stability, predictability, and survivability of the firm; they may want to be fiscally conservative about debt-equity ratios. The analysis for our partially altruistic decision maker is complicated, and it may be a mistake to perform quantitative analyses that are too restrictive in scope.

These are tough problems. One bit of advice for the analyst is to do a sophisticated *qualitative* structuring of the problem, coupled with one or more quantitative analyses that are more restrictive in scope. It would be nice if there were more case examples of good prescriptive analyses of these complexities. These concerns are especially important today in the era of corporate takeovers.

A metaquestion arises: For whom *should* the analyst be working? Descriptively, this question is often answered with another: "Who's paying for it?" Ideally, I would love to work in the middle, as an analytically oriented mediator among the stakeholders. Many joint gains can be achieved.

Cognitive Concerns along the Way

Decision trees often associate incremental monetary values, positive and negative, with branches of the tree. These incremental values along each path leading to a consequence at the tip of the tree are accumulated to give a net monetary value at that tip. Typically, however, the analysis ignores the psychological effects on the client along the way, such as joy, anxiety, peace of mind, regret, disappointment, envy, anticipatory dread or delight, and so on. If the decision maker is concerned about these psychological effects, then it may be appropriate for the analyst to incorporate them in his analysis. True, the analyst might discuss with his client whether some of these concerns are being inappropriately stressed, but the client should have the last say as to what is important to her.

Scott Cantor, a Ph.D. student in decision sciences at Harvard, is examining decisions about prenatal diagnoses of genetic abnormalities (e.g., Down's syndrome, Tay-Sachs disease). For women who would choose to abort their pregnancies after an unfavorable test result, the question arises whether information should be sought earlier or later in the pregnancy (say at twelve rather than eighteen weeks). Errors and complications may be more likely at the twelve-week stage. From a medical point of view that is concerned only with final health states, which often ignores trauma and anxiety, the eighteen-week alternative is preferred. But earlier knowledge has value for piece of mind. It may be psychologically and morally easier, as well as medically easier, to abort at twelve rather than at eighteen weeks. For many women the essence of this problem should not abstract away these cognitive concerns. In describing a consequence associated with a path through the decision tree, one should trace the time flow of psychological states—somewhat analogous to a time flow of monetary payoffs in an investment problem.

There are many anomalies, going back to Allais 1953, where the subjective expected utility (SEU) analysis gives advice at variance with descriptive empirical behavior. In examining—or should I say "in relishing"?—such behavior, psychologists have identified many cognitive concerns that are abstracted away in standard analyses. When the problems are analyzed by SEU theory, it's only money that counts. But subjects are concerned about psychological factors as well, such as postdecisional regret and disappointment (Bell 1985). From a descriptive point of view, it's important to recognize the shortcomings of SEU theory in predicting behavior and to try to modify the theory to be more accommodating of the empirical facts. One trouble is that as a theory becomes more complex, with more degrees of freedom to accommodate data, it may become a better rationalizer of past data but a poorer predictor of future behavior.

The SEU theory was not created by Ramsey or von Neumann to be a good predictor of the behavior of the public (of unaided, untutored subjects) but rather a coherent theory for rational, deliberative, highly intelligent individuals. It was designed from a normative perspective, but it is widely applied throughout economics and political science as

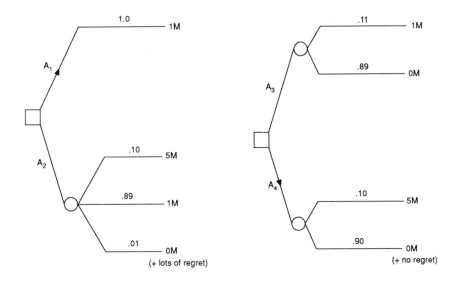

Figure 14.4
The Allais paradox

a descriptive theory. Not very surprisingly, it is not a very good descriptive theory in micro studies.

Let's examine the Allais paradox (see figure 14.4). If utilities are assigned to the monetary consequences $0, $1 million, and $5 million—there is no loss of generality of letting $u(0) = 0$, $u(5) = 1$, and $u(1) = \pi$ where $0 < \pi < 1$—then there is no numerical utility assignment for π that could result in the usual empirical observation that most people prefer Act 1 to Act 2 and Act 4 to Act 3. Most people assert that the consequence of $0 in Act 2 carries with it a negative charge of severe regret. "Why was I so greedy in choosing Act 2 over the sure thing of Act 1?" Whereas the $0 in Act 4 is psychologically benign: "If I had taken A3, I still could have ended up with $0. It's all chance." From a prescriptive point of view, the analyst should discuss with his client her a priori concerns about her anticipated posteriori regret. He could pose the problem several ways to help her understand the notion of regret. Ultimately, however, if she maintains that with the unfortunate outcome of $0 with A2, she will suffer the pangs of post-decisional regret, then it would be inappropriate and incomplete to describe this consequence in terms of final monetary assets alone. Ignoring regret would be like ignoring taxes—they are both part of reality.

In prescriptive analyses, there is no conceptual reason why consequences cannot be described in terms of cognitive as well as monetary concerns. This can be achieved operationally by adding another component in a multi-attribute utility analysis. By doing this formally, the analyst can help his client think more deliberatively about these psychological effects. Costing out the effects of regret (e.g., how much would it be worth to you to wave a magic wand to eliminate feelings of regret if $0 resulted from A2?) might reveal that a 0.01 chance at this imputed regret amount does not loom so large. But if fear of regret remains significant (and I know and respect some people for whom it does), then it's not the theory that has to be modified for prescriptive purposes, but the way that theory is applied. For such clients, consequences must be more fully described.

Suppose you are the decision maker, and if you had full control you would do A rather than B. But looking over your shoulder is an inescapable kibbitzer who will remind you, after the fact, of your stupidity if A turns sour. You can't get rid of that annoying kibbitzer who could reappear over time with snide remarks that would be painful. Of course, analysts would agree that the existence of the kibbitzer should be incorporated into the description of the consequences in a prescriptively designed study. But now the twist: suppose the kibbitzer is your more emotional self. He, she, or it is part of your reality. Your rational and emotional selves should communicate with each other, and your analyst friend might help with some therapy. But here again, this is not a blot against prescriptive analysis but an opportunity for such analyses. The internal kibbitzer is another case of a divided self.

Framing

George Katona, a famous sociologist, introduced me to the intricacies of framing with the following story. Priest A notices that Priest B is smoking and praying. "Father, your actions surprise me," he says. "Our good bishop told me that I shouldn't smoke while praying."

"That's odd," the other retorts, "the good bishop expressly told me I should feel free to pray while smoking."

Two alternately posed questions, containing the same logical content, often elicit wildly different answers. One reason is that the ques-

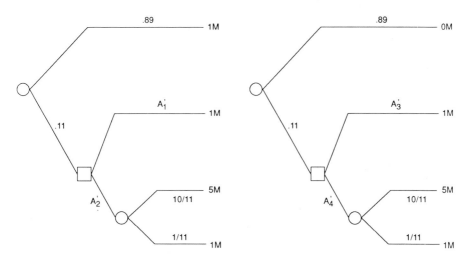

Figure 14.5
The Allais choice: alternate framing

tion itself may focus the respondent on one particular aspect of a multifaceted problem, anchoring on, or making salient, some particular set of attributes. An often cited example (McNeil, Pauker, and Tversky 1988) compares asking questions with lives saved versus lives lost.

Prescribers must be aware of the descriptive realities of framing. The process of eliciting subjective information is a central topic in prescriptive analyses, though it does not loom large in normative analysis. The analyst has a responsibility not to bias the elicitation of probabilities and utilities by selective framing. The phrasing of questions, the sequence of asking questions, the confrontation of incoherencies, the attempt to achieve coherency—these are important prescriptive and not normative concerns.

Framing is also an issue in drawing decision trees. A tree with a given logical content may not have a unique representation. Two seemingly different trees may be objectively but not subjectively equivalent. Take, for example, the decision trees in figure 14.5. Choices A'_i in figure 14.5 and A_i in figure 14.4 yield the same probability distribution of outcomes (for $i = 1,2,3,4$), but they look different. The alternate framing in figure 14.5 is designed to make transparent the substitution or sure-thing principle. The upper chance branches (with probability 0.89) are irrelevancies—according to the normative theory. But psychologically the choice between A_3 and A_4 looks different from the choice between A'_3 and A'_4. If a subject insists that A_4 is different from A'_4, the retort is, "O.K., which would you prefer?" or "How much would you pay to go from A_4 to A'_4?" These questions are designed to look at the same logical problem in different ways.

Conclusion

Decision analysis was not designed for descriptive purposes, and the observed actions of untutored subjects often violate the basic principles of the theory. But that discrepancy is not cause for modifying this normative theory. The theory could and should be (and has been!) modified to better account for descriptive purposes. The fact that subjects who are knowledgeable about SEU theory also deviate from it has more profound implications. Normative theorists have relaxed the desiderata of rational decision making to reflect the nuances of such behavior. Prescriptive analysts, such as myself, have a lot to learn from these descriptive anomalies. The real need, however, is not to alter the standard theory of decision analysis, but to apply it more flexibly and responsively. We have to do a better job of avoiding bias due to framing effects, incorporating cognitive concerns in the description of consequences, being sensitive about errors caused by incomplete trees, and applying a modest amount of therapy to decision makers who are excessively concerned about psychological effects.

And since a decision tree can never (well, almost never) be complete, we need to know the importance of what's left out and to make descriptive studies of how prescriptive analyses go awry because of incompleteness.

Here is some modest prescriptive advice about doing prescriptive analyses:

• Be sophisticated about the qualitative description and structure of the problem.

• Be pragmatic about doing tractable, formal quantitative analysis.

• Think about the potential effects of the factors excluded from the formal analysis.

• Iterate qualitative and quantitative analyses until intuition and formal analyses begin to converge.

• Encourage empirical research on how to do prescriptive analysis.

References

Allais, M. 1953. "Le comportement de l'homme rationnale devant le risque-critique des postulats et axiomes de l'école américaine," *Econometrica*, 21.

Behn, R. D., and J. W. Vaupel. 1982. *Quick Analysis for Busy Decision Makers*, Basic Books.

Bell, D. E. 1985. "Putting a Premium on Regret," *Management Science*, vol. 31, no. 1.

Bell, D. E., H. Raiffa, and A. Tversky, eds. 1988. *Decision Making*, Cambridge University Press.

Bell, D. E., H. Raiffa, and A. Tversky. 1988. "Descriptive Narrative, and Prescriptive Interactions in Decision Making," in *Decision Making*, Bell, Raiffa, and Tversky, eds., Cambridge University Press.

Black, Fisher, and Myron Scholes. 1973. "The Pricing of Options and Corporate Liabilities," *Journal of Political Economy*, vol. 81, no. 3.

Elster, Jon. 1979. *Ulysses and the Sirens*, Cambridge University Press.

Howard, R. A., and J. E. Matheson. 1984. "Influence Diagrams," in *The Principles and Applications of Decision Analysis*, vol. II, R. A. Howard and J. E. Matheson, eds., Strategic Decision Group, Menlo Park, CA.

Kahneman, D., P. Slovic, and A. Tversky. 1982. *Judgment under Uncertainty: Heuristics and Biases*, Cambridge University Press.

Keeney, R. L., and H. Raiffa. 1976. *Decision and Multiple Conflicting Objectives*, John Wiley and Sons.

McNeil, B. J., S. G. Pauker, and A. Tversky. 1988. "On the Framing of Medical Decisions," in *Decision Making*, Bell, Raiffa, and Tversky, eds., Cambridge University Press.

Raiffa, Howard. 1968. *Decision Analysis*, Random House.

Schelling, T. C. 1988. "The Mind as a Consuming Organ." In *Decision Making*, Bell, Raiffa, and Tversky, eds., Cambridge University Press.

Shachter, R. D. 1986. "Evaluating Influence Diagrams," *Operations Research*, vol. 34.

15 Strategic and Ethical Issues in the Valuation of Life

W. Kip Viscusi

Valuation Methodology

Many major contributions to economics, when first introduced, represented highly controversial shifts in perspective, but ultimately were perceived as the clearly correct solution to a problem. Such was the case with Thomas Schelling's classic 1968 essay, "The Life You Save May Be Your Own." By showing how the willingness-to-pay methodology could be applied to value-of-life issues, he extended the domain of economic inquiry to a topic that economists had largely avoided.

Traditionally, issues pertaining to the valuation of human life had been treated as strictly moral concepts, not matters to be degraded through economic analysis of choices and trade-offs. Schelling demystified these issues by extending benefit valuation procedures used in other policy contexts. In general, the appropriate benefit measure for risk reductions is the willingness-to-pay to produce the particular outcome.[1] Similarly, the selling price for changes in risk establishes the value for risk increases.

In many decisions—for example, determining what safety characteristics to provide in automobiles—the policy result to be assessed is an incremental risk reduction rather than a shift involving the certainty of life or death. This need to think in terms of statistical lives as opposed to certain lives defines the main character of the choice problem. In particular, the matter of interest is individuals' valuation of lotteries involving life and death.

Addressing value-of-life issues by focusing on our attitudes toward lotteries involving the risk of death provided a methodology for formulating these issues in a sound economic manner. Moreover, Schelling's approach of addressing the issues within the context of ex ante lotteries serves to diminish the bitterness of the value-of-life debate. Nevertheless, the concerns involved remain inherently sensitive, and we should not be too cavalier in making these judgments.

Perhaps the most important concern is that of the degree of volition of those bearing the risk. As Hammond (1982) has emphasized, if we impose risks on people involuntarily and do not provide them with compensation, then our ex ante value-of-life measure may not be a compelling guide for policy. This concern is, however, pertinent to all benefit valuation issues, not simply those involving the value of life.

A related ex ante–ex post valuation issue is that raised by Broome (1978), who suggests that if lives have an infinite value, the use of value-of-life lotteries cannot provide us with a solution to this intractable problem. This observation does not indicate a flaw in our methodology because an infinite value of life would be mirrored in an infinite value for a lottery involving a risk of death. The fact that we make a myriad of decisions involving life and death—including the animal fats we ingest and the risky but fuel-efficient cars we drive—indicates that we are willing to trade off risks of life for other valued objectives. The approach I will take here will adopt the value-of-life lottery approach, recognizing as did Schelling that this formulation structures the difficult choices, but does not eliminate them.

Because of the central role of individual preferences, individual values of life may differ considerably, just as do other tastes. A central concern is who is valuing the life and for what reason. As Schelling indicates, a particular life may have one value to the individual, another to his family, and still another to society at large.

As the willingness-to-pay methodology has become better understood, the controversy surrounding the entire line of research on the value of life has diminished. Much of the early opposition to the economic valuation of life stemmed from the reliance on value-of-life concepts that had been developed to inform decisions on compensating survivors rather than on reducing risks to life. Initial efforts consequently sought to value life using the human capital approach. In particular, analysts such as Rice and Cooper (1967) and Mishan (1971) estimated values of life based on various measures of earnings. This technique, which continues to be used throughout the United States court system to assess damages for personal injury, addresses only the financial losses involved. The death of a family member, for example, would impose a financial loss on survivors, which would be measured as the present value of the income he would have earned net of taxes and his consumption. Similarly, the present value of taxes he would have paid represents the financial loss to the rest of society.

Schelling (1968, p. 134) dismissed this widely used accounting approach altogether, observing that "it is doubtful whether the interests of any consumers are represented in a calculation that treats a child like an unfinished building or some expensive goods in process." The battle lines had been drawn between the willingness-to-pay approach and the human capital viewpoint.

Value-of-life issues raise a series of questions for research. The first, which was the focus of Schelling's original essay, is how we should think about these issues methodologically. The second class of issues involves estimating the risk-dollar trade-offs that, in effect, are the value of life. Third, how can individuals make sound decisions regarding the risks they face? Finally, what approach should guide choices when society is making protective decisions?

Although the role of altruism complicates all policy valuations, the final class of questions becomes most problematic when we depart substantially from the private market analogy. When the government is providing risk reductions to a group with similar preferences and similar risks, then matters are relatively straightforward. However, if preferences differ because of wealth, if individuals cannot make fully rational decisions with respect to a risk, or if the parties affected are not currently alive, the choice process involves a greater leap because we become less confident of how hypothetical markets would function if they were perfect.

This chapter will explore the development of Schelling's methodology and its broader ramifications. I begin by briefly reviewing the empirical evidence pertaining to the value of life. An instructive comparison is between the market evidence and the survey evidence that has been developed, including the original survey estimates presented in Schelling's article. As we will see, the general order of magnitude estimated in Schelling's paper remains approximately correct, but advances in empirical methodology have led to considerable refinement of these estimates.

Although Schelling's paper focused on private rather than public valuations of life, he did recognize the importance of public concerns. In practice, value-of-life discussions arise principally in the context of public decision making, which is the focus of the following section.

A continuing theme in Schelling's work has been the role of ethical and strategic issues in decision making. Although decisions involving the value of life can be analyzed as we would any other economic choice, many of the more intriguing aspects of the topic are related to the distinctive and highly sensitive concerns that may arise. One such set of concerns has to do with rationality and self-control. In particular, if individuals do not make sound decisions on their own behalf, what role should society play in influencing these decisions? Moreover, if we are going to intervene, how do we identify what Schelling terms the "authentic self?"[2] I extend the domain of these considerations from the individual and his alter ego to the mother and her unborn child. If we do not fully trust the decisions individuals make on their own behalf, to what extent should we allow mothers to make decisions on behalf of the fetus, especially if these decisions pose a risk to the child?

The recognition of disparities in wealth poses particularly controversial issues for valuation of life. How we treat this issue may depend on the context in which it arises whether, for example, we are talking about rich and poor groups who are alive today, or future generations that may differ in wealth from our own. I conclude this essay with observations about the appropriate role of economics in framing value-of-life decisions.

Estimates of the Value of Life

The ultimate purpose of the value-of-life literature is to provide some basis for sensitive social decisions. Before investigating how society should make decisions involving the saving of lives, we will first assess whether we can establish an empirical reference point for making trade-offs involving life and health. In the absence of such empirical information there will be few operational contexts in which economic analysis of value-of-life decisions is instructive. Some sense of the order of magnitude of the value-of-life estimates will also assuage many of the concerns expressed about the morality of this line of work. If the appropriate economic value of life is over $1 million, resistance to this methodology will probably be much less than if the estimate is, say, $200,000.

Schelling (1968) identified two ways to establish the value-of-life reference points: using information provided by the price system, and survey-based results. He noted potential inaccuracies with each approach, and similar concerns continue to be expressed in the literature. However, more detailed empirical data bases and more sophisticated statistical and survey methodologies have enabled us to refine these estimates considerably. The success of these efforts has been much greater than might have been expected two decades ago.

Market-Based Estimates

Since the time of Adam Smith, economists have observed that workers will require extra compensation for hazardous jobs. Similarly, safer products will command a higher price. The problem in analyzing these implicit markets for safety is to disentangle the premium for risk from compensation for other aspects of the job or product. For example, the most attractive jobs in society also tend to be the highest paid; as one becomes richer one will value safety more (provided that safety is a normal economic good). This income effect will make it difficult to disentangle the positive wage premium for job risk, because the level of risk chosen will be negatively related to one's lifetime wealth. These competing effects account for some of the mixed findings in the literature.[3]

Because of these difficulties, much of the early research on the link between job risks and wages found a positive relationship. With the advent of large data sets on individual worker behavior, economists were able to sort out the key relationships using detailed information on attributes of the worker, the job, and the structure of compensation.

The diverse sources of job risk information used in such studies have included information on occupational death risks by occupation,[4] industry death rates,[5] and self-assessed risk levels for the particular job.[6] Much of the variation in the empirical results obtained with this econometric methodology can be traced to specific aspects of the death risk and the estimation procedure. Establishing estimates of the value of life using benchmarks from the labor market is no different from other econometric endeavors such as estimating the elasticity of demand for a product or the responsiveness of worker commuting patterns to travel distance. More reliable data lead to better estimates. The progress made in this literature over the past decade owes much to the acquisition of more specific data relating to job safety and the recognition of other factors influencing the wage-job risk trade-off, notably workers' compensation.[7]

To obtain a sense of the range of the estimates, consider several studies from the literature. Thaler and Rosen (1976) considered wage-risk trade-offs for workers in very risky jobs. Their sample consisted of workers who had an incremental annual mortality risk of 1/1,000 per year, which is an annual death risk roughly ten times as great as the job-related risk for the typical worker. They found an implied value per statistical life on the order of $700,000 (in 1988 prices). Individuals with low rates of trade-off between risk and dollars should select themselves into risky occupations. As a consequence, Thaler and Rosen believed that their estimates of the implicit value of life were relatively low.

Other studies have focused on value-of-life estimates for a more representative group of workers who faced an annual risk of death of 1/10,000.[8] These studies imply a value of life on the order of $3 million, far higher than the original Thaler and Rosen figure. The difference reflects the variation in risk levels faced by the workers. These two sets of results have been reconciled by an explicit estimate of the heterogeneity in the value of life as a function of the job risk, indicating that workers in high-risk jobs place a lower value on life than workers in low-risk jobs.[9]

As Schelling (1968) observed, estimates of the market premiums for risk will be limited by inadequacies in the data. Random measurement error will bias the estimates of the value of life downward, so that market-based estimates are likely to be low. The occupational fatality data used by Thaler and Rosen were not ideal because they did not reflect industry differences in risk; nor did they distinguish risks of the job from other risks correlated with the activities of people in different occupations. Similarly, the Bureau of Labor Statistics (BLS) industry death risk statistics used in many other studies are not free of measurement error either, because they do not take into account occupational differences in risk within an industry. In addition, the BLS uses a sample of deaths to establish an economywide projection.

The reporting error problem was sufficiently serious that in the early 1980s the National Institute of Occupational Safety and Health undertook a census of every occupational fatality in the United States over a five-year period. This effort, the National Traumatic Occupational Fatality Project, yielded a new set of death risk statistics, which presumably should reduce the measurement error associated with the BLS estimates. Inclusion of the new job fatality variable in a wage equation to estimate compensating differentials doubles the value of life to $6 million.[10]

Other market contexts also can be used to estimate a risk-dollar trade-off and hence to construct a value-of-life figure. An ingenious effort by Blomquist (1979) inferred a value of life from data on individual seat belt use, with a result similar to that estimated by Thaler and Rosen. For the most part, however, estimates using data other than labor market information have not been as successful because not enough detail is available to isolate the individual's trade-off between risk and dollars. Labor markets are not only important sources of risk, but (at least now) the best documented; as a result, the market for risky jobs has provided the most fertile area for investigating how individuals in market contexts value risk.

Even if we accepted the reliability of the empirical estimates, they would not resolve all benefit assessment issues. Econometric studies yield estimates of an average valuation across a sample of individuals. Moreover, the risk being valued is a composite of all types of death. In general, our attitudes toward death from cancer, explosions, auto accidents, and other causes may be quite different, but current empirical efforts have not been sufficiently refined to distinguish these differences.

Survey Estimates

If market evidence is unavailable or inconclusive, one can turn to survey evidence to estimate risk-dollar trade-offs. Surveys, however, reflect stated preferences as opposed to actual preferences revealed through individual decisions. The correspondence between stated and actual preferences may not be direct.

The possibility that people may misrepresent their preferences for strategic reasons has long been a concern in the benefit evaluation literature. A more important practical consideration is that respondents may find it difficult to think about and give sensible answers to questions involving risks of death. In Schelling's (1968) original paper, for example, his sample was better able to address a lifetime risk of 1/10 than a lifetime risk of 1/1,000. For his respondents with an average 1968 income of $20,000 to $30,000, the implicit value of life was on the order of $1 million. In his 1984 revision of the paper,

Schelling updated his statistics to indicate that an implicit value of life of $2 million would be associated with an annual income in the range of $40,000 to $80,000.

These estimates tend to be somewhat lower than those estimated with market data, perhaps because of the more substantial level of the risks involved.[11] Most market studies of risks have focused on an annual risk of death on the order of 1/10,000, whereas Schelling's survey addressed risks of 1/10. In addition, whereas the market focuses on individual willingness to accept risk, Schelling's survey focused on willingness-to-pay for risk reduction. For extremely small increments in risk, willingness-to-pay values will equal willingness-to-accept values. However, for large risk increments willingness-to-accept values will exceed willingness-to-pay values, as has been borne out empirically.[12]

This relationship can be traced to a wealth effect.[13] As one purchases successive risk reductions in a willingness-to-pay context, one becomes successively poorer, thus reducing the risk-dollar trade-off for the next incremental reduction in risk. Similarly, if people are paid to bear risk, each additional increase in wage compensation increases their affluence, thus increasing the risk-dollar trade-off. These wealth effects induce a spread between the willingness-to-pay and willingness-to-accept values. Because Schelling's respondents addressed a very considerable risk, the spread is likely to be of substantial consequence.

Perhaps the main shortcoming of survey investigations is that unless a meaningful decision context is recreated for the subjects so as to induce thoughtful and honest responses, the estimates will not be reliable. In an innovative early study of willingness to pay for improved ambulance service, Acton (1973) found that individuals valued lives at less than $100,000. This estimate may have reflected strategic considerations with respect to prospective tax payments; a more fundamental problem may be that individuals were dealing with decisions they did not generally confront and as a consequence did not have a realistic sense of what the appropriate financial trade-off should be.

One way to circumvent this problem is to construct a survey situation that replicates a market decision context. For example, one could ask individuals how they valued differences in risks associated with risky products. This methodology was used for nonfatal risks in a

Table 15.1
Median trade-off rates based on surveys of individual preferences

Health outcome of interest	Survey trade-off	Median value of trade-off
Chronic bronchitis	Chronic bronchitis/auto deaths	0.32 probability of auto-mobile fatality
Chronic bronchitis	Chronic bronchitis/cost of living	$457,000
Automobile deaths	Automobile deaths/cost of living	$2,286,000
Chronic bronchitis	Chronic bronchitis/auto deaths, chained with auto death/cost of injuries on medical basis	$800,000

Source: See Viscusi, Magat, and Huber 1989.

chemical labeling study by Viscusi and O'Connor (1984). The structure of the survey methodology was replicated by Gerking, de Haan, and Schulze (1988) in the case of fatalities. They found a willingness-to-pay amount of $2.7 million, which they concluded was roughly in line with the job risk literature.

Construction of Utility Functions for Life and Death

Rather than focusing solely on local risk-dollar trade-offs, Schelling (1968) also suggested the use of hypothetical lotteries to establish utility functions for a variety of health attributes. One could obtain such a scaling by, for example, finding the death-risk equivalent of blindness. This methodology has since become more widespread and has been advocated by the leading textbooks in the area.[14]

This technique has also been implemented on a large scale in the case of individual valuations of severe chronic bronchitis, a major health effect of air pollution.[15] In particular, for the top set of estimates in table 15.1, the median individual in a sample of 400 respondents viewed chronic bronchitis as being equivalent to a 1 out of 3 chance of an automobile death. Chaining this response with the individual's risk-dollar trade-off between automobile deaths and cost of living, which implied a $2.3 million value of life, then establishes the implicit value of chronic bronchitis in terms of the risk-dollar trade-off.

Of course, survey respondents could be asked to put a dollar value on chronic bronchitis risk. It is often difficult to respond sensibly to such questions, however, because they require unfamiliar trade-offs across different classes of attributes. Moreover, survey questions regarding small risk reductions for ailments such as chronic bronchitis presuppose sophisticated abilities to think sensibly about such probability information. In practice, two samples that were asked how much they would be willing to pay for a 1/1,000 risk reduction and a 1/10,000 risk reduction might well give similar responses, even though the risk levels differ by a factor of 10.[16] When respondents' attention is focused on a risk-risk trade-off in which the risk probabilities are of similar magnitude, they can concentrate on the relative severity of health outcomes such as blindness or permanent disability in relation to other health outcomes such as death without having to deal explicitly with the probability information. Strategic considerations also could taint the responses, but at this stage of development the primary task has been simply to ensure that people understand the risky decision and give thoughtful responses. This literature should ultimately establish a variety of metrics that can be used to measure the attractiveness of different life-enhancing efforts. Although dollars are the usual denominator for economists, a lives saved metric could also be used to put health effects on a comparable basis. The findings in table 15.1 do this using automobile deaths as the reference point, but other approaches are possible as well.

Valuing Life for Policy Decisions

Adopting the willingness-to-pay approach and establishing empirical estimates considerably simplifies the task of addressing value-of-life issues in policy contexts. For private decisions, the dominant concern will be the private willingness-to-pay amount. For public choices, it will be society's overall willingness-to-pay for the risk reduction. One would expect that the greatest benefit from a life-extension policy will be that received by the individual whose life is directly affected, so private valuation provides a good starting point for assessing the value of life.

Although Schelling (1968) speculates that most externalities will be captured through accounting procedures that reflect an individual's broader impact on society, such as taxes, the extent and implications of altruistic concerns have yet to be estimated precisely.

Identified versus Statistical Lives

Consider the situation of identified lives that are highly publicized as being at risk. Society is willing to spend a considerable sum to rescue a child who falls down a well or a man who is trapped under a collapsed freeway after an earthquake. The valuation of identified lives involving 0–1 probabilities of life or death will, of course, be quite different from the valuation of statistical lives. On an economic basis, the willingness-to-pay per unit of risk reduction should be lower for large risks than for small risks. In practice, we often observe the opposite. Society exhibits greater life valuations when saving identified lives than for policies with small effects on statistical lives.

Which reaction better reflects our true underlying risk valuations? From an economic standpoint, the statistical life valuation is the more correct approach to valuing statistical lives, but if our individual decision processes cannot deal effectively with probabilistic events, then the valuation of identified lives might be a more meaningful index of our preferences. Because value-of-life questions involve a complex mixture of morality, economics, and decision making under uncertainty, ascertaining the true underlying preference structure that should be used for policy purposes will often be difficult.

The dilemma in ascertaining our true preferences can be illustrated by the following example. Suppose that improved water treatment facilities will reduce the rate of a fatal form of cancer by 1/10,000 for a municipality of 10,000, so that on average one life will be saved. Suppose that we knew in fact that exactly one life would be saved, but we did not know whose it would be. Should our benefit value remain the same as when there was one expected life to be saved? If we are applying a standard Bayesian decision theory approach, there should be no change.

Now suppose that the one life saved is known to be Joe. Should our answer change? Strict application of willingness-to-pay principles suggests that the collective valuation of a 1/10,000 risk reduction by 10,000 people will exceed the value to one person of a risk reduction from 1.0 to 0. The value we are willing to pay per unit of risk reduction is greater for small increments than larger changes because our resources become depleted when we must purchase a large decrease in risk. The role of altruism may, however, alter this relationship. In practice, the societal value for saving Joe's life may be greater since it is an identified life. Should society's valuation of Joe's life be allowed to reflect the identified aspect? A more appropriate and consistent basis for decision making would result if we were to value one certain life to be saved at random. However, it may be that the reality of dealing with probabilistic events may not be understood until there is more tangible evidence of the risk reduction benefits.

Ascertaining the Pertinent Preferences

Ostensible concern with value-of-life outcomes may actually be related to the process by which these estimates are made. As Zeckhauser (1975) has observed, we often choose not to confront individual beliefs with respect to the life-extending decisions that we make. In many situations we may be forced to make a ceremonial commitment to life extension (e.g., unproductive medical expenditures), even though we do not believe that such expenditures can enhance life substantially.

Questions about true preferences also arise when we observe large discrepancies between the buying and selling prices for risk reduction. People often react with alarm to a risk increase, but may not be willing to spend much to achieve a comparable risk reduction.[17] Substantial gaps cannot be reconciled with consistent, rational behavior. In such instances, which preferences should count, our complacency when faced with opportunities to reduce risk or our extreme reactions to risk increases?

Because of the special status of life-saving decisions, planners in pursuit of some social good may attempt to impose their preferences. As the U.S. smoking population has dwindled, policy efforts to restrict smoking in public places have greatly increased. These restrictions have not emerged from a precise tallying of the risk reduction achieved against the decrease in welfare of smokers. Rather, each side has attempted to convert the smoking debate into a question of rights rather than policy merits. Is it the smokers or the nonsmokers who have the property rights in this particular instance?

Safety regulations present a less dramatic but more prevalent example of this imposition of preferences. Job safety standards reduce the risks faced by workers, but they also reduce the market-based compensation that workers receive. If the worker has knowingly struck a bargain with his employer for extra wages in return for the risk of the job, then regulations that decrease or eliminate this risk will reduce the worker's well-being, as he perceives it. The fact that policy makers would not accept the risk for the same trade-off that workers are willing to accept does not imply that the market has failed or that the risk necessarily merits regulation. Such efforts at protection may not enhance the welfare of their intended beneficiaries.

Even if a risk is incurred voluntarily, society may be concerned if the level of the risk is high. Just as legislators have tried to put a floor under income levels by setting a minimum wage (although many economists claim that such efforts simply eliminate low-wage jobs), society may wish to have a ceiling on any one worker's level of risk. Nuclear power plant workers must rotate assignments so that no single worker receives too large a dose of radiation. Recently, there have been similar proposals to rotate airline flight crews to limit their radiation dosage. The resulting policy will not affect the total expected number of lives lost with a linear dose-response relationship, but no single worker will be substantially at risk. This example suggests that the motivations for societal action and the subsequent value of risk reduction benefits may be highly complex, involving attributes other than the expected health impacts, such as the distribution of the risk.

The nature of societal interests driving these concerns with health status may lead to seemingly inconsistent policies. Society does little to interfere with most labor market operations, such as the determination of promotions and job assignments. But the same market processes giving rise to these outcomes also govern the allocation of labor market risks. These special concerns arise both because health risks are accorded special status and because the decision processes involving risks are likely to be particularly flawed. Clearly, however, we are much more concerned with a failure to assess the risk of death properly than with an overestimate of the likelihood of promotion. The stakes are greater, and the altruistic concerns of society with health are stronger as well.

Rationality and Self-Control

Smoking Behavior

The relationship between personal values and individual decision making involving risk is often unclear. Schelling (1984a) chose cigarette smoking as a focus for discussion of these issues. Although a third of the U.S. adult population continues to smoke, most smokers either say they want to quit smoking or have attempted to quit in the past. Schelling asks whose preferences should matter.

Is the authentic self the smoker or the person who claims to want to be a nonsmoker? What does it mean when individuals express a desire to quit smoking? Are they physically dependent on nicotine, or is it the act of smoking that they cannot quit?

Nicotine chewing gum provides a ready substitute for those who want one. But it appears that most consumers enjoy smoking as a consumption decision. In 1988 R. J. Reynolds introduced the Premier cigarette. Externally indistinguishable from a traditional cigarette, the Premier had a burning charcoal ember at its tip which heated glycerine crystals coated with tobacco extract. The vapor from these crystals then passed through tobacco and was inhaled after going through a filter. Smokers of the Premier could enjoy the physical movements of holding a cigarette and the oral gratification achieved through cigarette smoking as well as the nicotine that smokers presumably desire. The Premier cigarette was available in regular and menthol flavors. Perhaps the only attribute on which the Premier fell short was its taste. The result was a marketing disaster, and the new product was withdrawn from the market.

The Premier provided an almost perfectly controlled experiment. All the carcinogenic risks of cigarettes were eliminated, with the "look and feel" left intact. The only drawback was in the cigarette's taste. Surely if cigarette purchases were driven by "addiction" alone, this product would have dominated the market. It seems clear that some fundamental taste on the part of consumers for the smoking experience is at play.

In recent years the addiction label has been liberally applied to a variety of behavioral phenomena. Most residents of Los Angeles claim to want to move out of the city but do not. Similarly, millions of workers profess a desire to leave their jobs, but they do not quit. Self-help psychology paperbacks provide guidance for overcoming addictive relationships.

Two factors appear to be at work here. The first is that the individual would like to purge a particular activity of an undesirable attribute, such as the risk associated with smoking, but such unbundling is not possible. Professing a desire to quit smoking may really mean that one wishes to avoid a particular attribute of the product, while keeping all of the remaining attributes. Second, making changes—

whether in smoking, diet, or exercise patterns—may impose important transactions costs.

To decide which of one's selves is the authentic self, it helps to
consider risk-taking decisions in other contexts. If smoking decisions
are rational, one would expect smokers to display a lower risk-dollar
trade-off than nonsmokers (unless the smoking decision is driven
simply by a difference in the taste for cigarettes). An intriguing set of
findings pertains to the variations in the job risk premiums workers
require with respect to smoking status and seat belt use.[18] Workers on
average receive compensation of $48,000 for each statistical injury
serious enough to lead to some loss of work. However, the group of
workers who are nonsmokers and who do wear seat belts require the
greatest compensation for bearing the risk (equivalent to $81,000 per
injury). Smokers on average receive compensation of roughly $26,000
per injury, or just over half of the comparable value for the entire
sample of smoking and nonsmoking workers. Although these results
do not imply that choices are fully rational, they do provide some
evidence of consistency. In particular, the same individuals who
accept the risks of smoking also are willing to accept a lower price in
exchange for risking their lives on the job.

Consistent biases in risk perception cannot account for these findings. Could the results, for example, be attributable to people systematically underestimating the risks of smoking and risks from their
jobs, thus gravitating to hazardous pursuits whose implications are
not well understood? The wage-risk trade-offs, however, are based
on the risk assessments by the particular workers. If smokers underestimate all kinds of risks, the statistical impact will be a *larger* estimated wage premium per unit risk rather than the smaller premium
that is observed. The given estimated wage premium will translate
into a high value of injury when coupled with a low risk perception.
One could advance the alternative hypothesis that smokers overestimate the risks they face, which would account for their smaller wage
premiums for jobs. If, however, smokers systematically overassess
risks, then their smoking behavior presumably is the result of a
strong taste for smoking rather than a failure to appreciate the potential hazards of this activity.

A variety of factors consequently influence smoking behavior.
First, smokers may have a different attitude toward risk, as reflected
in their willingness to take risks other than those of cigarettes. Thus,
there is at least some evidence that cigarette smoking is an action of

one's authentic self. Second, there is also substantial evidence that people would like to quit smoking, but the full implications of the survey responses are not clear. Changes in preferences, changes in health status, or information acquisition concerning cigarette smoking all may be involved.

Irrational Behavior and the Value of Life

Such controversies extend well beyond the case of cigarette smoking. Self-control is an issue in many areas, as Schelling (1984a) indicates, and it is often necessary to identify the preferences that should matter from a policy standpoint. A substantial recent literature has documented a wide variety of anomalies in decisions involving risk, in which the task of distinguishing the authentic self is once again important.

Irrationality involving choices made under uncertainty often stems from underlying inadequacies in the way risk perceptions are formed. For example, individuals overestimate the risks associated with low-probability events; they overweight events that lead to complete elimination of the risk (the "certainty effect"); and they overreact to highly publicized and dramatic risks. The irrational behavior in these instances does not stem from the underlying preference structure but rather the risk perceptions. The result is risk-dollar trade-offs that do not accurately reflect the preferences that individuals would have if they understood the risks better. As a practical matter, policy makers may have to overcome the political pressures generated by such preferences;[19] when formulating normative policy guidelines, however, one need not be concerned with excessive or inappropriate reactions stemming from inadequacies in risk perception.

More problematic are certain anomalies that cannot be attributed to simple misperception of the risk. One example is the phenomenon of regret.[20] Individuals may attach an additional negative payoff to an unfavorable lottery outcome above and beyond the stated terms of the lottery. Then decision making is complicated by making allowance for regret. Similarly, events associated with the "status quo"[21] or the current "reference risk level"[22] may have special properties as well. People generally avoid lotteries that could lead to a higher risk level. The level of the risk within one's total risk portfolio is not the central issue. Rather the main sensitivity is to an upward shift in a risk to which one has become accustomed.

These situations may involve a legitimate individual preference as opposed to a behavioral anomaly. To what extent should policies override these features of individual preferences? In addition, if individuals display various anomalous preferences, either in the market or in simulated market contexts presented by a survey, to what extent should we use these responses in formulating risk policy? Once risk policies have been framed in sound economic terms, making such distinctions will be a matter of increasing concern.

Regulation of Genetic Risks

One of the most sensitive areas of risk regulation pertains to genetic hazards. Controversies become particularly heated when risks are imposed involuntarily. To what extent, for example, should a woman be allowed to expose a fetus to potential birth defects as the result of her excessive drinking? Similarly, should pregnant women be allowed to work in situations involving the risk of potential birth defects (e.g., through exposure to lead in battery plants, or to excessive radiation)?

One would expect the mother to take into account the interests of the child. However, if self-control is a problem when individuals make decisions in their own behalf, how can we be sure that they will behave correctly with respect to the future well-being of the unborn? Society has chosen not to leave these matters to individual discretion. Instead, we regulate risks and control access to jobs on the basis of the risk exposure. These regulations reflect a complex set of concerns involving irrationality as well as a legitimate concern with the health of others.

One policy problem often posed as a matter of ethics is whether pregnant women should be barred from particular hazardous jobs or whether instead the employer should be required to provide positions safe enough for any worker, including pregnant women. This policy decision seems to have been miscast as one of ethics when it is really differences in safety productivity that are more relevant. If some workers pose a much higher degree of risk on the job, presumably the employer should not be required to reduce the risk so that it will be the same for all. Many factory jobs require heavy lifting, which can be done more safely by individuals with greater strength. To ensure that such positions would not impose dangerous back injury risks to any worker, all weight lifting tasks would have to be subdivided into small increments.

The basic principle of allocating individuals to positions in the labor market is that individual differences in productivity should be exploited, not suppressed. Differences in riskiness are just one aspect of productivity differences, and equalization of job risk is no more a matter of ethics than is equalization of other job attributes. Although I have long wished to be a Boston Celtic, I will be unable to fulfill this ambition until rules are instituted so that players who are nine inches shorter than Larry Bird and who cannot jump or shoot with any particular accuracy will be able to have the same productivity as people who can.[23] Indeed we owe our high standard of living and our overall good health to the fact that society has been organized to exploit differences in talents.

The case of alcoholic beverages illustrates the undesirability of equalizing risk levels. Alcohol poses a much greater risk to pregnant women than the adult population at large. The appropriate policy remedy is not to reduce the alcohol content of liquor so that it is equally safe for all to drink. Rather, the preferred policy course has been informational efforts aimed at reducing drinking by pregnant women. This approach recognizes that there is an inescapable heterogeneity in individual riskiness.

Changes in drinking patterns are, however, less costly to achieve than career shifts. When a woman who performs hazardous work becomes pregnant, transaction costs make it difficult for her to find a new job in the outside market. The employer can reduce those costs by providing alternative positions for employees who become pregnant. Because employers value workers' firm-specific skills, they have a strong interest in promoting such internal mobility.

The controversy surrounding pregnancy and hazardous jobs has not focused primarily on the situation of workers who already hold such jobs, but rather on the question of initial access to the risky jobs. Women who plan to have children want risk reduced so that they will face no greater risk on the job. Women who claim that they do not plan to have children want to choose better-paying, but potentially hazardous employment. Since women's preferences as to becoming pregnant may change over time, irrespective of verbal commitments and prior intentions, the reluctance of employers to expose future unborn to major risks, and themselves to substantial future liability, appears quite appropriate. There is a tremendous moral hazard problem involved, particularly given the million-dollar stakes in tort liability awards.

Some women have suggested that they should be permitted access to the positions after providing evidence that they have been sterilized or are otherwise unable to become pregnant. Sterilization prerequisites for jobs have, quite legitimately, evoked substantial controversy. But it must be remembered that it is not the employer who forces the women to become sterilized. (Indeed, women often have other reasons to seek sterilization.) Rather, if workers choose this course it is because they value the higher wage rate they will receive in this position more than the loss associated with sterilization.

Almost all of the complaints on this issue have arisen from people who are seeking promotion to a higher-paying, but potentially riskier job at the firm where they are currently employed. What is at stake here is not survival or avoidance of a poverty threshold, as hazard premiums average less than $1,000 annually for U.S. workers. Rather, the desire for economic advancement has generated a controversy over ethics and morality.

Such problems are likely to be less severe for entry-level jobs. Individuals seeking starting positions at firms have much greater mobility and many more diverse opportunities. Only when they have developed firm-specific expertise do workers become much more concerned with access to higher-paying positions. If society values access, it can approach this issue in the same manner used for the initial risk-dollar trade-off. In particular, we must balance our willingness-to-pay for increased access against the associated efficiency loss and potential increased risk. These are not strictly ethical questions beyond economic analysis. Rather, making such trade-offs lies at the heart of what economics is about.

Similar concerns regarding access occur in other contexts as well. Should we provide wheelchair ramps and parking spaces for the handicapped even when these policies fail a benefit-cost test? If the calculated benefits properly account for the entire value that society places on improved access, from an efficiency standpoint one cannot justify these efforts. The fundamental task is not to promote access at any price, but to acquire a much better basis than we now have for evaluating the benefits of improved access. These benefits are legitimate, but difficult to quantify, so that most policy decisions turn on speculative claims.

The ultimate policy question that must be addressed is what bases for discrimination are acceptable when differences in riskiness are present. Automobile insurance regulations generally preclude the use of race information in setting rates, and some states prohibit the use of age and sex information as well. Airplanes permit pregnant women to fly, even though the radiation risk to the fetus may be considerable and may not be well understood by the passenger. Overall, society has done very poorly at developing consistent guidelines for allocating risk and determining a sound basis for discriminating on the basis of differing riskiness. If we are to succeed in addressing these concerns, we must recognize that these are not simply issues of equity. Substantial efficiency gains can be reaped by proper allocation of risk, not only increasing productivity but more frequently saving lives and preventing genetic defects.

Affluence and the Value of Life

The starting point for any value-of-life discussion is the individual's own value of life. These values tend to be an increasing function of income. To what extent should we recognize this heterogeneity when making policy? Should one treat all individuals identically, as if they had the same values, or should we be guided by the values that the individuals themselves express?

Income Distribution at a Point in Time

Such distributional issues arise with all government programs, which inevitably benefit some parties more than others. Benefit assessment procedures are generally based on the willingness-to-pay of project beneficiaries, rather than on some systematic inflation of benefit values for the poor and compression of those for the wealthy. This approach does not mean that society has no concern for the poor, only that redistribution can be handled more efficiently through focused income transfer programs.

This kind of division of labor is consistent with the well-known Kaldor-Hicks compensation principle. If policy is based on willingness-to-pay guidelines, then the parties that benefit can potentially compensate the losers from the policy. To override the willingness-to-pay values and tilt the policy mix toward risk reduction and environmental preservation, when the poor want education and housing, does not seem to be in anyone's best interests.

Most policies do not better the lot of some individuals at the expense of others, but benefit one segment of the population disproportionately. Should we place a higher value on promoting airline safety because of the relative affluence of the passengers as compared with improved highway safety, which provides more broadly based benefits for the U.S. population? Reliance on willingness-to-pay would generate more stringent standards for airline safety, which in turn would raise the price that the (more affluent) airline passengers pay for their tickets. Somewhat paradoxically, however, the Federal Aviation Administration sets the least stringent safety regulations of any federal agency, because FAA regulations have been based on the present value of victims' lost earnings, as opposed to willingness-to-pay estimates of the value of life. Rather than raise its standards in areas where the private valuation of the publicly provided benefits is high, the government has for the most part ignored these concerns.

In some situations, of course, it would be difficult or undesirable to make distinctions along income lines. Schelling (1968) notes that the *Titanic* had enough lifeboats for the first-class passengers, but the others were apparently expected to swim ashore. One could imagine an economic argument for making such distinctions, if the wealthier passengers were willing to pay the extra fare needed to support the purchase of lifeboats, whereas the less affluent passengers were not. Of course, there is no evidence that such a rational market process drove the *Titanic* lifeboat decision. In any case such bargains will not hold up in practice, because once the catastrophe happens it is impossible to deny access to the lifeboats to those who did not pay. In situations that lead directly to a certainty of life or death rather than a small probability of death, denial of lifesaving alternatives based on income is highly controversial and objectionable to many. For similar reasons, if medical support measures can preserve a life that would otherwise be lost, society spares little expense in doing so, whatever the patient's income.

Differences in safety protection are less troublesome when death is not an inevitable prospect but remains a more modest probability. Because of the heterogeneity in the value of life, market pressures have led to the introduction of airbags and antilock braking systems for the luxury car segment of the market. Cars such as the Mercedes-Benz and the Acura have introduced such safety-enhancing measures because their more affluent customers value them, whereas the Yugo and the Hyundai have avoided such devices, which would lead to a dramatic price increase. There has been no public outcry that all cars should be equipped with the thousands of dollars' worth of extra safety equipment as in the luxury class. It is highly unlikely that less affluent drivers would favor requirements that all cars meet the highest possible safety standards.

Schelling (1984a, pp. 11–16) explores this class of issues, using as an example a policy that will improve airport runway lights. He grapples with both efficiency and distributional issues by proposing a sequence of tests. Whatever its distributional impact, the policy should not be pursued unless it passes a benefit-cost test: the total willingness-to-pay of the beneficiaries should exceed the cost.

Suppose that there are two airports, one serving affluent passengers and the other serving the poor. The affluent value safety highly, at a level that we will assume exceeds the costs of improved lighting, whereas the poor value the lights at less than their cost. If the ticket purchasers pay for safety and there is no evidence of irrational behavior, Schelling suggests that we let the private preferences decide the outcome, leading to lights only for the affluent airport. If, however, the money comes from public funds, the issue becomes much more controversial. An ideal solution in Schelling's view would be to install the lights for the rich and provide the poor with some other services that they value more highly. The difficulty is that single mission agencies cannot readily make such compromises in an effort to avoid selective provision of benefits to the more affluent.

Recognizing heterogeneity could have substantial implications for the design and targeting of risk policies. Individual value-of-life estimates range from $1 million to $10 million or more.[24] Moreover, for the range of risks now faced by American workers, risk valuations seem to be highly responsive to income (income elasticity is on the order of 1.0).[25] The role of individual income in assessing the value of life has long been accepted in legal contexts, where the basis for compensation is the present value of earnings or some other linear function of income, consumption, and taxes. As our estimates of the value of life become increasingly refined, policies will probably be designed to reflect these differences, thus replicating the outcomes that would be expected if individuals could express their attitudes toward risk in a market for safety.

Income Differences across Countries

Heterogeneity is particularly relevant to international trade policies. A desire to equalize risk levels throughout the world has led to proposals that the United States not export any products that violate any U.S. safety regulations, or import products from countries in which manufacturing processes are less safe than in the United States.[26]

Worldwide standards for risk are not appropriate, however, because individuals' attitudes toward risk are likely to vary considerably, depending on their countries' stage of development. Imposing the risk standards of an economically advanced society on less developed countries will reduce their welfare by retarding economic growth and the benefits it provides. The main reason for the United States's higher safety standards is not superior awareness of safety's importance but rather a greater ability to afford the luxury of greater safety. In many underdeveloped countries, increased income has a major impact on the individual's prospect of survival, and it would be highly detrimental to impose our regulatory standards on societies that have quite rationally made different risk-taking decisions. Indeed, America made similar decisions in its earlier stages of development.

The rationale for controlling the risks of exported goods is stronger than the rationale for not importing goods produced unsafely. Two considerations with respect to the export of hazardous goods are most salient. First, there may be an informational problem if foreign consumers purchase goods, believing that they meet U.S. quality standards. Exportation of substandard products may lead to unexpected welfare losses and may have damaging effects on the perceived quality of other U.S. products that meet high quality standards. Second, if the U.S. producer is the sole world supplier of a product, then the foreign purchasers are not buying in a competitive market. In such a context they should not suffer the imposition of a substantial risk because of the market power of the U.S. producer.

Neither of these rationales for regulating the export of risky products assumes an obligation to produce equally safe products for all markets. The assessment of the adequacy of the risk hinges instead on identification of a market failure in the recipient country. In particular, is regulation of product risk warranted from the standpoint of improving product market efficiency in the importing country? The resulting policies will not be of a caveat emptor variety but instead will require a careful assessment of the rationale for regulation. Automatically imposing U.S. standards is not appropriate, but neither is having no standards whatsoever.

Age-Related Variations

Differences in the value of life also could arise with respect to age. The young have more to lose than the old, and the special societal concern with averting risks to children reflects this difference.[27] Fine tuning life-saving decisions to reflect differences in life expectancy between thirty-year-olds and fifty-year-olds may not be of great consequence because of the offsetting effects of wealth increases over a lifetime and the discounting of future utility streams.[28] In addition, most life-saving policies benefit broad segments of the population— for example, all residents who drink water that may be contaminated by toxic wastes. Medical contexts offer the greatest potential for discrimination on the basis of age, but the issue has not become salient, because of the role of societal norms and patients' ability to pay for care through insurance and first-party payments.

Changes in Income over Time

Heterogeneity is also an issue with respect to valuing lives across time. If future generations are more affluent than we are, their value of life will be proportionally higher. Although in many cases we can simply let future generations spend more later, for irreversible effects on the environment or policies with long-term effects, decisions must be made now.

The growth of the benefit value over time will be indicated by the growth rate g, and the discount rate used will be r. If one recognizes the heterogeneity in the value of life, then the effective discount rate is approximately $1 + r - g$, but if one ignores the heterogeneity, the discount rate rises to $1 + r$. Even in the case in which heterogeneity is recognized, r will exceed g somewhat because of the presence of a pure rate-of-time preference for consumption now rather than later.[29] Thus, in each case there will be a positive rate of discount, but it will be greater when heterogeneity is suppressed than when it is recognized.

Recognition of heterogeneity in the valuation of life in this instance will foster more future-oriented policies. Policies addressing global warming and other long-term risks to society will appear more attractive. In contrast, if we ignore growth in the value of life over time as incomes rise, policies with deferred impacts will be put at a substantial disadvantage.

When making decisions with respect to our own internal welfare, we should not simply abstract from our own increases in well-being over time, because we will be richer selves in twenty years. The more appropriate economic procedure would be to consider our valuation of risk reductions at the time they will occur. Similarly, appropriate recognition of heterogeneity will lead to more stringent, less shortsighted environmental and risk regulation policies that will benefit future generations.

Appropriate recognition of the heterogeneity in the value of life could lead to either more stringent or less stringent risk regulation policies, depending on the situation. Adopting a uniform valuation of life is in no way more responsible or more stringent from a risk-management standpoint. Appropriate recognition of the heterogeneity of the value of life will permit more sensible and consistent policy choices that are based on the benefits provided.

Conclusion

The value-of-life literature has gone through a number of stages. The main thrust of the early efforts was to get our thinking straight on the general value-of-life issue and to begin casting the fundamental trade-off in meaningful economic terms. Much of the research throughout the 1970s was directed at developing an empirical basis for making these judgments, and in the 1980s we began to use these estimates for policy making. Indeed, the value of life approach is now required by the Office of Management and Budget as a standard practice for all new major federal regulations.[30]

Once an unmentionable issue, value-of-life trade-offs are now recognized as quite amenable to economic analysis. The substantial magnitude of the empirical estimates of the value of life, together with the proper valuation of policies based on willingness-to-pay principles (as opposed to earlier benefit techniques, such as lost earnings), has led to much more ambitious risk regulation efforts. Indeed, the first major application of value-of-life principles showed that the Occupational Safety and Health Administration (OSHA) hazard communication standard offered benefits ten times greater than OSHA had originally estimated using earnings-based measures of the value of life, enabling OSHA to overcome the original objections of the Office of Management and Budget and to issue the regulation.

Proper application of value-of-life principles will not necessarily make risk regulations less ambitious. It will put them on a sounder economic basis, however, so that we allocate our resources to the most appropriate risk-reducing policies.

As techniques for refining value-of-life estimates improve and as the use of these procedures spreads, more and more questions formerly seen as ethical issues will be structured through this methodology. At a broad level, reliance on willingness-to-pay principles and society's valuation of different outcomes raises no new ethical concerns not present in any other benefits area.

The fact that many of these issues are amenable to economic analysis does not imply that the answers are straightforward. One salient problem is the difficulty in ferreting out individuals' true underlying preferences toward risk in situations where their rationality is suspect. Society's willingness to make an appropriate commitment to the well-being of future generations is also likely to be controversial.

None of the major economic issues or policy debates will be resolved definitively in the near future. The terms of the debate, however, have now been framed in a meaningful manner. In this as in other areas, we owe a substantial debt to Thomas Schelling for extending the domain of economic inquiry.

Notes

Richard Zeckhauser, John Pratt, and several other anonymous readers provided helpful comments.

1. See any standard text such as Stokey and Zeckhauser 1978.

2. A discussion of self-control and determination of the authentic self appears in Schelling 1984a, especially pp. 107–109, 111–112, and 152–153.

3. For surveys of the literature on wage premiums for risk, see Smith 1979 and Viscusi 1983.

4. See Thaler and Rosen 1976.

5. Studies in this vein are reported in Smith 1979 and Viscusi 1979 and 1983.

6. See Viscusi 1979, Viscusi and O'Connor 1984, and Viscusi and Evans 1990.

7. The bias resulting from the omission of workers' compensation from a wage equation is documented in Moore and Viscusi 1990.

8. See Viscusi 1979. The risk measure used was based on Bureau of Labor Statistics estimates of the industry death risk. The econometric analysis also considered compensation for nonfatal injuries as well as a variety of other job attributes, so that one could more successfully disentangle the compensation for job hazards from other premiums that might be present.

9. See Viscusi 1983.

10. See Moore and Viscusi 1990.

11. Viscusi and Evans 1990 show that risk premiums required by chemical workers vary with the extent of the risk reduction.

12. Striking evidence of this spread appears in Viscusi, Magat, and Huber 1987.

13. Utility functions consistent with this effect have been estimated in Viscusi and Evans 1990.

14. See Stokey and Zeckhauser 1978.

15. See Viscusi, Magat, and Huber 1991.

16. See Viscusi and Magat 1987 and Viscusi, Magat, and Huber 1987.

17. See Viscusi, Magat, and Huber 1987.

18. See Hersch and Viscusi 1990.

19. This class of issues is discussed more fully by Zeckhauser and Viscusi 1990.

20. See Bell 1982 for an analysis of regret.

21. See Samuelson and Zeckhauser 1988.

22. See Viscusi, Magat, and Huber 1987.

23. It should also be noted that Larry Bird wishes he were three inches taller. See Bird 1989.

24. See Viscusi 1983.

25. See Viscusi and Evans 1990.

26. For advocacy of each of these proposals, see Ashford 1976.

27. See Zeckhauser and Shepard 1976 for development of the quality-adjusted value of life, recognizing both the duration of life and its quality.

28. Estimates of the quantity-adjusted value of life consistent with small differences in the value of life for thirty- and fifty-year-olds appear in Moore and Viscusi 1990.

29. Discounting issues are discussed in Fuchs and Zeckhauser 1987 and Moore and Viscusi 1990.

30. U.S. Office of Management and Budget 1988.

References

Acton, Jan. 1973. *Evaluating Public Programs to Save Lives: The Case of Heart Attacks*, Santa Monica, CA: Rand Corporation.

Ashford, Nicholas. 1976. *Crisis in the Workplace: Occupational Disease and Injury*, Cambridge, MA: MIT Press.

Bell, David. 1982. "Regret in Decision Making Under Uncertainty," *Operations Research*, 30: 961–981.

Bird, Larry. 1989. *Drive*, New York: Doubleday.

Blomquist, Glenn. 1979. "Value of Life Saving: Implications of Consumption Activity," *Journal of Political Economy*, 96 (4): 675–700.

Broome, John. 1978. "Trying to Value a Life," *Journal of Public Economics*, 9: 91–100.

Fuchs, Victor, and Richard Zeckhauser. 1987. "Valuing Life—A Priceless Commodity," *American Economic Review Papers and Proceedings*, 77 (2): 263–268.

Gerking, Shelby, Menno de Haan, and William Schulze. 1988. "The Marginal Value of Job Safety: A Contingent Valuation Study," *Journal of Risk and Uncertainty*, 1 (2): 185–200.

Hammond, P. J. 1982. "Utilitarianism, uncertainty and information," in *Utilitarianism and Beyond*, A. Sen and B. Williams, eds., pp. 85–102, Cambridge: Cambridge University Press.

Hersch, Joni, and W. Kip Viscusi. 1990. "Cigarette Smoking, Seatbelt Use, and Difference in Wage-Risk Tradeoffs," *Journal of Human Resources*, 25: 202–227.

Kahneman, Daniel, Paul Slovic, and Amos Tversky, eds. 1982. *Judgment Under Uncertainty: Heuristics and Biases*, Cambridge: Cambridge University Press.

Mishan, E. J. 1971. "Evaluation of Life and Limb: A Theoretical Approach," *Journal of Political Economy*, 79: 687–705.

Moore, Michael J., and W. Kip Viscusi. 1990. *Compensation Mechanisms for Job Risks: Wages, Workers' Compensation, and Product Liability*, Princeton: Princeton University Press.

Rice, D. P., and B. S. Cooper. 1967. "The Economic Value of Human Life," *American Journal of Public Health*, 57: 1954–1966.

Samuelson, William, and Richard Zeckhauser. 1988. "Status Quo Bias in Decision Making," *Journal of Risk and Uncertainty*, 1 (1): 7–60.

Schelling, Thomas. 1968. "The Life You Save May Be Your Own," in *Problems in Public Expenditure Analysis*, S. Chase, ed., pp. 127–162. Washington, D.C.: Brookings Institution.

Schelling, Thomas. 1984a. *Choice and Consequence*, Cambridge, MA: Harvard University Press.

Schelling, Thomas. 1984b. *Micromotives and Macrobehavior*, New York: Norton.

Smith, Robert S. 1979. "Compensating Differentials and Public Policy: A Review," *Industrial and Labor Relations Review*, 32: 339–352.

Stokey, Edith, and Richard Zeckhauser. 1978. *A Primer for Policy Analysis*, New York: Norton.

Thaler, Richard, and Sherwin Rosen. 1976. "The Value of Saving a Life: Evidence from the Labor Market," in *Household Production and Consumption*, N. Terleckyj, ed., New York: Columbia University Press.

U.S. Office of Management and Budget. 1988. *Regulatory Program of the United States Government*, Washington, D.C.: U.S. Government Printing Office.

Viscusi, W. Kip. 1979. *Employment Hazards: An Investigation of Market Performance*, Cambridge, MA: Harvard University Press.

Viscusi, W. Kip. 1983. *Risk by Choice: Regulating Health and Safety in the Workplace*, Cambridge, MA: Harvard University Press.

Viscusi, W. Kip, and William Evans. 1990. "Utility Functions That Depend on Health Status: Estimates and Economic Implications," *American Economic Review*, 80: 353–374.

Viscusi, W. Kip, and Wesley A. Magat. 1987. *Learning About Risk: Consumer and Worker Responses to Hazard Information*, Cambridge, MA: Harvard University Press.

Viscusi, W. Kip, Wesley A. Magat, and Joel Huber. 1987. "An Investigation of the Rationality of Consumer Valuations of Multiple Health Risks," *Rand Journal of Economics*, 18 (4): 465–479.

Viscusi, W. Kip, Wesley A. Magat, and Joel Huber. 1991. "Pricing Environmental Health Risks: Survey Assessments of Risk-Risk and Risk-Dollar Tradeoffs," *Journal of Environmental and Economic Management*, 20, in press.

Viscusi, W. Kip, and Charles O'Connor. 1984. "Adaptive Responses to Chemical Labeling: Are Workers Bayesian Decision Makers?" *American Economic Review*, 74 (5): 942–956.

Zeckhauser, Richard. 1975. "Procedures for Valuing Lives," *Public Policy*, 23: 419–464.

Zeckhauser, Richard, and Donald Shepard. 1976. "Where Now for Saving Lives?" *Law and Contemporary Problems*, 39: 5–45.

Zeckhauser, Richard, and W. Kip Viscusi. 1990. "Risk Within Reason," *Science*, 248: 559–564.

About the Contributors

Vincent P. Crawford is professor of economics at the University of California, San Diego. He was educated at Princeton University and the Massachusetts Institute of Technology, and has held visiting positions at Harvard, Princeton, and the Australian National University. His research has focused on game-theoretic questions in economic theory, with particular emphases on strategic communication, bargaining and arbitration, and coordination. He is a fellow of the Econometric Society and an associate editor of the *Journal of Economic Theory* and of *Games and Economic Behavior*.

Avinash Dixit is Sherrerd university professor at Princeton University. He was educated at Cambridge University and MIT, and previously taught at the universities of California (Berkeley), Oxford, and Warwick. His current research concerns the theory of investment under uncertainty, and his most recent book (with coauthor Barry Nalebuff) is *Thinking Strategically*.

Jon Elster is Edward L. Ryerson professor of political science and philosophy at the University of Chicago. He was educated at the University of Oslo and the Université de Paris V. Before coming to Chicago in 1985, he taught at the Université de Paris VIII and the University of Oslo. Among his recent publications are *Psychologie Politique* and *The Cement of Society*. His current work focuses on constitutional changes in the East European countries.

Robert H. Frank is professor of economics in both the Arts College and Johnson Graduate School of Management at Cornell University. Educated at Georgia Tech and the University of California, Berkeley, he was a Peace Corps volunteer in Nepal for two years. His books include *Choosing the Right Pond*, *Passions Within Reason*, and *Microeconomics and Behavior*.

Jerry R. Green is David A. Wells professor of political economy at Harvard University, where he has been teaching since 1970. His work concerns incentives and economic behavior under uncertainty. Educated at the University of Rochester, he is a fellow of the Econometric Society and an overseas fellow of Churchill College, Cambridge. In 1980–81, he was a fellow of the Center for Advanced Studies in the Behavioral Sciences, and in 1987–88 he held a John Simon Guggenheim Memorial Fellowship.

Dale Griffin was educated at the University of British Columbia and Stanford University. Since 1988 he has been an assistant professor of psychology at the University of Waterloo in Ontario, Canada. His research focuses on the role of situational context in determining an individual's representation of evidence.

Russell Hardin is Mellon Foundation professor of political science, philosophy, and public policy studies at the University of Chicago. A former editor of *Ethics: An International Journal of Social, Political and Legal Philosophy*, he is the author of *Morality within the Limits of Reason* (1988) and *Collective Action* (1982).

Richard J. Herrnstein is Edgar Pierce professor of psychology at Harvard University, where he has served on the faculty since 1958. He received his undergraduate degree at City College, New York, and his doctorate at Harvard. Much of his research has been concerned with choice processes in individual behavior.

Robert Jervis is Adlai E. Stevenson professor of international relations and a member of the Institute of War and Peace Studies at Columbia University. His most recent book, *The Meaning of the Nuclear Revolution*, won the Grawemayer Award in 1990 for the best ideas on world order.

Robert Klitgaard is a visiting professor of economics at the University of Natal, Pietermaritzburg. Educated at Harvard University, he has taught at the University of Karachi and the Kennedy School of Government, Harvard, and has been a consultant in twenty-one developing countries. His six books include *Adjusting to Reality: Beyond State versus Market in Economic Development* (1991) and *Tropical Gangsters* (1990).

Howard Margolis is professor of public policy at the University of Chicago, where he has been teaching since 1985. Prior appointments were at the University of California, Irvine, the Institute for Advanced

Study (Princeton), the Russell Sage Foundation, and MIT. He was educated at Harvard University and MIT, and was a journalist and policy analyst in Washington before entering academia.

Barry J. Nalebuff   is professor of economics and management at the Yale School of Organization and Management. Educated at MIT and Oxford, he taught earlier at Harvard University and Princeton University. His research has focused on voting, imperfect competition, and the application of game theory to business and politics.

Mancur Olson   is distinguished professor of economics at the University of Maryland and in 1990–91, a distinguished fellow of the U.S. Institute of Peace. His books include *The Rise and Decline of Nations* and *The Logic of Collective Action*. He is principal investigator under a cooperative agreement between the U.S. Agency for International Development and the University of Maryland on institutional reform and the informal sector.

Dražen Prelec   is assistant professor of managerial economics at the Graduate School of Business Administration, Harvard University. He received his Ph.D. in psychology from Harvard. From 1982 to 1985 he was a junior fellow in the Harvard Society of Fellows. His most recent work deals with the psychology of time preference.

Howard Raiffa   is Frank P. Ramsey professor of managerial economics at Harvard Business School. He has held joint appointments with the Harvard departments of statistics and economics, and with the Kennedy School of Government. Educated at the University of Michigan, he has done research in game theory, statistical decision theory, risk analysis, decision analysis, and negotiation analysis.

Amos Tversky   is professor of psychology at Stanford University, where he has been teaching since 1978. He received the Distinguished Scientific Contribution Award of the American Psychological Association in 1982 and the MacArthur Prize in 1984. He is a member of the National Academy of Sciences and of the American Academy of Arts and Sciences.

W. Kip Viscusi   is George G. Allen professor of economics at Duke University. Educated at Harvard University, he is the founding editor of the *Journal of Risk and Uncertainty*. His most recent books include *Risk by Choice, Reforming Products Liability*, and *Fatal Tradeoffs*. Viscusi's estimates of the value of life are used throughout the federal government.

Richard J. Zeckhauser is Frank Plumpton Ramsey professor of political economy at the Kennedy School of Government, Harvard University. His entire academic career has been spent at Harvard, including college, graduate school, and a term in the Society of Fellows. He exercises strategic choice at the bridge table, where he has won numerous regional and national championships. His present research investigates herd behavior among human beings, and information transmission in bargaining and decentralized allocation. His most recent edited books are *Principals and Agents: The Structure of Business* (1985), *American Society: Public and Private Responsibilities* (1986), and *Privatization and State-Owned Enterprises* (1989).

Index